USING
NETSCAPE®
COMMUNICATOR 4

USING
NETSCAPE®
COMMUNICATOR 4

Written by Peter Kent

Using Netscape® Communicator 4

Library of Congress Catalog No.: 96-71433

ISBN: 0-7897-0982-1

99 98 97   6 5 4 3 2 1

Interpretation of the printing code: the rightmost double-digit number is the year of the book's printing; the rightmost single-digit number, the number of the book's printing. For example, a printing code of 97-1 shows that the first printing of the book occurred in 1997.

Screen reproductions in this book were created using Collage Plus from Inner Media, Inc., Hollis, NH.

Contents at a Glance

Table of Contents

III | The Internet: More than Just the Web

13 Desktop Web Access: Using Netcaster   205

14 Accessing Files with FTP   215

21 Advanced Web Authoring   339

Credits

PRESIDENT
Roland Elgey

SENIOR VICE PRESIDENT/PUBLISHING
Don Fowley

PUBLISHER
Joseph B. Wikert

PUBLISHING MANAGER
Jim Minatel

GENERAL MANAGER
Joe Muldoon

EDITORIAL SERVICES DIRECTOR
Elizabeth Keaffaber

MANAGING EDITOR
Thomas F. Hayes

ACQUISITIONS EDITOR
Jill Byus

PRODUCT DEVELOPMENT SPECIALISTS
Jon Steever
Mark Cierzniak

PRODUCTION EDITORS
Patrick Kanouse
Tom Lamoureux

STRATEGIC MARKETING MANAGER
Barry Pruett

WEBMASTER
Thomas H. Bennett

PRODUCT MARKETING MANAGER
Kristine R. Ankney

ASSISTANT PRODUCT MARKETING MANAGER/DESIGN
Christy M. Miller

ASSISTANT PRODUCT MARKETING MANAGER/SALES
Karen Hagen

TECHNICAL EDITORS
Kyle Brant
Sunil Hazari
Troy Holwerda

MEDIA DEVELOPMENT SPECIALIST
David Garratt

TECHNICAL SUPPORT SPECIALIST
Nadeem Muhammed

SOFTWARE RELATIONS COORDINATOR
Susan D. Gallagher

EDITORIAL ASSISTANT
Virginia Stoller

BOOK DESIGNER
Ruth Harvey

COVER DESIGNER
Jay Corpus

PRODUCTION TEAM
Maribeth Echard
Bryan Flores
Nicole Ruessler
Donna Wright

INDEXER
Tim Tate

Composed in *Century Old Style* and *ITC Franklin Gothic* by Que Corporation.

About the Author

Peter Kent is the author of 33 computer and business books, including the best-selling *Complete Idiot's Guide to the Internet*. His work has also appeared in numerous newspapers and magazines, including *The Manchester Guardian*, *The Dallas Times Herald*, *Internet World*, and *Computerworld*. He's been testing and writing about computer software for 16 years. Peter lives in Denver, Colorado, and can be reached at **ntscp@arundel.com**.

We'd Like to Hear from You!

As part of our continuing effort to produce books of the highest possible quality, Que would like to hear your comments. To stay competitive, we *really* want you, as a computer book reader and user, to let us know what you like or dislike most about this book or other Que products.

You can mail comments, ideas, or suggestions for improving future editions to the address below, or send us a fax at (317) 581-4663. For the online inclined, Macmillan Computer Publishing has a forum on CompuServe (type **GO QUEBOOKS** at any prompt) through which our staff and authors are available for questions and comments. The address of our Internet site is **http://www.quecorp.com** (World Wide Web).

In addition to exploring our forum, please feel free to contact me personally to discuss your opinions of this book: I'm **mcierzniak@que.mcp.com** on the Internet.

Thanks in advance—your comments will help us to continue publishing the best books available on computer topics in today's market.

Mark Cierzniak
Product Development Specialist
Que Corporation
201 W. 103rd Street
Indianapolis, Indiana 46290
USA

Introduction

It's about two and a half years since Netscape Navigator appeared on the scene, and already we're on version 4. Not only that, but Netscape Communications has now "repositioned" Netscape Navigator. It's now simply one component of Netscape Communicator.

Netscape Communications is pushing a new vision of what the Internet and the World Wide Web should be. No longer are they selling a product used for "surfing" the World Wide Web. Now they sell a product that has a Web-surfing component but that is also used for communicating with other Internet users through e-mail, keeping in touch with your colleagues in discussion groups, composing your own Web pages, and "collaborating" with colleagues using a Voice on the Net program. All these components will be linked together, too, so you can view pictures in your e-mail, open a Web page from a discussion-group message, open a discussion group from a Web page, and so on.

If you've used Netscape Navigator in the past, though, you'll see that Netscape Communicator is not really a radical departure from the Netscape Navigator browser you are used to working with; in fact, you might be forgiven for thinking that it's pretty much the same thing, just renamed. It's certainly been updated, with lots of great new features, and a brand-new look, but if you're already a Navigator 2.x or 3.x user, you'll find that much of Communicator is already familiar.

What, then, is Communicator? It comprises these components:

- *Netscape Navigator*   The original Netscape browser.

- *Netscape Messenger*   An e-mail program. Of course, Netscape Navigator used to have an e-mail program, too, though the new one is greatly modified.

- *Netscape Collabra*   A newsgroup program. Again, Navigator had one of these, though this is a greatly modified version.

- *Netscape Composer*   Netscape Navigator Gold was the Navigator browser with a built-in Web-authoring tool. Composer is that tool.

- *Netscape Conference*   This is a Voice on the Net program, a system that enables you to talk to other people across the Internet. It also contains a "whiteboard," a chat (typed messages) program very similar to the CoolTalk program that was distributed with Netscape Navigator 3.x. In addition, though, it has a system for transferring files directly to another user and a collaborative Web-surfing utility, a program that enables one person to control a remote Web browser.

- *Netcaster*   This is something completely new, a "workspace" or "desktop" that you can use in place of your current operating system's desktop. This makes accessing the Web much easier, but it also incorporates "push" technology. "Push" is the name given to systems that can be configured to automatically retrieve information for you periodically. You don't need to go out onto the Web to get the latest news or weather reports, for instance; that information will come to you on its own.

- *Netscape Calendar*   This is in Communicator Professional Edition. It's a scheduling program that companies can use to manage employees, similar to many such programs already available with one important new feature; the program can communicate with other Calendar programs across the Internet.

- *Netscape AutoAdmin*   Another Communicator Professional component, this is used by system administrators to configure Netscape Communicator and keep it up-to-date for all the users for whom they're responsible.

- *Netscape IBM Host-On-Demand*   Yet another Professional Edition component. A program that enables computers to connect to IBM host computers through the Internet or an intranet connection.

Can you see where Netscape is going with this? A replacement for the operating system's desktop, eh (sounds a lot like Microsoft Internet Explorer 4, already released in "beta" form and due for a final release in mid-to-late 1997). Netscape Communications is trying to build a set of programs that will become a user's core suite. When users start their computers in the morning, they'll see the Netcaster desktop; they'll use Navigator to browse the Web, Messenger to manage their e-mail, Collabra to communicate in public or private newsgroups, and so on. When they want to open another program, a word processor or spreadsheet, for instance, it's back to the Netcaster desktop—they'll double-click a program icon to start work. Although Communicator won't be an operating system, it will act like a "shell," insulating the user from the operating system to some degree. ■

Netscape Navigator

You may or may not want Communicator to act as a "shell." That's okay; it's your choice. Regardless of what you decide to do, Communicator is still a suite of Internet programs, and the most important program of the suite is Netscape Navigator. If you've used the Web, you've probably used Netscape Navigator. That's an easy claim to make, as Netscape is the most popular Web browser around, used by around 75 or 80 percent of all Web users. It's one of the most popular software programs in history—the most popular, perhaps (that's certainly what Netscape Communications claims, and they're probably right if you exclude operating systems from the claim).

That's pretty good for a youngster. Netscape was first released late in 1994, and here we are, about two and a half years later, already on version 4 of Navigator, after literally scores of releases and beta "Preview Releases." (Remember the old days when software was released every 18 months or two years? And what does a beta release mean, when it's freely available to the general public—we'll discuss that in Chapter 1.)

Netscape has been fighting what's come to be known as the Browser War, a battle with Microsoft for the Web browser market. For the moment, Netscape is still winning that war, though Microsoft Internet Explorer seems to be making significant inroads. For now, Netscape Navigator remains the most popular Web browser.

But none of this really matters if you are using Netscape Navigator and Netscape Communicator. What counts is simple: How do you use the programs effectively and efficiently? That's what this book is all about. I'm going to explain how you can make the most of Communicator, how you can surf the Web at high speed and mess around in other areas of the Internet, too; how to search FTP sites, how to dig around in Gopher sites, how to read newsgroup messages, how to work with e-mail, how to talk to people across the Internet, and plenty more.

What Makes This Book Different?

This book explains how to work with Netscape Communicator, from the basics (installing it and moving around in Webspace), to more advanced stuff (FTP sessions, using newsgroups, working with Java applets, using frames, working with plug-ins, and creating your own Web pages).

You can use Communicator without my help; you'll quickly figure out how to click links to move around, even how to enter URLs to jump directly to a Web site. But will you understand what the cache is all about (and the dangers that the cache can pose to your career!)? Will you understand the how and why of drag-and-drop bookmark entries, how to manage newsgroup messages, or why another Navigator window just opened, even though you did nothing to make it do so? Can you work out how to automatically sort your e-mail into different folders? Will you understand how to create your own Web pages (or even why you should bother)?

By the time you finish this book, you'll know more about working on the World Wide Web than 99 percent of all Web users. You'll be able to use Communicator quickly and efficiently to find what you need when you need it.

You don't have to be a power user to work with this book. I'm assuming that you have a few basics down—how to use a mouse, how to open menus, and how to work in dialog boxes—but I won't give you abbreviated instructions that only a computer geek could understand. I'll tell you clearly what you need to do to get the job done. This is a book for people who want to understand how to use Communicator right now—with a minimum of fuss and a maximum of benefit.

How Do I Use This Book?

You can dip into this book at the point you need help—you don't have to read from page one to the end if you don't want to. I've put plenty of cross references in, so if you reach a point where you need some background information that I've covered earlier, you'll know where to go.

There are a number of ways for you to find information, too. There's a detailed Table of Contents—in most cases, you'll be able to skim through this and find exactly where to go. There's an index at the back, of course, to help you jump directly to a page.

It's a good idea to spend a few minutes just leafing through the book, finding out what's here. That way, when you run into a problem, you'll have an idea of where to go to find the directions you need.

How Is This Book Put Together?

I've divided this book into several parts, according to the different functions and procedures. Part I explains how to find and install Communicator and then get started with Netscape Navigator. Part II describes Netscape Navigator's more advanced features, such as multimedia, security, and Java. Part III explains how to use Communicator to work with non-Web Internet systems (newsgroups, FTP, e-mail, the Voice on the Net, the Netcaster desktop, and so on). And Part IV explains how to use Netscape Composer to create your own home page and even publish on the Web.

Part I: Caught in the Web

In Chapter 1, I describe where you can find Communicator, the different versions that are available, and how you can install it.

Chapter 2 explains how to begin moving around on the Web—the basic point-and-click moves. In Chapter 3, I explain the more advanced navigation techniques, such as entering URLs. I also explain the purpose and use of the cache.

Chapter 4 describes what you'll find as you move "further into the Web," some of the less common Web-page components, such as forms, tables, frames, Java applets, and more. Chapter 5 describes the two systems you can use to make finding your way around much easier—the history list and bookmarks—and how to create desktop shortcuts to your favorite Web pages.

In Chapter 6, I'll explain how to search for information on the Web—how to use the special directories and "search engines" that help you find the information you need.

Finally, Chapter 7 is all about the way that Netscape handles frames, a feature that improves the Web hypertext format by allowing documents to contain multiple, interactive panes.

Part II: Navigator's Advanced Features

This part of the book describes Navigator's more advanced features.

In Chapter 8, I'll tell you how to save what you find; how you can save documents, pictures, and URLs for future use. In Chapter 9, we'll get to the really fancy stuff. This chapter explains how to install the special plug-ins and viewers you'll need to hear music, view videos, read non-Web hypertext documents, and so on. Then, in Chapter 10, I'll describe specific plug-ins and viewers that you may want to install, and where to find them.

In Chapter 11, I'll explain how to use Communicator's security features to make sure your online transactions are safe. Chapter 12 describes built-in Java support. (Java applets are little programs that run in an associated Web document.) It also describes JavaScript, a simplified version of Java that even non-programmers can use to bring their Web pages alive, and ActiveX, Microsoft's answer to Java.

Part III: The Internet: More than Just the Web

There's plenty more on the Internet outside the Web, and in this part of the book I explain how you can use Communicator to work with other parts of the Internet. In Chapter 13, I'll talk about Netcaster, Communicator's replacement for your operating system desktop. In Chapter 14, I'll explain the different types of addresses that point out of the Web—such as ftp://, gopher://, and mailto: URLs. I'll also show you how to use Navigator to work at FTP sites, so you can transfer things from the Internet's vast file libraries. You can grab programs, sounds, clip art, documents, and more.

Chapter 15 explains a few more non-Web systems that you can access through Netscape: Gopher, Finger, Telnet, and Chat.

Chapters 16 and 17 discuss Communicator's e-mail system, Netscape Messenger. Chapter 18 describes how to work with Netscape Collabra, Communicator's newsreader. You can use this to read newsgroup messages, or work in your company's private message system. You'll learn what happens when you click a news link, a link to an Internet newsgroup, and how you can go directly to a specific newsgroup.

Chapter 19 describes how to use Conference, a program that enables you to literally talk to other Internet users (assuming you have a sound card, microphone, and speakers installed). You'll also see how to transmit pictures, computer files, and text while you talk and even how to go on a trip around the World Wide Web with the other party in the conversation.

Part IV: Creating Web Pages with Netscape Composer

In this part of the book, I'll explain a subject that you may not have considered quite yet—Web authoring. In Chapters 20 and 21, you'll learn how to create your own home page (it's really quite easy) and even how to set up your own Web site so other people can view your words of wisdom. Netscape Composer has the editing tools that make creating Web pages easy; you'll learn how to do it in literally a few minutes.

Information that's Easy to Understand

This book uses a number of special elements and conventions to help you find information quickly or to skip things you don't want to read.

Web addresses (URLs) and newsgroups are all in **bold type** like this: **rec.food.sourdough** and **http://www.netscape.com**, as is text that I'm instructing you to type. Messages that appear in message boxes and status bars are in `this special font`, as is link text (that is, the text in a Web document which, when clicked, takes you to another document or file). Program or HTML text is in `this special font`.

Throughout this book, we use a comma to separate the parts of a menu command. For example, to start a new document, you choose File, Open Page. That means "Open the File menu, and choose Open Page from the list of options."

And if you see two keys separated by a plus sign, such as Ctrl+X, that means to press and hold the first key, press the second key, and then release both keys.

 TIP Tips either point out information easily overlooked or help you use your software more efficiently, such as through a shortcut. Tips may help you solve or avoid problems.

CAUTION

Cautions warn you about potentially dangerous results. They will prevent you from doing something harmful.

N O T E Notes try to anticipate user questions that might come up and provide answers to you here.

Sidebars Are Interesting Nuggets of Information

Sidebars include information that's relevant to the topic at hand, but not essential. You might want to read them when you're not online. Here, you may find more technical details or interesting background information.

Caught in the Web

Finding and Installing Netscape Communicator

Before you can use Communicator, you've got to find it—it's available from many places, both online and off—and you've got to install it. There's more than one way to do that. In this chapter, we'll look at the things you've got to consider before you begin working with Communicator. If you don't yet have it, where can you get it? (You can download it straight from the Internet if you already have an Internet connection.) Do you have the version you want? (There are many different "flavors" of Communicator, so you need to know the differences.) What else do you need in order to connect to the Internet with Communicator? What's a proxy? What does Communicator do to your Windows file associations? All these questions will be answered in this chapter.

Where can you get Communicator? A variety of places. Perhaps you've been given a copy by your company. Many companies are now buying site licenses that allow everyone, it seems, to use Communicator—from the CEO to the cafeteria staff. (I know of one major company in the Denver area that bought a site license for several thousand copies of an earlier version of Netscape Navigator. I doubt if anybody did a cost-benefit analysis of having so many people surfing around the Web!)

The different Communicator versions

There are a number of different versions of Communicator to choose from: different security versions, release numbers, operating systems, and languages.

What sort of connection do I need?

Before you can use Communicator on the Internet, you need a TCP/IP connection to the Internet, either through a network or through a dial-up connection.

Downloading and installing Communicator

You can download Communicator from the Internet and install it on your system; you'll learn how to install it on Windows, Macintosh, and UNIX.

HTML and HTM associations

The Microsoft Windows versions of Communicator "associate" themselves with the .htm and .html file associations, along with some other file types.

Setting up proxies

If you're connecting to the Internet through a corporate network, you may need the system administrator to set up a "proxy."

You may have been given a copy by your Internet Service Provider; many service providers distribute Netscape products to their customers. Or perhaps you bought some software and got Communicator with it; I've seen the browser bundled with other Internet programs. Or maybe nobody's given you a copy, so you want to go get one. I'll explain where you can find it.

First, though, let me make a quick point about the different versions of Netscape Communicator and the primary program in Communicator, Netscape Navigator. Netscape Communications releases versions of its software every few weeks. I've seen dozens of beta versions (that is, "pre-release" versions) of various Netscape Navigator browsers. And even after the "final" version of Communicator is released, there may be further minor upgrades, too.

Netscape doesn't release versions for all operating systems at the same time, though. It may release the Windows 95 version one week, the Windows 3.1 version the next week, the Macintosh version a week or two later, and so on. Also, versions of the browser with the same version number may not have quite the same features. The Windows 95 Communicator, for instance, may have features that the Macintosh Communicator version doesn't.

Netscape Communications will also have multiple releases for each operating system. When you count Preview Releases, beta versions, the full release Communicator, then, quite likely, minor Communicator upgrades, and so on, you can figure that Netscape will release literally scores of different versions of this product.

In general you'll find that the version of Communicator that you are using will be very similar to what I've described in this book. But with scores of different versions around, you may find that your version of Communicator is just slightly different from the one described here. Not dramatically so, but in some small ways it might differ. It may be missing a feature (though the next upgrade may add that feature), may have a feature not covered here, or the feature may vary just a little.

Betas and Preview Releases

A *beta* release used to be a software release that a software company would give to a limited number of carefully selected users to help the company test the software before its final release. These days, in the Internet-software world at least, things have changed. Beta software is often released publicly to anyone who wants to download it. A beta program is one that the company doesn't regard as a true release. It's test software, and if you use it you risk running into problems. It's a good idea to avoid beta software because it's likely to crash frequently. On the other hand, if you really want to stay up-to-date and use the very latest browser features, you may want to throw caution to the wind and use a beta version—millions of people do. As for the term *Preview Release*, that's one that Netscape coined to mean a sort of early beta. The software's not good enough to be classed as beta, perhaps, but you can still download it and play with it if you want. Recently, though, the term seems to have completely replaced the term beta; Netscape no longer releases versions that it labels as beta, preferring the term Preview Release.

Communicator Versions

There are many different flavors of Communicator available. Here's a quick rundown of the differences.

The Main Versions: Communicator Standard and Communicator Professional

First, there are the two main versions of Communicator: the Standard and Professional Editions. Here's what the Standard Edition has:

Netscape Navigator 4.x (browser)

Netscape Messenger (e-mail)

Netscape Mail Notification (a small utility to tell you when e-mail arrives)

Netscape Collabra (newsgroups)

Netscape Conference (Voice on the Net and other remote-collaboration tools)

Netscape Composer (a Web-page creation tool)

Netscape Netcaster (an active "workspace" or "desktop")

The Professional Edition includes all the programs in the Standard Edition, plus these:

Netscape IBM Host-on-Demand (a tn3270 terminal-emulation program—see Chapter 15, "Gopher, Finger, Telnet, and More")

Netscape AutoAdmin (a Communicator configuration-management tool for system administrators, not covered in this book)

The Different Distributions

To complicate the issue a little, Netscape Communications is currently distributing two versions of the Standard Edition at its Web site: the Typical Install and the All Components Install. The Typical Install contains all components but Netscape Conference and the plug-ins (plug-ins are programs that display certain "multimedia" file types; see Chapter 9, "Sound and Video: Using Plug-Ins and Viewers" for more information). The All Components Install contains everything. (The Professional edition contains everything in the Standard All Components edition, plus Calendar and IBM Host-on-Demand.)

Release Version Numbers

Then there are the different releases. As Netscape Communications adds features to the browser, it releases an updated version. In fact, it begins releasing versions before the "true" released version. Here's how it works.

Netscape began by releasing private alpha and beta versions of the software. Then it posted a publicly downloadable version, known as the Netscape Communicator Preview Release Version

1, at its Web site. This release was followed by various other Preview Releases and then, sometime in mid-1997, the final released version.

But if past performance is anything to go by, it won't end there, because minor upgrades are almost certain. The Navigator 2.0 series had a 2.01 and a 2.02 release, for instance, and the 3.0 series had a 3.01 release. Communicator will quite likely have a 4.01 release and maybe others.

Which release should you use? The latest available. It will have more features and generally be more stable than earlier versions. So you may want to check back at the Netscape site periodically (you can periodically select <u>H</u>elp, <u>S</u>oftware Updates in the Navigator window to return to the Netscape site and check for upgrades) to upgrade your browser.

 TIP For a quick view of all the different releases and beta releases, see **http://home.netscape.com/ eng/mozilla/4.0/relnotes/** or **http://home.netscape.com/eng/mozilla/3.0/relnotes/**.

The Operating Systems

Then there are the different operating systems. Netscape Communications is currently trying to support these operating systems:

> Microsoft Windows 3.1 (16-bit Windows)
>
> Microsoft Windows 95 or NT (a single version that runs on both operating systems—32-bit Windows)
>
> Mac OS
>
> Mac OS—PowerPC
>
> IBM OS/2
>
> UNIX: HP-UX
>
> UNIX: IRIX
>
> UNIX: OSF/1
>
> UNIX: SunOS 4.1.3
>
> UNIX: Solaris 2.3
>
> UNIX: Solaris 2.4
>
> UNIX: AIX
>
> UNIX: BSD/386
>
> UNIX: Linux

N O T E There's a special program provided by Microsoft—Win32s—that enables you to run 32-bit programs in Windows 3.1 (a 16-bit operating system). However, note that even if you install Win32s, you still won't be able to run the 32-bit version of Communicator. If you're using Windows 3.1, you must use the 16-bit version of Communicator. ▪

The Languages

There are a number of language versions available. In other words, the browser has been translated into other languages—the menu options, buttons, and so on, are shown in that language rather than English, and Web pages shown within the browsers can display different character sets. The other languages currently available are: Dutch, French, German, Italian, Japanese, Korean, Portuguese, Spanish, and Swedish. At first, Communicator will only be available in English, but the other language versions will soon follow.

The Personal Edition

In the past, Netscape Communications has released a version of the Netscape Navigator known as the Netscape Navigator Personal Edition. This is a version of the program that is sold in retail stores (and can also be downloaded from the Netscape site if you buy it from Netscape's General Store), and distributed by Internet Service Providers. This version comes with the software you need to connect to the Internet; the TCP/IP stack and dialer. Communicator will also be available in an equivalent Personal Edition. We'll talk more about TCP/IP later in this chapter, under "Your TCP/IP Connection."

Export and Domestic Releases

There's another distinction between versions, one that is all but "hidden." Some versions are regarded as "export" versions, and others are regarded as domestic U.S. versions. The difference? Very little. All features in the export version are the same as the domestic, *except* the size of the "key" used for encryption while transferring data to a secure Web server. (We'll discuss this in Chapter 11, "Communicator's Security Features.") The larger the key, the more secure the encryption is. But the U.S. government has decided, in its infinite wisdom, that only small keys may be used for export software. The fact that the term "export" doesn't make much sense when related to software and the Internet doesn't matter. Under ITAR (the International Traffic in Arms Regulations), it's against the law to send software that uses very secure encryption out of the country.

> **NOTE** Shortly before we went to print, a federal judge ruled that these regulations were unconstitutional and that software publishers should be allowed to export encryption software. The issue is now in the hands of the courts, so it remains to be seen what effect this will have on exported software. ▨

So Netscape has created two versions, one that may be distributed within the U.S. (the one with the more secure encryption) and one that may be distributed outside the U.S. (the one with the weaker—though still very strong—encryption).

How do you know which version you've got? The easiest way to find out is to choose Help, About Communicator (on the Mac, choose About Netscape from the Guide menu) from any of Communicator's main windows. Scroll down the page that appears until you see the RSA logo (that's the company providing the security system incorporated into Netscape). If the note next to the logo says, "This version supports International security…," you've got the export version.

If you buy Communicator Personal Edition within the United States, you should get the domestic version, the most secure version. (However, note that even though you can just walk into a software store and buy the product or have the product shipped to a U.S. address from Netscape's online store, under ITAR it's illegal to do so unless you are a U.S. citizen or permanent resident!)

Netscape allows U.S. citizens and residents to download a free full-security version from the Netscape Communications Web site. You can apply online (you have to provide information that Netscape uses to check if you really are a resident or citizen of the U.S.) and download straight to your computer. I'll explain how to do this later in this chapter, under "Downloading the Full-Security Version."

There are actually three security versions, but unless you live in France, the third is not relevant. France recently banned the use of the form of encryption used by Communicator, so Netscape is releasing a special French version, available at French download sites, which has *all* encryption disabled.

Finding Netscape Communicator

You can download a copy of Netscape Communicator directly from the Internet, from a variety of Web and FTP (File Transfer Protocol) sites, so you must already have a browser of some kind or an FTP (File Transfer Protocol) program installed. If you already have Web access, start by going to the **http://www.netscape.com/** or **http://home.netscape.com/** Web page; you'll find information there about how to download Communicator. You can also try **http://www.download.com/**, which normally has links to Netscape's FTP sites.

You can download, without charge, a version that you can use to evaluate the software. Or you can go to the Netscape store and buy a fully supported version immediately (the free versions don't provide technical support). If you have an earlier version of Netscape Navigator, you can select Help, Software to see a Web page from which you can buy an upgrade to Communicator.

If you can't get through to the Netscape site (you probably will be able to, but it may be too busy now and again), try later. Or try the Netscape FTP sites:

> **ftp://ftp.netscape.com/pub/**
> **ftp://ftp2.netscape.com/pub/**
> **ftp://ftp3.netscape.com/pub/**
> **ftp://ftp4.netscape.com/pub/**
> **ftp://ftp5.netscape.com/pub/**
> **ftp://ftp6.netscape.com/pub/**
> **ftp://ftp7.netscape.com/pub/**
> **ftp://ftp8.netscape.com/pub/**
> **ftp://ftp9.netscape.com/pub/**
> **ftp://ftp10.netscape.com/pub/**

ftp://ftp12.netscape.com/pub/

ftp://ftp13.netscape.com/pub/

ftp://ftp15.netscape.com/pub/

ftp://ftp20.netscape.com/pub/

If you are comfortable working with FTP—see Chapter 14, "Accessing Files with FTP"—you may prefer using the FTP sites anyway, as you can go straight to the software you need much more quickly. (Some of the download files are very large, 13M or more, and a good FTP program will resume interrupted downloads. So if you get halfway through, and your connection drops, when you reconnect you don't have to start all over again.) Here are a few FTP mirror sites that you can try if the others are very busy:

ftp://ftp.pu-toyama.ac.jp/pub/net/WWW/netscape/

ftp://ftp.eos.hokudai.ac.jp/pub/WWW/Netscape/

ftp://ftp.nc.nihon-u.ac.jp/pub/network/WWW/client/netscape/

ftp://ftp.leo.chubu.ac.jp/pub/WWW/netscape/

ftp://ftp.cs.umn.edu/packages/ftp.netscape.com/

ftp://server.berkeley.edu/pub/netscape/

There are also a variety of mirror sites around the world that may allow you to download more quickly than from the U.S. Netscape site. Try the **http://home.netscape.com/comprod/ mirror/var.html** page to see a list of these mirrors.

N O T E A *mirror site* is a site that contains the same files as the site it is mirroring. Thus, Netscape's mirror sites should contain the same software as the main Netscape sites, so you can download software from a mirror site when you can't get into the main site. ■

Finding the software you need at the Netscape Web site should be quite easy. Right near the top of the page you should find a drop-down list box from which you can select the product you want to download; open the drop-down list box and click the version of Communicator you want to download. Then click the Try It or Buy It button below the list box and you'll be taken to a page with a form. (This will only work if you are using a Web browser that has JavaScript built-in and turned on; if you are not using such a browser, look around on the page for a link, something like Download Communicator.)

The form has several drop-down list boxes. You'll use these to choose the version of the product you want, the operating system you are using, the language you want to use, and your location. Then you'll click the Click to Display Download Sites button. After a few moments you'll see another page, with a few dozen links. Click a link to download the file. If one link doesn't work—the site may be busy—try another.

By the way, before you download the program, read the information displayed on the download page. It may include information about system incompatibilities, for instance.

TIP   To see which versions of Communicator are available for your operating system and in your language, go to **http://home.netscape.com/comprod/mirror/client_options.html**, or click the Configurations link at the download page. This page didn't include the Communicator versions at the time of writing, though they should be added soon.

Downloading the Full-Security Version

If you want the version of Communicator that uses the most secure encryption version, you must live in the United States of America, and you must be either a U.S. citizen or a permanent resident. You can download this software from the **http://www37.netscape.com/eng/US-Current/index.html** page. (If this link is not working, follow the normal procedure for downloading Communicator from the Netscape site. When you get to the form where you have to select the product, operating system, language, and location look for a Netscape Strong Encryption Software Eligibility Affidavit link. Click this link to find the U.S. version of Communicator).

You'll have to fill in a form, providing your name, address, phone number, and e-mail address. Netscape Communications can use this data to check on you with American Business Information, Inc., to confirm that you are who you say you are. (You'll be able to download the software immediately, but your application will be stored by Netscape and perhaps verified.)

Communicator's Registration Fee

You might have heard the rumor going around that Communicator is free software. In most cases, it's not. You can download Communicator and use it for free in two cases: if you are (to quote from the license agreement)

> ...a student, faculty member, or staff member of an educational institution (K–12, junior college, college, or library) or an employee of a charitable non-profit organization; or your use of the Software is for the purpose of evaluating whether to purchase an ongoing license to the Software. The evaluation period for use by or on behalf of a commercial entity is limited to 90 days; evaluation use by others is not subject to this restriction.

So, if you're not covered by the educational, charitable, or non-profit umbrella, after you've decided you like and want to continue using Communicator, you should register it; you can choose Help, Register Now within Communicator for more details.

Your TCP/IP Connection

To use Communicator you need a TCP/IP connection to the Internet. What's that? It's a *Transmission Control Protocol/Internet Protocol* connection, which is the "language" that computers on the Internet use to communicate with one another.

Two basic kinds of TCP/IP connections exist: LAN and dial-in connections. A *LAN connection* is one from a local area network to the Internet. Your company may already connect its network to the Internet. As long as you have access to the Internet from your computer, using the LAN's TCP/IP connection, you can use Communicator.

A *dial-in connection* is one that is made over telephone lines; you use your modem to dial a special number, and then your software sets up the TCP/IP connection. You may have heard this referred to as a SLIP, CSLIP, or PPP connection—these are simply different types of TCP/IP connections designed for use over the phone lines.

This book does not explain how to set up TCP/IP connections. If you want to use Communicator at work, talk to the LAN system administrator. If you want to set up a TCP/IP connection at home, you need to contact a service provider (a local provider or one of the major online systems). These days most service providers will help you set up a connection. You can also buy the Personal Edition from a retail store or from Netscape's General Store, which you can reach from the **http://www.netscape.com/** or **http://home.netscape.com/** Web pages. (Of course, you don't have access to the store unless you already have a TCP/IP connection; perhaps you can get a friend to download it for you.)

From here on, I'm assuming that you already have your TCP/IP connection and are ready to install and run Communicator.

N O T E If you're using the 32-bit version of Communicator on Windows 95 or Windows NT, you must also use 32-bit TCP/IP dial-in software. For instance, if your service provider or major online service has given you 16-bit dial-in software, you won't be able to run the Windows 95/NT version of Communicator. Some online services are still providing users with 16-bit TCP/IP software, even for Windows 95. However, both Windows 95 and Windows NT have built-in 32-bit TCP/IP software that you can use. ■

Installing the Program

If you have the Personal Edition of Communicator, follow the instructions that come with the program. If you've downloaded a version from Netscape Communications, use the following instructions.

Installing the Windows Versions

Follow these instructions to install the Windows versions of Communicator:

1. Create a directory (also known as a folder in Windows 95) to hold the Communicator file.
2. Transfer the file from the Netscape site to your hard disk and place it in that directory.
3. Open the directory and double-click the file name (for instance, in Windows 3.1 open File Manager and then open the directory and in Windows 95 use Windows Explorer).
4. If you are using a 32-bit Windows version (designed for Windows 95), as soon as you double-click the file the installation program will begin. Simply follow the instructions. If you are using a 16-bit Windows version (designed for Windows 3.1), when you

double-click the file it may extract a number of files into the folder or directory (the file is an archive file containing the required installation files). After all the files have been extracted, double-click the Setup file. Clicking this file starts the Communicator installation program.

5. Follow the instructions displayed by the installation program.

After Communicator has been installed, you can delete the original installation file or the files extracted from that file, if you want. You may want to keep the original file that you downloaded, though, in case you have to reinstall for some reason.

Installing the Macintosh Versions

Before you install a Macintosh version, read the information about program incompatibilities because previous versions of Netscape Navigator have run into problems with products such as SpeedDoubler, SurfWatch, and Open Transport. You'll find this information on the Web page that lists the download links. Also, Netscape recommends that you disable virus-detection software and non-essential Extensions and Control Panels before installing the software (you can virus check it before and immediately after you install the program).

At the time of writing, the only Macintosh version available was for the Power Mac (the 603e or 604e chip). However, at least one other version will be released, one for the 68000 Macintosh. Earlier versions of Navigator were also available in a FAT binary version, that would run on all types of Macintosh including the earlier 62000 series. At the time of writing, it was unclear whether this version will be available for Communicator.

The Macintosh file that you transfer from Netscape Communications may be a .bin or .hqx file (it seems to vary between download locations and program versions). The .bin file can be downloaded if you have StuffIt Expander installed (as you do if you have Netscape Navigator 3.x installed) or another utility such as Mac Binary II+. The .hqx file is a BinHex file—a binary file that has been converted to ASCII text. You'll also need to use some kind of utility to work with this—such as StuffIt Expander—to extract the Installer program from the .hqx file.

The FTP program or Web browser that you are using to transfer the file may be set up to automatically extract the file. For instance, if you configured StuffIt Expander as a Netscape Navigator 2.x "helper" (see Chapter 9), or if you have Navigator 3.x (which comes with StuffIt Expander built in), Netscape Navigator will automatically send the file to StuffIt Expander and expand the file.

1. Create a folder to hold the file, then transfer the file from the Web site to your hard disk, and place it in that folder.

2. If your Web browser or FTP program didn't automatically extract the Installer from within the .hqx file, use a utility to do so.

3. A folder named Communicator Pro will be created. Open this folder.

4. Double-click the Installer and the installation program will begin.

5. Click the Continue button in the Welcome/Logo screen, and you'll see the Netscape Installer box. Follow the instructions in this box to install the program.

Installing the UNIX Versions

Installing Communicator on a UNIX system is a little different, and a little more complicated. Place the file you transferred into a directory you've created for it. Currently all the UNIX files end with .tar.gz (at one time both this type of file and a file ending with .tar.Z were available, but Netscape seems to be using only the tar.gz version now).

At the UNIX command line type **gzip -dc filename.tar.gz | tar xvf** and press Enter. (If for some reason Netscape returns to using the .tar.z files, at the command line type **zcat filename.tar.Z | tar xvf** and press Enter.) The files held within the archive file will be extracted to the directory. (If this doesn't work, talk with your system administrator to find out what you need to do; you may not have the program you need set up so that you can extract from archive files, or you may need to use a different command. Or you can download the gzip program from **ftp://ftp.netscape.com/pub/unsupported/gnu**.)

When the files have been extracted, read the README file for more instructions. For instance, depending on which particular type of UNIX you are using, you may need to create an nl directory or even install "patches" (fixes) to your operating system. You can also find information in the Netscape Release Notes at **http://home.netscape.com/eng/mozilla/4.0/relnotes/**; look for the document related to the UNIX version of Communicator you are about to install.

Creating a User Profile

The first time you start Communicator, the New Profile Setup Wizard opens automatically and prompts you to create a user profile. A profile is a set of instructions concerning how Communicator will work. Each person using Communicator on your computer can have a separate profile so that each person's information remains separate: Your e-mail and newsgroup messages, preferences settings, bookmarks, and so on will be available only when you open your profile. This system provides convenience but not security. It doesn't stop others from accessing your information, rather it provides a simple way to separate information.

The wizard leads you through a very simple procedure. You'll begin by providing your name and e-mail address. If you have a previous Netscape Navigator installation, the wizard will ask you if you want to use the settings from that installation for this profile. (You can move the existing files to the new Communicator installation, copy the files, or simply start anew.) If you are setting up a brand-new profile, though, you can now set your Profile name (by default Communicator will use your e-mail name) and the directory in which Communicator will save your profile information. There's generally no need to change these settings. You'll also be asked to enter information used to set up Messenger and Collabra, the e-mail and newsgroup programs. You don't have to enter that information now—you can do so later if you want. (We'll look at this setup information in Chapters 16, "Messenger: World Wide E-Mail," and 18, "Collabra: From Newsgroups to Corporate Communications.") When you finish, the wizard completes its work and Communicator opens.

N O T E To create more profiles later, or to remove or rename an existing profile, use the User Profile Manager utility, available from the Netscape Communicator Utilities folder. ■

The HTML Association in Windows

When you install Communicator into Windows, it automatically changes your .html and .htm file association. The Windows file association system allows you to link data files to program types. For instance, the .Txt file extension is associated with the Notepad text editor. Double-click a .Txt file in Windows Explorer (the Windows 95 file-management program) or the Windows 3.1 File Manager, and Notepad opens and displays the file.

Communicator, then, associates itself with the .html and .htm file extensions, the file extensions used for Web documents. This means that if you see a Web document in File Manager or Windows Explorer, you can double-click it to open Netscape Navigator and view the document.

You should note, however, that another program may have been associated with .html and .htm previously. For instance, if you've been using Internet Explorer, Microsoft's Windows 95 Web browser, Communicator will remove the association between these files and Internet Explorer. The next time you open Internet Explorer, it will discover what has happened and get a little peeved. You'll see a message saying that it knows what has happened and asking if you want to "restore it [Internet Explorer] as your default browser." In fact, every time you try to use Internet Explorer, you'll see the same message, and, thanks to the way that Microsoft created Internet Explorer's bookmark system (the Favorites), bookmarks won't work in Internet Explorer. That's fine if you don't plan to use Internet Explorer any more, irritating if you do.

Communicator also modifies several other file associations. (You can choose which file associations it modifies during the installation procedure.) It will modify associations for .jpe, .jpg, and .jpeg files (JPEG image files); .gif files (GIF Image files); .js files (JavaScript source files); and .nsc (Netscape Conference Call files).

If you want to remove the Communicator association for some reason, open Windows Explorer and choose View, Options. In the Options dialog box, click the File Types tab. You then see a list of registered (associated) file types. When you click one, you'll see the association information below the list. Click the item you want to change and click the Edit button. Change the Description of Type, then click the Edit button, and change the Application Used to Perform Action. See your Windows 95 documentation for more information.

In Windows 3.1, you change file associations in File Manager. Click a file name with the .Htm association (in Windows 3.1 you can't use .Html associations because Windows 3.1 allows only three-character file extensions). Choose File, Associate, and then click the Browse button to choose the application with which you want to associate the program.

TIP If you want to revert to Internet Explorer, the quickest way to reassociate is to open Internet Explorer and click the Yes button when prompted. If you install Internet Explorer after Communicator, Explorer will take over the associations, but Communicator will display a similar message box, asking if you want to revert to using Communicator as the default.

If you remove Communicator's HTML association, though, certain procedures won't work. You won't be able to double-click an .htm or .html file in Windows Explorer to open it in Communicator, and you won't be able to use the Windows 95 Start, Run command to open Communicator and go to a Web document (see Chapter 2, "The Opening Moves").

Firewalls and Proxy Servers

If you are using a LAN/Internet connection, you may need to set up *proxy servers*. They are special "gateways" out of the LAN. Rather than provide a connection directly onto the Internet—like omitting a wall when building a house—system administrators can set up *firewalls*, which block the Internet (the outside world). Of course, doing so defeats the purpose of having an Internet connection, so they then set up *proxy servers*, which are special doorways onto the Internet.

The proxy servers take requests from your software, send the request out through the firewall, wait for a response, and then send it back to you. (After the proxies are set up, this process is all invisible to you; you just use your software as normal, and the network handles the rest.) Using a system like this provides a way to control communications between the LAN and the Internet and a way to keep intruders out (and sometimes to keep people on the LAN from using Internet services that the bosses have deemed a waste of time).

The proxies are set up in the Proxies area of the Preferences dialog box (choose Edit, Preferences, click the + icon next to Advanced in the Category list, then click Proxies). If you have to set up proxies, you'll be told what to do or, perhaps more likely, the system administrator will set it up for you. Talk with your system administrator if you need more information.

TIP Here are a few useful sources for information about Netscape Communicator. Try **http://help.netscape.com/** to get to the Technical Support page, where you can search a database of documents, find software updates, and connect to Netscape-related newsgroups (see Chapter 18, "Collabra: From Newsgroups to Corporate Communications," for information about newsgroups). And look in the top of the Communicator windows' Help menus for links to the help system installed on your hard disk (Help Contents) or to pages on the Web containing useful information (Release Notes, Product Information and Support, International Users, Security).

The Opening Moves

Now that you have Communicator installed on your computer, let's begin navigating around the Web with Navigator, Communicator's Web browser. In this chapter, we'll look at how to start Communicator, and what you'll find when you do. You'll learn how to begin moving around on the World Wide Web using Navigator's basic "navigation" techniques. You'll see what happens when you click links, and how to find your way back when you've finished your journey or have come to a dead end. And you'll learn how to set up a few basic configuration settings, too.

I'll assume that you have already connected to the Internet (you need a TCP/IP connection—a network, SLIP, or PPP connection) and Netscape Navigator installed. I'll also assume that you've already set up a Communicator profile (see Chapter 1). ■

Starting Navigator

There are a number of ways to start Navigator, especially for the Windows version. We'll see how to start the program, and what you'll find when you do.

Moving around the Web

Moving around on the Web is a matter of pointing and clicking.

Status messages

Watch Navigator's status messages; they say a lot about what's going on behind the scenes.

How do I find my way back?

It's easy to get lost on the Web; here's how to find your way back.

Changing Navigator's appearance

You can modify the manner in which Navigator displays Web pages in a number of convenient ways.

Starting Netscape Navigator

Depending on how you have configured your software and which operating system you are using, there are several ways to start Netscape Navigator. Use one of these methods to start:

- Double-click the Netscape Communicator icon on your desktop or in the Netscape Communicator folder. (Of course, in some operating systems, this may be a single click; if you're using the new Windows 95 or NT Active Desktop, for instance, it's a single click.)
- In Windows 95, click the Start button and select Programs, Netscape Communicator, Netscape Navigator.
- In Windows, you can open an .htm or .html file by double-clicking it in File Manager or Windows Explorer (Windows 95's file-management program) or by "running" it from the Windows 95 Start menu's Run command. Netscape Navigator will open and load the file so you can read it. (This assumes that the .htm and .html extensions are associated with Navigator, as they are by default; see Chapter 1, "Finding and Installing Netscape Communicator.")
- Double-click a Windows 95 desktop shortcut that refers to a Web page (you learn about shortcuts in Chapter 5, "History, Bookmarks, and Shortcuts"). Navigator will start and open the referenced Web page.

When Navigator opens for the first time, you'll see a license-agreement page—simply click Agree to continue. If you have created a single profile for Communicator (we talked about profiles in Chapter 1), Navigator will now open. If there are multiple profiles, you'll see a list box showing you the available profiles. Click the one you want and then click the Start Communicator button.

If you are working in Windows, you may also see the message box in Figure 2.1. This simply means that the .htm and .html file extensions are associated with another program, probably another browser that you've installed. If you double-click an .htm or .html file in a file-management program or try to use a Windows 95 Internet Shortcut (see Chapter 5), Navigator won't open; the other browser will instead. If you click Yes in this message box, the file associations will be modified to make Navigator open in such a situation.

FIG. 2.1
This means that the .htm and .html extensions are not associated with Navigator; click Yes to change file associations.

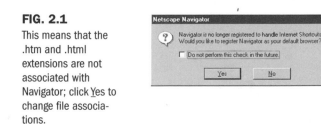

Which Programs Open?

Communicator is much more than just Navigator, as you'll see later in this book. If you find that you are frequently working with a number of Communicator's tools, you can set up the system to open several at once. When you use the Netscape Communicator icon or menu option, rather than Netscape Navigator, all the specified programs open at the same time.

To set this system up, choose <u>E</u>dit, Pr<u>e</u>ferences, and click the Appearance category. Then check the check box for each program you want to start: <u>N</u>avigator, <u>M</u>essenger Mailbox (see Chapter 16), Collabra <u>D</u>iscussions (see Chapter 18), Page <u>C</u>omposer (see Chapter 20), and N<u>e</u>tcaster (see Chapter 13).

It's also possible to set up Navigator to work "offline," but in order to do that you'll have to define a different home page. So we'll look at this issue later in the chapter, under "Working Offline."

Part

I

Ch

2

The Home Page

You should have Netscape Navigator open by now and you'll see what's known as the *home page*. This is the page that Navigator opens when you first start the program. What does the home page look like? At the time of writing, the default home page looked like the page shown in Figure 2.2 and 2.3. This page is stored on the Netscape Communications host computer, and they add and remove announcements as necessary.

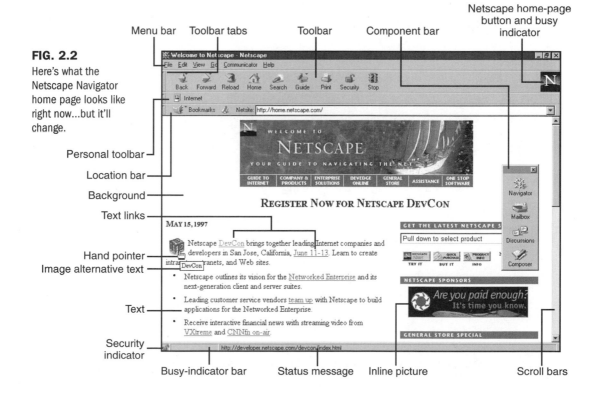

FIG. 2.2

Here's what the Netscape Navigator home page looks like right now...but it'll change.

FIG. 2.3

The Macintosh version of Communicator looks very similar to the Windows version.

T I P   For information on how to define a different home page, see "Setting a New Home Page," later in this chapter.

Let's take a look at the components of the Web document itself:

- *Background*   The background may be the default color of gray. But Web authors can create special background textures, patterns, and colors that are used instead of the browser's default color. And you can modify the background, too. (See "You Can Change Navigator's Appearance," later in this chapter.)

- *Text*   A Web document usually contains text. Not all the text you can see is true text, though. Some text may be part of an inline image rather than true document text.

- *Inline picture*   Web authors can place inline images into their documents. Such pictures are, in some cases, links to other documents. Notice the small hand pointer in Figure 2.2: It indicates that the image it's pointing to is a link to another document.

- *Image alternative text*   Some images have "alternative" text, text that appears in place of the image if the image itself is not displayed. If you hold the mouse pointer over the image for a moment, the alternative text will appear in a little pop-up box.

- *Text links*   Web documents can contain special text that, when clicked, cause the browser to display another document. This text is usually underlined and colored blue. The underlined words you can see throughout Figure 2.2 are links.

- *Hand pointer*   When the mouse pointer changes to a small pointing hand, it's over a link. When it's a normal arrow pointer, it's over an "inactive" part of the document.

Here are the components of the Navigator window itself, rather than the document shown within the window, starting at the top of the window:

- *Title bar*   Shows the title of the currently displayed document. (Web authors can—and usually do—provide each document with a title, which is not necessarily the same as the heading you see at the top of a document.)

- *Menu bar*   Select most of the Navigator commands here.

- *Toolbar tabs*   There are three toolbars in Navigator, but you can open and close them individually. Click the toolbar tabs to open and close a toolbar.

- *Back*   Click to see the previous Web document. Or click and hold the button down to see a list of previously viewed documents from which you can select. If you are using frames, the Back button takes you back to the previous frame's contents. (For more information on frames, see Chapter 7, "Navigator Frames.")

- *Forward*   Click to see the next Web document—the one you left by clicking the Back button. Or click and hold the button down to see a list of documents you've come back from. If you are using frames, Forward takes you forward to the frame that you just left when you used the Back button.

- *Reload*   Click to reload the currently displayed document from the Web again.

- *Home*   Click to return to the home page.

- *Search*   Click to view a Web page from which you can search for information on the World Wide Web.

- *Images*   This button appears on the toolbar only if you've turned off the automatic loading of inline images in Web pages (see Chapter 3). Clicking this button loads the missing images in the Web page.

- *Guide*   Click to open a menu; select an option from the menu (such as People, Yellow Pages, or What's Cool) to view a useful Web page.

- *Print*   Click to print the currently displayed document.

- *Security*   This button is used to access Navigator's security system, and to indicate when a secure document is displayed. When the button displays a locked padlock, you are working in a secure document. See Chapter 11.

- *Stop*   Click to stop the current procedure—to stop transferring the Web document or file.

- *Status Indicator*   As long as the meteors are shooting across the sky, Navigator is busy doing something: retrieving a document, trying to connect to a Web server, or transferring a file. Also, you can click the indicator to go to the main page at the Netscape Web site.

N O T E   A *Web server* is a computer that administers a Web site. When you use your browser to display a Web page, the page is transmitted to your browser by the Web server. ■

■ *Bookmarks*   Click here to open a menu showing the contents of the bookmark folder that you've set as the Bookmark Menu Folder (see Chapter 5). Select one of the entries to load that page. You can also use this menu to add and modify bookmarks, and to add buttons to the Personal toolbar.

■ *Document Link*   You can use the mouse pointer to drag and drop this icon:

Onto a blank Composer window (see Chapter 20, "Creating Your Own Home Page") to open the current document in the editor

Onto a document in the Composer window in order to create a link in that document to the Web page shown in the browser

Onto the Bookmarks window (see Chapter 5, "History, Bookmarks, and Shortcuts") to create a bookmark to the document

Onto the Windows 95 or Windows NT desktop to create a shortcut to the Web page.

Onto another Windows application to paste a copy of the current Web page's URL.

Or double-click the icon to copy the URL of the currently displayed document to the Clipboard.

■ *Location bar*   This contains a box that shows the URL (the Web address) of the document currently displayed (see Chapter 3 for more on using URLs). The bar's label changes. If it says `Netsite`, the current document is on a Netscape server; if it says `Location`, the document is on a non-Netscape server. When you start typing an URL into the box—so you can go to a specific document—the label changes to `Go to` (press Enter to go to the document).

■ *Personal Toolbar*   This is a toolbar to which you can add your own buttons. Clicking a button in this bar takes you to a specified Web page. (See Chapter 5.)

A page button takes you directly to a particular page.

A folder button opens a little menu that contains more bookmarks.

■ *Security Indicator*   Shows you the type of document you are viewing. There are currently two indicators (see Chapter 11 for detailed information about security).

The open padlock indicates that this is not a secure document. It may be held by a Web server that is not capable of secure transmissions, or it may be held by a server that *can* handle secure transmissions, but this particular page has not been set up to work securely.

The closed padlock indicates that the document uses "medium-grade" security. (As discussed in Chapter 1, this must be an export version of Navigator.)

■ *Component bar*   This little bar contains buttons that open the various Communicator applications. When you first start Navigator—or any other Communicator program—the bar will be floating (see Figure 2.4), but it can also sit on the Navigator status bar.

FIG. 2.4
This is the Communicator taskbar, with the right-click menu visible.

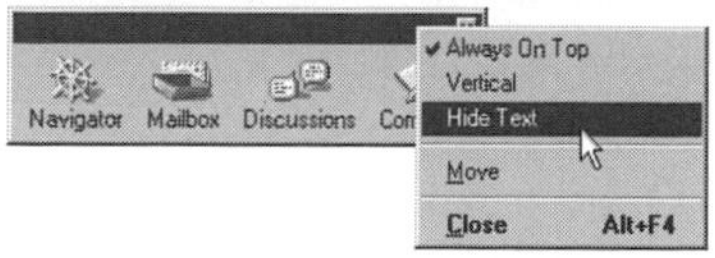

■ *Navigator button*   Click this to open a new Navigator window.

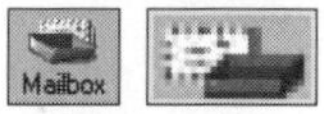

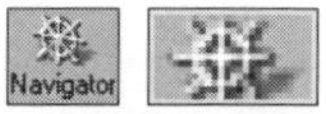

■ *Mailbox button*   Click this icon to open the Netscape Messenger window (see Chapter 16).

■ *Discussions button*   Click here to open the Collabra window to read newsgroup messages (see Chapter 18).

■ *Composer icon*   Click here to open a Netscape Composer window, in which you can create your own Web pages (see Chapter 20).

■ *Move to status bar*   Click this button to place the taskbar on Navigator's status bar.

■ *Status message*   Shows what's going on while a document is being transferred—when the Web server has been contacted, the percentage of the document that's been sent, and so on. Once Navigator finishes getting a document, it shows information about the link you are pointing to with the mouse.

■ *Busy-indicator bar*   Shows that the browser is busy receiving a Web page; you'll see a dark band move along this bar, left to right and back again.

■ *Scroll bars*   These are typical window scroll bars; use them to move around in the current document.

N O T E   Remember, as I said in Chapter 1, different versions of the browser have different features. At the time of writing, the Macintosh browser, for instance, did *not* have a Personal toolbar, the security icon in the status bar, the Bookmarks button, or the Location icon. ■

Using the Component Bar

The Component bar provides convenient access to all the Communicator programs and appears whenever you start any of those programs. When you first install Communicator, the taskbar is set up to be visible all the time, even when working in non-Communicator programs, that is, it's set to be Always on Top. (If you place the taskbar onto the Communicator window status bar, though, by clicking the little X button in the top right, it is no longer set to Always on Top—that is, it's only visible when one of the Communicator programs is open.)

In the Microsoft Windows browser, you can set up the taskbar to work differently, though. Right-click the "title bar" at the top of the Component bar (as shown in Figure 2.4), and a pop-up menu opens with the following options:

- *Always on Top*   Selecting this clears the check mark, so the taskbar is no longer always on top of other applications. You can switch to it using Alt+Tab or the Windows 95 taskbar.

- *Horizontal/Vertical*   The bar is placed on the screen vertically by default, but you can choose the orientation you prefer.

- *Hide Text/Show Text*   Select this to remove or replace the text labels under each button on the bar.

- *Move*   Use this to move the Component bar around on the screen. On the other hand, if you've just used the mouse to open this pop-up menu, why not use the mouse to move the bar?

- *Close*   The same as clicking the X button; moves the bar to the Communicator windows' status bar.

What Does a Web Document Contain?

Before we start moving around, let's take a closer look at the contents of a Web page. A Web document is really a simple ASCII text document that contains two basic components:

- Text that the author of the document wants your browser to display so you can read it

- Text that provides instructions to the browser, telling it how to display the document

You'll learn more about these special instructions in Chapters 20 and 21, when we talk about creating your own Web documents. For now, take a quick look at the following:

```
<A HREF="/que/software/"><IMG alt="Que's Software Library" WIDTH=460 HEIGHT=55
➥border="1" SRC="/ad_banners/ad_soft.gif"></A>
<img src="/general/pix/macpub_pix/head3_anim.gif" alt="Macmillan Publishing USA"
➥width="442" height="82">
<BR>
<a href="http://merchant.superlibrary.com:8000/search/simon.html">
<img src="/general/pix/macpub_pix/click.gif" alt="Click to search for books"
➥width="230" height="28" border=0></a>
<BR>
<font size="2">
<a href="/mcp/search/">Search</a> ¦
<a href="http://merchant.superlibrary.com:8000">Bookstore</a> ¦
<a href="/nrp/wwwyp/index.html">Yellow Pages</a>  ¦
<a href="/general/whats_new/">What's New</a>  ¦
<a href="/softlib/software.html">Software Library</a> ¦
<a href="/refdesk/index.html">Links</a> ¦
<a href="/survey/index.html">Win a T-Shirt</a> ¦
<a href="/general/support/index.html">Talk to Us</a>  ¦
<a href="/online/vendors">Advertisers</a>  ¦
<a href="/macpub/site_map.html">Site Map</a> ¦
<a href="/index.html">SuperLibrary Home</a>
```

```
</font>
</center>

<BR>

<font size="3">
Welcome to Macmillan Publishing USA, home of the world's largest computer book
➥publisher, the reference division of Simon & Schuster and the publishing
➥operation of Viacom Inc. Examples of Macmillan's most popular brands include
➥Betty Crocker,
Frommer's, Weight Watcher's, Que, Sams, Burpee, Lasser, Arco, and Webster's
New World. Here's where you'll find the right tools, topics and references for
➥all of your needs. Enjoy!
</font>
<p>
```

Part

I

Ch

2

This is part of the current main page at the Macmillan Publishing Web site (**http://www.mcp.com**), which you can see in Figure 2.5. All the text between the angle brackets (between < and >) are instructions. The rest of the text is text that you see on your screen.

FIG. 2.5
Here's what our sample HTML actually looks like in Navigator.

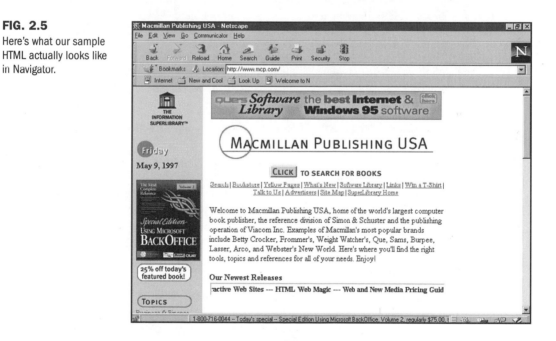

When a Web server sends a document to Navigator, the browser reads this text and *renders* the document. In other words, it looks at all the special commands inside the document, strips the codes out of the document, and then displays the text on your screen in the manner instructed by these commands. But what about the pictures, I can hear you ask? How do they get there? In the preceding example, you see a line like this:

```
<IMG alt="Que's Software Library" WIDTH=460 HEIGHT=55 border="1" SRC="/
➥ad_banners/ad_soft.gif">
```

This special instruction says, "Get the image file called ad_soft.gif, and place it right here."

Each Web document has its own address, an *URL* (Uniform Resource Locator). You can see it in the Location bar, immediately below the toolbar. The URL may look complicated, but it's really not; we'll look at how URLs are constructed in Chapter 3.

Finally, a Web document contains two basic forms of information. It contains the text and pictures that just sit there, for you to read or view. But the document also contains *links*, things that are *active*. When you click one of these links, something happens. Generally, clicking one of these links sends a message to a Web server asking for another document. However, it may also ask for an *external picture*, a picture file that is not embedded inside a document. Or it might ask for the Web server to transfer a file—a shareware program, perhaps—or some kind of unusual file format—a sound or video file, for instance. These links can be placed on both text and pictures.

How, then, do you know where these links are? In Figure 2.6 you can see several links. Links in text are shown with underlining and, at first, are colored blue. (As you'll learn in "Your Links Will Change Color" section, later in this chapter, after you've used a link it changes to purple, though you can tell Navigator not to use underlining and to change the default color.)

Links on pictures are not so easily identified. Some have a colored border around them, usually blue. This border appears in cases in which the Web author has turned the entire picture into a link, using the same technique that he might use to convert a word or sentence into a link.

But other image links don't use this method, so they don't have the blue border around them. Point to a picture using the mouse, though, and see if the mouse pointer changes to a hand pointer. If it does, you are pointing to a link. If it doesn't change, though, move the pointer around a little; some parts of a picture may contain a link, whereas others don't. You may also see the alternative-text message pop up if you keep the mouse pointer still for a moment. (I hate to complicate the issue, but in some cases, the mouse pointer won't change to a hand pointer when you point at a link on an image. Some image links are created in a special way, so Navigator can't tell what will actually happen until you click the image.)

Also, notice the status message at the bottom of the window. While you point to a link, whether a text or image link, information about that link is shown in the status message. Point to a simple link, and you see the URL of the document or file that the link points to, the document or file that will be transferred when you click the link. Point to a *hypergraphic* (also known as an *image map*), a picture with multiple hotspots (areas containing links) and you'll see the URL of the image itself, plus some numbers indicating the area of the image to which you are pointing. (In some cases, the link information may be obscured by a scrolling message in the status bar.)

FIG. 2.6
Text links are underlined and colored. You can identify picture links by pointing at the picture and looking for the hand pointer.

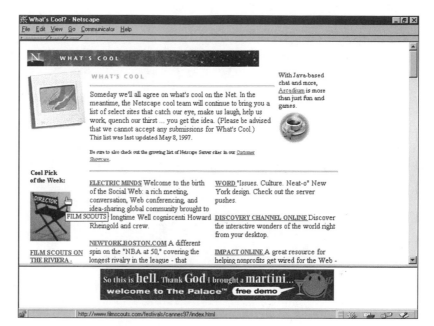

Your First Clicks

Let's begin with a few clicks. Here's a good place to start. Click the Guide button on the toolbar. A menu opens; select The Internet. (If the toolbar isn't there—it should be below the menu bar—choose View, Show Navigation Toolbar.)

A page showing links to interesting locations on the Web opens (see Figure 2.7). You can now begin clicking links to go to any site that takes your fancy. Simply move around, clicking link after link to see what happens. Note that when you click a link, the link may change color for a moment (if so, it changes to red). The color changes so that you can tell for sure that Navigator recognized your click on the link and that Navigator knows what you want to do. When you release the mouse button, the link changes back to the original blue and the transfer begins.

The way that a click actually works depends on which version of Navigator you are using and how long you click the link. If you are using the Windows browser, click quickly and the link works—Navigator begins transferring a Web page. But if you click and hold the button down, Navigator doesn't begin transferring a page. Rather, it waits to see what you will do; as you'll learn later in this book, you can drag links around. For instance, you could drag and drop it onto the desktop to create an Internet shortcut, a link to the Web page.

On the Mac, if you click quickly, the browser transfers the Web page. But if you click slowly, holding the button down for a little longer than necessary (experiment and you'll find out the interval required), a menu pops up. We'll learn more about these menu commands as we go through the book. However, you'll notice if you try this now that the Open command is selected, so, if you hold the mouse button a little too long and release it just after the menu has opened, the Open command is carried out. The effect is the same as if you had clicked slightly quicker; Navigator transfers (opens) the Web page referenced by the link. (As you'll see later, on the Windows version of Navigator you can right-click a link—and anything else in a page— to open this pop-up menu.)

FIG. 2.7

The main Guide page, a good place to begin exploring.

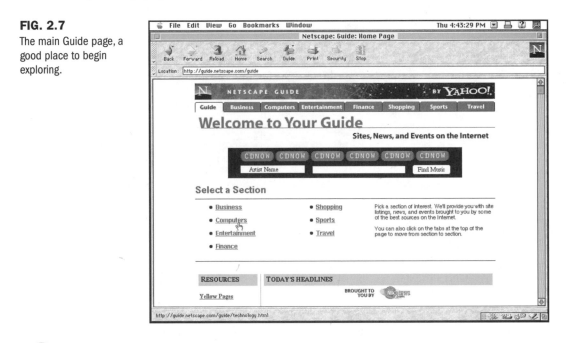

> **T I P**   For now, I want to stick with simple Web documents. You may click a link that displays a picture by itself or perhaps causes a sound to play; that's fine. But if you click a link and see a dialog box asking you to save a file or asking how to handle some kind of strange file format, cancel the dialog box and try some other link. (These subjects are covered in Chapters 8 to 10.)

Watch the Status Messages

When you click a link, you may want to watch the status messages in the status bar at the bottom of the window. You'll see a variety of messages, such as these:

- `Reading file`   Navigator is grabbing the document out of the document cache rather than from the World Wide Web itself. See Chapter 3 for information about the cache.

- `Connect: Looking up host: www.mcp.com`   This message tells you that Navigator is looking up the host address part of the URL (the Web address), trying to find the Web server specified by the link you clicked.

■ Unable to locate host www.ieee.com   If the link you click has a bad *host address*, you'll see a message saying that Navigator can't find the host. You'll also see a dialog box saying that The server does not have a DNS entry. This means that when Navigator contacted *DNS* (*Domain Name Service*, the Internet system that keeps track of all the host addresses), it was told that the host address did not exist.

N O T E   A host address is the information that identifies a particular computer connected to the Internet. Note that sometimes the URL may be correct, yet you still get this message. This may be because your TCP/IP connection is bad—if every site you try gives you an error, try logging off and back on again. Sometimes there are problems with the *nameservers*, too, the computers providing the addressing information used to locate things on the Internet. ■

■ Connect: Contacting host: www.mcp.com.   Navigator has sent a message to the server and is waiting for an acknowledgment that the server received the message.

■ Connect: Host Contacted: Waiting for reply   Navigator has received a message indicating that the host is available, and is now waiting for it to send the requested files.

■ Transferring data   The server has begun sending the document to Navigator.

■ 45% of 80k   A message, similar to this one, indicates how much of the document has been transferred and the size of the document. If the document contains inline images, you may see several of these messages, for the text itself and each image. In some cases, you'll also see information about how fast the data is being transferred and an estimate of how much longer it will take.

■ Document: Done   That's it; Navigator's got the entire document.

TIP   If you begin a transfer and decide that you want to stop (perhaps it's taking too long, or you realize you clicked the wrong link), click the Stop button or press the Esc key. On the Mac, you can press ⌘+. (that's ⌘+period). The Web page will display a Transfer Interrupted message below the last part of the page that transferred.

Don't Wait—Start Working Right Away

In the olden days on the Web—okay, a bit more than a couple of years ago—when you clicked a link, the document would start transferring, and you'd have to stare at a blank screen for a while, twiddling your thumbs. After all the information had been transferred, your browser would then display it on the screen.

That's all changed. Now, as soon as Navigator receives some text, it displays it on your screen. You can start scrolling around in the document, reading the text, while Navigator continues getting the rest of the text and then gets the pictures. For instance, Figure 2.8 shows a document with an incomplete picture: Navigator has transferred the text, put a "placeholder" in the document to show where the picture will go, and is now transferring the picture.

Part
I

Ch
2

In theory, Navigator has worked this way since the very first version of Netscape Navigator. In practice, though, this really didn't work well. The text wasn't always displayed while Navigator transferred files in the background. However, Navigator 4 really does a much better job of this, placing the text on the page fairly quickly so you can begin reading. (Though it's not yet perfect; sometimes you have to wait a few moments while Navigator displays a picture or two first, then displays the text, and then continues with the pictures.)

FIG. 2.8

Navigator is still transferring the pictures, though it's got all the text.

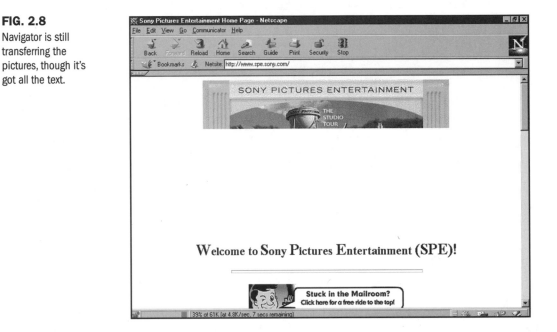

Two types of special images, designed to be used as inline pictures, transfer to Navigator very quickly: interlaced GIF and progressive JPEG. You can recognize interlaced GIFs by the fact that you see all the image very quickly, but it's fuzzy. Then, as more of the image is transferred, it gets sharper. The progressive JPEG image simply loads very quickly and smoothly. Of course, not everyone is using these special formats. If a Web author uses simple GIF and JPEG images (that is, non-interlaced and non-progressive versions), they transfer a little more slowly. (There are three basic image types that can be used for inline images: .gif, .jpg (sometimes seen as .jpeg or .jpe), and .xbm, a UNIX format that you don't run into very often these days.)

So what are you going to do while Navigator is transferring all the text and pictures? You can read the document and view the images that have already arrived. And if you find a link you want to use, don't wait. Simply click the link. Navigator will stop transferring the current document and start working on the document referenced by the link you clicked.

Moving Around the Document

You can move a document around so that you can view it all. Web documents have no set length: Some are visible in their entirety in the window; others may be hundreds of lines long, most of which will be off-screen.

You can use the window's scroll bars to move up and down, of course, and side to side. You can also use these keys:

- *Up and down arrows*   Move up and down a line or two at a time.
- *Page Up and Page Down*   Move up and down about a screenful at a time.
- *Spacebar*   Move down about a screenful at a time.
- *Ctrl+Home*   Move to the top of the document. (Windows only, not the Mac.)
- *Ctrl+End*   Move to the bottom of the document. (Windows only, not the Mac.)

T I P These keystrokes work only if the "focus" is in the content area. If you try to use the keys and they don't work, click inside the Navigator window—on text or background, not in a form—and then try again. Also, note that if the focus is on the Location bar, these keystrokes may cause Navigator to select another document.

Part
I
Ch
2

Using the Tab Key

You can often use the Tab key to move around in the document. Pressing Tab will move focus from link to link (on the Windows version—not on the Mac version at the time of writing). You'll see a faint dotted-line box appear around a text link when the focus moves to that link. If there's a form in the page (see Chapter 4), the Tab will also move focus into and through the form.

Focus will also move to links on images; again, you'll see the dotted-line box around the hotspot on the image. However, sometimes this doesn't work too well, and you may find that the Tab key takes you through hotspots on an image, but not to the text links, or it may miss some links if they're in a table.

Once a link has been highlighted by the dotted-line box, press Enter to select the link and view the document referenced by that link. Note also that in some cases pressing Tab moves the focus to the Location bar; if the last link in the page is selected, for instance, pressing Tab highlights the text in the Location bar so you can type a new URL. And pressing Shift+Tab moves focus in reverse, up the form.

Your Links Will Change Color

You may notice as you move around that links change color. At first, most links are blue, and then some of them become purple. The purple links are links to documents you've already seen—not just links you've clicked, but links to documents that you've visited. For example, suppose that you are in document A, and you click a link that takes you to document B. Later, while in document C, you see a purple link, one you've never clicked before (because you've never been in document C). You point to the link, then look at the status message, and see that the link points to document B. Navigator figures out these links when it transfers the document, and it changes the color accordingly.

How long will these links remain colored purple (or whatever other color you choose as the followed-link color)? By default, they stay that way for a few days (the actual number varies between versions). On Windows browsers, they stay purple until the page is removed from the history list (which you'll learn about in Chapter 5), and you can tell Navigator how long to keep pages in the history list, and even clear all the pages from the list immediately. Macintosh and UNIX browsers currently work a little differently; Communicator maintains a separate (and hidden) visited-links list that is not associated with the history list, because on those browsers the history list does not store information from previous sessions (though that may change in future versions).

N O T E Sometimes links *don't* change color, even if you have seen the page. Web authors can specify the link and followed-link colors used in their documents if they want, so they can force your browser to display the same color for both types of link. However, you can override these colors, as you'll see under "You Can Change Navigator's Appearance," later in this chapter. ■

Choose Edit, Preferences, then click Navigator in the Category list (this is labelled Browser in the current Macintosh version). At the bottom of the dialog box you'll find a Pages in History Expire After text box (Windows version) or Visited Links Expire After (UNIX and Macintosh). Use this to define the length of time that the visited links should remain colored. You can also click the Clear History (Windows) or Expire Now (UNIX and Macintosh) button to remove the color from all links immediately. Of course, on the Windows version you're also clearing the history list, which you may not want to do until you've read Chapter 5 and understand what the history list can do for you.

Lost Yet? Finding Your Way Back

Eventually, you'll reach a place in which you are stuck; you can't find a way forward—there are no more links to click. Or maybe you simply don't want to go forward; you want to return to where you've just been. So let's look at a few ways to return to a page you've seen earlier.

 Click the Back button to go to the previous document (or press Alt+left arrow in Windows and UNIX browsers, ⌘+[on the Mac). This takes you back through the history list, which we'll look at in Chapter 5. You can also press and hold the mouse button on the Back button to see the history list, from which you can select a previous page (see Figure 2.9). If you are using frames (see Chapter 7), the Back command takes you to the previous frame.

 Click the Forward button to go forward through the history list—to the document from which you've just come back (or press Alt+right arrow on Windows and UNIX, and ⌘+] on the Mac). Or hold the mouse button down while pointing at the button to see a list of pages.

 Click the Home button to view the Navigator home page.

N Click the status indicator to view the Netscape home page (**http:// www.netscape.com**).

Click the little triangle at the end of the Location drop-down text box, and then select an URL to go to that document. (Not available on all versions.)

Open the Go menu and select a document from the list. (This is the history list—see Chapter 5.)

Open the Go menu and choose Back, Forward, or Home.

Right-click in the document and choose Back or Forward (on Windows), or (on the Mac) click in the document and hold the mouse button down a moment until you see the pop-up menu, and then choose Back or Forward. (We'll cover the pop-up menu in more detail in Chapter 3.)

That's all the navigating we're going to be doing in this chapter; I'll explain a few more techniques in the following chapters. Before we move on, though, let's look at a few things you may notice as you travel around the Web.

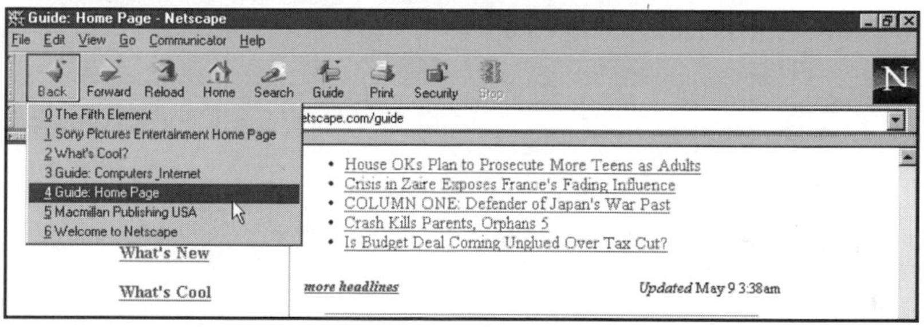

Part

I

Ch

2

FIG. 2.9

The Back and Forward buttons have a new feature; hold the mouse button down to see a list of pages.

Special Text, Special Backgrounds

Now and again, you may run across Web pages in which all the colors seem wrong. The text color is not the color you are used to, the links—are they links?—are different colors, the background is completely different, and so on.

Navigator has a series of default colors, but Web authors can override these colors if they want. They can make a particular word or paragraph a different color, or they can use a different color background or even a special pattern. In Figure 2.10, for instance, you can see that the document background is black with white dots, not the normal gray. And although you can't see it in this black-and-white book, the links are green. Even if I click a link, when I come back the link is still green; it doesn't change to the followed-link color. This author has defined a background and picked his or her own text colors.

You can override the author's overriding if you want. You can tell Navigator that you don't want to allow an author to pick backgrounds and text colors. You'll do this in the Colors area of the General Preferences dialog box. Choose Edit, Preferences, double-click Appearance, then click Color. Then select the Always Use My Colors, Overriding Document check box.

FIG. 2.10
The **http://www.kpig.com/** document shows an example of how an author may choose to pick a special background and text color.

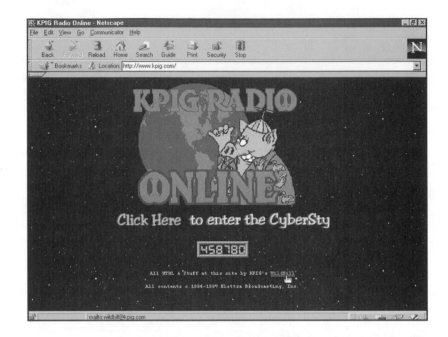

For an example of how you can override the author's wishes, see Figure 2.11. Notice that the background has gone, and the text has now changed back to the normal colors. (Well, actually it's not quite the normal colors; by default Navigator has a gray background. I'm using a white background in most illustrations to make them clearer.)

FIG. 2.11
We've overridden the author's overriding! Now we have default colors and have removed the background. Notice the black text now visible at the bottom, formerly covered by the background.

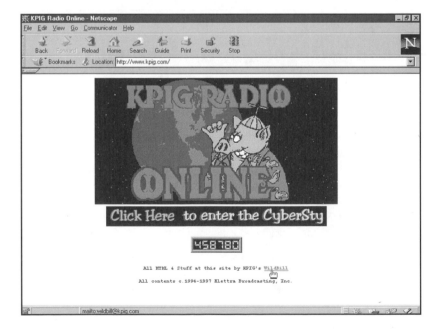

You Can Change Navigator's Appearance

Before we go on, I just want to discuss the different ways that you can modify Navigator's appearance. First, you can remove the three toolbars using a couple of methods:

- Select one of the View, Hide Toolbar commands to hide the Navigation, Location, or Personal toolbar. (Or choose a View, Show Toolbar command to reopen the bar.)

- Click the toolbar tab to open or close the toolbar (see Figure 2.12). These tabs provide a convenient way to provide the maximum amount of space for the Web page, yet keep the toolbars close at hand.

FIG. 2.12

Close the toolbars to maximize space; click a button to open a toolbar.

You can also move these toolbars around; simply press and hold the mouse button down while pointing at one of the bars, and then drag it up or down to move it above or below one of the other bars.

Additionally, you can reduce the size of the toolbar buttons. Select Edit, Preferences, click Appearances in the Category list, then choose one of the Show Toolbar As options: Pictures and Text, Pictures Only, or Text Only.

There are a few other ways you can change Web page appearance—you can create your own toolbar buttons, make language modifications, change fonts, and modify your screen resolution. We'll look at those in a moment. First, let's just see how the new Preferences dialog box works.

The New Preferences Dialog Box

Communicator has introduced a brand-new Preferences box system. As you can see in Figures 2.13 and 2.14, all the preference settings are now in one dialog box. And instead of having tabs at the top of the window, the box has a Category list on the left side. This list has a series of categories and subcategories. On the Windows versions, you can open a category, to see its subcategories, by double-clicking it or by clicking the little + icon next to the category name. The category is closed by double-clicking, or by clicking the - icon next to the name. On the Mac version of Communicator, the categories are opened and closed by clicking the little triangle next to the name, in the same way that the Mac uses these triangles to open and close subfolders displayed within folders.

The Preferences dialog boxes are much the same on all versions of Communicator, with a few differences where features are not present or work differently. (Also, note that there's a Navigator category in Windows, while it's called Browser on the Mac.)

Part
I

Ch
2

FIG. 2.13

The Windows version of the Preferences dialog box.

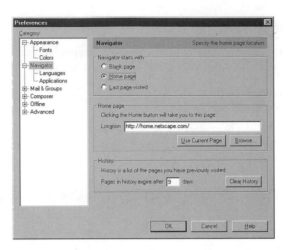

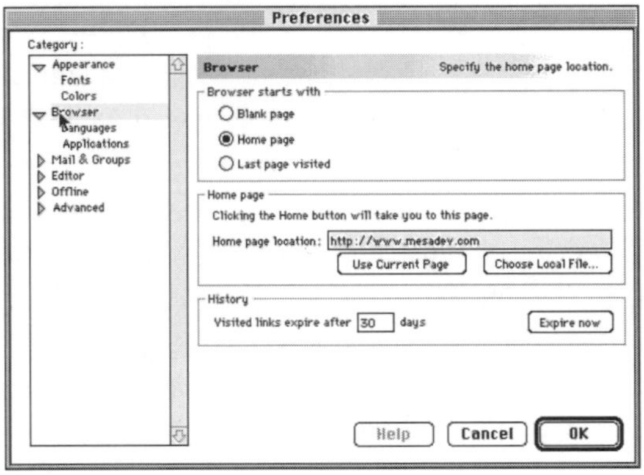

FIG. 2.14

The Macintosh version of the Preferences dialog box.

Changing Text, Link, and Background Appearance

To modify the colors of the text and links in the Web pages you view with Navigator, select Edit, Preferences, open the Appearance category, then click Colors (see Figure 2.15). To change link colors, simply click the button next to the type of link you want to modify: Unvisited Links or Visited Links. A Color box will open, from which you can select a color. You can also remove the underline from links if you want, by clearing the Underline Links check box.

You can also modify text and background colors. If you select the Use Windows Colors check box, the color scheme you've selected for all your other Windows applications will be used. Clear this check box, though, and you can click the individual Text and Background buttons to set those colors individually. On the Mac, there's a Use Default Colors button that lets you use the system's default color scheme.

Part

I

Ch

2

FIG. 2.15
Set link and background colors here.

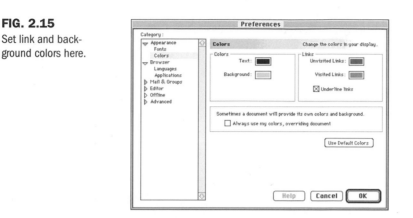

Remember, all these settings can be overridden by a Web author, so you won't always get your specified text, link, and background colors, unless you select Always Use My Colors, Overriding Document.

The Web Isn't Just English

Remember the full name of the Web? It's the *World Wide Web*. It's not the *U.S. Web*, not the *English-Speaking Web*, but an international system used by almost all nations of the world.

It's true that at the moment the vast majority of Web pages are in English, but it doesn't have to be that way and will probably change one day. Some Web servers can check to see what language your browser prefers to use and then send pages in the appropriate language. Right now few servers do this, so it's not an important issue, but Navigator has already added components to allow the browser to tell the server which language you prefer.

Choose Edit, Preferences, open the Navigator category (the Browser category on the Mac), and click Languages. You'll see the pane in Figure 2.16. Click the Add button open the Add Languages dialog box, from which you can choose which languages you want to use. Simply click an entry and then click OK to add it to the list. You can move the position of each language in the list using the arrow buttons. The language at the top of the list is the one you prefer to work with; if that's not available, the server can look down the list and find your next preference.

You can see the actual codes sent to the Web server in the Add Languages dialog box. For instance, there's English/United Kingdom [en-GB] and English/United States [en-US]; *en* is the language code (English), while *GB* and *US* are the region codes.

Document Encoding

Navigator uses a document-encoding system that allows it to display documents that have been created using different character sets; that is, document encoding tells the browser which computer codes represent which characters. For instance, most documents are currently created using the Western (Latin 1) character set, but documents may be created using the Central European (Latin 2) set or a variety of Japanese, Korean, Chinese, and Eastern European character sets.

FIG. 2.16

The Languages pane allows you to specify the order of language preference in which a server should send Web pages. (Right now, this is rarely used.)

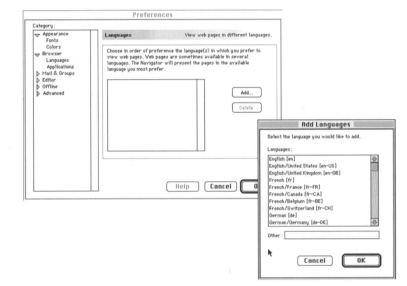

You can select which character set should be used by choosing View, Encoding; you'll see a drop-down menu with a list of options. Note, however, that you won't use these settings unless you are working with one of the foreign language versions of your operating system.

Changing the Fonts

You can also define which fonts you want to use in documents displayed by Navigator. Choose Edit, Preferences, double-click Appearance, then click Fonts. You'll see the information in Figure 2.17. The drop-down list box at the top, shown with Western selected, allows you to select the document-encoding system you're using on your browser. (You generally won't need to change this selection, unless you are using other character sets.) You can use the other two drop-down list boxes to choose the font types you want to use for that encoding system. You have two font types: the Variable Width Font (a "proportional" font, used for most of the text in Web documents) and the Fixed Width Font (used only when an author has defined text as fixed-width text).

It's now possible for a Web author to define which fonts are used in a page, though at present few Web pages define the font type. Still, we'll soon see the ability to set font types used throughout the Web, and Communicator provides a way to define what the browser should do when it loads a page in which the font has been defined. There are two types of fonts that an author can use; fonts built into the browser, or dynamic fonts, fonts that must be transmitted to the browser along with the Web page. The built-in fonts can be displayed very quickly, of course, but dynamic fonts will slow down the display of the page. (Dynamic fonts are not yet in use, but you can expect people to start using them very soon.) You can tell Communicator to:

- *Use My Default Fonts, Overriding Document-Specified Fonts* Your fonts will always be used, regardless of what fonts the author chooses.

FIG. 2.17
Tell Navigator which fonts to use, and whether to override the Web-page author's settings.

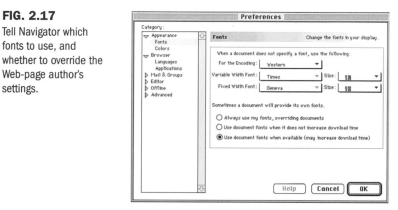

- *Use Document-Specified Fonts, But Disable Dynamic Fonts* The browser will use any built-in fonts specified by the author, but will *not* use any dynamic fonts.
- *Use Document-Specified Fonts, Including Dynamic Fonts* The browser will use all the author-specified fonts, whether built-in or dynamic.

N O T E A *proportional font* is one in which different characters may have different sizes; the letter "i" takes up less room than the letter "w". A *fixed font* is one in which all the letters are the same width. ■

By the way, you should also soon be able to enlarge or reduce the font size used in the window temporarily, using the View, Increase Font and View, Decrease Font commands. This makes it easy to quickly modify the text in a particular document to make it easy to use…but at the time of writing these commands do not work.

Changing Your Video Mode

Also, remember that Navigator's appearance is to some extent dependent on how you've set up your video monitor. If you're using a 16-color video mode, many images you see on the Web will appear rather murky. A 256-color mode is better. (Some images, though not many, use more than 256 colors.)

Also, you may find that the Navigator window is rather cluttered. Many people still use VGA resolution: 640×480. These numbers refer to the number of pixels (a pixel is the smallest part of the video image that can be displayed on your screen) across the screen and down the screen. But 640×480 isn't really very convenient because everything's very large using this resolution—you won't see much of the Web page. If you use 800×600, or even 1024×768, Navigator will be able to display more of each document inside the content area of the window.

The problem with using a higher resolution, however, is that a high resolution "squeezes" things. The text and pictures in the document will become smaller. (How do you think it gets more into the content area?) So there's a trade-off. The larger your screen, the higher resolution you can use comfortably; the smaller your screen, the more difficult high resolutions will be to work with. Also, the higher the screen resolution you use, the more work your video board has to do. At very high resolutions, you may find that things work more slowly. And with some old equipment, you may also find that you cannot use a 256-color mode at a high resolution.

So experiment a little. Try all the different resolutions you can, while still keeping 256 colors. See your system documentation for information on changing your screen resolution. (In Windows 95 and NT, for instance, you can modify your video modes using the Display Properties dialog box. Right-click the Windows desktop and then choose Properties. When the dialog box opens, click the Settings tab—you'll find the color and resolution settings.)

Working Offline

If you want, you can set up Communicator to work offline. In other words, it won't check for an Internet or intranet connection. Why would you want to do this? Perhaps you don't have a permanent connection to the Internet—maybe you're using Communicator from home, for instance. But maybe you want to open Communicator to look at your e-mail or newsgroup messages, or to view Web pages that are stored in your cache (more about that in a moment). So you may not want Communicator to try to connect to the Internet every time you start it.

To move around on the Web you have to be connected to the Internet through a TCP/IP connection. But you can open Navigator and view documents on your hard drive without being connected to the Internet (you'll see how to open files from your hard drive in Chapter 3, "Advanced Navigation"), and even view Web pages that you've seen in previous Navigator sessions.

Most browsers—Navigator included—have something called the cache (discussed in Chapter 3). The *cache* is a place on your hard disk where the browser stores copies of Web documents that were transferred from the Web earlier. In other words, when you ask the browser to retrieve a document from the Web, it not only displays it in the Web browser but also places a copy in the cache. Then, if you want to view the document again later, instead of grabbing it from the Web, it can grab it from the cache, saving a lot of time.

As you can see, it's possible (in theory) to move around on the Web without really being connected to the Web—as long as the pages are in the cache, Navigator can display them without retrieving them from the Web. In order to do this, though, everything has to be set up correctly. Before Navigator grabs a page from the cache, it checks the Web to see if the page has changed—to see if the page in the cache is the same as the one on the Web. In order to do that, of course, it needs to have a connection to the Internet. However, you can tell Navigator *not* to check the Web, but to grab pages directly from the cache without confirming that they're the latest version. You'll learn how to do that in Chapter 3. You'll also have to select a different home page, which we'll cover in a moment.

Unfortunately, this offline-work mode is marred by the fact that it doesn't actually work quite correctly. For instance, even if a page is in the cache, and even if you've set the cache so that Navigator is *never* supposed to check a page, Navigator may still try to connect to check a page. Nonetheless, you may want to experiment with offline-work mode, and it may work better in future versions of Communicator.

Setting Up Navigator for Offline Work

To set up Navigator to work offline, choose Edit, Preferences, and click the Offline category. You'll see the information in Figure 2.18. You can choose to work Online; Communicator will look for a network connection each time you start the program, and try to connect if there isn't presently an active connection. You can work Offline; Communicator won't bother to check for a connection or attempt to make a connection. Or you may select Ask Me, to get Communicator to display a dialog box asking if you want to work online.

FIG. 2.18

You have three Offline/Online work categories to choose from.

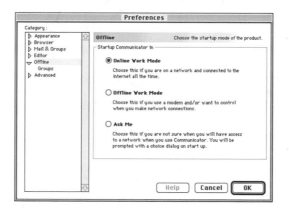

There are a few things to consider if you plan to start Communicator offline. First, you'll have to change the home page. The home page is the page that loads automatically when you start Navigator, and by default Navigator uses the **http://www.netscape.com/** page as its home page. But the system's set up so that each time you load this page, Navigator checks the Netscape Communications Web site to see if it has the latest version of the page; it checks regardless of how you've set the cache. So if you set up Navigator to work offline, and keep the default home page, each time you start Navigator it will tell you that it's unable to load the page. Instead, you should set the system to open with a blank page, the last page you visited, or a page on your hard disk (see "Setting A New Home Page," next).

Also, Communicator has File, Go Offline and File, Go Online commands. These allow you to switch mode. When you do so, though, you'll see the dialog box in Figure 2.19. As you can see, this mode-switching ability is primarily to allow you to grab e-mail and newsgroup messages and send outgoing messages (see Chapters 16 to 18), and then disconnect. If you simply want to connect with the browser to load a Web page, you need to clear the check marks first.

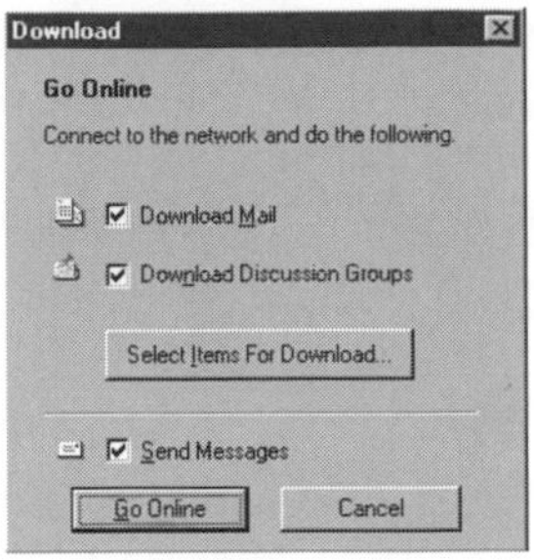

FIG. 2.19

When you go online or offline, you'll see this dialog box.

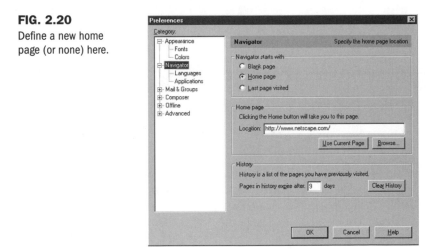

Setting a New Home Page

You can define another page as your home page—that is, you don't have to see the Netscape Communications page each time you open your browser. First load the page you want to use into the browser, then choose Edit, Preferences, click Navigator in the Category list (Browser if you're using the Mac), and click the Use Current Page button (see Figure 2.20) or you can type the URL of the document you want to use into the Location text box.

FIG. 2.20

Define a new home page (or none) here.

To use a document on your hard disk as your home page, click the Browse button and find the document (you can create Web pages and save them on your hard disk; see Chapter 20). You can also use the option buttons on this page to define the home page. If you select Blank Page, Navigator opens without loading a home page. If you select Home Page, it loads the page defined as the Home Page in the text box below. And if you select Last Page Visited, it loads whatever was the last page you viewed before closing Navigator the last time. ●

CHAPTER 3

Advanced Navigation

Now that you know how to use the basic browser navigation commands, we can move on to the more advanced moves. In this chapter, I'll explain how to work a little faster, how to run multiple Web sessions at the same time, how to go directly to a Web page, and so on. You need to know these advanced moves to work efficiently on the Web. ■

Speed up sessions by removing pictures

Inline pictures are part of the charm of the Web…and part of the problem. They can slow down Web sessions dramatically, so you may want to turn them off.

Using URLs (Web addresses)

URLs provide a way to go directly to the page you want to view.

Multiple Web sessions

If your computer has enough memory, you can load two or three or even more Web pages into separate windows.

What's the cache (and reload)?

The cache is an essential tool that dramatically speeds up your work on the Web. But you must know how to set it up properly.

Searching Web documents

The Find in Page command enables you to search a Web page.

Using pop-up menus

Pop-up menus provide a convenient way to access important commands.

Speeding Things Up—Removing Images

The Web is a very colorful place. Web authors really get into their work, in many cases including wonderful art in their works, photographs of themselves or their dogs, fancy buttons and toolbars. But all this colorful stuff is a double-edged sword. Sure, it makes the Web an interesting place to visit, but for many of us it also makes visiting the Web a very *slow* journey. Many people, perhaps most, are now working on dial-in lines, using modems to transfer the information from the Web back to their computers. And the really fancy stuff that's found on the Web can move very slowly, even with a fast modem.

After working on the Web for a while, when all these pictures are no longer a novelty, you may want to speed things up a bit by removing the pictures. You can then move very quickly through pages in which you have little interest and view the pictures only in the pages in which you want (or need) to view the pictures. You'll find you move around on the Web much more quickly.

Simply choose Edit, Preferences, click Advanced in the Category list, then clear the Automatically Load Images check box. The next time you go to a Web page, you won't see the pictures. Well, that's not quite true; if the page is in the cache (discussed in more detail later in this chapter) and if the page was originally retrieved with Automatically Load Images turned on, then you'll see the pictures. However, when you go to a Web page that is not in the cache, Navigator will not retrieve the pictures.

You'll discover, however, that not only do you sometimes want to view a missing picture, but sometimes you have to. Because so many Web pages these days contain images that are essential, you'll soon reach sites that you can't move through without viewing a picture first.

See, for instance, the example shown in Figure 3.1. This page has been retrieved with Automatically Load Images turned off, and you can see the little icons that Navigator uses to replace missing images. This page has no text links so, if you want to navigate "through" this page, you'll have to view these pictures.

Notice the pop-up menu on the Web page. You can display this menu by right-clicking the picture (in Windows), or by clicking and holding the mouse button down for a moment (on the Mac). There are several ways to display the missing images:

■ Open the pop-up menu, then select Show Image.

■ Open the pop-up menu and select View Image. This displays the image in a browser window by itself (you won't be able to use the links, if any, on the image).

 ■ Click the Images button on the toolbar to load all the missing images (this button only appears on the toolbar if Automatically Load Images is turned off).

T I P   Hold the mouse button over a placeholder for a missing image, and a small box may appear, displaying an associated "alternative-text" message giving you an idea of what the image shows.

FIG. 3.1
I retrieved this Web
page with Auto Load
Images turned off.
Notice the pop-up
menu.

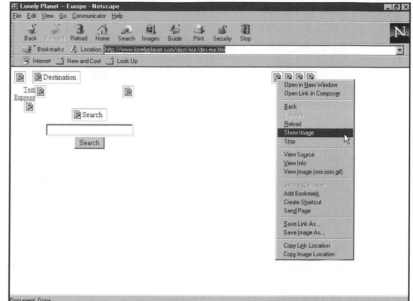

Stopping Animations

Netscape is adding a new image-related command to Navigator soon—the View, Stop Animations command. You'll often come across little flickering images displayed in Web pages. Most of these images are GIF89a images, created by "pasting together" several individual images and then displaying each one in turn. The effect is an animation.

These images can be very irritating to some people and, on a slow computer, can even be a real nuisance. If you want to stop the images from running, simply select View, Stop Animations. (This command is not currently working, though it should be soon.)

Traveling Directly to Web Pages with URLs

Now and then you may find an URL—a Uniform Resource Locator, or Web "address"—in a newspaper or magazine. Or perhaps you'll run across one in a newsgroup message, or a friend e-mails you something he's just found.

Now you need to know how to go directly from here to there. You don't want to follow links to this document; you want to go directly to it. Let's see how an URL is structured and then how you can use it.

URLs—The Web Address

Everything on the World Wide Web needs some kind of address; otherwise, how would you find anything? Each resource on the Web—each document, each image, and so on—has an address, an URL (or Uniform Resource Locator). Here's an example:

http://www.lonelyplanet.com/dest/eur/des-eur.htm

The URL starts with http://. This indicates the site is a normal HTTP (HyperText Transport Protocol) site; you are going to an HTML document. Sometimes the URL starts with something different. If it starts with ftp://, for instance, you are on your way to an FTP site. As you'll see in Chapters 14 and 15, Web browsers can access other Internet systems, not just HTTP.

Next comes the address of the host computer (the address of the computer that has the Web server you are contacting), in this case www.lonelyplanet.com. Following that is the address of the file directory containing the resource—/dest/eur/.

 In the world of Windows and DOS, directories are indicated with backslashes (\). In the UNIX world, however, they are indicated with forward slashes (/). Most Internet Web sites are running on UNIX computers (though that may change, thanks to the popularity of Windows NT servers), and the forward slash has become the standard for URLs.

Finally, you have the resource itself—des-eur.htm. In this case, you can tell that it's an HTML document. The .htm extension makes that clear. (Web documents often have .html extensions, too.)

Often the URL doesn't have a file name at the end; it just finishes with a directory name or perhaps doesn't even have a directory name—just the host name. That's not necessarily a mistake. For instance, if you want to go to the Macmillan Publishing Web site, you'll use the following URL: **http://www.mcp.com/**. This specifies the host, but no directory or document. That's okay; the Web server is set up to show you the document that the administrator wants you to see when arriving at the host.

Using the URL

Here are several ways to use an URL to get to the document you want to see:

■ Click inside the text box in the Location bar (remember, the Location bar is labeled `Netsite` if the current document is on a Netscape server); then type the URL. (When you click in the text box, the current URL is highlighted. When you type, the URL is replaced with the new one.) Then press Enter. For instance, type **http://www.mcp.com**, and then press Enter to go to the Macmillan Publishing Web site.

T I P   You can omit the http:// bit if you want; when you press Enter, Navigator will add it for you. In this example, type **www.mcp.com** and press Enter. In some cases, Navigator can even figure out where to go with less of an URL. If you simply type **mcp**, for instance, Navigator will look for http://mcp, discover it's not a real host name, and then take a guess and try http://www.mcp.com.

■ Copy an URL into the Windows Clipboard from another application. Then paste it into Navigator's Location bar, and press Enter. (You can press Ctrl+V—⌘+V on the Mac—or choose <u>E</u>dit, <u>P</u>aste.)

■ Choose File, Open Page. The Open Page dialog box appears. Type the URL and choose OK. (This dialog box is an alternative to the Location bar, in case you choose to remove the Location bar from the screen by choosing View, Toolbars, Hide Location Toolbar. It also allows you to open files from the hard disk—see "Opening Files on Your Hard Disk," later in this chapter—or place Web pages in Netscape Composer—see Chapter 20.)

TIP Sometimes you'll find that an URL doesn't work, perhaps simply due to a typo. Try this approach: Remove the rightmost portion and try again. For instance, if you try **http://www.mcp.com/author/pkent**, and it doesn't work, try **http://www.mcp.com/author/**. If that still doesn't work, try **http://www.mcp.com/**. (The first URL wouldn't work because there's a typo; it should be authors, not author. You can actually get to my Web page by using **http://www.mcp.com/authors/pkent**.)

Don't want to keep switching from the mouse to the keyboard? Here's a quick way to enter an URL. Simply press Ctrl+O (or ⌘+L on the Mac) to open the Open Page dialog box, type the URL, and press Enter. Or press Tab (you may have to press a couple of times) to highlight the URL in the Location box, type a new URL to replace the old one, and then press Enter.

By the way, Communicator now has a new feature that helps you quickly fill in URLs you've used before, a feature you may be familiar with from other programs (such as financial-management programs). When you begin typing an URL, Communicator looks through the list of URLs you've typed before, and sees if it has a match. So, for instance, if you've been to **http://www.mcp.com/** before, Communicator will be able find a match as soon as you've typed **www.m**, and will fill in the rest of the URL for you. If Communicator enters the wrong URL, keep typing and it may pick the right one (for instance, it will enter **www.macromedia.com** before it enters **www.mcp.com**, because that appears earlier in an alphabetically sorted list). Or if you are entering a brand new URL, simply continue typing to type over the URL that Communicator has entered for you. (This feature seems to work intermittently in the current version of Communicator, though presumably this problem will be fixed.)

Remembering URLs

Let's say you entered an URL a few days ago. Now you want to return to the same document, but you don't remember the URL. You can use a bookmark (if you created one for the document you want to view). You'll learn more about bookmarks in Chapter 5. But there's a quicker way. Notice the small down-pointing triangle at the end of the Location text box.

Click this triangle, or click inside the text box and press F4. The URL list opens up, as you can see in Figure 3.2. (Note that this feature may not be available on the Mac.) This list shows the URLs you've entered in the past; just click the one you want, and Navigator loads that document. (You can also use the down arrow to move through the list, though Navigator will attempt to load each document in turn as it is highlighted.)

FIG. 3.2
Select an URL that you've used earlier by opening the Location list.

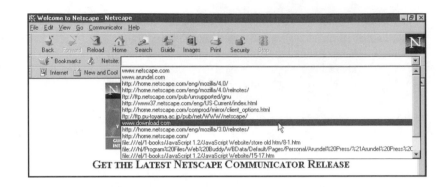

> **T I P**   The problem with selecting from the URL list is that you may not recognize the URL; URLs often are not very descriptive. If you can't remember the URL and you haven't placed the document in the bookmark list, you may be able to use the history list if you are returning to a document you've seen in the current session. The history list uses the document titles, which are much more descriptive and easier to remember (see Chapter 5).
>
> Note that only URLs that were entered into the Location text box—not the Open Location dialog box— are stored in the Location drop-down list box.

A reader of an earlier edition of this book had an interesting question: "What happens if I visit sites I don't want people to *know* I've visited? How do I remove the entries from the drop-down list box?" I didn't ask what sites he'd been visiting, but there is a solution to the problem: You can delete the entries from the configuration file in which they're stored. If you're using Windows 95 or NT, these listings are stored in the system Registry (run Regedit.exe to view the Registry, and search for one of the entries in the list; be warned, though, you can make your system unstable if you delete or modify something incorrectly). In Windows 3.1 versions, the entries are stored in an .INI file in one of the Communicator directories.

Sending URLs to Other People

You may want to share URLs that you've found. You can copy them from Navigator and paste them into letters, memos, e-mail, and so on. Here's how.

If you want to copy the URL of the page you are currently viewing, click in the Location text box. The entire text is highlighted. Then press Ctrl+C (Windows) or ⌘+C (Mac), or choose Edit, Copy. This copies the text to the Clipboard. Then you can change to another application and paste the text.

It's a lot safer to copy the URL than it is to retype it. Your spelling checker won't be able to help you with misspelled URLs, and, if even one character is wrong, the URL won't work.

If you want to copy an URL from a link—in other words, you haven't gone to the Web document, so the URL isn't in the Location text box—point to the link and right-click it (or hold the mouse button down on the Mac). When the pop-up menu opens, choose Copy Link Location.

The URL referenced by the link is copied to the Clipboard. You can then copy the link into an e-mail message—you'll learn about that in Chapter 16. (You'll also see how to send an entire Web page via e-mail.)

 Finally, you can drag the Document Link icon from Navigator's Location toolbar and drop it onto a document in another Windows application; the URL will be pasted into the document. (This feature won't work with all programs, though.)

Running Two (or More) Web Sessions

Navigator allows you to run more than one Web session at the same time. You can be loading a Web page into one browser window while you read another. Or maybe you need to find information at another Web site, but don't want to "lose your place" at the current one (see Figure 3.3).

Part
I
Ch
3

FIG. 3.3
You can open two (or more) windows so you can run multiple Web sessions.

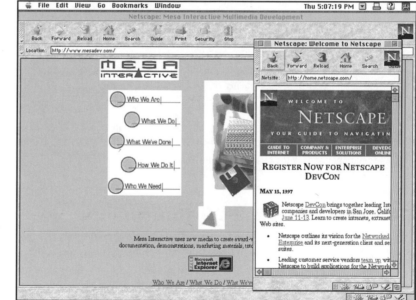

You can start new sessions a couple of ways. You can point to the link and right-click it or, on the Mac, click the link and hold the button down a moment. A pop-up menu then opens. Choose Open in New Window. A new Navigator window opens, and the referenced document opens in that window. You end up with two windows open, each displaying a different document. You can switch between these windows using the normal methods used by your operating system; click the window below, for instance, or if you're using Windows, press Alt+Tab. You can also use the Communicator menu (the Window menu on the Mac) to switch between open browser windows; at the bottom of the menu you'll see a list of these windows.

T I P   The ability to run multiple sessions can be very useful, but if you have a slow modem or an overtaxed server at work, the additional "bandwidth" that this requires will make all of the sessions a lot slower. Furthermore, Navigator eats memory like a pig at a trough; you may find that your system simply doesn't have enough memory to handle more than one additional window, if that.

The other method is to choose File, New, Navigator Window. Another Navigator window opens, displaying the first Web document that you viewed in the current session. This is the home page (unless you set up the General Preferences to display a blank page when Navigator opens, in which case it's the first document you went to after starting Navigator). You can then begin navigating through the window in a different "direction," so you have two sessions running at once.

T I P   If you want to view both windows at the same time, you can "tile" the windows. In Windows 95, for instance, right-click the taskbar, and then choose Minimize All Windows. Then click the buttons of the windows you want to tile together, right-click the taskbar again, and choose Tile Horizontally or Tile Vertically.

Also, it might be more convenient if the File, New, Navigator Window command opened a window and displayed the current document, not the home page. However, you can open the current document in the new window by selecting it from the new window's Go menu.

N O T E   A second window opened automatically; what happened? Navigator allows Web authors to open "secondary" or "targeted" windows for you. You click a link, and the referenced document opens in the new window. See Chapter 7 for more information. ▪

Opening Files on Your Hard Disk

Eventually, in your exploration of the Web, you may end up with .htm or .html files on your hard disk. You'll have them in your cache (which we'll discuss next); you may save documents using the File, Save As or File, Save Frame As command (see Chapter 8); or perhaps you'll even create your own (see Chapters 20 and 21). Navigator provides a way to open these files.

Choose File, Open Page. Then click the Choose File button, and the Open dialog box appears. Use this dialog box to find the .htm or .html file you want to open. Click the file name, and then click the Open button to place the file name into the Open Page dialog box. Click the Open button in that dialog box and Navigator displays the document.

T I P You can open other items, too. In the Open dialog box click the Files of Type drop-down list box to see a list of file types you can work with, such as:

.txt (text files)	.lam (Streaming Audio Metafiles)
.mid and .midi (MIDI music files)	.au, .aif, and .aiff (sound files)
.wrl and .wrz (VRML 3-D image files)	.wav (Windows audio files)
.mov (QuickTime video files)	.la and .lma (Netscape Packetized Audio files)

At the time of writing, this list wasn't complete; you can also open .gif, .jpg, .jpeg, and .xbm image files. In fact, you can open any file type for which you have configured a viewer or helper (see Chapter 9).

T I P If you know the exact path to the file you want to open, and if you can type quickly, click the Location text box and type the path. For instance, if you are working in Windows 95, you might type **C:/Data/About.html** to open the About.html document in the Data folder. (Note that you can type the forward slash or backslash; for instance, if you type **C:\Data\About.html**, Navigator stills grab the correct document, even though Web URLs generally use the forward slash.) Navigator will automatically open the file and replace what you've typed with a more formal URL, something like file:///c|/Data/About.html.

Part

I

Ch

3

Here's another way to open an .htm or .html file that you have saved on your hard disk, if you're using Windows 95. You can open Windows Explorer, find the file you want to open, and then double-click the file name. When you installed Navigator, it associated itself with the .htm and .html extensions, so, when you double-click one of these file names, Windows Explorer knows just what to do: open Navigator and display the file. You can also position Windows Explorer and Navigator so you can see both windows; then drag an .htm or .html file from Explorer and drop it onto Navigator. (The Mac has a similar associations system, though not quite as easy to work with; files may open in the application you think they will, but sometimes they don't.)

Understanding the Cache

Now you're ready to learn about the cache and the Reload command. I've mentioned it a few times already because it seems to touch on so many areas. So let's learn about it in detail.

When you go back to a Web document that you've previously viewed, you may notice that it's displayed much more quickly. That's because Navigator isn't taking it from the Internet; it's getting it from the cache, an area on your hard disk or in your computer's RAM (memory) in which it saves pages. This capability greatly speeds up working time on the Web.

Navigator has two types of cache: the disk cache and the memory cache.(The Mac version has only a hard-disk cache, not a memory cache.) The memory cache stores the most recent documents. Slightly older ones can be found in the hard-disk cache, which by default is the C:\Program Files\Netscape\Users*username*\Cache directory in Windows 95, or the System Folder::Preferences::Netscape folder::Cache folder on the Mac.

This cache can get very big—as big as you (and your computer) allow it. Choose Edit, Preferences; open the Advanced category; then click Cache. You'll see the information shown in Figure 3.4. Note that the Disk Cache Folder line shows which directory is being used as the cache. You can enter a different directory if you want. For instance, if your C: drive doesn't have much space, but your D: drive does, you may want to place the cache on that drive. First, create a directory for the cache. Then return to Navigator's Preferences dialog box, and click Choose Folder to select the folder you've just created.

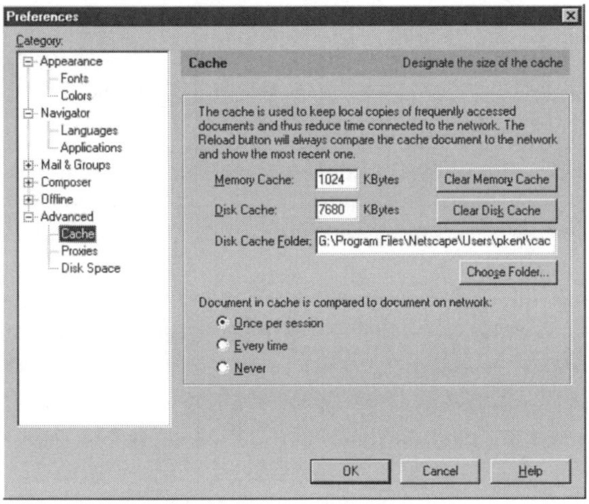

FIG. 3.4

The Network Preferences dialog box lets you determine the size of your cache.

You can also configure the cache size by entering numbers into the Memory Cache and Disk Cache text boxes. How large should these numbers be? Well, the larger the numbers, the better—though, as with everything involved with computers, there's a trade-off. The memory cache holds recent documents, so when you return to those documents—using the Back button or history list, for instance—Navigator can display them more quickly. The larger the memory cache, the more documents it can store.

If the document Navigator needs isn't in the memory cache, it looks in the hard-disk cache. The larger the hard-disk cache, the more likely a document is to be there. If your hard-disk cache is big enough, you can store documents for weeks or even months.

Note, however, that you are not reserving an area of your hard disk for the cache. For instance, if you have a 30,000K (almost 30M) disk cache, Navigator doesn't create a 30,000K file, so other programs can't use that disk space. Rather, it simply means that Navigator can use that much disk space for the cache, if available.

So what's the catch? Why not make your cache as large as possible? Because if you do so, you'll be using up resources that other applications may need. Fill up your hard-disk cache, and that much less disk space will be available to save files from other programs. Reserve a large area of memory, and other programs can't use the memory. Also, a very large disk cache may cause Navigator to close slowly.

TIP Navigator doesn't use the cache for everything. If it transfers files that it cannot display, it has to pass them on to a viewer (you'll learn about viewers in Chapter 9). These files are not placed into the cache. Rather, they are placed into your \Windows\Temp directory. For instance, when you transfer .Au sound files, Navigator places them in the \Windows\Temp directory before starting its internal sound program to play them.

Notice also that the Preferences dialog box has Clear Memory Cache Now and Clear Disk Cache Now buttons. Click these buttons to remove all the data from the respective caches. In the case of the disk cache, this button literally deletes all the files from your hard disk. Before you do that, though, read on, because in Chapter 8 I'm going to explain how to grab information from the Web—the cache can provide a storehouse from which you can extract information, even after you've logged off the Internet.

CAUTION

Be careful with that cache—it's a record of everything you've done! Let's say, for instance, that you like to sit in your cubicle at work and use Navigator to cruise around the naughty bits of the Web: the *Hustler, Playboy*, and *Penthouse* Web sites. Well, each time you view a picture of Candy or Bonita, that picture is placed in your hard-disk cache. That evening—or the next day, or next week, or next month, if the cache is large enough—your boss or coworkers can look through the cache and find out exactly what you've been up to! I would never advise that you spend time at these naughty sites—but if you do, use safe sex; click the Clear Disk Cache Now button afterward. You should also know that the history list provides a way to see where you've been in earlier sessions, too; see Chapter 5 for more information.

Navigator Verifies the Cache for You

In some cases, Navigator tries to verify the page for you, to see if the document on the Web has changed since the last time a copy of it was placed in the cache. That is, it sends a message to the Web server from which the document originally came, asking whether the document has changed. If the Web server responds that the document has changed, then Navigator asks the server to send a new copy; if it hasn't changed, Navigator simply retrieves it from the cache.

When does Navigator send this verification-request message? That depends on what you've selected in the Preferences dialog box.

The dialog box contains three option buttons under the Document in Cache is Compared to Document on Network heading: Once per Session, Every Time, and Never. If you choose the Once per Session option button, Navigator will ask for verification the first time you view a document after opening the browser. If you go to the document again, later in the same session, Navigator doesn't bother verifying the document; it assumes that the document hasn't changed during the session. For instance, let's say you visited the Dow Jones page (**http:// www.dowjones.com/**) yesterday. Today, you open your browser and go back to the Dow Jones page. Does Navigator ask the Web server if the page has changed? Yes, if Once per Session is turned on. And, if Navigator finds that the page has changed, it retrieves a new copy and places that page in the cache.

If you leave the Dow Jones page and return to it later, Navigator retrieves the document from the cache—it doesn't bother re-verifying the document.

Then there's the Every Time option button. This button tells Navigator to always verify the document, to see if any changes have been made, regardless of how many times you have viewed the document during the session.

Finally, you have the Never option button, which tells Navigator not to bother verifying documents; as long as the document is in the cache, Navigator will use that document. It will never check to see if a document has changed, so it will never automatically update the document. Documents will change in only two circumstances: if the document "falls out" of the cache (because the cache filled up and Navigator removed old documents to make room for new ones) or if you use the Reload command (as discussed later in this chapter).

Which of the cache options should you use? I prefer Never because it makes my Web sessions much quicker. Whenever I tell Navigator to go to a Web page that's already in the cache, Navigator loads the page from the hard disk right away, without sending a verification message to the server first. On the other hand, I have to remember to keep using the Reload command to make sure I'm viewing the latest version of the Web pages (and yes, sometimes I've forgotten and missed important information!). Some people may prefer to use the Once per Session option so that they can be sure of always looking at a version that is at the least very recent.

When Is a Page Verified?

Now that you've got the verification set up, you should be aware that the verification message is also dependent on *how* you access a page. Assuming you've turned on verification, Navigator will verify a document if you reach that document by clicking a link, choosing a bookmark, entering an URL into the Location text box, or clicking the Reload button. However, when you use the Back command or select an item from the history list (see Chapter 5), Navigator does not bother to verify the document. It simply grabs it from the cache.

What's Reload All About?

Reload is a "cure" for the cache. What happens if you return to a Web document that's stored in the cache? Navigator gets it from the cache, right? However, that means you are not getting the latest document. Now, getting the most recent document doesn't always matter, but in a few cases it does.

For instance, let's say you want to return to a site you visited several weeks ago. If you have a very large cache, that document may still be available. If you have the <u>N</u>ever option button selected in the Preferences dialog box, you'll be seeing the *old* document, though the corresponding document stored on the Web may have changed in the last few weeks. Or perhaps you are viewing a Web document that changes rapidly, such as a stock-quote page. Even if you viewed the page only a few minutes ago, it could already be out of date.

CAUTION

There's a serious reload bug in some versions of Navigator that we should mention—reloading does not always reload the document properly, particularly if something has changed in a form or a JavaScript (see Chapters 4 and 12). You can try to force a complete reload by pressing Shift when you click the Reload button. Or set a bookmark on the page and then open the document using the bookmark. Or, if you really have to have the latest version and Navigator just doesn't seem to be able to get it, your last resort is to clear the cache. This problem was present in earlier versions of Navigator, and some early 4.x versions. It may or may not still be present.

 The cure for old stale Web pages is to reload them. Click the Reload button, or choose <u>V</u>iew, <u>R</u>eload. Navigator overwrites the current document in the cache, replacing it with the latest version. You can also select <u>R</u>eload from the pop-up menu.

There are other related commands available. First, there's the pop-up menu's <u>R</u>eload Frame command. Right-click the frame (or click and hold the button if using the Macintosh), and then choose this command to reload only the contents of that frame (you'll learn more about frames in Chapter 7).

And there's also <u>V</u>iew, Re<u>f</u>resh. This command gets a new copy of the current document from the memory cache, not from the Web itself. Using this command is simply a way to "clean up" the document; if your computer is having some kind of video problem and displaying pictures or text incorrectly, this command "repaints" the screen.

TIP

The current Macintosh version of Navigator doesn't have a Refresh command, but it does have display problems now and again. There's one way I've found that sometimes fixes those problems. Turn on the Macintosh WindowShade utility. Then you can double-click window title bars in order to hide the window (the title bar remains visible, while the window itself disappears). Double-click the Navigator's title bar once to hide the window, then double-click again to open it, and the display problem *may* be fixed.

What Is LiveCache?

LiveCache is a feature coming to Navigator soon. It will allow the browser to load Web pages from a CD to the cache. For instance, a company might send a catalog on CD. You could view the contents of the catalog from the CD, with no Internet connection (or online fee) required. When you wanted the latest information, though—perhaps a price list—clicking a link would start your Internet connection and display a page at the company's Web site.

LiveCache has another important feature; if you begin to transfer a page and the transfer is interrupted, the cache will save what it can. The next time you try to display the page, it will grab what it has from the cache and then transfer the rest from the Web.

Searching Within Documents

Some Web pages are pretty big. In fact, some are *very* big—hundreds of lines long—with links from the top of the document to "sections" lower down. Many Web authors prefer to create one large page, rather than lots of small linked ones, because once the page has been transferred to your browser, you can use links to move to different parts of the page very quickly.

Navigator helps you search long documents. Choose Edit, Find in Page. The Find dialog box opens (see Figure 3.5). Type the word or words you are looking for, choose Match Case (in Windows) or Case Sensitive (on the Mac) if necessary, and then choose the direction (Windows has Up and Down option buttons, while the Mac has a Find Backwards check box). Choose Find Next, and Navigator moves the document so that the first line containing the word or words you are searching for is at the top of the window.

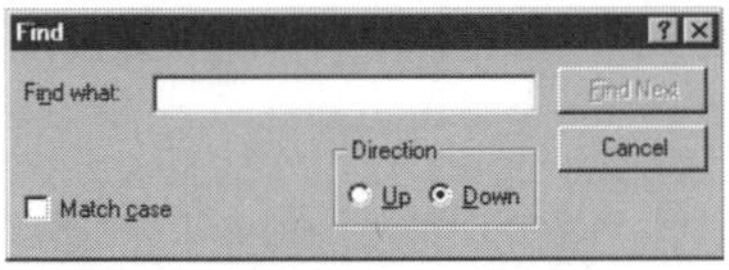

FIG. 3.5
Use the Find dialog box to search large Web documents.

If the first occurrence of the word isn't what you want, you can click Find Next again. Or you may want to close the dialog box and read what Navigator found for you. Then choose Edit, Find Again (or press F3 or Ctrl+G) to quickly continue the search. You can also leave the Find dialog box open and scroll through the document if you like.

T I P Don't forget the Find command. It can come in very handy for searching long Gopher menus and WAIS directories (see Chapter 15), FTP file listings (see Chapter 14), and large Web documents.

Remember the Pop-Up Menu

Remember to use the pop-up menu. Point at something in the Navigator window's content area, and then press the right mouse button (in Windows; if using a Mac, point and hold the mouse button down for a moment). Up pops the menu, as you can see in Figure 3.6. This menu provides shortcuts to a number of commands, some of which are duplicates of menu and toolbar commands, but others are available only through the pop-up menu. You won't see all of the menu commands in some cases; for instance, if you click in a blank area of the content area, you'll see fewer options than if you click a picture.

FIG. 3.6
The pop-up menu provides shortcuts to several commands.

We've already looked at the pop-up menu a couple of times, but let's quickly see what the other options on this menu can do for you (note that these menu-option names vary slightly between versions of Navigator):

Part

I

Ch

3

Pop-Up Option	Function
Open in New Window	Opens another Navigator window, and then opens the document referenced by the link in that window.
Open Frame in New Window	Opens another Navigator window, then loads the document shown within the frame in which you clicked.
Open Link in Composer	Opens the document referenced by the link in Netscape Composer, the HTML editor (see Chapter 20).
Back	Returns you to the previous document.
Forward	Takes you to the document you've just come back from.
Reload	Reloads the Web page.
Reload Frame	Reloads the page in the frame in which you've just opened the menu.
Stop	Stops loading the page.
View Source	Displays the Web page's source HTML file (see Chapter 8).
View Frame Source	Displays the source HTML of the document in the frame within which you are clicking.
View Info	Displays the Web page's information (see Chapter 4).
View Frame Info	Displays information for the Web page in the frame within which you are clicking.
View Image (Open this Image on the Mac)	Removes the current document and displays just the picture you are clicking.
Set as Wallpaper	Saves the image or background image you are clicking, and sets it as the Windows Wallpaper (see Chapter 8).

continues

continued

Add Bookmark	Adds a bookmark to the current page (see Chapter 5). If you are clicking a link, Navigator adds a bookmark to the document referenced by the link. If clicking a document inside a frame (see Chapter 7), the bookmark is set to that specific document, not the frameset.
Create Shortcut	A Windows 95 feature; creates a desktop shortcut that references the document you are clicking (see Chapter 5).
Send Page	Opens Messenger's Composition window, so you can e-mail a copy of the page to someone (see Chapter 16).
Save Link As	Saves the document referenced by the link you are clicking to your hard disk (see Chapter 8).
Save Image As	Saves the image you are clicking to your hard disk (see Chapter 8).
Copy Link Location	Copies the URL referenced by the link to the Windows Clipboard.
Copy Image Location	Copies the URL of the image you are clicking to the Windows Clipboard.
Save Background As	Saves the background image you are clicking to your hard disk (see Chapter 8).
Copy	This appears only if you've selected text in the document. Choose this option to copy the selected text to the Clipboard.

CHAPTER 4

Moving Further into the Web

You know how to move around the Web by now…but what are these strange things you keep running into? You'll soon find that Web pages are far more than just blocks of text with a few images inside them. That's the way it was just a couple of years ago, but the Web is in a state of continual transformation, as billions of dollars are poured into developing it into a more sophisticated system. In this chapter, you'll learn about other things you'll find in Web pages. You'll learn about Web pages that do things, pages that are divided into sections, forms you can enter information into, tables, and more.

What are tables and forms?

Web pages can display information in tables and use forms to interact with the user.

Secure sites and password protection

Not all Web pages are open to the public. In some cases, you must enter a user name and password before you can access a site.

Frames—multiple panes in your Navigator window

Navigator is able to display information in multiple frames within the main browser window, providing the Web author with more flexibility.

Java, JavaScript, multimedia, and live objects

Some Web pages "come alive" with animations, programs, sound, and much more.

Features that Navigator *can't* use

Navigator can't work with everything on the Web. Now and then you'll run across things that simply don't seem to work.

Viewing a document's info

You can view document information for any Web page and the images in it, information such as the image file names, the document last-modified date, the expiration date, and so on.

We've seen all the basics by now: the Web documents, links, pictures, and so on. But there are a variety of other items you'll find spread around the Web:

- Tables
- Secure sites
- "Secondary" or "targeted" windows
- Java applets
- Multimedia

- Forms
- Password-protected sites
- Frames
- JavaScript
- Push and pull commands

We'll look at each of these in turn. ■

Working with Tables

A *table* is…well, you know, a table. It's a set of columns and rows in which text—and some-times pictures—has been organized. You can see an example in Figure 4.1. (While Navigator can display tables, a few other, older, browsers cannot.) Often a table is simply used to format information in a document in a different way, placing text and images next to one another, for instance. Creating tables is currently the easiest way for a Web author to lay out pages with anything close to the degree of precision provided by a desktop-publishing program.

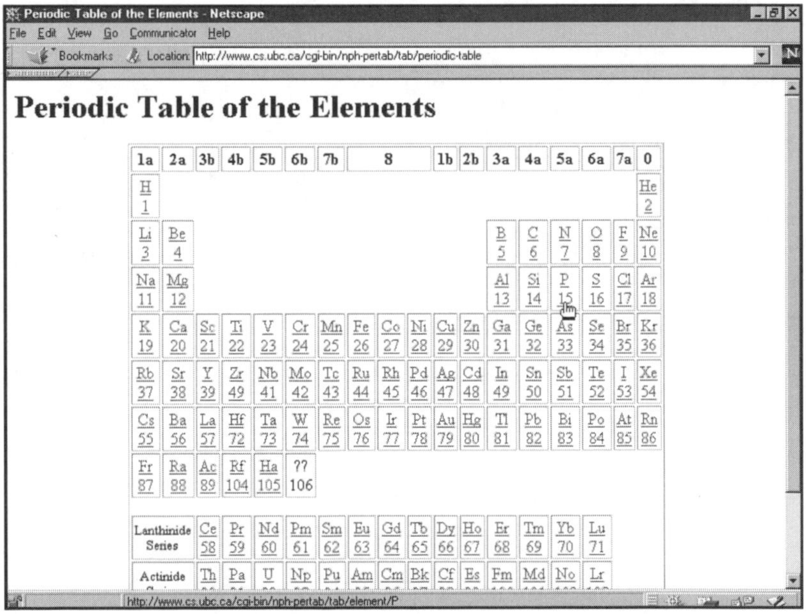

FIG. 4.1

Tables provide a convenient tool to help Web authors format information.

Tables may have colored border lines and colored or patterned backgrounds, even different backgrounds for each cell. (At the time of writing, Navigator 4 has trouble displaying internal border colors, though it can display the external border color and background colors and images.)

Interactive Web Pages Using Forms

A *form* is a special interactive Web document. It contains the sort of components that we've become familiar with while working in today's graphical user interfaces: text boxes, option buttons, command buttons, check boxes, list boxes, drop-down list boxes, and so on.

Figure 4.2 shows part of a form used to take information from you when you are buying something online; in fact, I found this particular form at the Netscape Store (**https://transact. netscape.com:443/ms_dom_bin/txsvr**). Want a Netscape T-shirt? A Mozilla mug? Better still, some Mozilla boxer shorts? (They seem to have discontinued boxer shorts, though; maybe they weren't selling well, but you can still get a stuffed toy.)

FIG. 4.2

Forms allow you to send information back to the Web server—so you can buy important stuff, for instance.

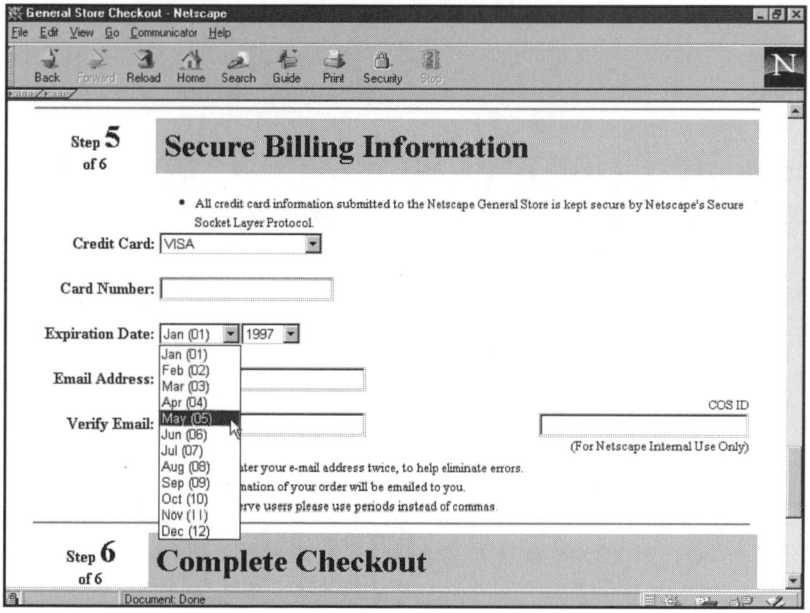

Part

I

Ch

4

N O T E Mozilla? He's the Netscape mascot, a little green, uh, lizard. (Yes, I checked; he's not a dragon or a dinosaur, he's a lizard.) ■

This form contains drop-down list boxes (click the little down triangles and a list of choices will appear), text boxes into which you type your credit card number and e-mail address, and a command button, which is used to submit the form.

Oh, what happens when you click a button? Well, you may see a message talking about security, which we'll get to right now.

Playing It Safe—Secure Sites

When you enter information into a form and send that information back to the Web server, what happens to the information between here and there? It could be intercepted by someone and read (actually it's not very likely that it'll be intercepted, but that's another story, which we'll get to when we cover security in detail in Chapter 11, "Communicator's Security Features"). If you've just transmitted your credit card number, or other information you don't want some snooper to see, and it does get intercepted, you're in trouble.

Navigator provides a special way to send information securely. If the form you are viewing comes from a special https:// server (a secure server), then when the information is sent back from the form to the server, it's encrypted. When the server receives the information, it then decrypts the information. Between your computer and the server, the information is useless; anyone intercepting the information will end up with a load of garbled rubbish. I'll explain more about how this all works in Chapter 11.

How Do I Get into Password-Protected Sites?

There's another form of security we should discuss: the *password*, which has nothing to do with encryption. It's simply a feature that allows Web authors to deny access to users unless they enter the correct password. For instance, you may have noticed by now that there are a number of, ahem, sexually oriented Web sites. Some of these contain "teasers," just a little bit of smut available to anyone who cares to view. But to get to the real stuff you have to register; once registered, you are given a password. (Getting a password generally requires forking over some bucks—that's how these sites make money.) You can then enter the "private parts" of the site using this password.

Well, okay, it's not just the sex sites using this system; there are many other by-subscription-only sites, too. Companies can use this system to create Web sites for their customers and reserve a special area for access by registered customers only, for instance. Anyone who wants to set up a "pay-per-view" site can use a password system to do so.

How do you use a password? Well, when you click a link that a Web author has set up to provide access to a restricted area, you'll either see a dialog box or a Web page with a form containing User Name and Password fields.

What Are "Secondary" or "Targeted" Windows?

Navigator now allows Web authors to open what might be termed secondary windows. I've used that term because it's an existing hypertext term that some readers may already be familiar with, and I'm not sure I like the term given to this feature by Netscape Communications; they've called it targeted windows. This feature allows a Web author to automatically open another Navigator window for you. In other words, when you click a link, another window opens and displays another document. You now have two windows open: the first one, in which you clicked the link, and the second one, displaying the document referenced by the link. We'll discuss this a little more in Chapter 7, "Navigator Frames."

Panes or Frames

Navigator allows multiple panes within a Web document; in Netscape-speak, these are known as *frames*. Figure 4.3 shows three frames: the top frame contains a sort of document title, the left frame contains a picture of the eye, and the right frame contains text. Click one of the callouts in the eye diagram, and the associated text in the right frame changes.

We'll look at this feature in more detail in Chapter 7.

FIG. 4.3
How We See is a great example of the way frames can make the Web look more like a CD encyclopedia.

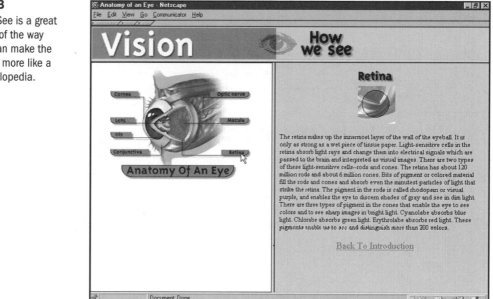

Part
I

Ch
4

Web Pages Come Alive—Java Applets

Java applets are special little programs that are associated with a Web document and created by using Java, a new programming language originally from Sun Microsystems. Java applets can provide Web documents with animation; interaction with the readers; and regular, automatic information updates. For instance, Figure 4.4 shows an interactive map, a demo of an applet that might be used by a travel agency (**http://www.eastland.com/travel.html**). We'll look at Java applets in Chapter 12, "Programs Built into the Web: Java, JavaScript, and ActiveX."

FIG. 4.4

Java at work. This is an interactive map; you can drag a flag to one of the headers on the right to get more information about a particular vacation package or to book the vacation.

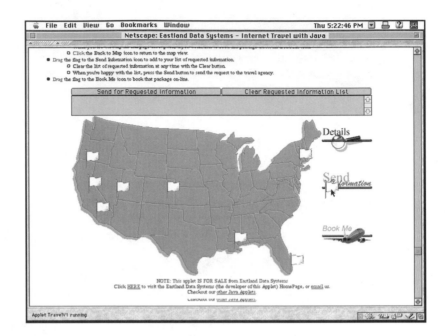

Poor Man's Java—JavaScript

Here's another programming feature: JavaScript. It's sort of a macro language for your browser (it's actually a simplified version of Java). A Web author can create simple scripts that link certain components together: Java applets, the Web document itself, inline plug-ins (special programs that help Communicator play various file formats—see Chapter 9, "Sound and Video: Using Plug-Ins and Viewers") and user events (mouse-clicking, document-opening, tabbing into a field in a form, and so on).

For instance, authors can use JavaScript to make their forms a bit smarter—when you try to submit a form, a JavaScript script can check the information you've entered into the form to ensure that it makes sense. It can check to see that your credit card number is in the correct format, or that you've entered all the information required.

Scripts can also be used to display or play special introductory information—perhaps music— when you first open a document, or play some kind of good-bye statement when you leave the document. We'll look at this in more detail in Chapter 12.

Pictures, Sounds, Video, and More—Multimedia

You'll find all sorts of different file formats on the World Wide Web. You'll find a variety of different still pictures, video and animation, sounds, electronic documents, 3-D images, and so on. Any file format that can be played or displayed on your computer can be linked to a Web page.

What happens when you click a link that takes you to one of these file formats? If Navigator can handle the file itself, it does so—it displays the document or picture in the window in the normal way, or plays the sound. But, if the file is a format that Navigator can't handle, it has two options. It may send the file directly to a program that can handle it (known as a *viewer* or *helper app*). Or it may ask you what to do. We'll take a look at this subject in Chapter 9.

> **N O T E**   You'll often see little pictures that move or flicker, or change from one image to another. These are usually GIF89a files, often known as GIF animations, which were designed a decade or so ago...but nobody could figure out what to do with them until the Web came along. Each file contains multiple images, along with instructions on how to display them (frequency and duration). Displaying images one after the other creates the illusion of motion. ▪

Pushing and Pulling

You may notice that some Web pages seem to do things by themselves. Rather than information arriving at your screen because you've directly requested it—by clicking a link or entering an URL—Web pages can use server push and client pull.

Server push occurs when the Web server continues sending information, even though you haven't requested it. For instance, you might click a link to display a Web page. Then, a few minutes later, the Web page changes; you haven't requested more information, but the server has sent updated information. And the server continues periodic updates until you close the page.

Client pull is similar, except that the request for updates comes from Navigator. For instance, suppose that you open a page. After a predefined interval, Navigator sends a request to the server asking for the information. Again, this will continue until you leave the page.

These systems appear very similar to each other—you usually won't know which method is being used. They are very useful for any information that changes rapidly, such as stock quotes, weather reports, news headlines, or auctions.

Enterprise Server Services

Netscape sells a special Web server called Enterprise Server. This server has been designed to allow corporations to make database information and corporate documents available through the Web or an intranet (an internal Web-like network). It allows the corporation to easily distribute information in a variety of formats—Word for Windows and Excel documents, for instance.

If a page is delivered to Navigator from an Enterprise Server Web server, special services may be available. You can load a page from which you can use these services by choosing View, Page Services.

Part

I

Ch

4

The Microsoft versus Netscape War

There's a war going on between Microsoft and Netscape Communications. You see, when Netscape was founded, not so many years ago, the company set out to create the very best Web browser that it could. But in order to make the browser really neat, they decided they'd also have to create new HTML codes. (You'll remember that in Chapter 2, "The Opening Moves," I explained how the source HTML document contains special codes—tags—that a browser reads in order to figure out how to format the document.) Well, the original idea behind the Web was that everyone would play by the same set of rules—that a governing body would publish a set of HTML codes that everybody could incorporate into their browsers if they wanted.

But Netscape Communications changed the equation by creating their own special HTML codes, designed to work with Netscape Navigator. That didn't stop other browser publishers from adding support for Netscape features, of course, but it did give Netscape a lead, and very soon Netscape Navigator was the most popular Web browser in the world—and still is. And all over the place little signs were appearing in Web documents, saying things like "Optimized for Netscape," or "This document looks better in Netscape," or whatever.

Microsoft wanted a bit of the Web pie, so it released Internet Explorer along with Windows 95 to give Netscape a real run for its money. Microsoft began creating its own HTML tags and then encouraging people to design their Web pages using these neat features and to put up little signs in their Web pages saying, "Optimized for Internet Explorer."

Not all browsers can do all things, however. There are some things that Internet Explorer cannot do—until recently it couldn't display frames or Java applets and still doesn't work with JavaScript as well as Netscape Navigator does, and there are a few text-formatting tags it can't work with, either.

But there are also features that Netscape Navigator cannot work with. Here are a few Internet Explorer features that, at the time of writing, Navigator can't handle:

- *Non-scrolling backgrounds (watermarks)*   This feature creates a background that doesn't scroll as you move down the document. Rather, the text simply scrolls over the top of the static background. If you find a document with this feature, you may not know it; Navigator simply treats it as a normal background.

- *Colored table borders*   Netscape recently added the ability to display table background colors and patterns to Navigator, but it's still unable to display interior cell-border colors.

- *Background sound*   A sound plays automatically when you display the document—it may play once, or may play over and over again as long as you are viewing the page. There are ways that Web pages can be created to play sounds in Navigator, but if they're created to use a special Internet Explorer method, they won't play in Navigator.

- *Floating frames*   A window within the browser window; clicking a link modifies the contents of the window. (It's similar to, but not quite the same as, Navigator's frames.)

Navigator won't display the referenced page in a floating frame, or an ordinary frame; it just opens another window. On the other hand, this feature isn't much used on the Web anyway.

■ *Marquee*   A piece of text that moves across a document, like text on electronic signs you see in airports and sports arenas. The text moves across the page, right to left. Navigator displays marquees as static text.

■ *Inline video*   A small movie that sits inside the Web document and runs automatically. Again, Navigator can be set up to display videos, but if a Web page uses a special Internet Explorer video system, it won't work in Navigator. Navigator may display the video as a static picture, or it may display a placeholder frame, showing where the video *should* be.

■ *Client pull*   There's a version of client pull used by Internet Explorer that Navigator doesn't seem to work with.

N O T E   Just to complicate the picture, it's possible that a Java applet or a JavaScript is being used to perform a procedure, or an embedded file is being played by a plug-in. For instance, although Navigator currently can't play background sounds, a site might use a Java applet to play a sound. Navigator can't play an Internet Explorer inline video, yet a Java applet can place a video inside a document. Or Navigator may have an installed plug-in (see Chapter 9) that will play video or sound within the browser. These are various ways to play the sound or video, though you may not be able to tell the difference. ■

Viewing Document Information

Before we move on, let's take a look at a special feature that provides information about a document. Choose View, Page Info; another Navigator window will open. You can see an example in Figure 4.5.

This window uses two frames. You can move the horizontal bar between the two up and down to provide more room in either frame. Here's the information you will find:

Top Frame

Document title	The title of the document you were viewing.
Document structure	The URL of the document, and the URLs of the objects (inline images, Java applets, and so on) inside the document. You can click any item to see that item's information in the bottom frame. If the document contains a form, you'll also see information about the form. If the browse window was displaying a set of frames when you chose the command, you'll see information for each of the documents displayed in the individual frames.

continues

continued

Bottom Frame

Netsite or
Location

The URL of the item for which information is displayed (you can click a link in the top frame to display information about that item in the lower frame). Click the link to view the document or image in the bottom frame. (Click the link in the top frame to return to the document information.)

File/MIME type

Shows the file type of the current item. Initially, it will show text/html, but if you click one of the links in the top frame, this will change—to image/gif, for instance. You'll learn more about MIME in Chapter 10, "More on Plug-Ins and Viewers."

Source

Shows whether the document is currently in the cache. It usually is, unless the cache is turned off (set to 0K).

Local cache file

If the file's in the cache, you'll see the name of the cache file (when Navigator places a document or image in the cache, it renames it by giving it an "M" name, such as M0parndl.gif.).

Last Modified

The date the file was last modified. You may see two Last Modified dates, one providing a local time and one providing the equivalent Greenwich Mean Time (GMT).

Content Length

The size of document, in bytes.

Expires

A Web author can add an expiration date to his documents using the `<META HTTP-EQUIV="EXPIRES">` tag (though few do); perhaps the Web document contains information that will be irrelevant or incorrect after a certain date. If there's an expiration date associated with the document, it's displayed here.

Charset

The character set that was used when the document was created. If you find a document with strange-looking text, look in the document info and see what character set is used. Most documents use ISO-8859-1. If the document you are viewing is using something else, it may be that your computer doesn't have that character set installed. For instance, documents in Japanese or Chinese will use a different character set.

Security

Tells you whether the document is secure or not, or whether Navigator knows about its security. If the document is secure, you'll be told what security level it has.

Certificate

If the document you were viewing is a secure document, you'll also see information about the site certificate (see Chapter 11, "Communicator's Security Features").

Image data

If the item is an image, you'll see a picture along with information about the image (the file size, dimensions in pixels, colors, and so on).

FIG. 4.5

The Document Info window shows useful information about the document you've been viewing.

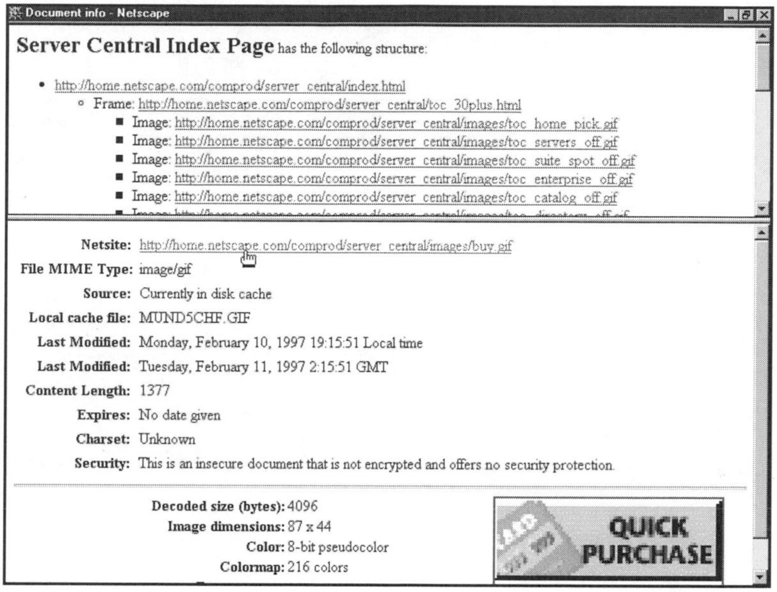

Server Central Index Page has the following structure:

- http://home.netscape.com/comprod/server_central/index.html
  - Frame: http://home.netscape.com/comprod/server_central/toc_30plus.html
    - Image: http://home.netscape.com/comprod/server_central/images/toc_home_pick.gif
    - Image: http://home.netscape.com/comprod/server_central/images/toc_servers_off.gif
    - Image: http://home.netscape.com/comprod/server_central/images/toc_suite_spot_off.gif
    - Image: http://home.netscape.com/comprod/server_central/images/toc_enterprise_off.gif
    - Image: http://home.netscape.com/comprod/server_central/images/toc_catalog_off.gif
    - Image: http://home.netscape.com/comprod/server_central/images/toc_directory_off.gif

---

Netsite:	http://home.netscape.com/comprod/server_central/images/buy.gif
File MIME Type:	image/gif
Source:	Currently in disk cache
Local cache file:	MUND5CHF.GIF
Last Modified:	Monday, February 10, 1997 19:15:51 Local time
Last Modified:	Tuesday, February 11, 1997 2:15:51 GMT
Content Length:	1377
Expires:	No date given
Charset:	Unknown
Security:	This is an insecure document that is not encrypted and offers no security protection.

Decoded size (bytes): 4096
Image dimensions: 87 x 44
Color: 8-bit pseudocolor
Colormap: 216 colors

QUICK PURCHASE

Part
I

Ch
4

CHAPTER 5

History, Bookmarks, and Shortcuts

The World Wide Web is enormous, containing tens of millions of pages. It's easy to get lost, and hard to find what you need. Navigator has several tools that make it easier to go back to pages you've been to before. In this chapter, we'll be looking at the history list, the bookmark system, the Personal toolbar, and Windows 95 shortcuts.

Hypertext has been around for a long time; it was invented years before the Web appeared on the scene. And it's long been known that one of the most serious problems with hypertext is that people tend to get lost. It's hard to get lost in a book; you read from the front to the back, or maybe dip into the book in the middle. The book has a direction, from page 1 through page 300 or 400 or whatever. But hypertext has no direction. Or rather, it has almost limitless directions.

There are literally billions of different paths that you can take through the World Wide Web. To make it worse, the paths are constantly changing. New ones appear every minute, and some pages that were there yesterday are gone today. Play around on the Web for a while and you'll soon find that you can get lost, that you're not exactly sure where or how you found that interesting document about

Using the history list

The history lists contains an entry for each Web page you've been to in the current session or, in some versions of Navigator, even Web pages you've visited in previous sessions. Use the list to find your way back.

Creating bookmarks

The bookmark system provides a way to find your way back to pages you think will be useful later.

Exporting and importing bookmarks

You can create bookmark files, then give them to friends and colleagues, or save them for later use.

Using drag and drop

Navigator has a number of drag-and-drop procedures to make working with bookmarks quicker and easier.

Using the Personal toolbar

You can use the Personal toolbar to create buttons that will take you to frequently used Web pages.

Creating Windows 95 desktop shortcuts

Windows 95 allows you to put shortcuts on the desktop; double-clicking a shortcut automatically opens the referenced Web page.

aliens and UFOs at Groom Lake (try **http://www.ufomind.com/area51/**), or how to get back to the page that lets you search for a word in 63 dictionaries at the same time (**http://www. onelook.com/**).

Navigator can help you out. It has three essential features that will assist you in your travels around the Web: the history list, bookmarks, and the Personal toolbar. We'll start with the history list. ■

Where've You Been?—Using the History List

A *history list* is, quite simply, a list of documents you've viewed during the current Web session. The history list is created automatically. Each time you view a document, that document is added to the history list.

T I P | Until recently, Navigator had a rather weak history-list system. It only listed documents from the current session, not previous sessions. And it didn't even list all the documents from the current session. The Windows version of Navigator has just been given a much better history-list system, and it's that system we're going to look at here. For now, the UNIX and Macintosh history systems remain unchanged; they don't list sites from previous sessions. That should, presumably, change very soon.

Note, however, that there is also a "hidden" history list. Type **about:global** into the Location text box and press Enter, and you'll see a list of URLs of pages that you've viewed (no page titles, unfortunately), not only in the current session but previous sessions, too. The list doesn't contain links, but you can copy the URLs from the page and paste them into the Location box if you want.

T I P | You can also choose <u>G</u>o, <u>B</u>ack, or <u>G</u>o, <u>F</u>orward; or use Alt+left arrow or Alt+right arrow (on the Mac you'll use ⌘+[for Back, and ⌘+] for Forward). And, if you right-click inside a document (or simply click and hold the mouse button down on the Mac), you'll find <u>B</u>ack and <u>F</u>orward commands on the pop-up menu.

There are a few ways to use the history list. The quickest and easiest is to use the Back and Forward buttons. They move you back and forward through the list. Back to the previous document, back to the one before that, forward to the one you've just come from, and so on.

In Navigator 4, there's a new feature built into these buttons; press the mouse button while pointing at one of the buttons and hold the button down. You'll see a little menu open, showing the documents in the history list before (for the Back button) or after (for the Forward button) the currently displayed document. Simply click the one you want to go to (see Figure 5.1).

Another way to use the history list is to open the <u>G</u>o menu and select a page from the bottom of the menu. You'll find a list of documents that you've viewed recently. Simply click one to display that document.

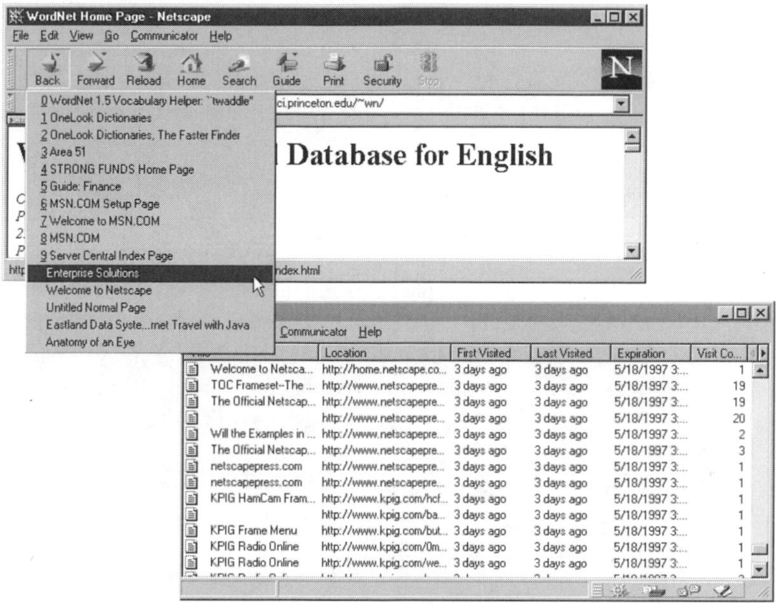

FIG. 5.1

Two ways to use the history list: Click the Back or Forward button and hold the mouse button down, or select Communicator, History.

Finally, you can also select Communicator, History. A window opens (refer to Figure 5.1), displaying the entries in the history list, showing both the titles and URLs of each entry in the list. This new history list is a great improvement over the original Navigator history system. It makes the history system much easier to use and much more useful. Here's what you can do in this window:

Go to the selected page	Double-click an entry; right-click and select Go to Page; or click once and choose File, Go to Page.
Place a bookmark on the selected page	Right-click and select Add to Bookmarks; or click once and choose File, Add to Bookmarks.
Place a button on the Personal toolbar	Click once and choose File, Add Page to Toolbar.
Copy the URL to the Clipboard	Right-click and select Copy; or click once and choose Edit, Copy.
Search for a Web page	Select Edit, Search History List; you'll be able to search for a particular title or URL.
Search a directory	Select Edit, Search Directory; you'll be able to search for a person or FedEx package. Why is this here? I don't know, but we'll look at it again in Chapter 17.
Change the sort order	You can make it easier to find entries by changing the sort order. Select View to sort by Title, Location, the number of hours or days since your first or last visit to the Web page, the expiration date, or the "visit count" (the number of times you've been to the page).

In particular, the capability to change the sort order is very important, as it can help you find exactly the page you need. Want to find a page you visited a great deal some time ago? Sort by Visit Count. Want to find a page you know the name of? Sort by Title. Do you need to find a page you visited three days ago? Sort by Last Visit, then look for 3 days ago in the Last Visited column.

The "expiration" date is the date on which the entry will be removed from the history list. You can adjust that date in the Preferences dialog box. Choose Edit, Preferences, and click Navigator in the Category list. In the main pane, you'll see the History area, with a box labelled Pages in History Expire After. Simply enter the number of days you want to keep entries in the history list. If you want, you can clear the history list entirely by clicking the Clear History button. (You can also clear the list from the History window itself, by choosing Edit, Select All and pressing Delete.) Remember, if you're visiting Web sites that you'd rather someone else with access to your computer didn't *know* you are visiting, it's a good idea to clear the history list!

T I P You can't just leave the History window open and use it to return to pages you've seen during the session. The window is updated when it opens, so you must close it and reopen it to add the entries for pages you've seen since you first opened it.

Not All the Documents!

I stated that the history list is a list of documents viewed during the current session. But it's not always a list of all of the documents you've viewed, unfortunately. In the browsers using the simple, old-style history list (at the time of writing, the UNIX and Macintosh browsers), some entries are thrown away. And even in the browsers with the full history list, some entries are not available from the Go menu or the Back and Forward buttons.

Here's how it works. Let's say you are in document A, and click a link to go to document B, then go to C, then to D, then to E. Now you use the history list to return to document B. In document B, you select another link that takes you to, say, document 1. Now take a look in the Go menu. You'll find that documents C, D, and E are no longer there; they've been thrown out of the list.

This is a little confusing, because the history list doesn't take you back in an exact line, and you can't view a list of all the documents you've seen in the current session. The history list truncates your short excursions, and only maintains a list of the current route. In fact, this is downright irritating at times, when you simply can't use the history list to get back to a page you've seen earlier in the session. Now, if you have the Windows version of Navigator 4, you can go to the History window and see *all* pages listed. The UNIX and Macintosh browsers, though, currently don't have a full history list in their History windows, so you can't view "truncated" entries there, either. By the time you read this, however, those browsers may have the new style—the greatly improved history list.

Remember the Location Bar?

Remember that there's another form of history list: the Location bar's drop-down list box. This shows you a list of URLs that you have entered into the Location text box. This does go back to prior sessions, by the way. Its main problem, though, is that it only shows URLs, not document titles, so it can be a little difficult to use sometimes. And it only shows URLs that you've typed into the Location bar, not those typed into the Open Location dialog box or the URLs of pages that you reached by clicking links.

The Bookmark System

Though Navigator's history list is a little weak, the bookmark system is much more helpful. *Bookmarks* are just what they sound like; they are markers for Web pages. Just as you might place bookmarks inside a paper book to find your way back to a particular page, Navigator's bookmarks allow you to quickly return to a Web page. (You are not literally adding a bookmark to a Web page, of course; you are creating a list of URLs and Web addresses, and using that list to help you find your way back to the pages.) Bookmarks stay until you remove them; they are not limited to the current session, and you'll be able to use them weeks, months, even years later.

Some versions of Navigator come loaded with a collection of bookmarks to some of the best and most popular Web sites. You can add to this list, but it's a great place for a Web beginner to start browsing. These sites are all "G-rated" and safe to let your kids explore. (Of course, where they go from there is another question.)

You can use a bookmark by clicking the Bookmarks button on the Location bar; a menu opens, showing you your bookmarks. Click the one referring to the document you want to view. You can also open this menu by selecting Window, Bookmarks.

There are a variety of bookmark procedures: You can add bookmarks, select a bookmark from the Bookmarks menu, open the Bookmarks window and select a bookmark from there, create a hierarchy of bookmark folders, and create bookmark files. Note that I'm describing the bookmark system in the Windows version here; the Mac browser currently has an earlier, much simpler, bookmark system, though it may be upgraded soon.

Adding a Bookmark

This is the simplest procedure. If you find a Web page that you think you'll want to return to later, you can use one of these methods to create a bookmark:

- Click the Bookmarks button (on the Location bar) and then select Add Bookmark from the menu that opens. The bookmark is added to the bottom of the Bookmark menu.

- Click the Bookmarks button and then select File Bookmark from the menu that opens. A submenu appears; select a folder into which you want to place the bookmark. (Selecting the first entry in this submenu places the bookmark on the bottom of the Bookmark menu, the same as the previous procedure.)

- Right-click the page to open the pop-up menu and choose <u>A</u>dd Bookmark (make sure you don't right-click a link, that you click the background or plain text).

That's it, the bookmark has been added. If you now open the Bookmarks menu (click the Bookmarks button on the Location bar or choose <u>C</u>ommunicator, <u>B</u>ookmarks), you'll see that the document title has been added to the menu, either at the bottom or in the submenu you specified. You'll be able to return to the document at a later date by simply opening the menu and clicking the entry.

TIP You can add a bookmark to a document you haven't viewed yet. Right-click a link and choose Add Bookmar<u>k</u> to create a bookmark to the document referenced by the link; the link text will be used as the bookmark title. Or, if the Bookmarks window is open, you can drag a link from the browser and drop it into a bookmarks folder, a quick way to get the bookmark exactly where you want it. Also, you can drag the little link icon on the Location bar and drop that into a bookmarks folder; a bookmark to the current page is created.

Or add a bookmark for a document you viewed earlier in the session. Choose <u>C</u>ommunicator, <u>H</u>istory, right-click the document in the history list, and choose Add to Bookmar<u>k</u>s.

There are a few problems with the menu entry, though. You may not want to use the document title. Some are too vague or verbose, and it's nice to be able to modify them. Also, the list in the menu is not in alphabetical order, making it hard to find things after a while. And although there's a bookmark hierarchy of submenus, it might not be quite what you want. Don't worry, though; we can solve all these problems in the Bookmarks window.

Modifying Your Bookmarks

Open the Bookmarks window by clicking the Bookmarks button and then clicking Edit Bookmarks, or by choosing <u>C</u>ommunicator, <u>B</u>ookmarks, Edit <u>B</u>ookmarks. (On the Mac, you currently must select Window, Bookmark.) You'll see something like the window in Figure 5.2. As you can see, Navigator comes with a hierarchy of bookmark folders, but we're going to see how to create new folders, so you can organize the bookmarks the way that's most suitable for you.

Each folder in this window represents a menu or submenu on Navigator's Bookmarks menu. To create a new folder—and, therefore, a new menu or submenu—click the folder of which you want the folder to be a subfolder (the menu of which you want it to be a submenu), and choose <u>F</u>ile, New <u>F</u>older to open the Bookmark Properties dialog box. (Or right-click the folder and select New <u>F</u>older from the pop-up menu.) Type a title for your new folder into the Name text box: Sports, Politics, Aliens, Conspiracies, Business, Shopping, or whatever other kind of category you care to create. You can also enter a description, a few words explaining what the category is intended to hold. Click the OK button, and your new folder will appear inside the Bookmarks window.

FIG. 5.2

The Bookmarks window allows you to create bookmark hierarchies.

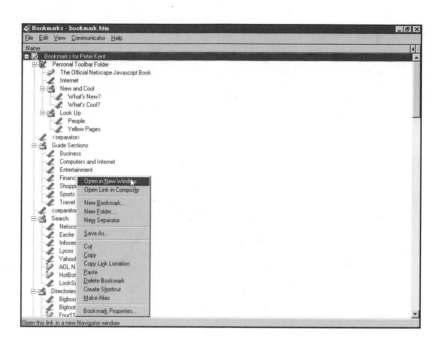

Now you can move bookmarks into the folder:

- Click a bookmark and hold the mouse button down for a moment; then, while still holding the button down, drag the bookmark onto the folder and release the button.

- You can move several bookmarks at once. Hold Ctrl while you click each one that you want to move, and when you click the last one hold the mouse button down and drag them into the folder. (On the Mac, you can press Shift as you click each one, to select them all; then release Shift and drag them.)

- You can also select a contiguous block of bookmarks by clicking the first in the block, holding the Shift key down, and clicking the last in the block.

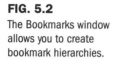

TIP You can also move bookmarks using the menu commands. Select them and then choose Edit, Cut (or select Cut from the pop-up menu). Then click the folder into which you want to place them and choose Edit, Paste.

Create as many folders as you want. Remember that when you create a folder within your Bookmarks window, you are automatically modifying the Bookmarks menu, too. When you open the menu, you'll see that each folder is represented by a cascading menu. The folder name appears in the menu with a small triangle to the right; click the entry and you'll see another menu open, displaying the contents of the folder.

Part

I

Ch

5

More Bookmark Operations

Once you've created a bookmark hierarchy, you may want to modify your bookmarks. Here's what you can do in the Bookmark window:

- *Rename a bookmark* Click the bookmark, choose Edit, Bookmark Properties, and type a new Name. You can also modify the URL and add a description (see Figure 5.3). On the Mac, you'll choose Edit, Get Info to see the bookmark's properties box.

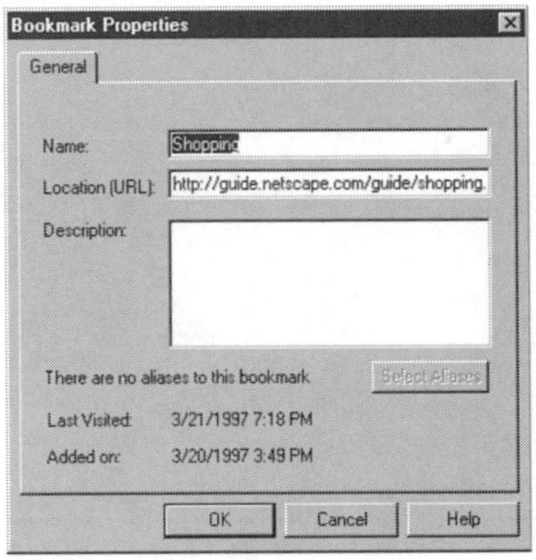

FIG. 5.3

The Bookmark Properties dialog box, where you can change an item's name and URL, and add a description.

TIP You can also open the Properties dialog box by right-clicking the bookmark and choosing Bookmark Properties. (There's no pop-up menu here on Mac versions, though. Use Edit, Get Info.)

- *Copy a bookmark to another folder* Hold down the Ctrl key while you drag the bookmark to another folder. Or click the bookmark; choose Edit, Copy; click in the folder you want to copy to; and choose Edit, Paste. (On the Mac, you'll have to use the Edit menu commands, as you can't drag copy.)

- *Delete a bookmark* Click it, and press Delete.

- *Find a bookmark* Choose Edit, Find in Bookmarks, type a word (part of the bookmark title or the URL), and press Enter. This will even find bookmarks in closed folders.

- *Open or close a folder* Double-click it, or click once the + or - icon to the left of it.

- *Insert a menu separator* To place a separator line on the Bookmarks menu between items (remember, the menu reflects the Bookmark window's format), click the entry after which the line should appear and then choose File, New Separator. (Or use the pop-up menu.)

- *Add a bookmark manually* Click where you want to place the bookmark, and then choose File, New Bookmark. Type a name and the URL, and a description if you want. Remember that the URL must be entered exactly—it's a lot safer to copy the URL and paste it in, or set it while browsing.

■ *Create aliases*   You can create *linked* copies of bookmarks if you want and place them in other folders. Each time you modify the original or one of the copies, all associated bookmarks are changed. (You might change a bookmark name, for instance, or use the Update Bookmarks feature to see if the bookmarked Web page has changed—we'll look at that later in this chapter.) Select the bookmark and then choose File, Make Alias, or right-click the bookmark and choose Make Alias. A copy of the bookmark with an italicized title appears below (the italic text identifies it as an alias). You can now drag the alias to another folder. (You can't copy aliases, though.) You can quickly find aliases, or the original of an alias, by opening the bookmark's Properties dialog box, clicking the Select Aliases button, and clicking OK. All associated bookmarks are highlighted—folders are automatically opened if necessary. (This feature wasn't working well at the time of writing. The aliases may not be selected until you close the dialog box, and it may not select the original bookmark if you use it on an alias.)

■ *Sort the bookmarks*   Choose View, then select one of the sort options. You can sort by name, creation date, last-visited date, or location (URL). (However, at the time of writing this feature didn't work correctly.)

■ *Create a Windows 95/NT desktop shortcut*   Right-click the bookmark and choose Make Shortcut, or click once and choose File, Create Shortcut.

■ *Save the text or HTML source code from a document referenced by a shortcut*   Right-click and choose Save As. See Chapter 8 for more information about saving files from the Web.

TIP When you get a lot of bookmark folders, you can make sure they are sorted in a convenient manner by changing the names of frequently used folders so that they begin with 1 or _ (underscore), and renaming the seldom-used folders to begin with Z_. That will move the frequently used folders to the top of the Bookmark menu and Bookmark window, and the infrequently used ones to the bottom.

Part
I

Ch
5

Where Do You Want Your Bookmarks?

By default, when you set a bookmark from the browser window, that bookmark is automatically placed in the main folder (if you use one of the simple Add Bookmark commands, that is, rather than one of the commands that allows you to drop the bookmark directly into a folder). Wouldn't it be nice if you could tell Navigator where to place the bookmarks, though? For instance, if you are out browsing through music sites, couldn't all the bookmarks go into a Music folder?

Well, you *can* tell Navigator which folder to use. Click the folder, and then choose View, Set as New Bookmarks Folder. Or select that command from the right-click pop-up menu. All subsequent bookmarks created using the simple Add Bookmark command will go into this folder—until you change the setting again, of course.

Which Folder on the Menu?

How about telling Navigator which folder should be displayed in the browser's Bookmarks menu? Well, you can do that, too. Click the folder you want to be used in the menu, and choose View, Set as Bookmark Menu. Or select that command from the right-click pop-up menu.

TIP What about the Set as Toolbar Folder command? That refers to the Personal Toolbar, which is part of the bookmarks system. We'll look at that later in this chapter, under "Using the Personal Toolbar."

 Switch to the browser and click the Bookmarks button, and you'll see the contents of this folder. Of course, this means that any folders higher up the bookmark hierarchy won't be available on the menu—folders lower down the hierarchy will still be available, though, as submenus.

Using the Bookmarks

How do you actually use your bookmarks? You've seen how you can select a bookmark from the Bookmarks menu. To go to a bookmarked document from the Bookmarks window, you can use several methods:

- Double-click the entry.
- Click an entry once and press Enter.
- Right-click an entry and choose Open in New Window.
- Right-click an entry and choose Open in Composer to open the referenced document in Communicator's Web-page editor (see Chapter 20).
- Click an entry once and choose File, Go to Bookmark.
- Drag the bookmark from the Bookmarks window and drop it onto the Navigator window.

Creating Bookmark Files

You can create and import bookmark files. This provides several benefits. It allows another hierarchical level; for example, you might have one bookmark file for business-related Web sessions, and one for your personal interests. Or one for each member of the family, or each coworker using the computer. You can then load the bookmark file you need for a particular session.

Being able to create bookmark files also provides a convenient way to share bookmarks. Create a bookmark file, put it on a floppy disk, and take it home to load into your personal copy of Navigator, or give it to a friend or colleague. And it allows you to import other lists of links, perhaps from other programs, and use them as bookmarks.

There are three basic procedures:

- *Create a bookmark file*   Choose File, Save As to create an HTML document containing all of your bookmarks.

- *Import a bookmark file*   To add the contents of a bookmark file to your current bookmarks, choose File, Import.

- *Open another bookmark file*   Choose File, Open Bookmarks File to use a different bookmark file.

Dragging and Dropping Bookmarks

Not only can you drag and drop bookmarks within the Bookmarks window, but you also can drag and drop between windows, too. If you drag a bookmark from the Bookmarks window onto Navigator, Navigator will load the document referenced by the bookmark. If you drag a bookmark to, say, a WordPad or Word for Windows window, the URL will be copied into the word processing document. You can also drag a bookmark onto the Windows 95 desktop to create a desktop shortcut (which we'll look at under "Creating Desktop Shortcuts," later in this chapter). You can also drag bookmarks onto a Web document that you are creating in order to quickly make links—see Chapter 20.

You can use this feature on the Mac, too. Drag a bookmark onto the desktop to create an icon. You can click that icon later to open a Web page.

N O T E   Note that you can only drag and drop to Windows OLE client applications. *OLE* stands for Object Linking and Embedding, which is a special system used by Windows for sharing data between programs. WordPad and Word for Windows, for instance, are OLE programs; Notepad is not. WordPad is what's known as an OLE client, a program that can accept data from an OLE server. ■

Part

I

Ch

5

Smart Bookmarks

Wouldn't it be nice if there were an easy way to know when your favorite Web pages have changed? Or when there's more information added to a page, when a new song is available at a music site, or when new shareware is added to a shareware site? Well, there is.

Choose View, Update Bookmarks (choose View, What's New? on the Mac), and you'll see the dialog box in Figure 5.4. You can click the All Bookmarks option button (to tell the system to check all of your bookmarks), or click the Selected Bookmarks option button (to check just those bookmarks that you've selected). Then click the Start Checking button. The bookmarks system will send a request to each Web server that contains the documents you want to check, asking for information about the Web document. If it finds that documents have been changed, it shows you by adding a special icon. You can see these icons in Table 5.1.

Table 5.1   The Bookmark Window Icons

Icon	Function
	This represents the root bookmarks folder, the folder in which all others are stored.
	This is the Personal Toolbar folder (see the next section, "Using the Personal Toolbar").
	This is a closed subfolder.
	This is an open subfolder.
	This is the folder that appears as the main Bookmark Menu.
	This is a bookmark to an unchanged page (the same symbol also represents a separator line between entries on the menu).
	This is a bookmark to a page that the bookmark system has no information about; it does not know if it has changed.
	This is a bookmark to a page that has changed.

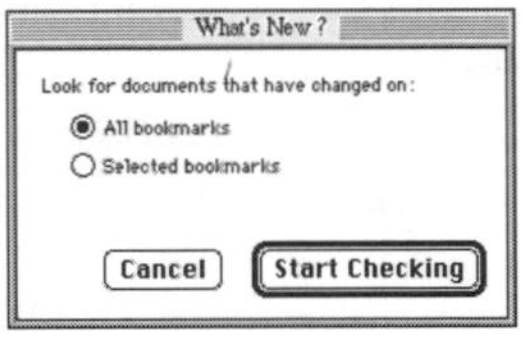

FIG. 5.4

You can ask the bookmark system to search for changes for you; it marks the bookmarks that reference the changed documents.

Using the Personal Toolbar

Navigator has another feature that is, in effect, a form of bookmark system: the Personal toolbar. You can add buttons to this bar and define which Web page each button will open. This is very handy for setting up shortcuts to Web pages you view frequently. (At the time of writing, the Mac browser did not have a Personal toolbar.)

The Personal Toolbar is, by default, the third toolbar down from the top of the window (though, of course, you can move it to another position if you want, by dragging it up and down). This toolbar is a Bookmark folder. There's already a folder called Personal Toolbar Folder, but in fact you can place whatever folder you want on the toolbar. Click the folder in the Bookmarks window, then choose View, Set as Toolbar Folder (or right-click the folder and choose that command from the pop-up menu).

If you pick a folder with a lot of entries, they won't all fit on the toolbar, of course. But you can shift buttons around on the toolbar by dragging them into the positions you prefer; simply click and hold the mouse button down, then drag the button to another place on the Personal Toolbar.

Note also that you can put menu buttons onto the Personal Toolbar; that is, buttons that open a menu when clicked upon. To do this, simply put a subfolder inside the folder you've designated as the Personal Toolbar folder.

To add buttons to the Personal toolbar you add them to the folder you've specified as the Personal Toolbar folder. By default you would open the Bookmark menu (click the Bookmark icon on the Location bar, or select Communicator, Bookmarks...Window, Bookmarks on the Mac), then choose File Bookmark, Personal Toolbar Folder, Personal Toolbar Folder. That's right, there's a submenu named Personal Toolbar Folder, and a menu option in that submenu named Personal Toolbar Folder. Why? Because, as you've just seen, you might have subfolders within this folder. You could select one of those folders if you wanted to place the new bookmark on a menu that opens when you click a button on the Personal Toolbar. But to create an actual button on the toolbar itself you must select the Personal Toolbar Folder menu option. Of course if you've selected a different folder as the Personal Toolbar Folder, this procedure is a little different. You'll be adding the bookmark to that folder rather than the one named Personal Toolbar.

TIP Note that at present the Macintosh version of Communicator does not have a Communicator menu; in its place it has a Window menu. When I refer to the Communicator menu, look at the Window menu on the Mac.

FIG. 5.5
Create your own toolbar buttons; each button is linked to a specified Web page, or opens a submenu.

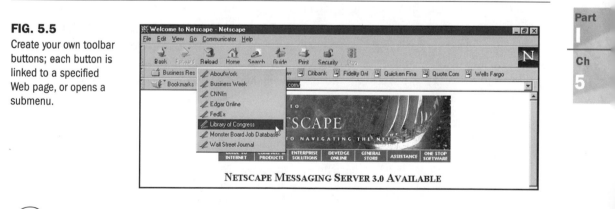

TIP Here's a quick way to add buttons, and to add a bookmark to the folder, too. Display the page for which you want to create a button; then drag the page icon next to the Location text box onto the Personal toolbar, in the position in which you want the button.

Creating Desktop Shortcuts

If you are using Windows 95 or Windows NT 4.0, Navigator also allows you to create desktop *shortcuts*. A shortcut is a special icon placed on the Windows 95 or NT desktop that, when double-clicked, carries out some kind of operation. In this case, when you double-click an Internet shortcut, Navigator will open and display the referenced document. You can create a shortcut to a document you are viewing in Navigator, to a document referenced by a link in the document you are viewing, or to a document referenced by a bookmark. Here's how it works:

■ To create a shortcut to the current document, right-click in a blank space and choose Create Shortcut from the pop-up menu. In the dialog box that appears (see Figure 5.6), modify the Description if you want and click OK.

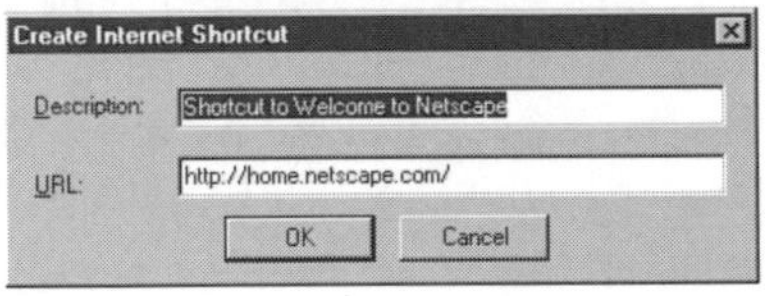

FIG. 5.6

When you create a shortcut, you may want to modify the description to help you remember the document.

Create Internet Shortcut	
Description:	Shortcut to Welcome to Netscape
URL:	http://home.netscape.com/
OK	Cancel

■ Another way to create a shortcut to the current document: Drag the document-link icon over the desktop and release the mouse button.

■ To create a shortcut to a document referenced by a link in the document, right-click the link and choose Create Shortcut.

■ To create a shortcut to a document referenced by a bookmark, open the Bookmarks window, right-click the bookmark you want to use, and then choose Create Shortcut; or click once and choose File, Create Shortcut.

■ Another way to create a shortcut to a bookmarked document: Drag the bookmark over the desktop and release the mouse button.

You can also create a shortcut to a document referenced by a link by dragging it onto the desktop. First, position the Navigator window so that you can see your Windows 95 or NT desktop. (You can also place shortcuts in desktop folders or in Windows Explorer—open the folder or Explorer, and position the shortcuts so they are visible.) Now, point at a link in a Web document, and then press and hold the mouse button down. With the button held down, drag the mouse pointer off Navigator and onto the Windows desktop (or over a desktop folder or Windows Explorer folder), and release the mouse button. The shortcut is created.

How do you use these shortcuts? Simple. Double-click a shortcut at any time to open Navigator and display the referenced document. You can open these shortcuts and see the shortcut properties, by the way. Right-click the bookmark, and choose Properties to see the Properties dialog box. Click the Internet Shortcut tab to see the URL of the referenced document.

TIP If you drag a link and drop it into an OLE application, such as Word for Windows, the URL will be pasted into the program.

 TIP As I mentioned before, you can also use the drag-and-drop feature on the Mac. Drag a bookmark onto the desktop and an icon is created. You can click the icon later to open the Web page.

Part
I

Ch
5

CHAPTER 6

Searching for Information on the Web

The Web is huge, comprising literally tens of millions of pages, on millions of subjects, published by millions of people. How can you possibly find what you need? There are a number of ways to track down subjects of interest on the Web, and to find other things, too, such as other Internet users, software, and newsgroup and mailing list messages. In this chapter, you'll learn how to stop looking at the Web as a needle-in-the-haystack system, and start regarding it as a tremendous source of information.

The Web is enormous, and thousands of new pages are added every week. How can you possibly know what's out there, and how can you find the information you need? For example, I recently wanted to find information about a particular printer that I was considering buying. I was sure that the company that made the printer must have a Web site—most companies in the computer business seem to these days. But what URL did I need to get to the site? I also wanted to find the public television Web site so I could search for a particular show I was interested in. How would I find this site?

Searching the Internet with search engines

Communicator puts search engines and directories close at hand to help you quickly find what you need.

Using a site sampler for convenient searching

A site sampler is a search box that remains on your screen while you move around on the Web.

Using Internet directories

The Web directories make finding things a little easier; they categorize the pages, and sometimes even sift through them to find the best.

Finding people

You can search the Internet for people—colleagues and old school friends, for instance.

Searching newsgroup messages

Want to know what people are saying about you, your product, or your area of interest in the newsgroups?

Searching mailing-list messages

You can search some mailing lists.

Finding software

The Web has become a shareware distributor's dream. Here's how to find the shareware, demoware, and freeware.

Of course, I could have spent several years wandering through hyperlinks on the Web, and maybe eventually I would have wandered into the pages I needed. Or I could have gone to a search or directory site, and then searched a vast index of Web sites or viewed lists of sites broken down by category.

How about tracking down people? If I needed to find another Internet user—an old school friend, a former colleague, or a long-lost relative—where could I start? ■

Navigator's Search Tools

Navigator provides you with several search tools; well, they're not really Navigator's tools, but Navigator puts them a click away, making them quickly available. You can use the following buttons and commands to find sites:

TIP Some versions of Navigator come with scores of helpful, preloaded bookmarks that can take you to many useful destinations. Refer to Chapter 5, "History, Bookmarks, and Shortcuts," for more information on bookmarks.

■ *Search*   Click this button to see a Web page from which you can search the entire Web. Navigator picks the first search engine at random from a choice of Excite, Yahoo!, Infoseek, or Lycos—but you can switch to one of the others if you want. You can also add a fifth service, and define one as the service to be used each time. See "Searching for Web Sites" later in this chapter.

■ *The Internet*   Click the Guide button and a menu appears; select The Internet to see a page containing links to a variety of Web directories, categorized by subject: finance, sports, travel, and so on.

■ *People*   Click the Guide button and select People to see a search form that lets you search any of six different directories of Internet users. See "Finding People" later in this chapter for more information.

■ *Yellow Pages*   Click the Guide button and select Yellow Pages to see a search form that lets you search any of seven "yellow-pages" directories. These contain information on businesses around the world—real world addresses and telephone numbers. See "Searching the Real World with the Yellow Pages" later in this chapter for more information.

■ *What's New*   Click the Guide button and select What's New to see Netscape's selection of interesting new Web sites.

■ *What's Cool*   Click the Guide button and select What's Cool to see a selection of Web sites that Netscape's staff regards as cool or exciting.

N O T E What's the difference between a Web-page directory and a Web-page search site? A *directory* provides categorized lists of Web pages—you select a category, then a subcategory, then another subcategory, and so on, until you find the site you want. A search site lets you use a *search engine*, a program that searches a database of Web pages. Type a keyword and then click a Search button or press Enter, and the search engine searches the database for you. Some sites—such as Yahoo!—contain both directories and search engines.

By the way, you can also access the Web pages I've just mentioned through the Bookmarks menu. You'll find a New and Cool submenu, which contains two bookmarks, What's New and What's Cool. There's a Guide Sections submenu, which is the equivalent of the Internet selection on the Guide button; each bookmark takes you to one of the categories available in The Internet page. There's a Look Up submenu, with bookmarks to the People and Yellow Pages Web pages. And there's a Search submenu; the Netscape Search bookmark takes you to the page that's displayed when you click the Search button, while the other bookmarks take you directly to a particular search page.

Searching for Web Sites

Let's begin by seeing how to search the Web for the information you need; this information might be about a product you want to buy, one of your hobbies, a research project, or any other need you have.

 Click the Search button. You'll see something like what's shown in Figure 6.1.

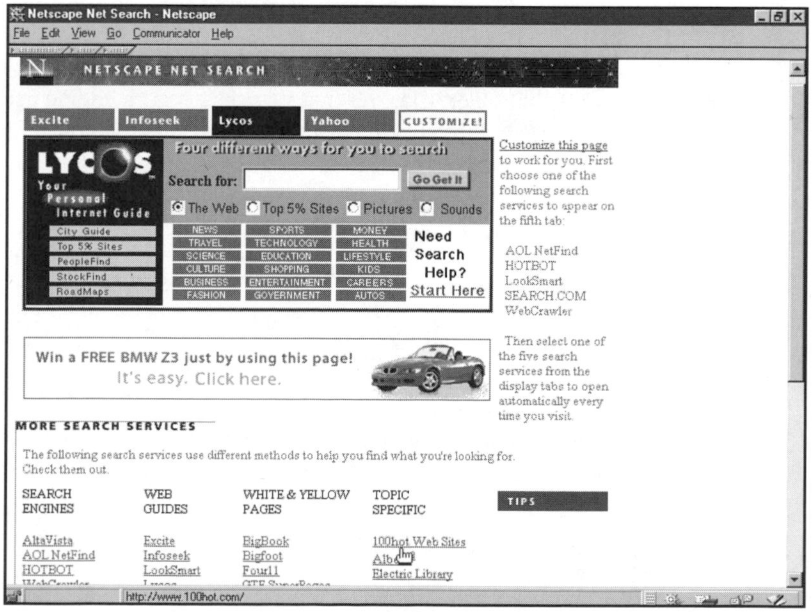

FIG. 6.1
The Internet Search page lets you use five different search engines to go to various search sites.

Part

I

Ch

6

If you've been to this page several times, you might have noticed that you see a different setup each time. This page randomly selects one of the following search engines: Yahoo!, Infoseek, Lycos, and Excite. If it picks one you don't want, you can select another from the bar above the search box.

If you want, you can choose another search engine for the fifth tab above the box; click the Customize tab and a secondary window opens (see Figure 6.2). You can then select another search engine (AOL.NetFind, HotBot, LookSmart, Search.Com, or Webcrawler). Then you can define this search engine (or one of the others) as the one to be used each time you open this page; in other words, Navigator won't pick a search engine randomly if you make this choice. Click Submit and your search system is configured.

FIG. 6.2

Customize your search system to work with the search engine you prefer.

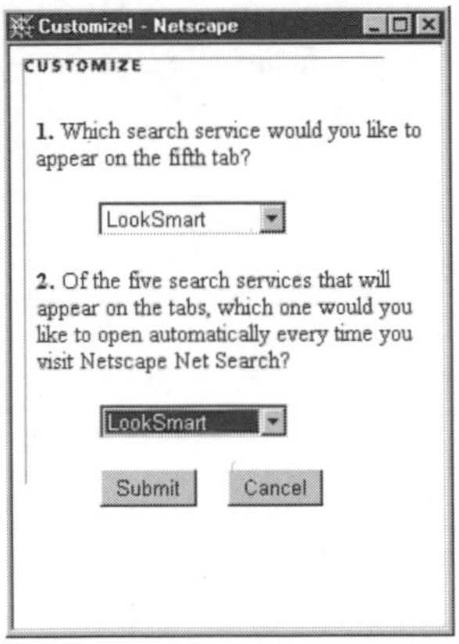

To carry out a search, you need to type a search term into the text box. What are you going to type, though? You can just type a single word and then click the Search button (or the GO GET IT button or Seek button or whatever that particular search engine uses). You can, in some cases, narrow the search by clicking an option button first. Lycos, for instance, allows you to search the entire database of Web sites, the "top five percent," for pictures, or for sounds.

You may, however, want to get fancy and do a more sophisticated search. Search engines generally allow you to combine search terms to do a more refined search. To find out what rules the search engine uses, click the search system's logo that appears next to or above the search box. You'll go directly to the search site itself, where you can find detailed search instructions. (Look for links that say things like Custom Search, Tips, Help, and Advanced Search.)

For example, here are a few things you can enter when you are using Infoseek:

- Words between quotation marks—This format tells Infoseek to find the words only when they appear in that exact order, right next to each other (example: "the here and now").

- Words separated by hyphens—This tells Infoseek to find the words as long as they appear close together in the document format (example: diving-scuba).

- Words in brackets—This format (tells Infoseek to find the words as long as they appear together, even if they're not in the order you've entered (example: diving scuba).

- Proper names—You should capitalize all proper names correctly (examples: Colorado, England, CompuServe, and Gore).

Infoseek also provides some unusual forms of searching, such as the following:

- link:*hostname*   You can, for instance, enter link:mcp.com to find Web pages that contain links to the Macmillan Computer Publishing Web site. This is a great way for companies to find out who's linking to their site.

- site:*hostname*   You can, for instance, enter site:mcp.com to find pages that contain mcp.com in their URL. This is a good way to limit your search to particular sites.

- url:*word*   You can, for instance, enter url:geo to find pages that contain the word geo somewhere in the URL.

Each search engine is a little different, allowing different kinds of search terms. You can always search by simply entering a single word, but the more you know about each search engine, the more efficiently you'll be able to search. When you first go to a search engine, look around for some kind of link to a help document.

What happens when you search? Navigator sends the information to the search engine, and, with a little luck, you'll see a result page soon, as shown in Figure 6.3. On the other hand, you may see a message telling you that the search engine is busy; try again in a few moments and you may get through. (Or try another search engine.)

FIG. 6.3
Infoseek here has found thousands of links to Web pages related to Greenland.

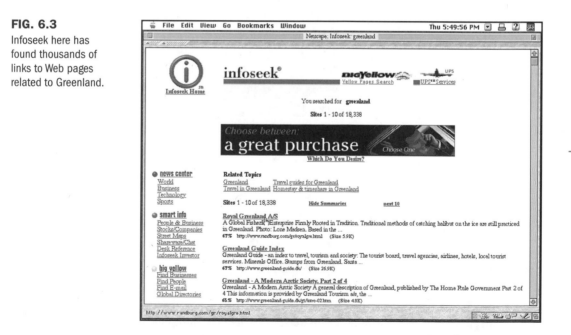

Part
I

Ch
6

What, then, has Infoseek found in this example? Well, when I searched for "greenland," it found thousands of links to Web sites that contain information about Greenland.

The document I'm viewing doesn't show me all the links. It shows me the first few, but there's a link on the right side, at both the top and bottom of the page, to show me the next few (see the link that says Next 10). It has found links to information about the Greelandic telephone company, the music of Greenland, the geography of Greenland, the city of Narsaq, and much, much more (18,338 entries' worth)! If any of these links interests me, all I need to do is click that link, and away I go, over the North Atlantic and into Greenland.

But this offers me way too many entries to be of any use! Luckily, I can search again. At the bottom of the page (see Figure 6.4), there's another search text box, above an option button that's labeled Search only these results. If I enter another word—in this case hiking—and then click Seek, Infoseek will search those 18,000 or so entries for just the ones related in some way to geography; this time I end up with just 180 entries, including *An Introduction to Africa*, which goes to show that nothing's perfect. Then I can, if I want, further refine the search, by searching for something like Ivittuut (a town in Greenland). Now I end up with just 14 entries, a much more manageable number.

FIG. 6.4

Further refine your searches to get just what you need; Infoseek allows you to search within the previously found entries.

Using a Site Sampler

You may notice a Site Sampler label on the Net Search page. This is not always present, but if it is there you can click it to open another Navigator window. This window will contain the current search form. (If it's not there, you can sometimes find a link to a site sampler at the search site itself—click the search-site logo to go to the site. At Yahoo!, for instance, you'll find a Yahoo! to Go link that opens a site sampler.) You can minimize this window, continue your travels around the Web, and then restore the window at any time to do a quick search (see Figure 6.5).

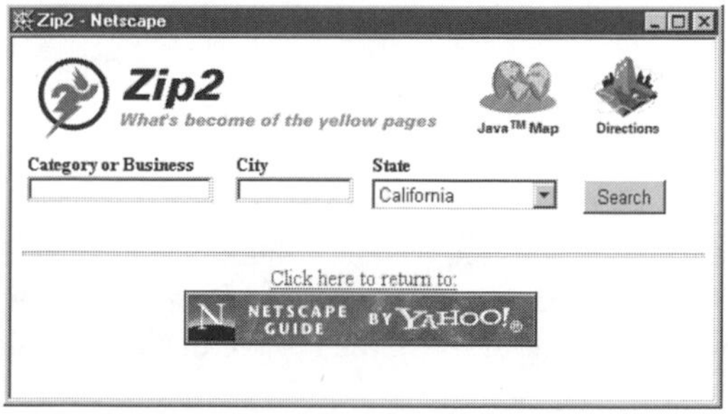

FIG. 6.5
Click the Site Sampler label to open another Navigator window containing the search form. This one is actually one of the Yellow Pages search sites, Zip2.

Load More Search Engines

Try all five of these search engines to find the one you prefer; each is a little different. But these are only a handful of the search engines on the Web. If you click the Net Search button again and then scroll down the page, you'll find links to dozens of services such as GTE SuperPages, AccuFind, Disinformation (a search system that helps you find information about "current affairs, politics, new science, and the 'hidden information,'" including cults, conspiracies, and UFOs), and HotBot.

There are plenty more not listed here. For a good place to find all sorts of search systems, try the following:

http://www.yahoo.com/Computers_and_Internet/Internet/Searching_the_Net/

You can also try the following page:

http://www.nosc.mil/planet_earth/Library/sei_room.html

Search Multiple Engines Quickly!

There are many more search engines, and you can quickly search dozens of them using special forms. Try these sites:

- *W3 Search Engines*   This is neat; not only will you find a list of many search engines, but you can search directly from the W3 Search Engines form.

- *CUSI (Configurable Unified Search Interface)*   Another great site for searching, CUSI allows you to search a variety of engines from one form, and also allows you to search for people, software, dictionaries, and so on. It's perhaps a little easier to use than W3 Search Engines. The URL is:

http://web.nexor.co.uk/susi/cusi.html

N O T E   There is no "best site." I like to start my searches with Yahoo! (**http://www.yahoo.com/**) and then go to AltaVista (**http://altavista.digital.com**) if I still can't find what I want, but you may prefer other sites. Each works differently and each provides different results. Try a few and see which you like. ■

Browse the Internet Directories

Many of these search sites contain not only search engines (programs that allow you to search a database) but directories that you can browse. Yahoo! (see Figure 6.6) is one of the best of these; follow Yahoo!'s link on the Net Search page, or go to **http://www.yahoo.com** (you can go to **http://www.yahooligans.com** if you want to see the kids' version).

FIG. 6.6

Yahoo! provides lists of Web sites, broken down by category.

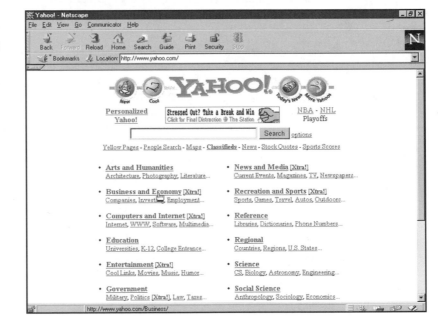

At the top of the page, you'll find a text box into which you can type a search term. But notice the category links: Art, Education, Health, Social Science, and so on. Each link points deeper into the Yahoo! system, to a lower level in the hierarchical system of document categories. For example, click Recreation and Sports and you'll see a document from Yahoo! with a list of more categories: Amusement and Theme Parks@, Aviation, Drugs@, Motorcycles, and so on.

What does the @ symbol at the end of some of these mean? It means that this entry is a sort of cross-reference, and that you will cross over to another category if you select this link. For example, click Drugs@ and you'll see the page shown in Figure 6.7, which is in the

`Health:Pharmacology:Drugs` category and contains links to other drug-related categories. This page also contains links to Web pages related to recreational drugs (from alcohol to XTC), political and legal issues involving drugs, pharmacology, and many other subjects.

FIG. 6.7
Finally you arrive at a page with links out across the Web.

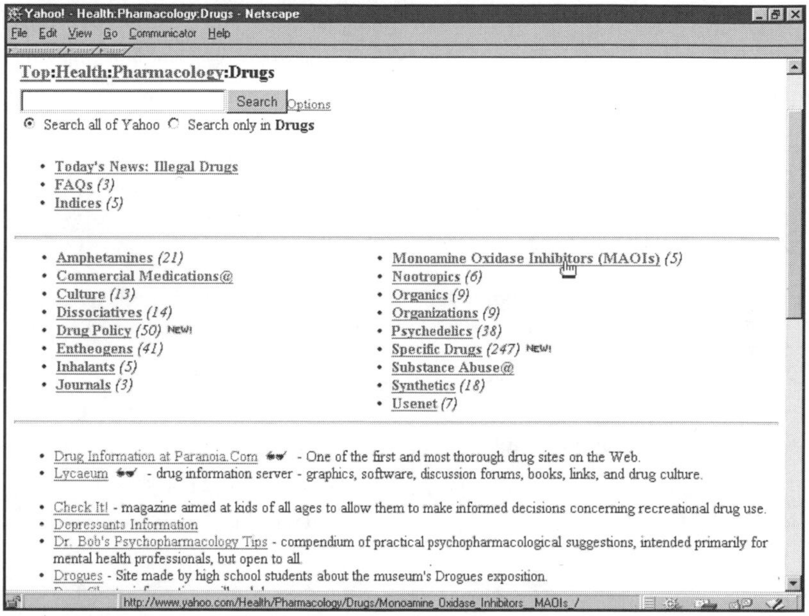

Notice that Figure 6.7 contains links that are in bold text with numbers in parentheses after them (such as `Monoamine Oxidase Inhibitors (MAOIs) (5)`), as well as links that are not in bold (such as Dr. Bob's Psychopharmacology Tips). The bold links take you further down the Yahoo! hierarchy; you'll see another document that contains more links. The number in parentheses after the link indicates how many links you'll find in that document.

The non-bold links are links across the Internet to Web documents containing the information you're looking for. Click `Dr. Bob's Psychopharmacology Tips`, for example, and you'll find yourself viewing a document on the use of drugs, intended for people who work in the mental health field.

A Navigator Shortcut

Here's a nice shortcut you can use for searching. Simply type a search term into the Location box and press Enter. You must type something that cannot be interpreted as an URL; if you just typed greenland, for instance, Navigator would look for **http://www.greenland.com/**. So you must type at least two words. You could type something like greenland greenland. Currently you shouldn't type find greenland, or, as Internet Explorer allows, go greenland. If you did,

Part

I

Ch

6

Navigator would actually search for both words. You could type s greenland or f greenland, though. Because it's two items, the browser will interpret it as a search term, but because the first part is a single letter, the search engine will ignore it and just search for greenland.

You can search for combined terms like greenland geography or greenland tours. Netscape will take your search term and send it to one of the search engines shown in the Net Search page (at the time of writing at least, Navigator would *not* automatically pick the search engine you defined as the one you want to use each time you click the Search button). In a few moments, you'll see the results in the Navigator window. This is a very handy feature, if you don't mind allowing Navigator to pick the search engine.

Finding People

Now, how about tracking down people, including old friends and colleagues, who probably have Internet access but for whom you don't have e-mail addresses?

Many of the search systems we've looked at so far can help you find people. For instance, if you're using Yahoo! or Excite, you can click the `People Search` link. With Lycos, you can click the People Find button.

 But the easiest way to get started is by clicking the Guide button in Navigator and then selecting People. This brings up the page shown in Figure 6.8.

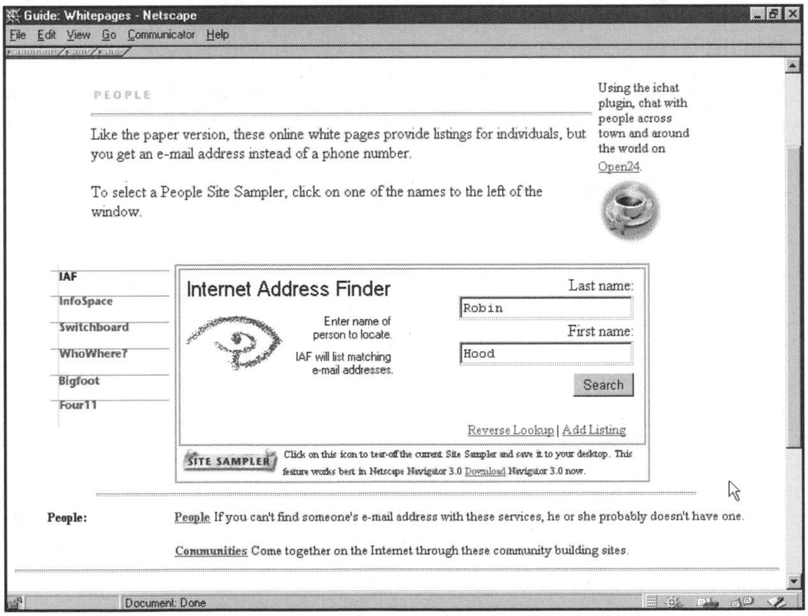

FIG. 6.8
Here you can begin your
search for that special
someone.

This page works in a manner similar to the search page. There are six major directories you can search (WhoWhere?, Bigfoot, Four11, Internet Address Finder, InfoSpace, and Switchboard), and when you select the People menu option Navigator picks one of the six at random. You can click one of the names on the left to use another, if you want.

TIP Netscape Communicator's Address Book has a built-in directory-search system that helps you quickly search these directories (see Chapter 17 for more information).

You'll find that tracking down people is very difficult. There is no single directory of Internet users. Imagine trying to find someone's phone number if you didn't know what country—let alone what city—he lived in. It's a similar situation with the Internet—lots of independent directories, none of which are comprehensive.

Still, the Internet is getting better, and you may locate people if you try various directories. You'll find that some of these directories have nice little features such as services that will e-mail you if they later find the person you're looking for, systems that search directories of phone numbers and street addresses, systems that find personal Web pages or Internet phone addresses, and so on.

Look back at Figure 6.8 and you'll see a link that starts with `People` and continues with the following note:

`If you can't find someone's e-mail address with these services, he or she probably doesn't have one.`

This note is incorrect; it's quite possible for someone to have an e-mail address yet not be listed in any directory. However, the link takes you to another list of places you can use to track down people—everything from the World Alumni Page to Telecom New Zealand. If you can't find whom you're looking for with the main People page, keep going through these directories and you may get lucky.

Finding Newsgroup Messages

Another form of search can be very useful at times, especially if you're in the "public eye" at all, or sell a product. You can find out what people are saying about you or your product in the Internet newsgroups.

To do so you need to find a search engine that also searches UseNet newsgroups (you'll find out more about these in Chapter 18, "Collabra: From Newsgroups to Corporate Communications"). You may have to go to the actual search site to do this, rather than use the Net Search form. For instance, if you go to Infoseek (**http://www.infoseek.com/**) you'll find a drop-down list box below the search box, from which you can select UseNet Newsgroups. At Excite (**http://www.excite.com/**), you can select (again, from a drop-down list box) either UseNet Newsgroups or UseNet Classifieds (these are newsgroups that carry classified ads). There's also a search system dedicated to searching newsgroups; it's called DejaNews, and you can find it at **http://www.dejanews.com**.

Part

I

Ch

6

Search the same way you would when searching for a Web page—type a word, or combination of words (read the system's instructions to find out how to combine words). Type your name, your product's name, or some other subject you're interested in researching. Figure 6.9 shows an example of what you might see as a response.

FIG. 6.9
DejaNews will search
newsgroup messages
for you.

You can click one of the returned links to view the actual message and see what people have been saying.

Searching Mailing Lists

Mailing lists are discussion groups based on e-mail. If you subscribe to a mailing list, you'll receive a copy of each message sent to the list; in turn, any messages you submit are sent to all the other users.

Searching mailing list messages is not easy—because of the decentralized way in which mailing lists are handled, there are few mailing-list search sites. You can try **http://www.reference.com**, though. This site lets you search newsgroup and mailing list messages at the same time. This system has another advantage—if you register with this site (it's free), you can create an "active query." This means the system will automatically run your search every few days and e-mail you if it finds any new matches.

There are 80,000 or more Internet mailing lists, and no system can search all of them. Reference.com, the only mailing-list search system I've found so far, currently searches a relatively small number of lists.

Searching the Real World with the Yellow Pages

Netscape has added a new search feature, a Yellow Pages search page. Click the Guide button, then choose Yellow Pages. You'll see the page in Figure 6.10. This page works in a similar manner to the other search pages, but this time it searches business directories such as ON'VILLAGE Yellow Pages+, WorldPages, Zip2, and the GTE SuperPages. You'll find links to sites that list businesses in North America, and throughout the rest of the world. These are not simply Internet Yellow Pages; they don't just list e-mail addresses and Web URLs. Rather, they provide real-world addresses and telephone numbers.

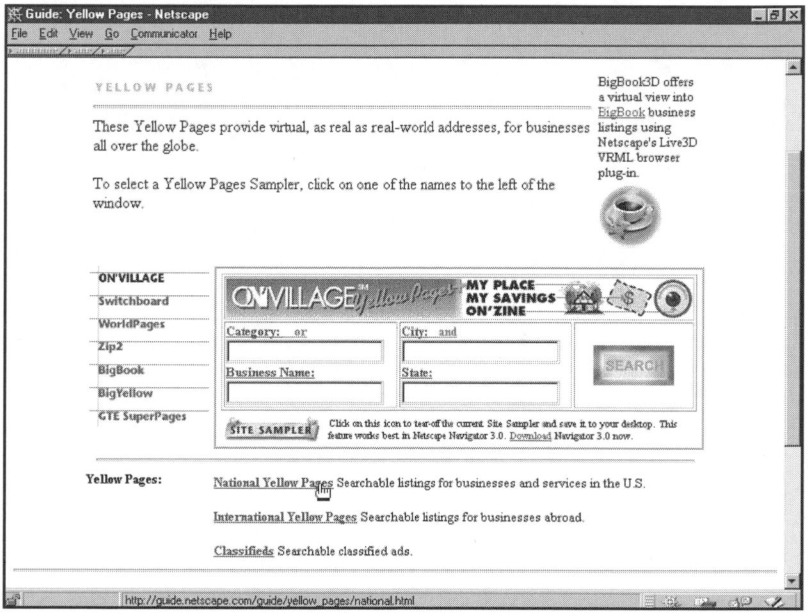

FIG. 6.10
Navigator's Yellow Pages Web page provides links to search systems that will help you find businesses throughout the world.

Finding Software

If you want to find useful shareware programs—one of the most popular uses of the Web— you'll find that some of the search systems we've already looked at have features that help you track down programs.

There are also a number of sites dedicated to distributing shareware:

Shareware.com	**http://www.shareware.com** (all operating systems)
Jumbo	**http://www.jumbo.com** (all operating systems)
Tucows	**http://www.tucows.com** (Windows only)
The Ultimate	**http://www.velodrome.com/umac.html** (Macintosh only) ●

CHAPTER 7

Navigator Frames

Now and then you'll see the Navigator window split into different sections, each section containing an image or document. Occasionally you'll even notice that a new browser window opens automatically. Frames and secondary windows provide a way for Web authors to make the Web's giant hypertext system easier to handle…but when misused, frames and secondary windows actually make it harder to work with!

Despite all the excitement surrounding the World Wide Web, until recently it was still a relatively primitive form of hypertext. I'm not talking about all the multimedia stuff—sound, video, pictures, and so on. I'm talking about the way in which documents are handled. Until fairly recently, Web browsers could display only one document at a time. Click a link, and the current document would disappear and another would appear.

The best that you could do was to open another window in which to display a new document. For instance, in Navigator you can right-click a link and choose Open <u>N</u>ew Window. A new Navigator window opens and displays the document. But what you are really doing in this case is starting a new Web session. You end up running multiple Web sessions, but the documents within are still single-view documents.

Panes and frames

Frames were originally known as *panes* in the hypertext world.

Different uses for frames

Frames can be used for a variety of purposes, from providing tables of contents that remain in view, to creating banners and "ledges."

Using frames

There are a few simple techniques you need to know about how to work with frames.

Sample frames

I'll show you a few sample frames from around the Web.

Targeted windows

Targeted windows (or secondary windows) are windows that the Web author opens for you.

Some other forms of hypertext, such as Windows Help files and the Microsoft Multimedia Viewer format that many multimedia CDs use, handle documents differently. They may enable the hypertext author to open *secondary windows,* for instance—the reader can click a link, which opens another window showing the referenced document. The first window remains open.

At first glance, this appears to be the same as Navigator's Open in <u>N</u>ew Window command. It's not, though, because in this case the *author* is determining that a new window should open, so it's the author who can determine the flow of the session. The user is not opening another hypertext session; he's merely following the flow of the document according to the wishes of the author.

Some hypertext systems use multiple panes. While you are viewing only one window, there can be two or three individual areas within the window—maybe more. One pane may contain special controls needed, another may contain a picture, and another may contain a list of cross-reference links.

Well, Netscape has introduced both these concepts to the Web: Web authors can create documents that open multiple panes within a Navigator window (in Netscape-speak these are known as frames), and can also tell Navigator when to open a new window. ■

How Are Frames Used?

The following list describes a few ways you'll see frames used:

- Authors can add banners to their documents. The banner at the top (a corporate logo, for instance) remains static, while you can scroll through the contents of the lower frame. Static areas such as this are known as *ledges.*

- A form in one frame may be used to accept data from you, while another frame displays results after you've submitted the form. For instance, you might enter information you want to search for in the form, submit the form, and then view the results in the second frame.

- An author may add a control bar in one frame and a document in the other. Clicking the control bar might take you out of the current document, into another part of the same document, or to a different framed document. This is another form of ledge.

- A table of contents might be displayed in the left frame, with the full document in the right frame. Clicking an entry in the table of contents would display the requested content in the right frame.

- A company might choose to keeps its copyright information in a frame, as a constant reminder to the reader.

Different framed documents work in different ways. Here are a few things to look for:

■ Frames may be fixed in place.

■ Frames may be movable. Point at a border between frames; if the pointer changes to two parallel lines with two arrows (see Figure 7.1), you can drag the border to reposition it.

■ Links within documents can be set up to take you away from the framed document to a completely different document, to replace the contents of the current frame, or to replace the contents of a different frame.

■ Frames may be independently scrollable; that is, you may be able to scroll through the contents of one frame while the contents of other frames remain static. An author can fix the contents of a frame, though, so that you cannot scroll the document within that frame.

TIP Some commands act on the selected frame. For instance, on the File menu you'll find the Save Frame As, Edit Frame, Send Frame, and Print Frame commands. And there's also Edit, Find in Frame.

Simply click the document inside the frame to select that frame (make sure you click an inactive part of the document, of course). When a frame is selected, an outline is placed around the inside of the borders around that frame. On the Mac, the border is a thick yellow line; it's quite obvious which frame has been selected. On the Windows browsers, it's a thin black line, not quite so obvious, but still visible if you look closely.

A Table of Contents

Figure 7.1 shows a good example of frames used to create a table of contents. The left frame is the table of contents. When you click an entry in the left frame, the referenced document appears in the right frame. Notice that the mouse pointer on the border has changed: This means you can move the border.

A Table of Contents and a Ledge

The Web page shown in Figure 7.2 contains three frames. The upper frame is both a ledge containing the site name and a Table of Contents for the city selected in the lower-left frame. The lower-left frame is a Table of Contents listing the cities for which information is available, and the lower-right frame is the content area. Both the content area and the table of contents are scrollable. (Notice the mouse pointer on the horizontal border; it hasn't changed form, so these are non-adjustable borders.)

Part

I

Ch

7

The pointer changes to show
that you can move the border.

FIG. 7.1

The left frame provides
a permanent table of
contents; click a link in
the left frame to change
the document in the
right frame.

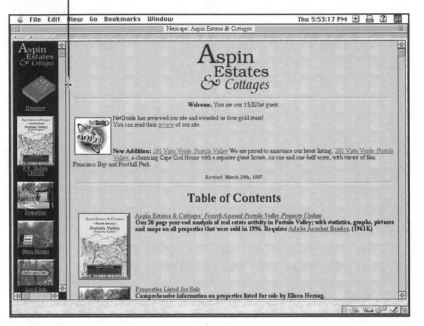

FIG. 7.2

Besides the content
area, this document has
a table of contents (a
list of cities) on the left
and a ledge containing
other links at the top.

The mouse pointer
hasn't changed, so you
can't move this border.

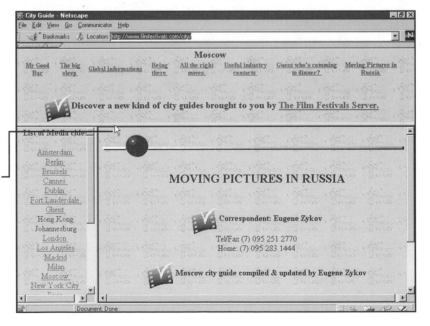

My Favorite Example

One of the nicest framed documents I've seen is a demo document. It's the How We See document located at the following URL:

http://home.netscape.com/comprod/products/navigator/version_2.0/frames/eye/

The lower-left frame contains a picture of the eye, with callouts pointing to the eye's various components. Each callout is a link; click a callout to change the contents of the lower-right frame. The upper frame is a static banner. Figure 7.3 shows this document.

FIG. 7.3
The How We See demo document is an excellent example of how frames can work.

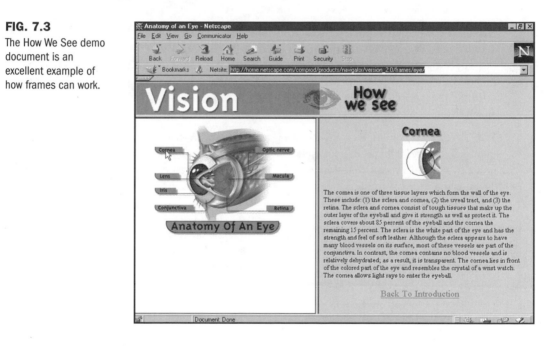

The Problem with Frames

Frames can often be irritating if they're not used properly. There's a tendency for many Web authors to use every neat toy that's available, without considering whether it's really appropriate. Frames can clutter the Navigator window, especially on a small monitor.

When frames were first introduced late in 1995, the consensus on the Web was that they were a Good Thing, something that we all should use. In the best "it's a cool new feature, so let's use it" spirit of the Web, all sorts of Web sites suddenly popped up with frames over a period of just a few weeks.

Since then, many Web authors have realized that new is not always good, and have either stopped working with frames or at least have provided non-frame options. Even Netscape Communications, which for a short while forced everyone coming to their site to use frames, now doesn't use frames by default.

Part

I

Ch

7

Early versions of the frames feature were buggy; frames borders sometimes disappeared, Navigator sometimes crashed at framed sites, and so on. The feature now works much better, but people are realizing that frames are not always appropriate. Frames are often a nuisance when viewing Navigator in low-resolution modes—each frame is too small to fit much into, and many users simply don't like them. Frames are often appropriate for tables of contents, but not for many other situations.

Especially annoying in earlier versions of Navigator was the problem with the history list; using the Back command would often take you all the way out of the framed document to the document viewed immediately before entering the frames, rather than showing you the previous document displayed within the content frame.

Netscape has fixed this problem, though. The Back command now goes back through each document you've seen; in other words, it includes documents within frames, not simply the main documents. Note, however, that the history list itself does not list all the different documents at the framed site; look at the Go menu and you'll see that it includes the main frame document, not each document you've seen. So at a framed site, the Back button is using a special, hidden "frame history" list.

There's another, completely unnecessary problem. Many Web authors work with large computer screens set to high screen resolutions. They create wonderfully attractive Web pages, using two, three, or even four frames. They often set these frames to be non-scrollable, too. Then, when a user working with a low screen resolution tries to view the page, it's unusable. It's too cramped, some of the data is off-screen, and, if the author has set the frames to be non-scrollable, the user can't even move through the document to read it all. If you run into this problem, though, you can right-click within the frame to open the pop-up menu (or, on the Mac, click and hold the button down), then choose Open Frame in New Window. You'll see the contents of the frame in another window, so you should be able to read the entire page; if necessary, you can scroll through the frame, too.

TIP You'll run into framed sites quite often, as they're fairly common. If you want to find some now, you may be able to track them down from the Companies Using Frames document:

http://home.netscape.com/comprod/products/navigator/version_2.0/frames/frame_users.html

This page is a little old, however, and for the reasons discussed earlier, many of the sites this document links to no longer use frames!

Targeted Windows

The other feature I mentioned earlier—allowing Web authors to automatically open another window and place the referenced document in that window—is known as *targeted windows*. In other hypertext systems, it's often known as secondary windows. The Web author can assign documents to windows by name. When you click a link, Navigator looks for a window with that particular name (you can't see the window names, because they're hidden), and then, if the window is already open, places the document in that window. If the window is not open, Navigator opens another window, gives it the required name, and then places the document inside.

For example, an author may have a list of subjects in a window. When you click a link in that window, an appropriate document may appear in a separate window. Clicking another link in the first window may open yet another window, or it may replace the document in the second window with the new document.

There's a drawback to this feature, though. Many Web authors open their targeted windows full-screen, completely covering the original browser window. If you're using a fast computer and glance away for just a moment, you might not even realize that you're working in a new window.

Here's the telltale sign that you're working in a new window: You try to use the history list and find that it's gone! Targeted windows do not inherit the original window's history list. The Back and Forward buttons won't do anything, and you won't see pages listed in the Go menu.

Some authors have taken to using JavaScript to automatically open a targeted window when the user simply points at a link. In other words, you may simply move the mouse pointer across the page, and a new window opens; you've no idea why or how it opened, but there it is. This is a really irritating trick, but there's not much you can do about it but close the window and move on. ●

Navigator's Advanced Features

Saving Documents and Images from the Web

After the novelty of traveling around on the Web has worn off, you may begin to actually use it for day-to-day work. Web pages are more than things to look at for a moment and move on. With tens of millions of Web pages you'll find a lot of trivia, but you'll also find some very useful and interesting information. Inevitably the question arises: "How do I save that?"

Navigator provides lots of ways to save information; you can save the text and pictures from a page, save the Web page's HTML "source" code, save files referenced by links, print the document, and so on. You can even use a few fancy tricks, like creating desktop wallpaper from a document's background image or an inline image within the document, or embed a Web page into a word-processing document. ▪

Saving documents as text and HTML files

It's an easy task to save documents you find on the Web; you can save them as plain text or with their HTML codes.

Saving images and backgrounds from Web documents

Images you find can be saved on your hard disk.

Printing documents

You can print Web documents and read them later at your leisure.

Saving URLs

You may need to copy URLs so you can send them to friends and colleagues.

Transferring files across the Web

The Web contains millions of computer files that you may want to save.

Embedding documents in a word processor

Web pages can be embedded into word-processing documents in Windows 95 and Windows NT.

What Can You Save?

Navigator provides a number of ways for you to copy information from a Web document into your other Windows applications or save it on your hard disk. You can perform the following operations:

- Save the document text
- Save the HTML source document
- Save the text or HTML source for documents you haven't even viewed
- Save an inline image as a graphics file or as your desktop wallpaper
- Save the document background as a graphics file or as your desktop wallpaper
- Print the document
- Save URLs to the Clipboard so you can copy them into another program
- Grab files directly from the cache
- Save computer files referenced by links
- Embed Web pages into other applications

CAUTION

Remember, much of what you come across on the Web is copyrighted material. In fact, unless you are sure that what you are viewing is not copyrighted, you should assume it is. You can take this material for private use, but not for publication. (In other words, accord Web information the same respect you would information in a book in your local library.) For information about what you can and can't do with copyrighted material, refer to a book on copyright law. (Many writers' references contain copyright law information or visit The Copyright Website at **http://www.benedict.com/**.)

How Can I Grab Document Text?

Let's begin by looking at how to get text out of a Web document. (Note that these methods save just the text; you'll lose the images from the document, but as you'll see in a moment, you can save those separately.) Use the following methods:

- Choose File, Save As (or, if viewing a framed page, click in the frame containing the document you want and choose File, Save Frame As). In the Save As dialog box, select Text (*.txt) from the Save as Type drop-down list box, select the directory you want to place it in, enter a file name, and click Save. Navigator will save all the text from the document (not the underlying HTML codes, though).

 TIP Some versions of Navigator may not carry out this operation correctly. If you find that the document is saved with all the HTML tags inside, and with an .html extension, go back and try again. This time don't bother selecting Text (*.txt) from the drop-down list box. Instead type a file name and include the extension .Txt. This bug has been in Navigator for a long time, so it may be there for some time more.

- In the History window, click an entry and choose File, Save As; you'll be able to save the file referenced by that history entry.

- Highlight the text; choose Edit, Copy or press Ctrl+C (Windows) or ⌘+C (Mac); or select Copy from the pop-up menu. The text is copied to the Clipboard, so you can now go to another application and paste it.

T I P To highlight text, choose Edit, Select All. Or point at the beginning of the text you want to highlight and click the mouse button, hold the button down, and drag the pointer across the text. (Make sure you're not clicking inside a link, of course, or you won't highlight the text—you'll see another document.) You can also click in the document. At the point at which you want to start copying text, press Shift, and click at the ending point. This is a good way to select text if you want to copy text that spans more than one screen.

If you are viewing a framed document, you'll need to use File, Save Frame As. Navigator will save only the selected document, so before you use the command, click the frame containing the document you want to save. You'll notice, though, that there's still a File, Save As command available. At the time of writing, this does exactly the same as the File, Save Frame As command—it saves the document in the frame you selected. This doesn't make a lot of sense, so I suspect that eventually this command may save the *frame-definition* document. That's the document that tells your browser how to create the frames: how many frames it should make, where and how large they are, and which document to place into each frame.

Saving the HTML Source Document

Why would you care about the *source* document? Most people won't want the source document, but if you're interested in creating your own Web pages, you will. If you view a source document, you can learn the techniques that other Web authors have used to create documents.

The source document is the ASCII text document that is the basis of the Web page you are viewing. As you saw in Chapter 2, "The Opening Moves," each Web document is an ASCII text document with special codes, or *tags*, that tell Web browsers what to do. When you transfer a document to the browser, the browser renders the document; that is, it takes a look at all the codes, then figures out what it has to do to turn the document into something you can read.

To save the source document, choose File, Save As (or File, Save Frame As). Enter a file name, choose a directory, and make sure that HTML Files (Source on the Mac) is displayed in the Save As Type drop-down list box. Then click Save. (If you're using Windows 95 or Windows NT, Navigator automatically saves the document with the .html extension, not .htm, since Windows 95 and Windows NT accept file extensions over three digits. If you're working with Windows 3.x, you'll have to use the .htm extension.)

Viewing the Source Document

To see the HTML codes before you decide whether to save the file, choose View, Page Source, and another Navigator window will open, displaying the document source. Unfortunately, there's no menu bar, so you can't use File, Save As. You can, however, either highlight the text in the window and press Ctrl+C (Windows) or ⌘+C (Mac) to copy it, or close the window and use the File, Save As command.

> **TIP** At one time Navigator allowed you to pick a different program to display the source; for instance, you could tell the browser to display the source in Windows Notepad. The advantage was that you then had all the tools of the chosen program available to work with the source; you could search, save, copy, and so on. At the current time, Navigator no longer allows you to pick the program, but perhaps this will return sometime (soon, I hope). Look in the Preferences dialog box, probably in the Applications pane.

If the browser is displaying frames, this command will display the frame-definition document, the one that tells the browser how to set up the frameset. To see the source of a document in a frame, right-click in the frame (or click once and hold the button on the Mac) and select View Frame Source.

Saving Documents You Haven't Even Seen

You don't have to view a document before you save it. As long as you have a link to the document, you can save it without viewing it first. Simply right-click the link (in Windows) or click and hold the button down until you see the pop-up menu (on the Mac), and then choose Save Link As. You'll see the Save As dialog box and can choose HTML Files or Text (*.txt), as described earlier (refer to "How Can I Grab Document Text?"). After you've entered the document title you want to use, select the directory and click Save. Navigator will transfer the document. It won't display it, though; it will simply save it as instructed.

How Can I Save Inline Images?

You can save pictures that you find in Web documents. Right-click the picture (or click and hold the button if using the Mac) and choose Save Image As. You'll see the Save As window. Enter a file name and click Save to save the image to your hard disk. It will be saved using the original format: if the picture is a .gif file, Navigator will save it as a .gif; if it's a .jpg or .xbm, it will be saved as such.

> **TIP** If you want to save an entire document, including both text and images, you can open the document in Composer, then save the document. Select File, Edit Page, or File, Edit Frame to place the document in Composer...then see Chapters 20 and 21 for information about working with that program.

By the way, there's a way to remove all the text from around the picture, displaying the picture in Navigator as if it were in a document by itself. Right-click the picture (or click and hold the button if using the Mac) and choose View Image (*image name*). Navigator will request a copy of the picture from the Web server that has the picture, and then display the picture in a document by itself. In other words, even though the picture is in the cache, Navigator will get a fresh copy. You won't see the original text or document background; all you'll see is the image you've selected. (This can be handy because it's not always clear where one image ends and another begins.)

The Mac also has a way that you can quickly save an image to your desktop. Simply drag it from the Navigator window and drop it on the desktop.

TIP You can quickly copy a picture of an image into another application. In Windows, press Alt+Print Screen to place a copy of the Navigator window in the Clipboard. Then go to the application in which you want to paste the image, place the cursor where you want it, and press Ctrl+V to paste the image. You may, depending on the capabilities of the program into which you've pasted it, be able to cut away the area around the image, leaving just the inline picture. On the Mac, you can press ⌘+Shift+3. This creates a file named Picture 1 (then Picture 2, then Picture 3, and so on), which is placed on your hard disk. The file contains a snapshot of the screen, and can be opened in another program.

Using the Image as Wallpaper

If you are using Windows, you can take an inline image and use it as your desktop wallpaper. Simply click the image and then choose Set As Wallpaper. Navigator creates a wallpaper file, then sets up Windows to use that file as the wallpaper. Each time you use this command, the old wallpaper is replaced with the new.

To remove the wallpaper, see your Windows documentation and use the normal wallpaper commands. (In Windows 95 and Windows NT, right-click the desktop and choose Properties; you'll find the Wallpaper settings under the Background tab. Select None in the Wallpaper list box to clear the wallpaper.)

Saving Document Backgrounds

A relatively new feature that has become very popular on Web pages is the *background* image. A Web author can add a special background to his documents; the background may be a plain color or some sort of pattern. Many Web sites use a company name or logo as a sort of watermark in the background. Others use some kind of marble or rock effect. (Some authors aren't doing a good job here. I've noticed that a lot of Web pages are almost illegible, thanks to a poorly chosen background image or color.)

In a previous edition of this book, I said that although Navigator had no *direct* way to save the background image, it might soon, thanks to the Microsoft versus Netscape Communications "war." After all, if Internet Explorer can do this, shouldn't Netscape? I'm glad to say that one of my predictions has finally come true, and Navigator can now store background images; just right-click the image (or click and hold the button if using the Mac) and choose Save Background As. If you're using Windows, you can even save the background as your Windows wallpaper; right-click and choose Set As Wallpaper.

From Web to Paper—Printing the Document

If you want a paper copy of something you've found in a Web document, you can print the document directly from Navigator. First, define your default page setup (you only have to set this up once, not every time you print). Choose File, Print Setup to see the dialog box in Figure 8.1.

FIG. 8.1

You can define margins, headers, and footers and tell Navigator how to print text.

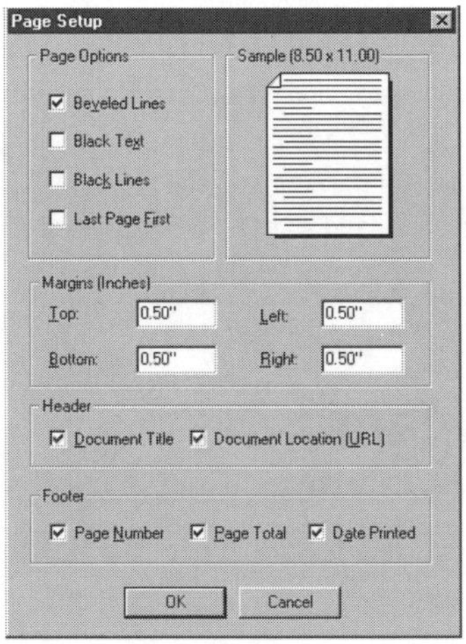

This box lets you select a variety of options, as follows:

- *Beveled Lines*   Many Web documents contain dividing lines across the page (these are created by Web authors using the <HR> tags). Select this option if you want to print these lines as beveled lines, more or less as they appear on-screen—a sort of 3-D effect. (Well, okay, it just looks like two lines close together on my printouts.) If you don't use this option, the lines will appear as single black lines.

- *Black Text*   Select this option to print all the text, even colored text, in black. This is only needed if you are using a color printer, of course.

- *Black Lines*   Select this option to print all lines, even colored lines, in black.

- *Last Page First*   If you select this, Navigator will print the document back-to-front, last page first.

- *Margins*   This sets up the margins (the distance from the edge of the paper to the edge of the text). If you enter a number and then tab out of the field, you'll see that the sample at the upper right of the box changes to show you the new margin.

- *Header*   You can print two items in the header (the line at the very top of the page): Document Title and Document Location (URL). These are handy because they help the reader identify and find the original Web document.

- *Footer*   You have three choices for the footer: You can print the Page Number, Page Total, and Date Printed.

The Mac version of this dialog box is different (you can see it in Figure 8.2). You have fewer options, and you select some of the options from drop-down list boxes rather than by using check boxes. (You actually have more options for setting up the header and footer.) Because Windows and the Mac handle printing differently, the Mac dialog box also has what, in Windows, would be regarded as Print Setup (as opposed to Page Setup) options (paper choice, orientation, and so on).

FIG. 8.2
The Mac's Page Setup box is a little different, but it has most (though not all) of the same options, plus a few extras.

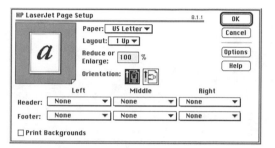

Before You Print—The Preview

Before you print a document, you may want to look at a preview to see how it will turn out. Choose File, Print Preview to see something like the window shown in Figure 8.3. You can see more or less how the document will turn out on the printed page. You'll see the header and footer, the images, and the text. (You *won't* see any background graphics, though, because Navigator strips the background out before printing.)

N O T E   You cannot print, or preview, all the documents held in a frameset at the same time; in other words, you can only print or preview one of the framed documents at a time. So before you choose File, Print Preview, click in the frame you want to preview first. ■

Notice the following buttons at the top of the window:

- ■ *Print*   If you like what you see, go ahead and print the document.
- ■ *Next Page*   If there's more stuff than will fit on one sheet of paper, click this button to see the next page.
- ■ *Prev Page*   This button takes you back to the previous page.
- ■ *Two Page*   This displays two pages on your screen.
- ■ *Zoom In*   Click here to zoom in on the document. You can zoom in twice, which gets you pretty close. You can also click inside the document to zoom in (notice that the mouse pointer is a small magnifying glass).
- ■ *Zoom Out*   Click here to zoom back out.
- ■ *Close*   Click here to return to the main document.

FIG. 8.3

The preview shows you how the printed document will look.

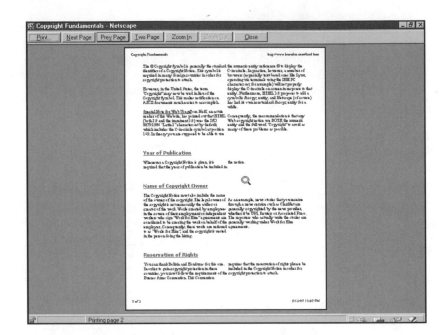

Printing the Document

When you are ready to print the document, choose File, Print to see a Print dialog box, or simply click the Print button on the toolbar. You can pick the printer you want to use, select the pages you want to print (you'll have to guess here a little, because a Web document is a single—perhaps very long—page while it's on-screen), and decide how many copies you want to print.

Saving URLs to the Clipboard

After you're a regular Web user, you'll find that you want to save URLs, or Web "addresses." Perhaps you want to share them with a friend or colleague. Perhaps you want to include an URL in a memo or article you're writing, or want to save the URL in a database with other research materials. Navigator provides the following ways to save URLs:

■ Drag the link icon from the Location bar onto another application; the URL is dropped into the document in that application (it won't work with all Windows applications).

■ Click in the Location text box, and the URL of the current document will be highlighted. Then press Ctrl+C (Windows) or Command+C (Mac); the text is copied to the Clipboard.

■ Right-click a link (text or graphic), or click and hold the button if using the Mac, and then choose Copy Link Location from the pop-up menu. This is a very handy method for copying an URL without even going to the referenced document.

- To copy the URL that identifies a picture, right-click the picture (or click and hold the button if using the Mac) and choose Copy Image Location.
- In the History window, right-click an entry and select Copy (or to remove it from the History window at the same time select Cut). Of course, you can also use the other Copy and Cut commands; use the Edit menu or the keyboard shorcuts.

Stealing Directly from the Cache

Long after you've been to a Web document—days or weeks later, depending on how big your hard-disk cache is (see Chapter 3, "Advanced Navigation")—you can grab information from that document by digging around in the cache. However, the cache is not always easy to work in.

First, to see where your cache directory is, choose Edit, Preferences, open the Advanced category, then click Cache. The Disk Cache Folder text box shows where your cache has been placed.

Now view the contents of that directory (in Windows Explorer or File Manager if using Windows, or by opening the appropriate folders on the Mac). You'll find all the inline images—.gif, .xbm, and .jpg files—from your cached documents, along with the .html documents themselves. You can simply open them in another application or copy them to another directory.

Unfortunately, though, these files have all been renamed, and it's quite difficult to figure out what they are. They've all been given a special M number; for instance, M0o7j0pl.html. Double-click the .html files, and they'll open in Navigator—though the links to the inline graphics won't work. If you have some kind of file viewer, you can use that to quickly view entries. For instance, if you're using Windows 3.1 and have PC Tools, you know that the PC Tools File Manager has a good file viewer; after you've opened the file viewer, each time you click a file, the image or text within the file is displayed in the viewer. Or try this trick; type **about:cache** into Navigator's Location box and press Enter. You'll see a list of the files in the cache, with the original URLs identifying where each cache file comes from. You can click the links to view the files.

N O T E The term *viewer* is interchangeable with the word *helper.* The term viewer is perhaps more commonly used on the Web than helper, but Netscape uses the term helper most—but not all—of the time. Both terms refer to a program that has been set up to accept files from the browser; the program will display or play files that the browser is unable to work with. ▪

Of course, you can also use Navigator itself to open these files; simply choose File, Open Page and then click the Browse button and select a file—.htm, .gif, .jpg, or whatever—from the cache. Or simply drag the file from the cache onto the Navigator window to open the file.

More convenient, though, would be to obtain a utility designed just for this purpose, one that lets you "browse" the cache and save the files you want. You can find such a utility at shareware libraries on the Web, such as **http://www.shareware.com** and **http://www.jumbo.com** (all operating systems) or **http://www.tucows.com** (Windows only). Search for something like netscape cache and you'll find a variety of cache utilities. Or, if it's mainly the graphics you're interested in, find a graphics utility like ThumbsPlus (see Figure 8.4).

FIG. 8.4

Utilities such as ThumbsPlus (**http://www.cerious.com**) can help you find graphics in the cache.

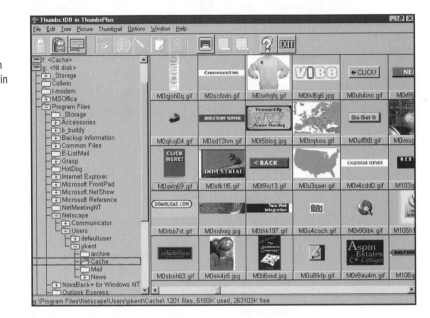

TIP Here's a quick way to view the contents of the cache if you're using Windows 95. Open Windows Explorer and position the window so you can also see the Navigator window. Find the cache directory and then drag the directory icon from Explorer onto Navigator. When you release the mouse button, Navigator creates a Web page (see Figure 8.5) displaying the cache directory, showing each file as a link—as if you were at an FTP site (see Chapter 14, "Accessing Files with FTP"). The files are listed in chronological order, from oldest to newest (it may take a while to display the list, especially if you have a large cache). Now you can just click links to view files. Set a bookmark so you can quickly return to view the cache directory. Of course, this works with all hard-disk directories, not just the cache directory.

FIG. 8.5
Drag the directory icon from Explorer onto Navigator to view the cache.

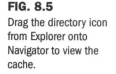

Part
II

Ch
8

Directory listing of /g|/Program Files/Netscape/Users/pkent/Cache - Netscape

File   Edit   View   Go   Communicator   Help

Bookmarks   Location: file:///g|/Program Files/Netscape/Users/pkent/Cache/

Directory listing of /g|/Program Files/Netscape/Users/pkent/Cache

Up to higher level directory

M007D8PR.GIF	261 bytes	Thu May 08 15:10:18 1997	GIF Image
M008NTOV.GIF	6 Kb	Tue May 13 09:21:56 1997	GIF Image
M00K2QCG.GIF	1 Kb	Sun May 11 11:53:45 1997	GIF Image
M00LFQMM.GIF	2 Kb	Fri May 09 17:51:13 1997	GIF Image
M00M3VI7.GIF	291 bytes	Mon May 12 13:46:44 1997	GIF Image
M00NFDSR.GIF	4 Kb	Mon May 12 11:45:38 1997	GIF Image
M00PC7VB	2 Kb	Tue May 13 09:32:15 1997	
M00PE9A0.GIF	593 bytes	Tue May 13 09:05:01 1997	GIF Image
M00QC887.JPG	39 Kb	Fri May 09 17:51:31 1997	JPEG Image
M00QEMBK.GIF	490 bytes	Fri May 09 15:57:09 1997	GIF Image
M011PD5L.GIF	1 Kb	Tue May 13 12:02:45 1997	GIF Image
M011QD7H.GIF	1 Kb	Thu May 08 14:56:10 1997	GIF Image
M011S8R2.GIF	2 Kb	Mon May 12 14:15:22 1997	GIF Image
M012CN2O.GIF	8 Kb	Fri May 09 17:50:34 1997	GIF Image
M013CLSO.JPG	17 Kb	Mon May 12 11:54:02 1997	JPEG Image
M013J6AD.GIF	7 Kb	Mon May 09 09:57:16 1997	GIF Image
M014N2TN.HTM	5 Kb	Mon May 12 13:38:58 1997	Hypertext Markup L
M015KBTL.GIF	436 bytes	Fri May 09 15:57:11 1997	GIF Image

file:///g%7C/Program%20Files/Netscape/Users/pkent/Cache/M00NFDSR.GIF

How Do I Grab Files from the Web?

Many links on the Web point not to other Web documents, but to computer files of various kinds. You can group these files into the two following types:

- Files that you want to transfer to your hard disk—For instance, a link may point to a program that is in an .exe, .zip, .sit, .sea, .gzip, or .hqx file. You want to transfer this program to your computer and then install it. (These are various forms of archive files, for different platforms: .exe and .zip are commonly used on Windows; .sit, .sea, and .hqx are common Mac formats; and .gzip is one of several UNIX formats.)

- Files that you want to play or view—These include sound files (music and speech), video, graphics of many kinds, word processing documents, Adobe Acrobat documents, PostScript files, and so on.

Of course, in order to play or view a file, it has to be transferred to your hard disk, and you may then choose to save it. So in one sense, there's no difference between these two types of files—in each case, a file is transferred to your computer. But if you want to play or view a file, that's part of the *hypermedia* or *multimedia* experience of the Web, so the purpose of the transfer is different.

But it's also different in another way: For the second type of file, you may have to configure a special plug-in or viewer (also known as a helper) so that when Navigator transfers the file, it knows how to play or display it. (For the first of these file types—files you want to save on your hard disk—Navigator doesn't care what happens to the file; it's simply going to save it to your hard disk and let you figure out what to do with it later.) You'll look at viewers in Chapters 9, "Sound and Video: Using Plug-Ins and Viewers," and 10, "More on Plug-Ins and Viewers." For now, we're only interested in the first type of file—one that you want to transfer and save on your hard disk.

File Transfers

Why transfer files back to your computer? In Chapter 14, you'll learn how to use Navigator to run FTP (File Transfer Protocol) sessions. FTP is an Internet-wide system that allows you to copy files to your computer from software archives all over the world. You can get shareware programs, clip art, various documents, sound clips, and more. There are literally millions of files waiting for you at these archives.

But Web authors can also distribute computer files directly from their Web documents. They create special links from their documents to the files that they believe their readers may want to transfer. Clicking such a link begins the transfer to your computer. The following are a few reasons for grabbing files from across the Web:

- Many sites are run by companies that want to distribute their shareware, freeware, or demo programs. (We'll look at one of these in a moment.)

- Some authors want to distribute non-Web documents. They may create links to PostScript, Word for Windows, Adobe Acrobat, and Windows Help documents, for example.

- Some authors have placed clip-art archives on the Web. You can transfer the files and then use them in your own Web documents.

As you can see, there is some overlap here between the two types of files mentioned before. This list points out that a Web author may want to distribute an Adobe Acrobat file (Acrobat is a hypertext document format). But Acrobat files fall into the second category of files: ones that are part of the multimedia experience that Navigator wants to "play."

Well, they may be files that can be played, depending on the following two factors:

- How is the document formatted? If the file has its original extension and is in its original format, the Web author has set it up so that it can be played. For instance, the Acrobat extension is .pdf, and when the file is transferred, Navigator can automatically send this file to an Adobe Acrobat plug-in or viewer so that you can view the document immediately. But the Web author may have saved the file in a compressed, or archive, format. The extension may be .zip (a PKZIP compressed file), .exe (a self-extracting archive file), .sea (a Macintosh self-extracting archive file), .sit (a Macintosh StuffIt file), and so on. This means that the Web author expects people to transfer the file, extract the software, and then load the file into another program. (Just to confuse the issue, you can set up programs such as WinZIP to act as a "viewer" for .zip files or StuffIt Expander to act as a viewer for .sit files. That way you can quickly expand the files once they're transferred.)

■ Have you set up Navigator to play the file? That is, have you installed a plug-in or viewer? If you haven't set it up to play a particular file (I'll discuss that in Chapter 9), the only thing Navigator can do is transfer it to your hard disk. So even if the file extension is .pdf, for instance, if you haven't configured Navigator to "call" an Adobe Acrobat viewer, it can't do so. Navigator will want to simply transfer the file and drop it onto your hard disk.

Here's How It Works

Exactly how this works depends on the type of file being transferred. If it's a type that Navigator recognizes, Navigator will do one of two things:

■ It may ask you where on your hard disk you want to save the file. That's what happens, for instance, in the Windows versions if you are transferring an .Exe file; Navigator assumes that you want to put it on your hard drive, so it displays a File Save dialog box. Simply pick the directory in which you want to place it, and then click OK.

■ Navigator may transfer the file and pass it to another application, a plug-in or viewer. For example, let's say you're using the Mac version and have installed StuffIt Expander as a helper (see Chapter 9), or the Windows version and have installed WinZIP as a helper. When you click a link to a .sit file (in the Mac case) or a .zip file (in the Windows case), Navigator begins the transfer and sends the file to the appropriate helper. WinZIP, for instance, opens and displays the contents of the .zip file.

What if you haven't configured one of these viewers, though? For example, if you've clicked a link to a .zip file, but you haven't configured WinZIP—or any other .zip-file utility—as a helper? Well, you'll see the dialog box shown in Figure 8.6.

FIG. 8.6

The Unknown File Type dialog box appears whenever you begin transferring a file that Navigator doesn't recognize.

Why has Navigator displayed this dialog box? Because it doesn't know what to do with the file. Navigator can't do anything with the file itself because it's not one of the file types that has been designed to work with Navigator. It doesn't have a viewer installed for this file type, so it can't send the file to another program. It needs your help. You have the following four choices:

■ *More Info* Click here to open a new window containing a page at the Netscape Web site. It has a link to a page where you can download a plug-in (see Chapter 9). Although this in effect cancels the transfer, the original page remains open so you can switch back to it if you want.

■ *Pick App* Click here to tell Navigator which program to send the file to (but I'll cover that in Chapter 9).

- *Save File*   Click here to see the Save As dialog box, in which you can tell Navigator where to put the file once it has transferred it.
- *Cancel*   Click here to remove the dialog box and return to the document.

If you've clicked Save File, you'll see a Save As dialog box in which you can tell Navigator where to save the file. Click Save and Navigator begins transferring the file. You'll see the window in Figure 8.7, which has all sorts of handy information: the name of the file being transferred, the directory into which it's being placed, the file size, the percentage already transferred, and an estimate of how much longer it will take to transfer the file.

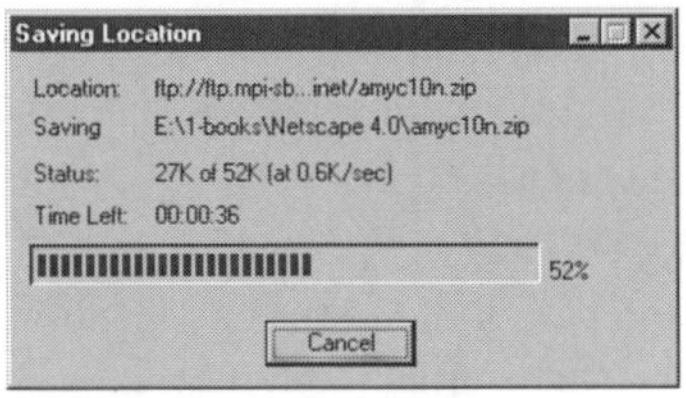

FIG. 8.7
Navigator provides plenty of useful information while transferring a file.

Note that you don't have to wait for this transfer. You can simply click the Saving Location window's minimize button (the third from the right on the title bar), and continue working in the Navigator window—selecting another file to transfer or moving to another document.

CAUTION

It's a good idea to check programs you transfer with a virus-checking program before using them. Many sites on the Internet don't check for viruses, so you don't always know for sure what you are getting. There are a number of commercial and shareware virus-checking programs available.

Embedding Web Pages in Other Documents

Now we'll get really fancy. We're going to use *OLE* (Object Linking and Embedding), a Windows feature, to embed Web pages in other programs. The Windows versions of Navigator are OLE *servers*, programs that can provide information to OLE *clients*. We're going to use Word for Windows (only because that's the word processor I use—you can use any OLE client program).

Follow these steps:

1. Choose Insert, Object. (That's the command in Word for Windows; in other programs, the menu option may be different, so check your documentation.) The Object dialog box opens.
2. In the Object Type list box, find Netscape Hypertext Document.
3. If you want, click the Display as Icon check box (see Figure 8.8). With this selected, Navigator will insert an icon to represent the document; if it isn't selected, Navigator will

insert an actual document that you can view. If you select this check box, you can also click the Change Icon button to select a different icon to represent the document. (There were not many choices last time I looked, though you can pull an icon from a different application if you want.) Right now you're going to look at what happens when you don't use the icon.

FIG. 8.8
Select Netscape
Hypertext Document
and then click OK.

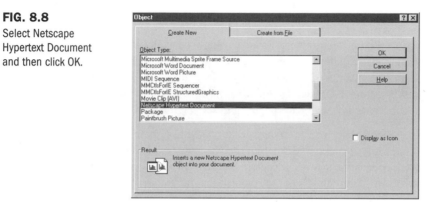

4. Click the OK button and your application will change to show the Navigator toolbars. You can now navigate to the Web page you want to embed in your document. In the Location bar, type the URL of the document you want to embed, and press Enter. (You can also select the URL from the drop-down list box, or use a bookmark.)

5. The page will be loaded into a box within the document in your application, as you can see in Figure 8.9.

FIG. 8.9
This is a Word for
Windows document,
but it's got the
Navigator toolbar and a
Web document inside.

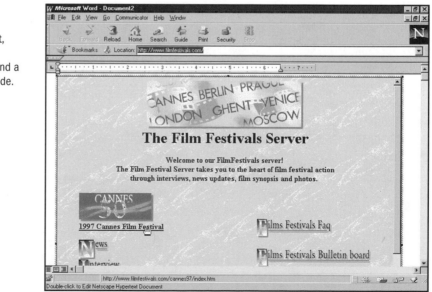

6. Click outside the Web document, but within the word-processing document, to remove the Navigator toolbars. Well, if you're lucky, they'll disappear and your application's toolbars will reappear. On the other hand, they may just change color and stay in place; this feature doesn't work quite properly.

7. You can double-click the box in which the Web page is stored to reopen it. The normal word-processor menu and toolbars are removed again, and you'll see Navigator's toolbars in their place.

That's the theory. At the time of writing, it wasn't working too well, though. In fact, although this feature has been in Navigator for quite some time, going back to Navigator 2, it has never actually worked properly, though it's much better in Navigator 4 than it was. By the time you read this, it might be completely fixed, though it might work in a slightly different manner. If you think this feature would be useful to you, try it to see if it functions.

What good is an embedded document? Well, you can read and view the visible contents. But you can also double-click the document to bring the Navigator components back again. You can now navigate the Web using your word processor as the browser! That's right, the links in the document work. When you are finished, click outside the document to remove the Navigator components.

Note that you can size this window. There are little black *handles* on the corners and in the middle of each side; drag a handle in or out to modify the size of the image in your word-processing document. Or point to an edge, wait until the mouse pointer changes to a four-headed arrow, and then drag the edge to move the entire window.

You'll also find several menu options that let you do things to the document. Click in the document and then, in Word for Windows, choose one of the following (the options may vary between applications):

- *Edit, Hypertext Object, Edit*   Choose this to edit the document within the word processor; this is the same as double-clicking the object.
- *Edit, Hypertext Object, Open*   Choose this to open Navigator and place the document within the Navigator window, where you can begin navigating from the document.
- *Edit, Hypertext Object, Convert*   You may be able to convert the document into another format—then again, you may not.

T I P You may also have some right-click menu options. In Word for Windows, if you right-click the document you can select Edit Hypertext and Open Hypertext. You can also Cut or Copy the document to the Clipboard, add a border or caption, or place the item in a frame.

If You Use an Icon

What happens if you choose to represent the document as an icon (that is, if you click the Display as Icon check box in the Options dialog box)? When you click the OK button, a Navigator icon appears in your document, and the Navigator window opens. Find the Web document you want; then close the window by choosing File, Exit and Return.

The document is now represented by an icon. You won't be able to view the document within your word processor, but if you double-click the icon (or choose Edit, Hypertext Object, Edit or Edit, Hypertext Object, Open), the Navigator window opens and displays the document. Well, again, this is just the theory; at the time of writing, this didn't work. When you double-click the icon, you'll find that there's no Web page saved, though the Navigator window does open. Perhaps this feature will be fixed soon; if you need the feature, try it. ●

Sound and Video: Using Plug-Ins and Viewers

The World Wide Web is—at least in theory—a multimedia system. It's a lot more than text and inline pictures. I say "in theory" because it's really not a true multimedia system. A lot of new Internet users have been convinced by television advertising that the Internet is full of pictures and sounds, video and animations. As a friend's daughter said recently: "I thought the Internet was going to talk to me!" In the multimedia arena, the Web cannot compete with CDs and programs running on hard disks, with television and VCRs. Mainly because of bandwidth limitations and network bottlenecks, the Web is still overwhelmingly text-based—with a lot of static pictures thrown in to brighten it up—and will remain so for some time.

Nonetheless, the Web *does* have a wide variety of file formats available, from sound and video to animations and three-dimensional imagery. In this chapter, you'll learn how Navigator handles these different types of media.

The different file formats

There are hundreds of different file types on the Web. We'll look at the most important ones.

How Navigator decides what to do with different file types

When a file is transferred across the Internet to your computer, Navigator has to decide what to do with that file type. We'll see how it makes this decision.

Plug-ins and external viewers

Plug-ins and viewers are used to work with file types that Navigator can't handle.

Working with plug-ins— BubbleViewer and Shockwave

We'll look at a couple of example plug-ins, the BubbleViewer and Shockwave plug-ins.

Installing viewers on-the-fly

Navigator can tell you when you need to install a plug-in or viewer.

Installing viewers through the Preferences dialog box

You can install viewers through the Preferences dialog box, too; I'll explain how.

What happens when you click a link in a Web document? Well, it might take you to another Web document, or it might point to an image of some kind that Navigator knows how to display—one of the .gif, .jpeg, or .jpg files that are often placed inside Web pages. The link might also transfer a .zip, .sit, .sea, or .exe file, an archive, a program, or a self-extracting archive file that you want to transfer to your hard disk (covered in Chapter 8, "Saving Documents and Images from the Web"). That's pretty much what this book has been about so far.

But the link might point to something different, a file format that must be played or displayed in some manner, but a format that Navigator is unable to play or display itself. Such files must be opened in a *plug-in*—a special add-on program that works within Navigator and uses the Navigator window to display the file—or a *helper* (also known as a *viewer*), a program that opens separately from Navigator and handles the file. Table 9.1 describes the way Navigator works with a variety of file formats. Remember, though, there's some variation between versions of Navigator.

Table 9.1   File Formats that Navigator Can Handle

File Format	What It Does
.exe	This is a program file or a self-extracting archive file. (You saw .exe files in Chapter 8.) Navigator will let you save the file to your disk.
.gif, .jpg, .jpeg, .jpe, .xbm	These are graphics files. They share one thing in common: They are the formats used for inline graphics images. But a Web author may also place one of these files at a Web site with a link pointing to it. The file will be transferred, but it won't be *inline*; that is, it won't be part of a Web document. As a graphic separate from a document, it's often known as an external image. These files will be displayed in the Navigator window. There's a special form of .gif, by the way, a GIF89a format, which allows several images to be stored in one file and displayed in sequence, to create animated images. Navigator can work with this format, too.
.jfif, .pjpeg, .pjp	These are a few more variations of the JPEG format that Navigator can display, though they're quite rare.
.htm, .html, .htt, .htx, .css	You know all about the first two of these files; they're the basic Web-document format. The others are special HTML formats sometimes created by Web servers in response to some action the user takes at a site; these formats are also displayed in the browser.
.txt, .text	These text files are displayed in the Navigator window.

The Navigator browser can't handle the following files directly, but when you install Navigator some special plug-ins are installed that *can* handle them. (However, remember that there are differences between versions of Communicator, so some versions of Navigator may not handle all these file types.)

File Format	What It Does
.au, .aif, .aiff, .aifc, .snd, .wav	Sound files of various kinds—Navigator uses the LiveAudio plug-in to play these.
.avi	Video for Windows. Navigator's AVI plug-in will play these.
.hqx	A BinHex file, a format often used to archive Macintosh files. Navigator will ask you where to place the file that's stored within the .Hqx file, and then automatically extract the file for you—even on Windows versions of Navigator.
.la, .lma	The new Netscape Packetized Audio format, played by the LiveAudio plug-in.
.lam	LiveAudio Metafiles. These can be played in the Netscape Media Player plug-in that is installed with some versions of Communicator. These are "streaming" files, sound files that play in your browser as they're being transferred, rather than after they've transferred. (For more information see "RealAudio (.Ra and .Ram) files" in Chapter 10.)
.mid, .midi	MIDI (Musical Instrument Digital Interface) sounds—also played in the LiveAudio plug-in.
.mov, .moov, .qt	The QuickTime video format, originally a Macintosh format but now fairly common on the Internet (see Figure 9.1). Some of these files are in QTVR (Quick Time Virtual Reality) format; that is, they are 3-D images in which you can "move around." The QuickTime plug-in handles these. (At the time of writing, it didn't handle it very well, though; it might be necessary in some cases to install a new plug-in.)
.wrl, .wrz	A VRML (Virtual Reality Modeling Language) 3-D object. The Cosmo Player plug-in displays these.

Part
II

Ch
9

FIG. 9.1
A tornado touches down in Miami; a QuickTime video from CNN (**http://www. cnn.com/**).

You'll have to add a plug-in or helper (viewer) to work with the following files:

File Format	What It Does
.arj	A compressed-file format from the DOS world. This can be opened in the ARJ program or in programs such as WinZip.
.bmp, .pcx	Common bitmap graphics formats. These can be displayed in Windows Paintbrush and many other graphics programs.
.dir, .dxr, .dcr	Macromedia Director animation files. These can be played by the Macromedia Shockwave for Director plug-in.
.doc	These document files can be opened in MS Word, in Windows 95's WordPad program, in a free viewer from Microsoft called Word Viewer, and many word processors.
.flc, .fli, .aas	Autodesk Animator files. These can be played in Windows Media Player.
.gzip, .gz	UNIX compressed files. Some archive utilities, such as WinZIP, can work with these files.
.lzh	Another type of compressed file, from the DOS world. This can be opened in programs such as WinZip.
.hlp	Windows Help files. The Windows Help-system program opens them—that's built in to all versions of Windows, so you don't need to find a special utility.
.mmm	Microsoft Multimedia Movie Player files. Again, these run in Media Player.
.mng	A variety of the .png format (see below) specifically designed for multiple image files, the sort that create animations (like the GIF89a format—see .gif, earlier). This file format is currently in development, but it may appear on the Web in the future.
.eps	A PostScript image.
.mpeg, .mpg, .mpe, .m1v	The MPEG (Motion Pictures Expert Group) video formats.
.mp2	An MPEG audio format.
.png	The Portable Network Graphics file type. Designed as a replacement for .gif files; for various technical reasons it's said to be better than the .gif format, and it's also slightly smaller. Netscape has said that the .png format will work in Navigator 4. At the time of writing, it did not, but there is a PNG plug-in.
.ppt	Microsoft PowerPoint presentation files. You'll need MS PowerPoint or a PowerPoint viewer for these.
.pdf	The portable document format, an Adobe Acrobat hypertext file. This format is becoming a very popular way to distribute electronic documents.

File Format	What It Does
.ps	A PostScript document.
.ram, .ra	RealAudio. This is a popular sound format that plays while it's being transmitted. Click a link to a RealAudio file and it begins playing within a few seconds, rather than making you wait for the entire file to be transferred before starting.
.rtf	Rich Text Format files are word-processing files that work in a variety of word processors.
.sea	A Macintosh self-extracting archive file.
.sit	A StuffIt archive file, created by the Macintosh StuffIt program.
.sgml	A document format.
.tar	A UNIX tape archive file. It's a sort of "container" for multiple files, though it's not compressed.
.tsp	TrueSpeech, a sound format similar to RealAudio.
.tif, .tiff	A common graphics format.
.wri	Windows Write word processing files. These can be opened in WordPad, Windows Write, and some other word processors.
.xdm	The StreamWorks webTV and webRadio format. Similar to RealAudio, although it allows real-time playing of video in addition to sound.
.Z, .z	UNIX compressed files.
.zip	PKZIP archive files. These files contain other compressed files within them. They can be opened with PKUNZIP, WinZIP, and various other Windows and DOS programs. On the Mac, you can use StuffIt Expander to unzip these files, if you also have DropStuff with Expander Enhancer installed.

Part II
Ch 9

TIP You'll find compressed files in a variety of formats. If you find a .zip, .arj, .lzh, or .arc file, it's probably for a DOS or Windows computer. (The .zip format is currently the most-used archive format by far; you'll rarely find the other formats these days.) The .exe self-extracting archive is very common in the DOS and Windows world, too. If the file is an .hqx, .sea, or .sit file, it's for the Macintosh. The `.Z`, `.z`, `.tar`, `.gzip`, and `.gz` files are generally for UNIX computers. (Although the `.gz` format can work on all three of these computer types, you'll probably never find a `.gz` file for the PC or Mac.)

I've mentioned a few common programs that could work with these files, but these aren't your only options; as you'll see, you can find other plug-ins and helpers to work with these file formats.

Have I missed some formats? Sure, there are as many possible file formats on the Web as there are file formats in existence. But the ones I've mentioned here are the ones you'll most likely find. (In fact, even some of the ones I've mentioned are not used very often on the Web, so I think I've covered the ground pretty well with this list.) ■

What Plug-Ins and Viewers Do You Have?

As you've seen, when you install Navigator a few plug-ins are installed for you: depending on which version of Communicator you have installed, you may have the QuickTime, Cosmo Player, LiveAudio, AVI, and Media Player plug-ins. There are a couple of ways to see which file types Navigator can handle. First, you can choose Help, About Plugins. (On the Mac, this menu option is currently Apple, About Plugins. And note that you can also display this page by typing **about:plugins** into the Location bar and pressing Enter.) This page shows a list of installed plug-ins, with a list of the file types that each can handle. (If this page appears and then immediately disappears, click the Reload button and it should come back.)

Most file types will be handled by viewers, and although there used to be a quick and easy way to check which viewers are installed and how different file types are handled, the Windows versions of Navigator 4 have a brand new way to handle file types, and it's not quite so easy. (On the Mac and UNIX, it will probably still be fairly straightforward, as you'll see—though at the time of writing, the mechanism used for working with viewers was not yet functioning.) Choose Edit, Preferences, then open the Navigator category (Browser on the Mac), and click Applications. You'll see the information shown in Figure 9.2. (At the time of this writing, the interface to the Applications was not active on the Mac and UNIX versions of Navigator, so it remains to be seen exactly how this procedure is handled in those browsers.)

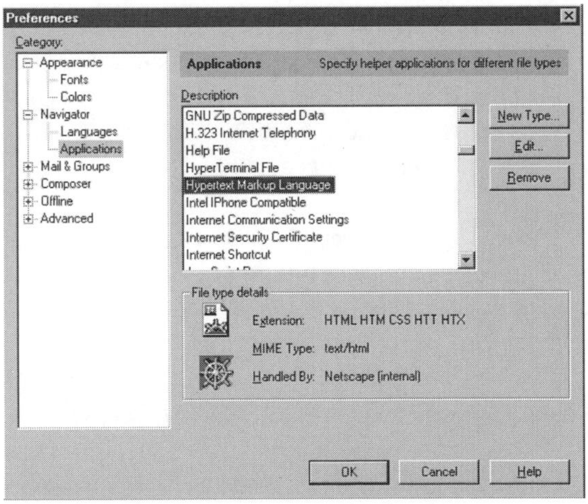

FIG. 9.2

Here's where you can see which file types Navigator can handle.

In earlier versions of Navigator, the browser decided which viewers it could use by referring to its own internal list of viewers. But this system has completely changed for the Windows browsers. Now Navigator refers to Windows' own internal "association" list, the same list of associations that all other Windows programs use. So the list shown in Figure 9.2 is the same list you'd see if you went to Windows Explorer and opened the File Types list there (select View, Options and click the File Types tab).

In Figure 9.2, you can see that the list box contains entries for each file type for which an association has been created. In the example, the Hypertext Markup Language entry has been selected. You can see below the list box that there are three pieces of information shown: the file extensions that this file type uses; the file's MIME type (which we'll discuss later); and the program that this file type is handled by (in this case, Netscape Navigator).

The Macintosh and UNIX operating systems don't have the same sort of associations list that's present in Windows, so their viewers' configuration will probably be different when it's finally added to the browser. You may see that you can select a file type, and view several radio buttons that are used to define how the file type is handled. These radio buttons will probably be something like the following:

- *View in Browser* If this radio button has been selected, either Navigator can handle the file format itself, or a plug-in that can handle the format has been installed. You can't modify this setting, except by installing or removing plug-ins.

- *Save to Disk* Navigator will assume you want to save the file onto your hard disk, and display the Save As dialog box.

- *Unknown: Prompt User* Navigator has no idea what to do, so it displays the box you saw in Chapter 8 asking you what to do.

- *Launch the Application* Navigator starts a viewer or helper. You'll see several ways to install a viewer, starting under "Installing Viewers" later in this chapter.

What Happens When Navigator Transfers a File?

When you click a link, the Web server sends information about the file that is about to be transferred. Navigator looks at this information to see what type of file is being sent. The Web server may send the MIME information (I'll get to that later in this chapter—see "What Is MIME?"), which tells Navigator exactly what the file is. If the server doesn't send the MIME information, Navigator takes a look at the file extension and uses that to figure out what sort of file it is. The procedure is as follows:

1. If the file is a Web document (MIME type `text/html`, extension .htm or .html), it knows just what to do: Display the file in the Navigator window because it's a Web document.

2. If the file is a text file (MIME type `text/plain`, extension .txt or .text), it's not a true Web document, but it can be displayed easily (it's a text document), so Navigator displays it in the window. (You'll often find .txt files when working in Gopher sites—see Chapter 15, "Gopher, Finger, Telnet, and More.")

3. If the file is an inline image file (MIME types `image/jpeg`, `image/gif`, or `image/ x-xbitmap`, extension .jpg, .jpeg, .jpe, .gif, or .xbm), Navigator displays the file in the Navigator window; all of these are graphics types.

4. If the file is an .hqx file (a Macintosh BinHex file), Navigator transfers the file and extracts the file held within.

5. If the file is none of these, Navigator looks at its list of plug-ins and viewers to see if any have been configured. For instance, if the file is an .mid music file or a .wav Windows audio file, Navigator can use the LiveAudio plug-in to play it.

6. If Navigator doesn't have a plug-in or a viewer configured for the file type, Navigator is stuck; there's nothing more it can do, so it has to ask you, as you saw in Chapter 8 and as you can see in Figure 9.3.

FIG. 9.3

If Navigator doesn't know what to do with a file, it will have to ask you.

You have four choices. You can click Save File to save the file to your hard disk—absolving Navigator from any further responsibility. You can click Pick App to tell Navigator which application it should use to open this file type (we'll look at this in a moment). You can click Cancel to remove the dialog box and return to the Navigator window. Or you can click More Info to open a secondary (targeted) window with a page from the Navigator Web site, from which you'll be able to look for a plug-in or viewer.

In some cases, depending on how the Web author has coded his Web page, you may see a dialog box telling you that you need a particular plug-in, and asking if you want to get the plug-in. Click OK, or in some cases the Get Plugin button, and the Web page specified by the author will appear; presumably the Web page from which you can download the plug-in you need.

Plug-Ins versus Viewers

In a moment, we'll look at how to configure a plug-in (see "Installing Plug-Ins"). But first, I want to make sure the distinction between plug-ins and viewers is clear. There are two different types of programs you can use to display file types that Navigator can't handle, as follows:

- *Plug-ins*   A plug-in is a program that is "plugged in" to Navigator. Instead of opening another program and sending the file to that program, Navigator will use a special program that you've added to display or play the file *within* the Navigator window. You may not even realize that a plug-in is at work; it appears that Netscape itself is handling the file.

- *External viewers (helpers)*   Viewers are more properly called *external viewers*. They're sometimes known as *helpers*. An external viewer is a separate program that Navigator opens when it needs it. Navigator sends the file it's just received to the viewer, and the viewer displays or plays it. For instance, you might configure MS Word as the program to be used to display .doc files.

You might think of plug-ins as *internal* viewers, and viewers and helpers as *external* viewers. The concept of plug-ins is similar to that of Windows OLE (Object Linking and Embedding), in which one Windows program can use program code from another Windows program to display a file within itself. For instance, using OLE, Word for Windows can display Excel spreadsheet data, or Excel can display Word for Windows word processing data. Plug-ins are not OLE programs (and are not limited to only the Windows operating systems), but the idea is the same: They allow Navigator to display data that it normally would be unable to handle. The Navigator window changes a little in some cases—a different toolbar may appear, with special buttons for the form of data you're currently viewing. But you remain viewing the Navigator window, not another program's window.

If there's a plug-in available for a particular file type, it's probably more convenient than using an external viewer program. Rather than waiting for another program to launch and display a file, the file will be displayed within Navigator (though there may be cases in which you prefer to have the file type played or displayed *outside* Navigator). For instance, if you want to view .pdf files, use the Adobe Acrobat plug-in rather than installing the Adobe Acrobat reader program. On the other hand, you may find that some viewers have more features than the equivalent plug-ins. There's no rule that says a plug-in must be better designed than a viewer!

Two Types of Objects

There are also two different types of objects: external objects and what has sometimes been called *live objects*. An external object is a file that is not embedded into a document. You click a link, and the Web server sends the file referenced by the link. For instance, the link may "point to" an Adobe Acrobat .pdf file (an Acrobat hypertext file, which you'll learn more about in Chapter 10, "More on Plug-Ins and Viewers"). Click the link and the Web server sends the .pdf file, which is then displayed by the plug-in or sent to the external viewer.

Live objects, though, are embedded into a document. They're sometimes called embedded objects, or, rather ambiguously, plug-ins; the Web author uses the `<embed src="file">` tag so that when you open the document containing the tag, the embedded object is displayed within the document. Navigator will run the appropriate plug-in, which will display the document. For instance, an .mpeg file can be embedded in a Web document. When you click a link that takes you to the Web document, Navigator automatically opens some kind of MPEG player plug-in— if you have one installed, that is—and the video begins playing in a rectangle within the Navigator window.

> **T I P**
> Right-click inside a live object displayed in the Web page, or, if using the Mac, click and hold the mouse button down. You'll often find a pop-up menu containing plug-in controls (Stop, Start, Properties, and so on).

Installing Plug-Ins

Navigator maintains a plug-in registry to keep you abreast of the latest and greatest plug-ins and how you can download them; this is the best place to start when you're hunting for a new plug-in. You can see the registry at **http://home.netscape.com/comprod/products/ navigator/version_2.0/plugins/** (yes, I know the URL says version_2.0, but that's where the inline plug-ins page is currently located). A quicker way to get there is to choose Help, About Plugins, and then, when the installed plug-ins page opens, click the For more information on Netscape plug-ins, click here link just below the page heading. You can also find plug-ins at many shareware sites on the Web, such as **http://www.jumbo.com/**, **http:// www.tucows.com/**, **http://www.shareware.com**, and **http://browserwatch.iworld.com/ plug-in**.

Plug-ins are proliferating like rabbits. When I finished the first edition of this book late in 1995, there were only three or four. By the end of 1996, there were 113. Now there are reportedly about 135, with more on the way. What do all these plug-ins do? Table 9.2 shows a quick summary of just a few of the plug-ins I found at the Navigator site.

Table 9.2   Types of Plug-Ins and Brand Names

Type	Brand Names
3-D and animation players	BubbleViewer, Cosmo Player, FutureSplash, Live3D, mBed, Narrative Enliven, Play3D, Shockwave for Authorware, Shockwave for Director, Sizzler, TopGun, Topper, Viscape, VRScout, Vrealm, WebActive, WebExpresso, Whurlplug, Wirl
Audio players	Crescendo, EchoSpeech, Koan, MIDIPlug, RapidTransit, RealAudio, Talker, ToolVox
Video-and-audio players	Action, CineWeb, CoolFusion, FlashWare, MacZilla, MovieStar, PreVue, VDOLive, ViewMovie QuickTime, VivoActive, QuickTime
Graphics viewers	ABC QuickSilver, BubbleViewer, CMX Viewer, DWG/DXF, FIGLeaf Inline, Fractal Viewer, InterCAP Inline, KEYView, Lightning Strike, Shockwave for Freehand, SVF, ViewDirector Imaging, WaveLet Image Viewer, Whip
Presentations	ASAP WebShow, Astound Web Player, HyperPage, PowerMedia, PowerPoint Animation Player and Publisher, PointPlus
Document viewers	Acrobat Reader, Envoy, Word Viewer

Here are a few unusual things that don't fit anywhere:

Name	What It Does
CarbonCopy/Net	Controls a PC across the Web
Chemscape Chime	Displays chemical models
Concerto	An advanced Web forms utility
EarthTimeDisplay	Provides the time in eight time zones around the world
Formula One/Net	Adds a spreadsheet to Navigator

Name	What It Does
Ichat	A chat system
ISYS Hindsight	A super-history list that lets you search the text of pages you visited long ago
Look@Me	Can view what's happening on another user's computer screen, across the Web
NET-Install	A software distribution system
OpenScape	An Internet application-building utility
PenOp	A signature-verification program
PointCast	A service that transfers information to your computer desktop; news, weather, stock prices, and so on
QuickServer	Runs programs within the Navigator window
QuickView Plus	Allows you to view, copy, and print files in 200 different formats
Techexplorer	Works with the Tex/Latex publishing markup language
WebBasic	An application-development tool

Part

II

Ch

9

Is that enough for you? If not, that's okay, because there are plenty more, and by the time you read this, there will be more still!

NOTE A couple of quick comments. First, most of these viewers are for Windows, with just a few for the Mac, and fewer for UNIX. Sorry, that's life! Second, most of these viewers are for file formats that are very rarely found on the Web. Every software company feels that it has to have a plug-in for its special file formats, or it won't be competitive. That may be true, but for the moment most of these plug-ins are part of a war for Web territory, not tools that every user really must have. Pick the ones you want carefully. ■

Installing a Plug-In—BubbleViewer

How are plug-ins installed? It's really quite simple. Let's take a look at the BubbleViewer plug-in, which you can get from **http://www.omniview.com/plugin.htm** (it's also available as an external viewer from **http://www.omniview.com/viewers/viewers.html**). This is used to view special 3-D images that let you "experience" sitting in a car, for instance. (Toyota is using this system on its Web site so you can "sit" inside their cars and see what they look like.) This viewer is available in both Windows and Mac versions. Download the file to your hard disk (see Chapter 8), then run the program and a setup program will begin. Follow the instructions and the plug-in is installed. Is that easy enough for you? No messing around with configuration data—the setup program will do it for you. Most plug-ins are the same; run a setup program and the plug-in is installed.

T I P In some cases, the installation is a little cruder. For instance, you may have to copy a Windows .dll file into the Communicator Plugins directory. Just follow the instructions that come with the program.

On the other hand, we may soon see automatically installing plug-ins; you'll click a link to the plug-in, and the file will be transferred to your computer and automatically installed for you. That's the promise; though, at the time of writing, it was not yet in action.

After you've got your plug-in installed, how do you use it? Simply click a link to the appropriate object type, and the plug-in takes over. For instance, I went to the **http://www.toyota.com/bubbles/** site and then clicked the RAV4 link, which took me to a bubble view of a Toyota vehicle (see Figure 9.4).

FIG. 9.4
The BubbleViewer in action.

This system really works remarkably well. You'll notice a little pointing hand in the picture; by pressing the mouse button and moving the hand, you can swing around to any angle. Look up at the roof, down from the roof to the seats, or even look through the rear or side windows. It works very quickly (at least, on a fast computer). Click right in the middle of the image (the pointer changes to a plus sign), and you'll zoom in closer. Right-click to see a pop-up menu. This is very similar to using the Apple Quick Time VR plug-in, except that the BubbleViewer format users photos, while QuickTime VR format uses computer-generated images.

BubbleViewer is one of the better plug-ins available. It works well, and can be more than just a toy. For instance, are you moving to another town where you'll need to rent an apartment? You can take a look inside a few apartments (**http://www.rent.net**) before you send your check. BubbleViewer can be used by museum Web sites, by tourism agencies to show local sights (take a look at the pyramids at Giza and various other tourist sights—**http://www.omniview. com/destinations/destinations.html**), by news agencies to add real dimension to news stories, and so on. This technology is not used much as yet, but the possibilities are tremendous. Go to **http://www.omniview.com/** and follow the links (in particular, the Destinations and Partners links) to find other examples.

Another Popular Plug-In—Shockwave

One very popular plug-in is the Shockwave plug-in. This plays animations, games, music, interactive news and sports pages, and so on. I've got to admit, however, that I'm a little cynical about this—Shockwave animations are often not worth the wait. All too often, they're added to a Web site to amuse the Web-site developer more than the Web-site user.

Still, if you really must try Shockwave, you can find the Shockwave plug-in at **http://www.macromedia.com/**. It's very simple to install; just transfer the file and double-click to run it. Then go back to the Macromedia site (an option at the end of the plug-in installation program offers to take you there) and use the Gallery link to find some "shocked" sites. In Figure 9.5, you can see an example of Shockwave in action.

FIG. 9.5

This is a Shockwave CD player.

Different Types of Plug-Ins

There are basically three types of plug-ins:

- *Embedded*   An embedded plug-in is one that runs an embedded object. It appears as a rectangular area within the Web document, just as an inline image appears as a rectangular area. The difference is that while the inline image is static, the embedded plug-in will "do stuff," such as play a video, and is interactive—you may be able to use mouse clicks, for instance, to determine what's happening in the plug-in.

Part

II

Ch

9

■ *Full-screen*   The full-screen plug-in takes over the entire Navigator content area. When an external file is transferred to Navigator, the full-screen plug-in opens and displays the file contents (it may be an Adobe Acrobat hypertext file or Apple QuickTime video file, for example). The normal Navigator controls will generally remain in view, but the plug-in may add controls, too (a video-player plug-in, for instance, would have start, stop, pause, and rewind buttons).

■ *Hidden*   A hidden plug-in is one that runs without any visible sign. A plug-in that plays sounds, for instance, may be hidden.

Security Warnings

Now and then, when Navigator is about to transfer a file, you'll see a warning message. The warning tells you that files downloaded from the network (meaning the Internet, generally speaking, though Navigator can be run on a network that is not connected to the Internet) can contain `malicious programming instructions`—in other words, a virus. The dialog box allows you to save the file to disk, or "open it" (in other words, to transfer it and then open it in whatever viewer or plug-in is configured). At the bottom of the dialog box, you'll see an Always Ask Before Opening This Type of File check box. If you clear this check box, the next time Navigator tries to transfer this file type, you won't see the warning message again.

Why turn off the warning message? Some file types are *not* dangerous. If the file type can't do anything, it's not dangerous. What file types can do something? Executable files (also known as program files, such as .exe and .com files), script files (such as .bat files), and document files from programs that allow internal macros. (Many word processors these days allow users to create macros—mini-programs—that run when the document is opened.) But many file types are not dangerous because they are essentially nothing but dumb data. For example, bitmap files—such as .bmp and .tif files—can't do anything. They can be displayed by a program, but they can't do anything themselves.

Unexpected File Types

What happens if you come across a file type that you don't recognize and for which you don't have a plug-in installed? You may see a dialog box like the one we saw earlier, in Figure 9.3, asking you what to do with the file.

But you may open a page in which the file has been embedded using the `<embed>` tag I mentioned earlier. In that case, soon after the page starts to load in the browser window, you'll see the dialog box in Figure 9.6. This explains that you need a plug-in to view the file type that is about to be transferred, and asks if you want to get the appropriate plug-in. You might want to simply click Cancel and move on. But, if you really want to see what the file is, you'll have to click Get the Plug-in.

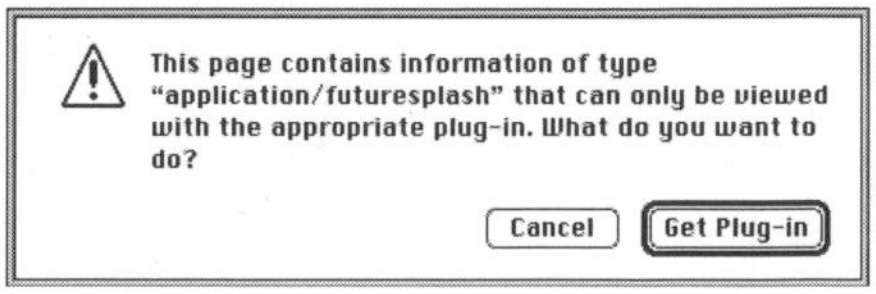
This page contains information of type "application/futuresplash" that can only be viewed with the appropriate plug-in. What do you want to do?
Cancel
Get Plug-in

FIG. 9.6
Navigator wants to load a file, but you don't have the required plug-in.

Unfortunately, this system doesn't always work well. What happens next depends on how the Web author has set up the embedded plug-in. The author may have included a special instruction in the `<embed>` tag explaining where to go to find the plug-in; when you click the Get the Plug-in button, the dialog box closes and Navigator opens the specified Web page. If the Web author has done his job properly, you'll now see instructions on how to download the plug-in.

If the author hasn't provided the special instruction telling the browser which Web page to load, the browser will load a Plug-in Finder page from the Netscape site instead (see Figure 9.7). With luck, this page will show you the plug-in you need; Navigator uses the MIME information to figure out which one that is (see "What Is MIME?" later in the chapter). You can now click the link to download the plug-in.

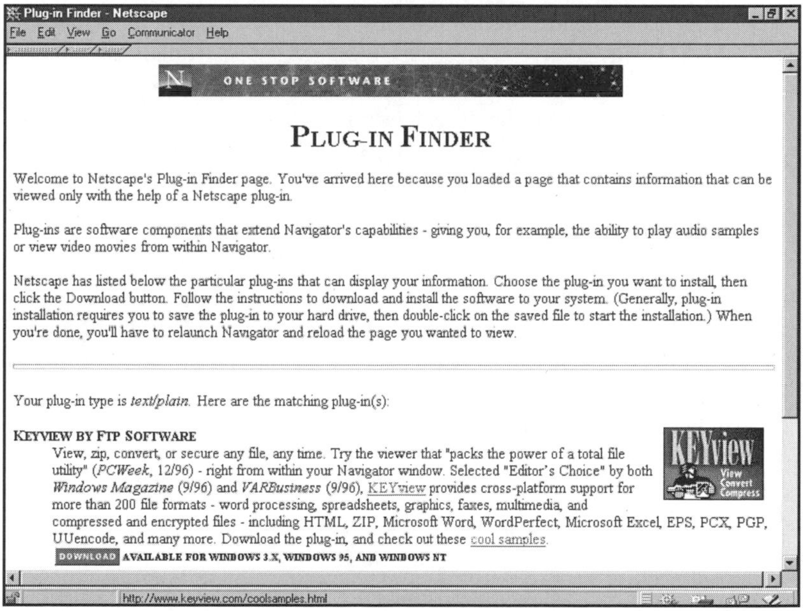
Plug-in Finder - Netscape
File Edit View Go Communicator Help
ONE STOP SOFTWARE
PLUG-IN FINDER
Welcome to Netscape's Plug-in Finder page. You've arrived here because you loaded a page that contains information that can be viewed only with the help of a Netscape plug-in.
Plug-ins are software components that extend Navigator's capabilities - giving you, for example, the ability to play audio samples or view video movies from within Navigator.
Netscape has listed below the particular plug-ins that can display your information. Choose the plug-in you want to install, then click the Download button. Follow the instructions to download and install the software to your system. (Generally, plug-in installation requires you to save the plug-in to your hard drive, then double-click on the saved file to start the installation.) When you're done, you'll have to relaunch Navigator and reload the page you wanted to view.
Your plug-in type is text/plain. Here are the matching plug-in(s):
KEYVIEW BY FTP SOFTWARE
View, zip, convert, or secure any file, any time. Try the viewer that "packs the power of a total file utility" (PCWeek, 12/96) - right from within your Navigator window. Selected "Editor's Choice" by both Windows Magazine (9/96) and VARBusiness (9/96), KEYview provides cross-platform support for more than 200 file formats - word processing, spreadsheets, graphics, faxes, multimedia, and compressed and encrypted files - including HTML, ZIP, Microsoft Word, WordPerfect, Microsoft Excel, EPS, PCX, PGP, UUencode, and many more. Download the plug-in, and check out these cool samples.
KEYview
View
Convert
Compress
DOWNLOAD
AVAILABLE FOR WINDOWS 3.X, WINDOWS 95, AND WINDOWS NT
http://www.keyview.com/coolsamples.html

FIG. 9.7
The Plug-in Finder page *may* tell you which plug-in you need.

Unfortunately, two things can go wrong. First, Navigator may have received the incorrect MIME information, in which case you'll be presented with the wrong plug-in. So read the information carefully to figure out if that's the case. Second, the Netscape Web site may be unable to find a matching plug-in, in which case you'll see a message telling you that you're on your own!

Installing Viewers

Plug-ins are not the only game in town. You'll find that there are no plug-ins for some formats, and you may find that you simply don't like some of the plug-ins. You can install a viewer (or helper) instead.

We're going to quickly install a viewer; we'll set up Navigator so that whenever it transfers a .zip file (a PKZIP compressed file), it opens the WinZip utility, a Windows program. If you're using the Mac, you can do the same thing using StuffIt Expander and DropStuff; with both of these utilities installed you can open .zip files. Of course, the techniques we're using here are the same for installing any type of viewer.

TIP Why would a Mac user want to work with `.zip` files? Although .zip files come from the DOS and Windows world, Mac users may now and again want to open them. They often contain document or image files that can be used on the Macintosh.

When you first install Navigator, it may not know how to handle .zip files. You can find out if it does, though. Choose Edit, Preferences, open the Navigator category (Browser on the Mac), then click Applications, and you'll see the dialog box we looked at earlier (in Figure 9.2). This list is really inconvenient, at least on the Windows versions of the browser, as it makes finding particular file types very difficult in some circumstances; sometimes the file descriptions are hard to match with the file extensions (the old system was much easier to work with). Still, you can look down the list for an entry that refers to .zip files. If you find one, click it and look below the list to see what program has been configured to handle .zip files.

At the time of this writing, the Macintosh and UNIX browsers provided no way to set up viewers. This system will be added soon, but will probably vary slightly from what is described here (you can see the current Macintosh dialog box in Figure 9.8). It may actually be easier to work with; you may be able to look in the list for `application/x-zip-compressed`. If so, click that entry and look at the associated information to see what the browser does with such files. It may say something like `Ask User`, and, perhaps, `Unknown: Prompt User`. In other words, when you click a link to one of these file types, Navigator will ask you what it should do with the file.

FIG. 9.8

The Mac's Applications pane is not yet active, but will be similar in some ways to the Windows version. You may be able to find viewers and file types more easily in this list, though.

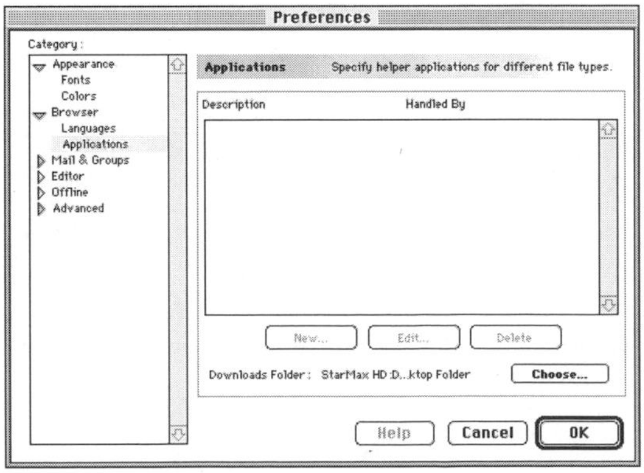

What Is MIME?

When you look in the list of file types in the Applications area of the Preferences dialog box, you'll see various MIME types shown, things like `application/x-zip-compressed`. These are the *Multipurpose Internet Mail Extension* types. Originally, this system was designed to allow Internet e-mail programs to transfer binary files, and it's still in use today for that purpose. But it's also used on the Web as a way for a Web server to identify a file type. A Web server, when transferring a file to a browser, sends the MIME description to the browser so the browser knows what it's receiving.

Navigator can use this MIME information to identify the file type and figure out what to do with it (which viewer to send it to or which plug-in to use). If the server doesn't send the MIME information, Navigator looks at the file extension and identifies the file that way. (Using the MIME information is the preferred way to handle files; a single file type may be identified using a range of different extensions.)

There are two parts to the MIME description: the type and the subtype. For instance, here's a MIME file description: `video/mpeg`. The type is `video` (the file is a video file), while the subtype is `mpeg` (just one of several different types of video files). If you look in the Helpers list, you may see more `video/` subtypes, depending on what viewers you have installed: `video/quicktime` (an Apple video format) and `video/x-msvideo` (a Microsoft video format).

Some MIME types have the letter "*x*" in the name—`x-msvideo`, `x-gzip`, and so on. The x means that the MIME type is nonstandard. Someone has created this MIME type, and it may be in common use, but it hasn't been approved by the IANA (Internet Assigned Numbers Authority).

T I P Where can I find out more about MIME types? Try these URLs: **http://sd-www.jsc.nasa.gov/mime-types/** (where you'll find a large list of types) and **http://home.netscape.com/assist/helper_apps/mime.html**.

Finding the Viewer

Okay, it's time to install the viewer. Go to any shareware site you want (for instance, try **http://www.jumbo.com** and **http://www.shareware.com** for Windows, Mac, or UNIX; or **http://www.tucows.com** for Windows). Then search for and download the utility you want to install. If you are working in Windows, search for and download WinZIP or a similar utility that can handle .zip files. (Search for WinZIP or simply ZIP.) If you are using a Macintosh, search for stuffitexpander and dropstuff.

How do you extract these files if you don't yet have an extraction utility installed? They'll be in self-extracting format. The files for Windows computers will have an .exe extension. The ones for the Mac will probably have a .sea.hqx extension (Navigator will automatically extract the file from within the .hqx file, leaving a file with the `.sea` extension). Both .exe and .sea files are self-extracting archive files; simply double-click them to expand the files from within them. Then follow the instructions that will appear, or that are held within text files extracted from the archive file.

The best way to configure a Navigator viewer in Windows is to simply run the installation program for that viewer; in most cases, the viewer will configure itself as the associated application. For instance, to configure WinZip, a popular .Zip utility, simply run the program and it will automatically associate itself with .zip files, in effect becoming the Navigator .zip viewer. You can also configure the viewer "on-the-fly," as you'll see in a moment (that is, configure the viewer during a Web session, when the browser reaches a file for which there is no viewer installed). In fact, that's the easiest way to set up a viewer for the Macintosh and UNIX systems, which don't have the same sort of file-association system as Windows.

Setting Up the Viewer On-the-Fly

You can set up viewers "on-the-fly," that is, when the browser informs you that it's about to transfer a file type that it can't handle. Assuming that you've found and installed a program that *can* handle the file type, you can quickly tell Navigator where that viewer is stored.

For instance, let's say you are at one of the shareware sites and find a .zip file you'd like to download. You click the link to that file, and Navigator will display the dialog box we saw earlier (refer to Figure 9.3), asking what to do with the file. Follow this procedure:

1. In the Unknown File Type dialog box, click the Pick App button.

2. The Configure External Viewer dialog box opens (see Figure 9.9). All you need to do is tell Navigator which program you want to use to open files of this type.

FIG. 9.9

Click a link; then click Pick App, Configure a Viewer, Browse, and find the program.

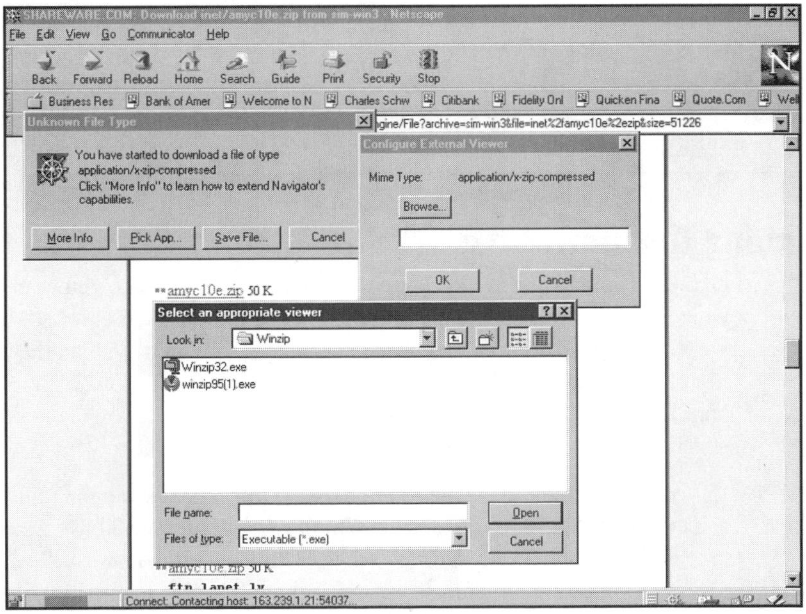

3. In the Mac version, you can now select the application you want to use. In the Windows version, you must click the Browse button and the Select an Appropriate Viewer dialog box opens—this is a typical File Open box.

4. Find the program you want to use as the viewer, click its name, and then click the Open button to place the program name into the Configure External Viewer dialog box.

5. Click OK, and Navigator begins transferring the file. When it's finished, the viewer opens and handles the file (in the case of WinZIP, for instance, it displays the contents of the .zip file so you can select the files you want to extract).

Adding Viewers Manually

There's another way to add viewers. You don't have to wait until you click a link to a file type that Navigator doesn't recognize. Instead, you can go to the Preferences dialog box and add viewers beforehand.

In the Windows browsers, you may never do this, because in most cases installing a program will automatically set it up as a viewer, by associating the program with the particular file extensions. If, for some reason, you have to configure the viewer by hand—perhaps you have a viewer you want to use that doesn't automatically associate itself with a file type—click the New Type button in the Applications area of the Preferences dialog box to see the dialog box in Figure 9.10. Then enter all the information: a Description of Type (make it easy to remember and identify); the File Extension (or file extensions; type the extensions—without periods preceding them—separated by spaces); and the MIME type. Then click the Browse button to find the viewer program that you want to handle this file type.

FIG. 9.10

You can configure viewers manually if you want.

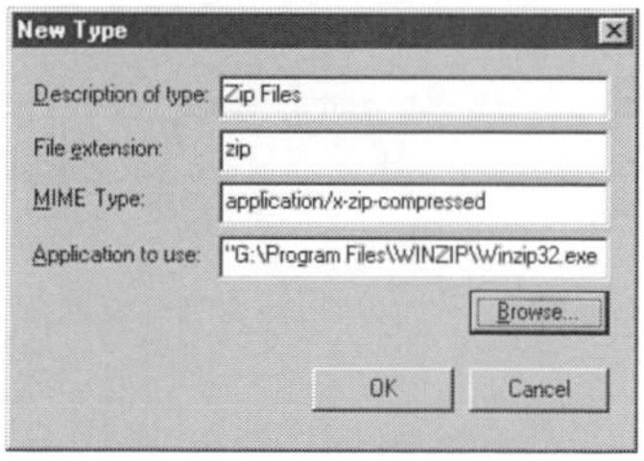

Part
II

Ch
9

CHAPTER 10

More on Plug-Ins and Viewers

You'll need a number of plug-ins and viewers to make the most of the multimedia World Wide Web. There are programs that play "streaming video," Adobe Acrobat hypertext files, videos, 3-D images, and just about any other file format you can image. I'll show you where to find these plug-ins and viewers, and also explain how to save the files for future use after they've transferred to your computer. ▪

Saving the multimedia files you play

After a file has played through a plug-in or browser, you may want to save it for future use. I'll explain how.

Where can I find more viewers?

There are literally thousands of different viewers available, and we'll look at a few places you can find them.

RealAudio, real cool

RealAudio is the best known and most popular of the streaming audio file formats. You may want to download a viewer for RealAudio, and perhaps some other streaming formats, too.

Adobe Acrobat and KeyView

Adobe Acrobat is a fairly common hypertext system incorporated into many Web sites, so you may need the Acrobat reader. And KeyView, though little known, is a great way to add the capability to view 200 different file formats to your browser.

Videos and 3-D images

Video and 3-D images are the "cool" things that the media likes to concentrate on. You ought to get viewers for these file formats so at least you'll have the chance to let the novelty wear off.

Saving What You've Played

After you've played a file, you can save it for future use. Most viewers have a command to help you save the file. After all, a viewer may be one of your everyday programs, such as your word processor, graphics program, sound program, and so on. After the file has been placed into the viewer, you can use the normal commands for saving it, generally File, Save.

But some viewers don't provide a way to save files, nor do many plug-ins. For example, the Navigator's LiveAudio plug-in doesn't give you a chance to save the sound files that it plays. Nor does the Bubble Viewer that we saw in Chapter 9. So how can you save a file that's been played by a program that doesn't let you save it? Grab it from the hard disk.

When Navigator transfers a file, it has to place it on your hard disk. In some cases, it places the file in the cache directory (see Chapter 3 for information about the cache). For example, when it transfers a Bubble file (a .bub file) to the Bubble plug-in, it puts it in the cache directory. You can copy the files from the cache to another directory to save it. For instance, if you are using Windows 95, use Windows Explorer to look in your cache directory, and sort the files by date using View, Arrange Icons, By Date. Near the top, you'll find the file that was just transferred and played (when it's placed into the cache, it's renamed). Or type **about:cache** into Navigator's Location bar and press Enter; after a little while, you'll see a list of files stored in the cache, with links to them. You can click the links and view the files in the browser to confirm what the files actually are.

> **N O T E**   If you save these files, how can you play them later? You can open them from Navigator
> itself. Use File, Open Page, and then click the Browse button. Find the file you saved (the
> .bub file, for instance), and select it. Navigator will open the plug-in and display the file. ■

Navigator doesn't place all the files in the cache, though. If you are using Windows and the file is being played by an external viewer, for instance, it's placed in your Temp directory—look in \Temp or \Windows\Temp. It should have the original file name.

TIP   Navigator doesn't rename files it places in the Temp directory. If you are using Windows 3.1, however, it may have to shorten the name to restrict it to the DOS eight-character file name rule.

What Viewers Do I Have?

You probably have plenty of viewers already. As you've already seen, Navigator can, depending on the version, deal with a wide range of files, including the most common sound files (.au, .aiff, .wav, and .midi), common movie files (.avi and .mov), 3-D image files (.wrl, .wrz, .mov), and so on. But what about other types of files? You may have lots of programs already on your system. On Windows, for instance, you have a variety of built-in viewers—Sound Recorder, Media Player, and WordPad. You may have installed more viewers without realizing it, too. For example, I installed Hijaak Pro, a graphics program. That program can work with loads of file formats, including .tif and .eps, two common graphics formats.

I Need More Viewers!

In Chapter 9, I told you where to find plug-ins. But don't forget external viewers. Just because a program is a plug-in doesn't mean it's better than an external viewer—you may find viewers that are much easier to use, and more convenient. Most viewers will allow you to save the file that's just been played, for instance. And in many cases, you simply won't find a plug-in for the file format you want to handle.

You can find more general-purpose viewers and plug-ins on the Internet. These are often freeware or shareware. You may want to take a look at the following Web sites to see what you can pick up:

- **http://home.netscape.com/comprod/products/navigator/version_2.0/plugins/ index.html** (Netscape's Inline Plug-ins page)
- **http://home.netscape.com/assist/helper_apps/** (The Netscape helper applications page)
- **http://www.jumbo.com/** (Jumbo!, programs of all sorts for Windows, UNIX, and Mac)
- **http://www.ncsa.uiuc.edu/SDG/Software/WinMosaic/viewers.htm** (The Mosaic External Viewers page)
- **http://www.shareware.com/** (Shareware.com, all types of programs for Windows, UNIX, and Macs)
- **http://www.browsers.com/** (c|net's Browsers.com, a large collection of plug-ins)
- **http://www.tucows.com/** (The Ultimate Collection of Winsock Software page— Windows only)
- **http://www.winsite.com/** (Winsite, a huge archive of Windows software)
- **http://www.windows95.com/** (Windows95.com, a large archive of 32-bit Windows software)
- **http://www-dsed.llnl.gov/documents/WWWtest.html** (The WWW Viewer Test page)
- **http://www.iuma.com/IUMA-2.0/help/help-windows.html** (The IUMA Microsoft Windows Utilities page)
- **http://wwwhost.ots.utexas.edu/mac/main.html** (The University of Texas Mac Archive)
- **http://hyperarchive.lcs.mit.edu/HyperArchive.html** (Info-Mac HyperArchive)
- **http://www.velodrome.com/umac.html** (The Ultimate Macintosh Site)

If you can't find what you need through these sites, you might try searching the Web (see Chapter 6) or use Archie (see Chapter 14). On the other hand, you might not; if you can't find what you need at the sites I've just listed, it's probably not available.

Part
II

Ch
10

RealAudio (.ra and .ram) and LiveAudio (.lam)

RealAudio is a popular format that greatly improves the way sound is played over the Web. With other sound formats you've looked at, you click a link and then wait. Twiddle your thumbs for a while or go get some coffee because it can take a long time to transfer a sound file. Once the transfer has finished, Navigator plays the file or sends it to Sound Recorder.

RealAudio, on the other hand, begins playing almost immediately. Navigator begins the transfer and then starts the RealAudio player within a few seconds. (You don't have the RealAudio player yet—I'll explain how to find it in a moment.) The music begins playing right away and continues playing while the file is being transferred. (It doesn't have to be music; National Public Radio uses RealAudio files for its news broadcasts—go to **http://www.npr.org/**). In fact, isn't this the way that a radio works? The radio receives a signal over the airwaves and plays the signal immediately (it doesn't wait until it has received the entire song and then play it). On the Internet, the procedure of transferring a file at the same time that it is being played is known as streaming. There are streaming sound formats, streaming video formats, and so on.

If you want to try RealAudio, go get the player. You can find it at the RealAudio Web site (**http://www.realaudio.com/products/player.html** or **http://www.realaudio.com/**). There are actually two versions: RealPlayer plays audio, and RealPlayer Plus plays both audio and video. (RealPlayer is free; RealPlayer Plus is $30.)

Once you've downloaded the file, close Navigator. Run the RealAudio Player installation program, and follow the instructions. The Setup program looks for various Web browsers on your hard disk and asks if you want to install the RealAudio player for those browsers, too. Make sure you select Navigator, of course, so RealAudio can configure itself for that program. Finally, the RealAudio player opens and informs you—vocally—that the setup is complete.

That's it; RealAudio is ready to play. Now you can go to a site that uses RealAudio and try it. You can find links to such sites at **http://www.realaudio.com/**, or try the Rolling Stones site (**http://www.stones.com/audio/index.html**), or NPR (**http://www.npr.org/**). You might try IUMA, too, the Internet Underground Music Archive (**http://www.iuma.com/**).

Playing RealAudio

At one of the sites I just mentioned, find a RealAudio link and click it. The RealAudio program will open (it may take a few moments), Navigator starts transferring the file, and the music (or newscast or whatever) begins (see Figure 10.1). RealAudio is, however, a plug-in paradox. Although it calls itself a plug-in, and although it's configured as a plug-in rather than a viewer, it looks like a viewer! A separate program opens—it's not built in to the browser window.

T I P   If you increase the volume, yet it's still too quiet, look for other audio controls. For example, in Windows 95 look in the *taskbar tray*, the small panel where you'll find the clock and various small icons. Click the speaker icon to open a small volume control.

NOTE Streaming audio doesn't always sound so good. RealAudio often doesn't sound as good as some other sound formats, but that's because it's a compromise between instant gratification and sound quality. (Recently, RealAudio has greatly improved, so you may hear quite a range of RealAudio quality.) If you have a slow connection to the Internet—a 14,400 modem, for instance—it may not work well. Also, if you have a low-quality sound card and cheap speakers, you'll get low-quality sound. Finally, sound files can vary in quality, depending on how they were recorded. ■

FIG. 10.1
Listening to National Public Radio news over the Internet using RealAudio.

Click here to rewind or wind forward

Click here to display the RealAudio page in Navigator

Click here to start or pause the sound

Click here to stop and move back to the beginning

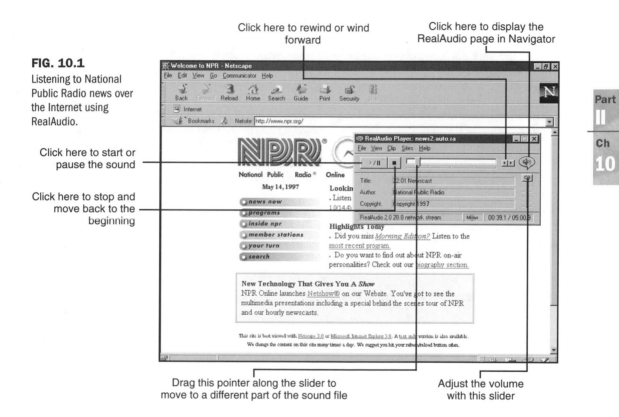

Drag this pointer along the slider to move to a different part of the sound file

Adjust the volume with this slider

Netscape Media Player and the LiveAudio Metafile

Netscape has recently entered the streaming-sound game. Some versions of Communicator come with a plug-in called Media Player, which plays .lam (LiveAudio Metafiles). If your version of Communicator doesn't have Media Player, you can download it from the Netscape Inline Plug-Ins page listed earlier in this chapter, or from **http://home.netscape.com/comprod/announce/media/demos.html**. It's similar in many ways to RealAudio, with good quality, but one major problem...right now, you'll have trouble finding .lam files that are not merely demonstration files (you can find demo files at the URL I just noted). Of course, situations like that can change in the blink of an eye on the Internet, and in a few months it might be the new sound format.

Media Player also comes with a special control panel, the Configure Media Player program, which you'll find in the Utilities folder within the Netscape Communicator folder. This allows you to make a variety of advanced settings: Bandwidth, Connection, Proxy, Clip, and Local Playback. You may not need to adjust these settings, but if you do, open the utility and click the Help button for more information.

TrueSpeech (.tsp) Files

RealAudio is not the only program that plays a sound at the same time it transfers, though it is currently the most popular. You may want to also take a look at the TrueSpeech program, which plays .tsp files. These files are much clearer than most RealAudio files.

Go to **http://www.dspg.com/** to find more information and to download the free TrueSpeech player. At one time, TrueSpeech seemed likely to become very popular on the Web, not only because of the high quality but also because a variety of companies, such as Microsoft, Cirrus Logic, and Sierra Semiconductor like the product. So far, though, RealAudio has maintained its lead, perhaps even pulled farther ahead partly because RealAudio quality has improved greatly, though perhaps also because it had the momentum that comes from being the first on the market.

 TIP Another product, called StreamWorks, allows you to play a sound at the same time it transfers and can do the same thing for video, too. (These are .xdm files.) Go to **http://www.xingtech.com/**.

Adobe Acrobat (.pdf) Files

The Adobe Acrobat .pdf format is fairly popular on the Web. Adobe Acrobat files are self-contained hypertext documents, with links between pages. Unlike HTML, though, Acrobat files allow the author to determine exactly what the document will look like.

When a browser renders an HTML file into the document you see on your screen, the browser decides how to display the different document components—the headers, body text, pull quotes, and so on. (To render means convert the source HTML file into something that the user can read.) But with Acrobat, this control is left in the hands of the author; the Acrobat viewer displays the document just as the author intended. Also, Acrobat files are independent of the Web. You can take an Acrobat file and send it to anyone with an Acrobat reader; they don't need a Web browser. In fact, Acrobat began its life far from the Web; it was intended to help companies distribute online documentation to a variety of different computer systems. The same document can be read by Acrobat readers on Windows, DOS, Macintosh, SunOS, and Solaris computers, with more viewers to be added soon. It also allows companies to produce online documents that look the same as their paper documents.

Adobe also has a system called Weblink (go to **http://www.adobe.com/Acrobat/Plug-Ins/** for information) that will allow Acrobat authors to add links from their Acrobat files to Web sites. Users will be able to click a link in Acrobat, causing their Web browsers to retrieve the specified Web document.

The Acrobat plug-in makes Acrobat files appear within the Navigator window itself, though the window's controls are changed. You'll find the Adobe Acrobat reader in a variety of places, but you might want to try the source first, Adobe itself, at **http://www.adobe.com/prodindex/ acrobat/readstep.html** or **http://www.adobe.com/** (as with most plug-ins, the Acrobat reader is free; Adobe wants to sell the authoring tool, so they've made the viewer easy to get). After you've installed the program (just run the file you download and follow the instructions), go to **http://www.adobe.com/prodindex/acrobat/atwork.html** and you'll find links to loads of Web sites using Adobe Acrobat documents.

You can see an example of an Adobe Acrobat document in Figure 10.2.

FIG. 10.2
The Badger Books Quarterly, shown inside the Adobe Acrobat Reader plug-in. I found this at **http:// www.execpc.com/ ~badgerb/**.

Part
II

Ch
10

KeyView—200 File Formats

I think KeyView is worth mentioning, although you'll have to buy it (it's $49.95, though you can download a free evaluation version from **http://www.ftp.com/mkt_info/evals/ choice.html**). This plug-in will display 200 different file formats: word processing files, loads of graphics formats, video files, spreadsheets, fax files, and even various compression files. KeyView also converts between many of these formats. You can use it outside Navigator, too, to work with files you receive through e-mail, that you are given on floppy disks, and so on.

In Figure 10.3, you can see an example of KeyView at work; I've found a UNIX Compression file, a .gz file. Inside that .gz file is a .tar file, a tape archive file. And inside that .tar file are scores of other files. KeyView displays the contents of the .tar file. I can right-click any stored file to print or view the contents of that file or to save it on my hard disk.

There's a lot of hype on the Web, loads of plug-ins that are more toys than tools. A plug-in like this, though, can be a real blessing to someone who spends a lot of time working on the Web.

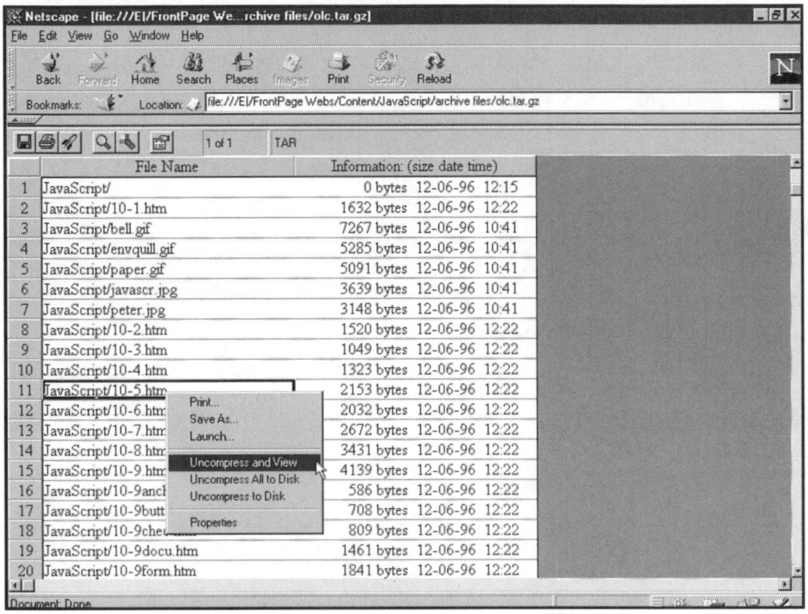

FIG. 10.3

The KeyView plug-in, displaying a UNIX Compression file (olc.tar.gz).

scriptActive—Add ActiveX to Navigator

In Chapter 12, you'll learn a little about Java and JavaScript, two programming languages that are being used on the Web to add programs and advanced multimedia to Web pages. There's another system that's being introduced, called ActiveX. It's currently less popular than Java and JavaScript because the only Web browser that supports it is Microsoft Internet Explorer. However, it does seem to be gaining in importance. (Microsoft says it plans to lose a billion dollars on the Internet over a three-year period, and that kind of money buys plenty of influence!) It's often used to create animated signs and images, though it can be used to create actual programs, too. Figure 10.4 shows an example of a spinning cube sign.

Although Navigator itself won't work with ActiveX, you can add a plug-in that will. The scriptActive plug-in from NCompass is available from **http://www.ncompasslabs.com/ products/scriptactive.htm** for $21, though you can get a free 30-day evaluation. After you've installed the plug-in, go back to **http://www.ncompasslabs.com/** and follow the links to see examples in action. In effect, the scriptActive plug-in makes Netscape run like Internet Explorer where ActiveX controls are concerned. Well, almost like Internet Explorer; if you go to the MSN site (Microsoft Network: **http://www.msn.com**), you may see a message telling you that your browser won't work at that site. That's because sites that use ActiveX may check to see which browser you are using, and automatically route you to a non-ActiveX page if you're not using Internet Explorer.

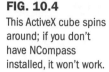

FIG. 10.4
This ActiveX cube spins around; if you don't have NCompass installed, it won't work.

Part
II

Ch
10

Motion on the Web—Video Viewers

You'll find a variety of video images on the Web. Perhaps the most popular are the MPEG (.mpeg, .mpg, .mpe), Video for Windows (.avi), and QuickTime (.mov) formats. Navigator already has plug-ins installed for the AVI and QuickTime formats. There are plenty of plug-ins available for MPEG, too, and a number of external viewers as well. You can find them at shareware sites or at the Netscape Inline Plug-Ins page (select Help, About Plug-ins, and then click the link at the top of the page that appears).

As neat as video on the Web might be, it can get old fast. The problem is that transferring video across the Internet is very slow, even if you're using a 28,800 bps modem. If you have an ISDN (Integrated Services Digital Network) connection or a LAN connection, you're okay (perhaps), but many people are still working with 14,400 or 28,800 bps modems, which take a long time to transfer the 5M or 6M that many videos on the Web take up. A small video can easily take an hour, or several hours, to transmit when using a slow modem! (When the transfer begins, wait a few moments for the transfer speed to settle down, and then look at the Saving Location dialog box to see what the estimated transfer time is.)

You can see an example of an MPEG movie in Figure 10.5, playing in the InterVU MPEG player (**http://www.intervu.com/**). This is a *streaming video* player, which means that it will play the video as it's being transferred (just as RealAudio plays sounds as the sound files are being transferred), rather than waiting for the entire file to transfer first.

FIG. 10.5
The Shuttle lifts off, played in InterVU (from the Space Move Archive at **http://www.univ-rennes1.fr/ASTRO/anim-e.html**).

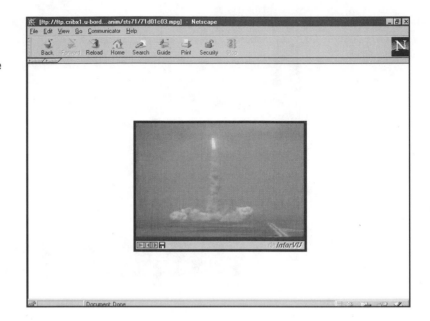

 T I P Where can I find MPEG videos on the Web?
Try the **http://www.powerweb.de/mpeg/**, **http://www.islandnet.com/~carleton/monster/monster.html**, and **http://www.intervu.com/partners/mpegsites.html** sites. You'll find links to dozens of MPEG-related sites. You can also find links to video at the sites belonging to companies that create video plug-ins. Or search for video, MPEG, and MPG at Yahoo! or another search site.

More Sounds on the Web—MPEG Audio

MPEG audio is another MPEG format (these files have the .mp2 extension). *MPEG* stands for the Motion Picture Experts Group, after the people who came up with the file format. MPEG files provide a great way to play sound; the files are compressed, so really high-quality sounds can be squeezed down into quite a small space. You won't find a lot of these on the Web, though—most sounds are in the .au, .aif, .wav, or .ram formats.

I installed XingMPEG, which you can get from **http://www.xingtech.com**, the home site. It was very easy to install and works well, playing both audio and video MPEG.

VRML 3-D Images

A year or so ago, the new fad on the Web was 3-D images known as *VRML* (Virtual Reality Modeling Language). Click a link in a Web page, and up pops your 3-D viewer with a 3-D image inside. Move around in this image, or "walk around" the image. Some images are of landscapes and buildings you can "move through," others are of objects that you can rotate. The only problem is that working in 3-D images is often painfully slow, especially over phone lines and with slow computers.

Right now, VRML still seems to be a developer's toy, fun for the people who create the images, but not terribly interesting or exciting for Web users. Most of the VRML images I've seen on the Web are fairly underwhelming, hardly worth the wait.

Navigator comes with Live3D, a VRML plug-in, but there are many more. You can find a lot at the plug-in page at Netscape. Or check these sites for plug-ins and viewers:

To Find This Viewer...	...Go to This Site
WorldView	**http://www.webmaster.com/vrml/**
WebSpace	**http://webspace.sgi.com-/WebSpace/**
Pueblo	**http://www.chaco.com/pueblo/**
VRWeb	**http://hyperg.iicm.tu-graz.ac.at/Cvrweb/**

Part
II
Ch
10

Note that not all of these programs are available for all operating systems; as usual, it's mostly Windows, then a few Mac, and then hardly any UNIX.

You can also check the following page to see a list of dozens of plug-ins and viewers:

http://www.3dsite.com/cgi/VRML-index.html.

NOTE Just to confuse you a little...programs that display VRML images are often known as VRML browsers rather than viewers. ▪

Note that working in 3-D often requires relatively powerful computers. You'll need a fast computer, lots of RAM, and a video mode using lots of colors— and it still may not be enough! When you are talking about 3-D images, the more power, the better.

Download a viewer or plug-in and install it. Read the installation instructions carefully. Then go to one of the following Web pages, where you can find links to VRML objects you can test:

▪ **http://www.3dsite.com/cgi/VRML-index.html** (The 3Dsite page)

▪ **http://www.aereal.com/boom/** (Aereal BOOM!)

▪ **http://www.virtpark.com/theme/proteinman/home.html** (Proteinman's Top Ten VRML1.0 Worlds)

▪ **http://www.vrmlsite.com/** (VRMLSite Magazine)

▪ **http://www.vrmlsite.com/resource/anchor.html** (The Most Complete List of VRML 2.0 URLs, at VRMLSite Magazine)

When you've found a link to a VRML object (it will usually have the .Wrl or .Wrz extension; look in the status bar), click it and Navigator will transfer the file and load your viewer. You'll then be able to move around in (or about) the 3-D picture (see Figure 10.6). You'll generally press the mouse button and move the mouse to move into and around the 3-D image. You'll be able to rotate some images or move around other images, sometimes even moving inside buildings. 3-D plug-ins have toolbars and pop-up menus to provide further control.

FIG. 10.6
The Central Plaza at the Active Worlds site (**http://www. marketcentral.com/ univar/plaza.wrl**). You can walk around and into the buildings. Right-click to see a control menu.

> **TIP** This Web page is a good place to try out all sorts of viewers (including VRML viewers): **http://www-dsed.llnl.gov/documents/WWWtest.html**. You can also find unusual viewers here—viewers for .pdb "chemical objects," .ma Mathematica files, .v5d dataset objects, and so on.

You'll find that some images have Web links inside them. For example, you can walk through a museum, click a door, and go into another room. For more information about VRML, go to the **http://vag.vrml.org/www-vrml/** and **http://www.3dsite.com/** Web pages.

Note that VRML is still young. There was a lot of fuss about it early in 1995, and then it stalled—probably because it's such a hog. Few people have the sort of hardware necessary to make using VRML quick and easy. We keep hearing how VRML is the next thing on the Web, and then something else comes along and becomes popular. Still, VRML development continues, with the release of a new language specification and Microsoft showing interest. Maybe VRML will revive and eventually live up to its promise…. It probably won't be soon!

> **TIP** There's another Virtual Reality/3-D system available, QuickTime VR (QTVR). This system is from Apple Computers, though viewers are available for Windows, not only the Mac. The QuickTime plug-in built in to Navigator will display QTVR files (sometimes; at the time of writing it wasn't working well). You can find the latest plug-ins and viewers, along with links to QTVR sites, at the **http:// qtvr.quicktime.apple.com/** Web page.

Voyager CDLinks

Here's a format that's an interesting combination of CD-ROM and Web site and shows that just when you think you know what the Web can do, it does something you would never have thought of. Voyager CDLink provides a way for Web authors to link their Web sites to a music CD in your computer's CD-ROM drive. These CDs don't have to be created to work with a Web site. A Web site can be created to work with an existing CD. You can read a review of a CD, for instance, and then click links in the review to play specific portions of the music (see Figure 10.7). You can download Voyager CDLink from **http://www.voyagerco.com/cdlink/**.

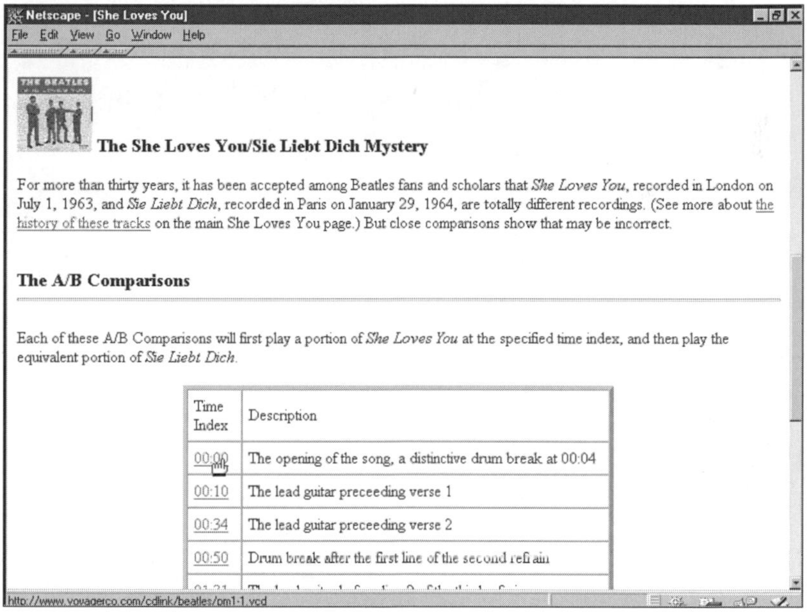

FIG. 10.7
This Web page attempts to solve an old Beatles mystery; are "She Loves You" and "Sie Liebt Dich" really different recordings? Put the Beatles Past Masters Vol. 1 CD into your computer's CD drive, and then click the links to hear matching portions of both songs played one after another.

Part

II

Ch

10

T I P To find a registry of Web sites that use the CDLink program—and the music CDs they work with—go to **http://www.voyagerco.com/cdlink/registry/registry.html**. You'll find sites working with CDs from Selena, Amy Grant, Bach, Bob Dylan, The Traveling Wilburys, The Beatles, Bon Jovi, and plenty more.

CHAPTER 11

Communicator's Security Features

The big question on the Web these days seems to be, "Is it safe?" People are concerned that information they send out across the Internet can somehow be intercepted by someone between the Web browser and the Web server. We'll look at the ways you can use Communicator to ensure that information you send across the Web reaches nobody but the intended recipient.

Imagine that you want to buy something from an online mall; you fill out a form, entering your name and address, the product you want, and your credit card number. You click the Submit button, and off that information goes, across the Internet, to the Web server that is managing this particular Web store. What happens to that data between here and there? Where is "there," even? It might be the other side of the country, the other side of the continent, or even the other side of the world. Could someone take a look at that message as it shoots by and grab your credit card number?

The dangers of Web transactions

When you send information across the Web, what could go wrong? What sort of information could be stolen?

How real are the dangers?

It is possible for information sent across the Web to be stolen...but not very likely.

What is public-key encryption?

Communicator's security system is based on something called public-key encryption. You're probably already familiar with some form of private-key encryption, but the public-key system is very different.

Working with site certificates

Communicator has a brand new "site certificate" system that allows Web sites to prove their identity before you divulge information to them

Personal certificates and e-mail

Similar to the site-certificate system, personal certificates identify individuals, and are the basis of the e-mail security system.

Well, yes, perhaps. Yes, it can be done. And we've heard a lot in the last year or two about the dangers of sending information across the Internet. In fact, we've heard so much about this that many people refuse to divulge their credit card information in cyberspace. But, in fact, very few people would know how to steal credit card numbers online. The security threat has been greatly exaggerated. There is a threat, and I think companies such as Netscape should be coming up with solutions, but I don't think that at present it's much of a threat to individual Web users. (Do I practice what I preach? Yes, I've sent my credit card numbers via e-mail to purchase something, and I didn't lose a moment of sleep.) ■

It's Not That Dangerous!

I know people who wouldn't dare to send their credit card numbers across the Internet. They seem to have this strange idea that every host computer has some evil soul lurking around, checking every e-mail message for credit card numbers.

Of course, these same people would give their credit card to a waiter in a restaurant, or to the guy in the 7-11, or even read the number over the phone to someone they've never met. They don't know what's happening to that credit card while it's out of their sight. They don't know whether the guy at the corner store is copying down the number from the receipt, for instance.

In fact, the most dangerous point in a transaction is not while the message is winging its way across the Internet, but when it gets to the other side. Relatively few credit card numbers are stolen online, for a couple of reasons. Very few people know how to do it, yet just about anyone could figure out how to steal a number in the real world. And credit card numbers simply aren't very valuable because they are so easy to steal in the real world. You wouldn't know it from all the "Ohmigosh-I-can't-use-my-credit-card-online" hype, but at the time of writing it is actually safer to use a credit card in cyberspace than in the "real" world—at least according to the credit card companies, who should know!

Public-Key Encryption

Nonetheless, it does make sense that the companies building software for the Web should do everything they can to reduce the risks, even if those risks are currently minor for most people. The more transactions made over the Web, the more potential for trouble. And after the Web has been made secure, it can be used for transmitting data far more valuable than credit card numbers: corporate financial and management data, research data, even government communications.

Netscape Communications has incorporated something called *public-key encryption* into its browsers and servers to ensure the safety of online transactions.

I don't have a lot of room to explain public-key encryption, which is unfortunate, because it's a concept that few people have heard of and fewer still understand. I'll just spend a few moments explaining the basics.

First, let me describe *private-key encryption*, which most people do understand. A computer file can be encrypted—turned into a jumble of garbage characters that makes it useless—using a program that works with a *private key* (also known as a *secret key*). The private key is a sort of code word. Tell the program the name of the file you want to encrypt, tell the program the private key, and the program uses a mathematical algorithm to encrypt the file. How can you decrypt the file? You do the same thing: Give the program the name of the encrypted file, give it the private key, and it uses the algorithm to reverse the process and decrypt the file.

Public-key encryption uses two keys: a private key and a public key. Through the intricacies of mathematics, these keys work together. When you encrypt a file with one key (the public key, for example), the file can be decrypted only with the other key! Sounds a little odd, but that's how it works. (Don't ask me how; as far as I'm concerned, it's magic!)

How, then, does this apply to Navigator? Navigator can use public-key encryption to encrypt information from a form before it sends it to the server. Here's how. When you load a secure Web document—a form, for instance—the Web server sends its public key along with the form. (That's why it's called a public key; it's available publicly, and no attempt is made, or needed, to protect the key.) You fill in the form and click the Submit button, and your browser takes the public key and encrypts the data in the form. It then sends it back to the server.

The server uses its *private* key to decrypt the message—remember, any file encrypted with the public key can be decrypted only with the private key. Because the people running the server keep that private key secret, your information is safe. If anyone intercepts it, they can't decrypt it.

TIP Remember, there are two required components in this procedure. Your browser has built-in security software, but not all servers do. Only special https servers (also known as *Secure Sockets Layer* servers) have the security software required for secure transactions. You'll find out how to recognize when you are connected to an https server under "How do I actually use this?" later in this chapter.

Part **II** Ch **11**

Different Size Keys

There are actually two different versions of the Navigator security software: a 40-bit version and a 128-bit version. These numbers refer to the length of the key—the code—that is used to encrypt data. The longer the key, the more secure the transmission. The 128-bit software is built into the Netscape servers and browsers sold to customers within the United States. The 40-bit software is built into Netscape servers and browsers that are sold to customers outside the United States; it's also built into most of the browsers that can be downloaded from the Netscape Web site and FTP sites and the various mirror sites.

You can download the 128-bit software from Netscape's site (previously, you could get it only by buying it at a store or having it shipped to you), but you'll have to fill out a form and provide information that Netscape can check (using the American Business Information Inc. service) to show that you are a resident of the U.S. (Only citizens and resident aliens—green-card holders—who are living in the U.S. are allowed to download the software.) You have to provide your name, address, phone number, and e-mail address. (See Chapter 1, "Finding and Installing Netscape Communicator," for information on tracking down the 128-bit version.)

Does it really matter which version you use? In most cases, no. The 40-bit software is strong enough for all but the most critical of applications. A government department using the Web to transfer information throughout the world would probably want to use 128-bit encryption, ensuring that the message was unbreakable. But, for most uses, 40-bit keys are fine.

Why, then, are there two different versions? For one reason only: ITAR, the United States Government's International Traffic in Arms Regulations. Encryption software using keys over 40 bits long is, as far as ITAR is concerned, on a par with armaments—SAM missiles and the like—and cannot be exported. Ridiculous, but true. (How can you stop the export of software, something that can be exported without physically moving anything?) This situation may change soon, as a federal judge recently ruled this regulation unconstitutional, so the issue is now in the hands of the courts. Note, by the way, that some other countries have laws that are as bad or worse. France, for instance, has banned the use of the 40-bit version of Communicator's encryption, so Netscape Communications now produces a special "security-free" Communicator for that country.

So there are two parts to the security equation: the browser and the server. What happens if you have a 40-bit browser, and you connect to a 128-bit server? The data encryption will be carried out using a 40-bit key. What if you have a 128-bit browser, and you connect to a 40-bit server? The encryption is still carried out using a 40-bit key. You'll only get full security when both browser and server use the 128-bit security software.

Is Communicator's Encryption Really Safe?

Is the encryption system safe? Well, that depends on what you mean. The encryption method itself is very secure. Data encrypted using the U.S. version, the 128-bit key, is essentially unbreakable. (That's why various U.S. lawmakers have suggested banning this form of encryption; in a number of countries it's already illegal.) Messages encrypted with the 40-bit key can be broken, but at a very high price. It takes about 64 MIPS years to break (a million instructions per second for 64 years). A French student recently broke a 40-bit-encrypted message by using spare time on several computers. Netscape estimated that it cost $10,000 of computing time to do so. That's a high price to grab one credit card number! Note that the 128-bit system is not simply three times as strong as the 40-bit system, it's thousands of times stronger; there's no known way to break it.

However, a little while before this book was published, another security flaw was discovered. The encrypted data itself is unbreakable. But what if you could masquerade as a Web site, so that someone submitting sensitive information, thinking it was going to the correct person, was actually sending it to you? This is known as *spoofing*. A special Web server can be placed between you and the rest of the World Wide Web, intercepting data as it goes both in and out of your computer. So when you think you're communicating with a particular online store, you're really communicating with the spoofer. When you send encrypted information back, the spoofing server can decrypt that information—because you're using that server's public key.

How likely is this to happen? Not very. How concerned should you be? If you're sending your credit card number across the Internet, not very. If you're sending national security secrets, be careful. As the people who discovered this problem point out (**http://www.cs.princeton.edu/ sip/pub/spoofing.html**), spoofing happens in the real world, too. Criminals sometimes set up fake cash machines; when a user enters the card and types in the number, the machine records the number and either copies or keeps the card. And again, carrying out a spoof is really nothing simple, nowhere nearly as simple as stealing a credit card number in the real world.

Using the Security Features

There are several ways that Communicator uses public-key encryption. We'll start by seeing the simplest way in which the Navigator uses this system—communications between your browser and a secure Web server.

Go to the Netscape store; you can get to it from the Netscape home page or go directly to **http://merchant.netscape.com/netstore/index.html**. You're going to go through the process of buying something. (Don't worry, you can cancel the operation at the last moment.)

TIP If your system administrator has set up your connection to the Web behind a *firewall*—a security system that limits the type of communications between your network and the outside world—you may find that Navigator is unable to communicate properly with a secure server. If so, talk with your system administrator about modifying the firewall.

Part
II

Ch
11

When you get to the store, click a link to select the type of product you want to buy: Navigators, Publications, or Logo Products (T-shirts and so on), for example. Continue following links until you come to a product that is for sale. If you have a baby, maybe you should buy the Mozilla Baby Bib, for instance. Make the appropriate selection—color, size, quantity, and so on—then click the Place in Shopping Basket button. In a few moments, you'll see the dialog box in Figure 11.1. This informs you that you are entering a secure form and that the data you enter into the form will be transmitted back to the server in an encrypted format.

FIG. 11.1
You'll see this message box when you enter a secure document.

Click the Continue button. (If you don't want to see these message boxes each time you enter a secure form, clear the Show This Alert Next Time check box, or on the Mac click the Don't Show Again button.) Now you'll see the secure form; you'll see that the URL shows https:// rather than http://.

You'll also see that the Security button on the toolbar has changed (it's now a locked padlock) as has the icon in the lower left corner of the browser (on the status bar). You *won't* see a blue bar across the top of the document; that feature of earlier Netscape Navigators has been removed.

 There's also a padlock icon in the status bar, on the left side. When you're viewing an insecure document, the icon is open; when you're in a secure document, it's closed.

> **N O T E** At the time of this writing, the Macintosh and UNIX versions of Communicator do not have all the security features in operation. From here on, we're looking at the Windows program, though these features will soon be incorporated into the versions for the other operating systems. ■

 You can now view information about this secure page. Click the Security button or the padlock icon in the left side of the status bar, and the box in Figure 11.2 opens. This box allows you to check the site certificate. (The message in the box is ambiguous. The certificate belongs to the Web site sending the page, not the page itself; it's like the site's "signature.") Click the View Certificate button to see the certificate, or the Open Page Info to see the Info window we looked at earlier (in Chapter 4).

FIG. 11.2

Click the padlock icon or Security button to see information about the displayed page.

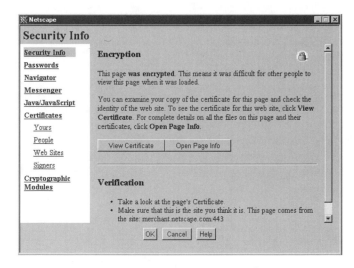

You can see a sample certificate in Figure 11.3. This shows two main things: information about the certificate itself and whom it belongs to, and the company that issued the certificate. We'll come back and discuss certificates a little more later in this chapter.

What do you have to do to send information from the Web page using encryption? Nothing. Just leave it up to Navigator. Use the form as you normally would: Type the information, click the Submit or Send button, and so on. Navigator quickly encrypts the data and sends it to the server. It's all transparent to you.

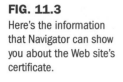

FIG. 11.3
Here's the information that Navigator can show you about the Web site's certificate.

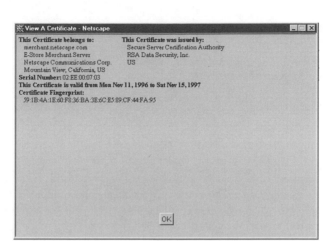

CAUTION

Just because Navigator provides security features doesn't mean you are totally safe. There are other things that can go wrong: Someone at the receiving end could steal the information, for instance. You have no control over what happens to information you send across the Internet after it's received and decrypted by the Web server.

N O T E Some secure servers have pages that don't show the security indicators. You may view a secure page at a secure site one moment and then click a link and find yourself at a page without the usual security indicators. In fact, you'll also see a message telling you that you are leaving a secure area. What's going on? Well, just because a server is capable of secure transactions, it doesn't follow that all the pages at the server will be set up as secure pages. System administrators can choose which pages to make secure, so they often secure only the ones that allow the user to submit important data. ■

Using Site Certificates

A *site certificate* is a special document that is used to *authenticate* a site or person. It's all part of the public-key encryption system. Here's how it works.

A company that's setting up a secure site on the Internet has to get a certificate—otherwise, the server can operate only in an insecure manner. The company applies to a *certificate authority*. Netscape has arranged for a variety of companies, including RSA Certificate Services (which is owned by the company that created the encryption system used by Netscape) to issue certificates.

The company applying for a certificate uses special software to electronically create the certificate (this is an electronic, not paper, certificate), and sends it to the certificate authority, which then verifies that the company applying for the certificate is really who it says it is. The authority then digitally signs the certificate.

TIP

This public-key encryption thing can get very involved. You can sign a document by using a private key to encrypt it. If someone wants to check the authenticity, he can use the associated public key to decrypt it. Because the private key is secret, and because only the associated public key can decrypt documents encrypted with the private key, that person can be sure that the document is authentic.

The company now has a valid https security certificate and can install that in its server. When you display a secure document, the certificate is sent to your browser, and you can view the certificate, as we did earlier (refer to Figure 11.3).

N O T E   To find a few secure servers to practice on, go to the Netscape Galleria: **http:// home.mcom.com/escapes/galleria.html**. You can search for sites in different businesses. These are sites using Netscape servers, many of which are secure servers. Dig around a bit for order forms and other types of forms. Or use Netscape's General Store, as I did in my examples. ▪

What good are these certificates? A site certificate identifies the site and says, in effect, "We are who we say we are." That's going to become much more important as more money is spent on the Web. Considering how easy it is to set up a Web site (you'll see just how easy in Chapters 19 and 20), anyone can set up a site, take orders for a nonexistent product for a few weeks, and disappear. Or someone could set up a site purporting to belong to another company or organization for various nefarious reasons—to muddy the water, distribute false information, even gather information from that company's or organization's employees, clients, and members.

The ability to identify a site will be very useful, then. But the positive identification depends on the level of trust you have in the certifying authority, of course. Actually, the certificate isn't quite a "we are who we say we are," statement; it's more of a "we are who we say we are, and the certifying authority agrees with us and has checked us out." This is known as *server authentication*. So when you look in the certificate and see the company's address, you know that the address is (or at least, should be) on record with and verified by the certifying authority.

Using the Security Dialog Box

You can view information about the security configuration and security certificates by choosing Communicator, Security Info, or by clicking the Security toolbar button or security icon on the left side of the status bar. When you first open the Security Info box, it shows information about the currently displayed Web page; as we've just seen, if the page is from a secure server, it allows you to view the certificate; if it's not, the information in the dialog box tells you that it's not, and lets you view the Page Info window.

In the left column, you'll see a list of headings; click a heading to see more information about a particular category:

Security Info—The information about the currently displayed Web page.

Passwords—You can set a password here to control use of your personal certificate, or modify the password. You can create the password when you obtain a certificate, or later. See "Changing the Keyfile Password," later in this chapter.

Navigator—You can define the security warnings shown to you by Navigator, when to identify yourself to a Web site, and the security configuration. We'll look at this later in this chapter. (See "Keeping You Informed—The Security Messages.")

Messenger—Defines how to work with Messenger's e-mail encryption system; see Chapter 17.

Java/JavaScript—A brand-new feature, not in use at the time of writing, allows Java and JavaScript programmers to "sign" their programs using private keys. You'll be able to store their public keys, then selectively allow certain Java and JavaScript programs to carry out certain procedures on your computer, procedures that you would allow to be carried out only by programs you are sure you can trust.

Certificates—Click here to see some basic background information about certificates.

Certificates: Yours—As you'll see later in this chapter ("Using Personal Certificates"), you can obtain a personal certificate which you can use to identify yourself. That certificate (or perhaps multiple certificates) will be stored here.

Certificates: People—In this area, you'll find other people's personal certificates, which allow you to send these people encrypted e-mail. See Chapter 17.

Certificates: Web Sites—This stores the site certificates we've discussed already.

Certificates: Signers—This lists the certification authorities, the companies that can sign certificates to verify that they are valid. In other words, if you receive a personal or site certificate signed by one of these companies, Communicator will assume that the certificate is valid. (However, you can modify a signer to block their authorization, or warn you when you receive a certificate signed by that authority.)

Cryptographic Modules—There are many different ways to encrypt data, and Communicator has been set up so that different modules may be installed. Installing a module adds new encryption capabilities to Communicator. Few users will ever have to install a new module, though.

Editing Site Certificates and Certification Authorities

You can modify the manner in which Communicator uses a certificate. Click a certificate and then click the Edit button. For instance, open the Signers pane, where the certificates from the certifying authorities (the organizations signing people's certificates) can be found. Click, say, United States Postal Service, then click the Edit button. You'll see the dialog box in Figure 11.4.

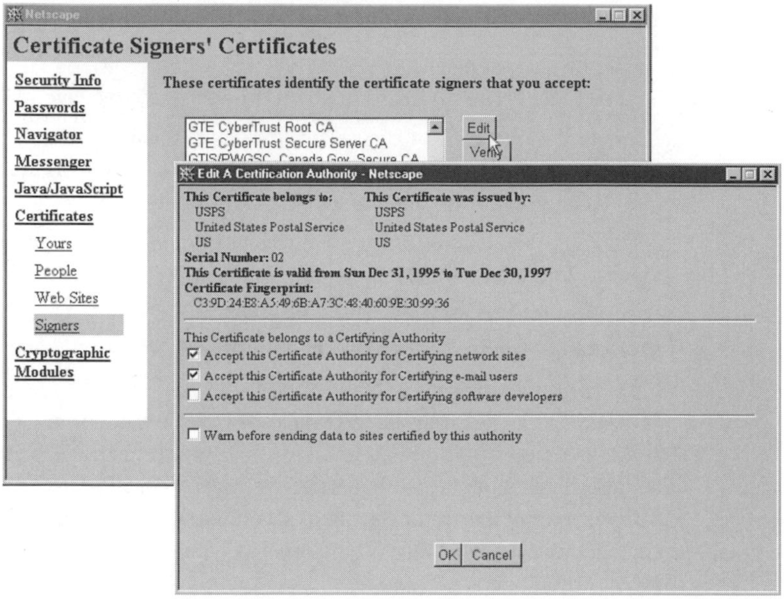

FIG. 11.4

The Edit a Certification Authority window allows you to tell Navigator whether to accept sites authorized by this authority.

At the top, you can see information about the site certificate; it tells you who owns the certificate and who issued it (in this case both by the same organization, because this is an authorized certification authority, the United States Postal Service).

You'll see the certificate's serial number, its valid dates, and its *fingerprint*. The fingerprint provides a physical way to check the authenticity of a certificate. A company could publish its fingerprint if they wanted, in print ads, brochures, even on business cards. Anyone who wants to confirm that they really have connected to the correct site—and not one masquerading as the site—could compare the fingerprint in the dialog box with the fingerprint in the company's publications. There's no practical way to add a forged fingerprint to a forged certificate. So if you're looking at a business card sent to you by a colleague, and the fingerprint on the card matched the fingerprint on the certificate, you could be certain that the Web page you were looking at was held at your colleague's Web site.

You have three option buttons in this dialog box:

> Accept This Certificate Authority for Certifying Network Sites—In other words, if your browser connects to a secure site, and that site sends a certificate that has been signed by this certifying authority, the browser should assume that it's safe. (How does Navigator know? You won't see any of this and don't need to worry about it; the site sends the certificate to Navigator when you connect to the site, and Navigator can read the digital signatures on that certificate.)

> Accept This Certificate Authority For Certifying E-mail Users—If this is checked, you will also accept personal certificates issued by this certifying authority. Personal certificates are used to encrypt e-mail to the owner of the certificate, and to check the digital signature on an e-mail message that you've received.

Accept This Certificate Authority For Certifying Software Developers—As I mentioned earlier, it is now possible for software publishers to digitally sign JavaScript and Java applets. If this box is checked, Navigator will accept applets that have been created by any company with a certificate issued by this certification authority.

You can clear the check boxes if you *don't* want to accept certificates issued by an authority. Why would you ever use this? If, for some reason, you suspect that the certifying authority has certified sites incorrectly. Or perhaps the site accidentally issued certificates to a company that is carrying out fraudulent transactions, or somehow the certification procedure was subverted and certificates were issued incorrectly. Either way, you can block this certifying authority.

N O T E How will you hear about certification problems? I don't know; this is all in its infancy. Perhaps Netscape Communications will issue warnings via e-mail, or post such news at its home page, at the certifying authorities' pages, and so on. ■

Finally, there's a check box at the bottom: Warn Before Sending Data to Sites Certified by This Authority. This tells Navigator to display a warning message if the server you are about to send data to was certified by this authority. Again, there may be a problem with *some* of the certificates issued by this company, and you want to know whenever you come across one.

In Figure 11.5, you can see an example of what happens when Navigator needs to warn you about a certificate; in this case, the Web site is using a certificate that it's not authorized to use (probably by accident; if a company is using more than one domain name, the administrator can accidentally configure the system to send the certificate for the wrong domain).

Part
II

Ch
11

FIG. 11.5
A Web site has sent an invalid certificate.

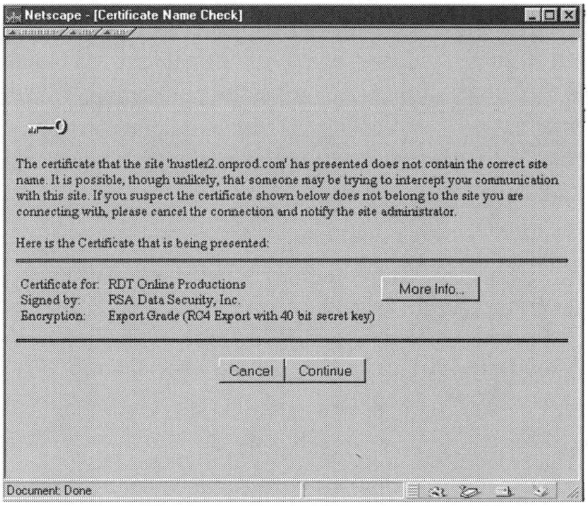

Using Personal Certificates

Now let's look at personal certificates, certificates that identify a user (you), rather than a site. You can apply to a certifying authority for your own certificate, so that you can identify yourself positively to a Web site.

Where do you get your certificate? From a key server, a site with the necessary software to issue certificates. There are both public- and private-key servers. Right now, you can get one from the public VeriSign key server (though other authorities will, presumably, be issuing them, too). There are two ways to do this. You can open the Security Preferences dialog box (click the Security button, or choose Communicator, Security Info), then click the Yours heading in the list box on the left side of the dialog box. Scroll down to the bottom of the Your Certificates pane, and then click the Get a Certificate button. Navigator should now open another Navigator window and connect to a Web page (**https://certs.netscape.com/client.html**) that has links to certification authorities—well, just to VeriSign right now, but there may be more soon. (You can also go directly to VeriSign's Digital ID page—**http://digitalid.verisign.com/**—or to VeriSign's main page at **http://www.verisign.com/**.)

T I P Netscape Communications sells a product called the Netscape Security Server. Your company can use this server to set up its own key server and issue certificates to its employees.

When you arrive at the VeriSign site, go to the Digital ID Center; you may find a `Go to Digital ID Center` link, or a drop-down list box from which you can select that page. Then go to the `Enroll: Request an ID` area; then, in the next page, select the `Netscape` link in the Individual/Browsers category.

You'll then have to select the type of certificate you want. There are currently two types available (with maybe a third being added soon). Remember, a certificate identifies you as the person you say you are. But how does the certifying authority know who you are? The certification authority uses different methods to identify you for the different classes:

- *Class 1*   VeriSign confirms that you have access to the e-mail address you claim as yours. In effect, this certificate says, "This e-mail address belongs to the person communicating with you." It's a limited identification, but it does confirm that the person is not masquerading as another e-mail user (which happens often on the Internet). This is currently free, though it may be $10 a year or so later on. It is also available to anyone in the world.

- *Class 2*   VeriSign requests identifying information from the applicant and then checks that information against the Equifax consumer-credit company. In effect, this certificate says, "This person gave us enough credit information to confirm that he is who he says he is." You have to provide your Social Security number, driver's license number, spouse's first name, previous address, credit card number, and so on. Of course, if someone really wants to masquerade as you, he can find the information he needs. These cost $20 a year and are currently available only to U.S. and Canadian residents.

- *Class 3*   In order to get one of these certificates (not yet available), you'll have to appear before a notary public with identifying documents. This says, "A notary public claims that the person who applied for this certificate has provided enough information to positively identify himself."

No system is perfect, and clearly *any* of these systems can be subverted to some degree. However, there is one thing that all these certificates do. If you use a certificate to identify yourself to a Web site (or an e-mail user—see "E-Mail Encryption," later in this chapter), then identify yourself later on using the same certificate, the site (or person) receiving the certificate can be fairly sure that it is receiving information from the same person. The only way that another person could use the certificate would be if he had access to your computer *and* knew the password that protects the certificate.

To obtain your certificate, simply follow the instructions on your screen (see Figure 11.6). (Click the image link with the big black ID letters to get to the form you need.)

FIG. 11.6

This form is used to apply for a Class 1 Digital ID from VeriSign.

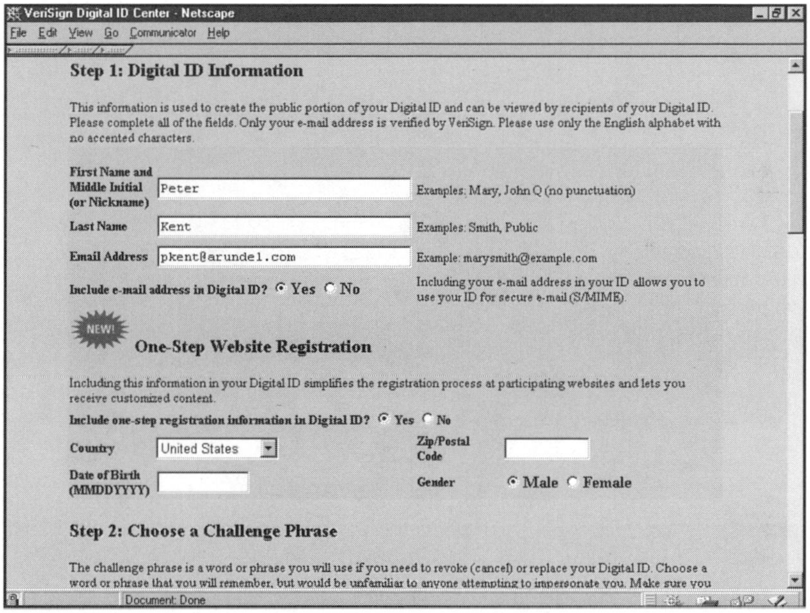

Enter the information requested by VeriSign, and then submit the data to them. (Note, by the way, that one of your options is to pick the encryption strength that your personal certificate will allow; if you have the U.S. version of the browser, the one with the full-strength security system, you can select a 768-bit or 1,024-bit key—the longer the key, the stronger the encryption.

When you submit the data to the certification authority, Navigator begins the process in which your private key is created (see Figure 11.7). Follow the instructions you see.

Remember, the private key is used to decrypt messages that are sent to you, messages that are encrypted with your public key. It's also used to identify you; it's used to "digitally sign" messages, as you'll see in Chapter 17. Before it creates your key, it asks you if you want to provide a password (see Figure 11.8). This password is used to unlock the private key; without the password, it's not possible to use the private key to decrypt data. However, you have the option of not providing a password, in which case anyone who can get to your computer and start Navigator can use your private key both to impersonate you and to decrypt messages sent to you! If you're not absolutely sure your computer is secure from unauthorized use, *don't* work without a password.

FIG. 11.7

When you submit the information to VeriSign, Navigator begins creating your private key.

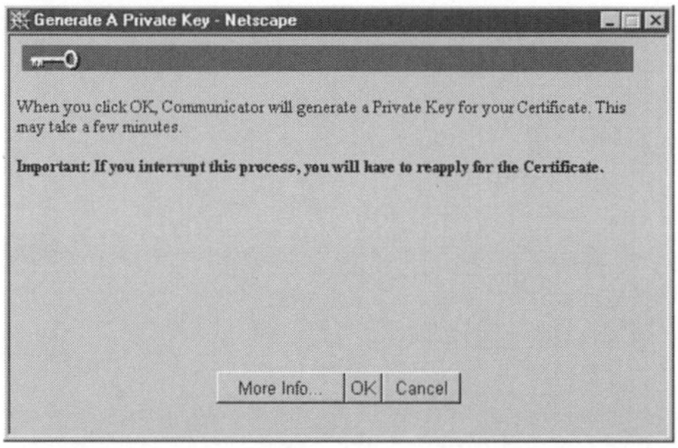

Generate A Private Key - Netscape

When you click OK, Communicator will generate a Private Key for your Certificate. This may take a few minutes.

Important: If you interrupt this process, you will have to reapply for the Certificate.

More Info... | OK | Cancel

FIG. 11.8

To make sure nobody can use your private key, use a password.

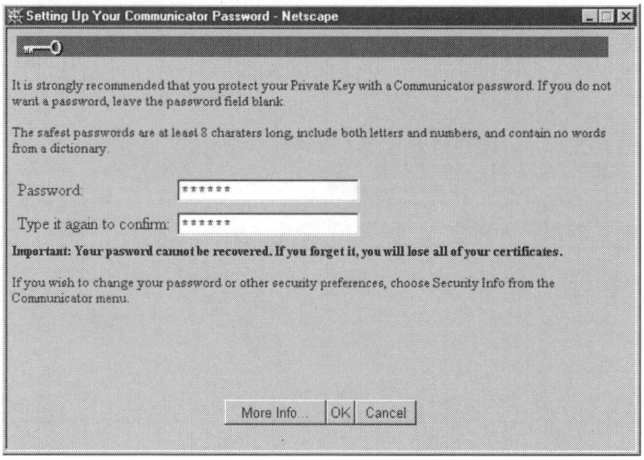

Setting Up Your Communicator Password - Netscape

It is strongly recommended that you protect your Private Key with a Communicator password. If you do not want a password, leave the password field blank.

The safest passwords are at least 8 charates long, include both letters and numbers, and contain no words from a dictionary.

Password: ******

Type it again to confirm: ******

Important: Your pasword cannot be recovered. If you forget it, you will lose all of your certificates.

If you wish to change your password or other security preferences, choose Security Info from the Communicator menu.

More Info... | OK | Cancel

This password is known in encryption lingo as the *keyfile password*. The keyfile password allows you to use the private key to sign or decrypt things. If you don't add a keyfile password now, you can do so later (or modify the one you created); see "Changing the Keyfile Password," later in this chapter.

Here's an analogy that might help you understand this. Think of your certificate as a paper certificate, a special document that identifies you. You can lock away the certificate in a secure lock box, so secure that the only way to get the certificate out is to use a very special key, a key that only you possess—the private key. But the private key is very unwieldy; it's much too heavy to carry around. (In fact, the real private key is a very large and complicated string of numbers, far too complicated for you to remember.) So you keep the key itself locked away in an impregnable safe. Of course, you have another key to open this safe. This key is the equivalent of the keyfile password. Without it nobody can get to your private key, so they can't use your certificate.

In other words, to identify yourself or to decrypt messages that you receive, you must a) know the keyfile password, b) use the keyfile password to unlock the private key, and c) use the private key to unlock the certificate. So don't forget your keyfile password, or you can't use the certificate!

When you've finished the process, VeriSign sends an e-mail message to you (it may take a little while to get to you, of course). Read this message for instructions on how to install the permanent certificate in Navigator.

To retrieve your certificate, you'll have to go to a particular Web page (the e-mail explains which—it's currently **https://digitalid.verisign.com/getid.htm**) and then enter an identifying number (again, included in the e-mail). When you submit the number, VeriSign generates the certificate for you and sends it to Navigator. Navigator then begins "importing" the certificate. It displays a series of boxes; read the messages and follow the instructions (you'll have to enter the keyfile password if you created one earlier). You'll also be asked to enter a Certificate Name, or accept the one provided (see Figure 11.9). This is simply the name you use to identify the certificate, in case you have several for different purposes. You can also choose to Make This The Default Certificate For Signed And Encrypted E-Mail; if you leave this box checked, this certificate will be selected automatically each time you digitally sign e-mail; see Chapter 17.

FIG. 11.9
Provide a nickname to identify this personal certificate; then Navigator will install it for you.

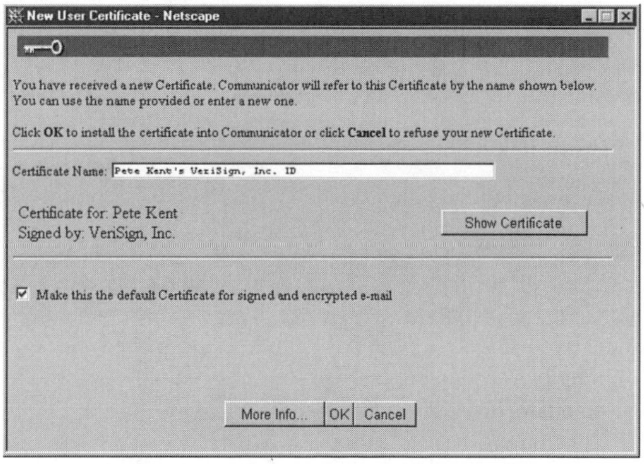

At the end of the process, you'll see a dialog box from which you can save a copy of the certificate. This can be saved on a floppy disk, or used to install the certificate on another computer (see "Importing and Exporting Certificates," later in this chapter). You might want to save the certificate in a safe deposit box, in case you lose it (perhaps your computer dies, is stolen, or burns) and want to reload it. These files are saved with a .p12 file extension.

When you finish importing the certificate into your browser, you can check to see what happened; open the Security dialog box (click the Security toolbar button), then click Yours in the list box on the left side of the dialog box (see Figure 11.10).

You'll see your certificate name in the list box; click the name and then click View. You'll see something like Figure 11.11. All this information is sent to a Web site requesting your certificate when you are identifying yourself to the site, or included with e-mail when identifying yourself to a recipient. Notice the comment box, by the way. This explains the type of authentication. In this case, the certificate is a Class 1, so the comment points out that VeriSign has simply authenticated the e-mail address, but that the certificate owner may be using a fake name.

FIG. 11.10

Now you'll find your personal certificate in the Security dialog box.

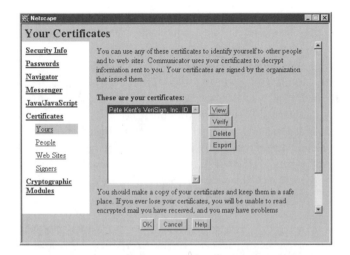

FIG. 11.11

You can view information about your certificate from the Security Preferences dialog box.

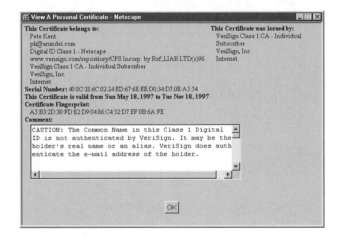

Importing and Exporting Certificates

If you have to completely reinstall Navigator for some reason, or need to use your digital ID on another computer (such as your laptop), you can copy the ID from one browser to another. Click your certificate in the Security dialog box, then click the Export button. You'll be able to save the file on your hard disk, or on a floppy disk (it's quite small), then transfer it to another computer.

Be careful when copying these files, though. They contain your private key. If you told Navigator not to use a password, then the private key can be used by anyone!

To install the certificate on another computer, open Netscape on that computer and then open the Security dialog box. Click the Yours heading, then scroll down to the bottom of the Yours pane. There you'll find an Import Certificate button; click this and select the certificate file—it has the .p12 file extension.

Using Your Certificate

How, then, can you use your certificate? You can use it to sign an e-mail message, to prove it comes from you. We'll learn more about that in Chapter 17. You can also use it to identify yourself to a Web site. When a site wants you to identify yourself, you'll see a dialog box asking for your certificate. You'll select the certificate you want to use and then enter your keyfile password to "unlock" the private-key part of the certificate and send a digital signature, a little file that says, in effect, "I've been signed by this guy's private key, so he must be who he says he is."

 TIP For more information about working with personal certificates, see the **http://digitalid.verisign.com/ ask_veri.htm** and **http://digitalid.verisign.com/info_ctr.htm** Web pages.

You can see an example in Figure 11.12 of the sort of message you'll receive when a Web site prompts you to provide your certificate. Web servers using this system may simply turn you away if you don't provide a certificate, or perhaps allow you access to certain non-secure portions of the site. You can choose which certificate you want to use and then click Continue. You must then provide your keyfile password, if you created one.

FIG. 11.12
Here's what you'll see when a site asks you for your certificate.

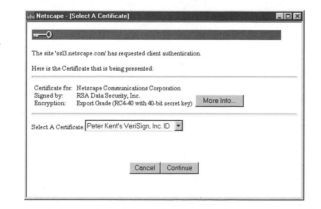

How often will a Web site request your certificate? Not often, at least not now. This is a new service, so it will be a while before you see it in wide use.

Changes and Revocations

After you have a Digital ID, you can't change it. If you forget your keyfile password, you can't create a new password for the certificate. You'll have to get a new one. And if you change your e-mail address, you'll have to get a new certificate, too; it can't be switched.

Before you can get a new certificate, you'll have to revoke the old one, because VeriSign won't issue duplicate certificates for the same person and e-mail address. You can revoke your certificate at the VeriSign site (**http://digitalid.verisign.com/**). Revoking a certificate not only allows you to create a new one, but it also removes it from the VeriSign keyserver, the Web site that keeps all the VeriSign public-key portions of the certificates (I'll discuss that more in a moment, when we look at e-mail encryption).

> **CAUTION**
>
> If, for some reason, you need to delete Communicator, export your certificate and save it somewhere safe, or you won't have a copy of it and will have to reapply if you need it later. Upgrading Communicator will not damage your certificates.

Changing the Keyfile Password

Navigator allows you to modify your keyfile password—or add one if you didn't create one in the first place. Choose Communicator, Security Info, or click the Security button. Then click the Passwords heading in the list box on the left side of the Security dialog box (see Figure 11.13). Click the Change Password button (it says Set Password if you didn't create one earlier), and then follow the instructions for modifying or creating the password.

FIG. 11.13
You can create a keyfile password, if you haven't already done so, or modify the one you have.

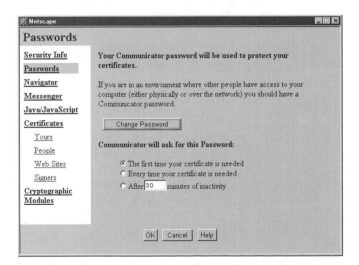

Notice that you can also tell Navigator how often to prompt for the keyfile password: The First Time Your Certificate is Needed means that after you've used the certificate in a session, you won't have to use the password the next time (not too secure if you're in an office in which others can use your computer); Every Time Your Certificate is Needed (the most secure method), and After *nn* Minutes of Inactivity (so, if you walk away from Navigator, after the specified number of minutes, the private key is locked up).

E-Mail Encryption

Perhaps the most useful feature of personal certificates will be the ability to encrypt e-mail. You'll be able collect other people's certificates, then use those certificates (which contain those people's public keys) to encrypt messages to the certificate owners; a message encrypted with the public key can only be decrypted with the corresponding private key. So messages that you encrypt with a friend's or colleague's public key can be decrypted only by that person's private key, which provides, in effect, completely secure e-mail transmissions.

Where will you be able to get other people's certificates? The easiest way is directly from those people. Get someone to send you a message with the personal certificate attached to the message. When the message is received, Messenger will be able to extract the certificate and save it (see Chapter 17; I'll explain how to attach certificates to outgoing messages, and how to save them from incoming ones).

Another way to get a certificate is to obtain it from a directory. Open the Security dialog box (click the Security toolbar button), then click People in the list box on the left side of the dialog box. Scroll down to the bottom of the Other People's Certificates pane, and you'll find the Search Directory button. You can then select a directory, enter the e-mail address of the person whose certificate you are looking for, and click Search. If the certificate is found (it probably won't be!), you can automatically save it. This is a great system, but because few people are using personal certificates yet, it's difficult to find them on these directories!

You can also find certificates at a key server, a Web site containing a list of public certificates. For instance, VeriSign maintains a key server (go to **http://digitalid.verisign.com/** and choose the Find: Search the ID Database link, or something similar). You can use this service to find the public key belonging to someone with whom you want to communicate—a form allows you to search for the person by name, e-mail address, or digital-ID serial number. When you find the person, VeriSign displays a complicated-looking link, something like this:

```
Locality = Internet, Organization = VeriSign, Inc., Organizational Unit =
➥VeriSign Class
1 CA - Individual Subscriber,
    Organizational Unit = www.verisign.com/repository/CPS Incorp. by
Ref.,LIAB.LTD96, Organizational Unit = Digital
    ID Class 1 - Netscape, Common Name = Peter Kent, Email Address =
➥pkent@arundel.com
```

Click this link, and you'll see more information about the person. Make sure it really is the person you want; then, at the bottom of the page, find the download controls. Select Netscape Navigator from the drop-down list box, and then click the Download Certificate button. Navigator will then import the public-key certificate.

Using the Certificate

In Chapter 17, I will explain in detail how to use certificates to encrypt messages. Here's a quick summary of what happens, though. Once you've got someone's certificate stored in Communicator, when you want to send an encrypted message to that person, you simply create the message and then select the certificate. Messenger will automatically encrypt the message before sending it. The recipient will then use his copy of Messenger to decrypt the message by using his private key.

A person for whom you have a personal certificate can also sign messages he sends to you. He uses his private key to sign the message (in effect, encrypting a small part of the message). Then, when you receive the signed message, Messenger will verify the signature for you; it will use the public key stored in that person's public certificate to decrypt the signature.

Keeping You Informed—The Security Messages

Here's a simpler aspect of Communicator's security system: its security messages. By default, Navigator will display message boxes informing you of certain operations:

- When you enter or leave a secure (encrypted) Web document
- When you enter a document with a secure and insecure mix (part of the information will be submitted securely, part insecurely)
- When you submit information insecurely—for instance, if you click a Send or Submit button in a form that is not on a secure server

You can turn these message boxes off if you want; open the Security dialog box (click the Security toolbar button), then click Navigator in the list box. You'll see several check boxes that you can use to turn the messages off. (You can also clear the Show This Alert Next Time check box that appears inside a message box when it pops up.)

The most irritating of these messages is the Sending Unencrypted Information To A Site message. Most forms on the Internet are insecure, and in most cases you won't submit anything of importance. If you submit messages in a form used by a Web site in an online discussion group, or if you search at one of the sites I mentioned in Chapter 6, you'll see the message. There's no security risk, though. The Internet is full of such forms, systems in which you enter data that is not particularly "sensitive." So you may want to turn this message box off.

TIP   You can save secure documents or view their source, but Navigator won't save them to the hard-disk cache for you. There used to be an Allow Persistent Caching of Pages Retrieved Through SSL check box in the Preferences, which would tell Navigator to cache secure pages, but this option has gone, at least for the moment. Who knows, it might reappear in a later version of Communicator.

There are a number of other messages, some of which you have no control over; the following list contains a few messages you're likely to see:

- Navigator will inform you if a document comes from a secure server, but submits your data to an insecure server. (In other words, the Web page itself is held by the secure server, but it submits the data to a different, insecure, server.)

- Navigator will inform you if a document comes from a secure server, but the script that is used to generate the form (the *CGI*—Common Gateway Interface—script) is not secure. (Perhaps the CGI referred to by the document is on a different server.)

- Navigator will inform you if the form you are using is submitting the data you've entered by e-mail. (Some forms use something called CGI scripts; others use e-mail. Currently e-mail forms are not encrypted.)

- If a Web page sends you a *cookie*, you *may* see a warning. (The warning box is turned off by default; choose Edit, Preferences, then click Advanced in the Category list to see the cookies options.

Working with Cookies

"What's a cookie?" you're no doubt asking. That's a piece of information that a script on the Web page wants the browser to save, initially in the computer's memory and then, when you close the browser, on your hard disk in the cookie.txt file. It can be used to find out the last time you visited the site, for instance, or choices you made in a form the last time you were there.

Many, many Web sites set cookies these days. If you want to see how many, check the Accepting a Cookie check box in the preferences and you'll start to see lots of warning boxes as you move around on the Web.

If you allow Web sites to set cookies on your system, you may, in some cases, be providing more information to the Web site than you want to. By looking around in your Cookie.txt file, Web sites can figure out which pages you've seen at their site and what you've been doing there—useful marketing information if you also provide your e-mail address at some point. Any information you volunteer to the Web site in forms may be written into the cookie.txt file, thus identifying you the next time you come to the site. If you are concerned about this, you might want to leave the message box turned off—so you don't have to mess with all those messages continually—and use the Disable Cookies checkbox to completely stop cookies from working. However, some sites use cookies to determine the best way to display pages on your browser, so refusing cookies occasionally means that pages won't display properly.

Note also that there are certain safety features built into the cookie system. There are limits to how large cookie.txt can grow, to the size of a cookie, to how many individual cookies a Web site can set, and so on. And Web sites are not supposed to be able to view cookies set by other sites.

N O T E Why are they called cookies? According to the preliminary specification for cookies, "for no compelling reason." ■

Part

II

Ch

11

By the way, there are some products that help you manage cookies. For instance, there's PGPcookie.cutter, available soon for both Windows and the Macintosh (**http://www.pgp.com**), and NSClean (**http://www.wizvax.net/kevinmca/**), both of which help you manage cookies much more effectively—by blocking and allowing domains from particular sites, specifying the type of information you will allow to be sent to a server, allowing you to use an alias, and so on. On the Macintosh, there's also a product called Cookie Cutter. ●

CHAPTER 12

Programs Built into the Web: Java, JavaScript, and ActiveX

One of the most exciting new technologies on the Web is *Java*. This is a programming language from Sun, a language based on the C++ programming language. It allows a programmer to create a small program that can run "within" a Java viewer. And Navigator has the viewer (more properly known as an *interpreter*) built into it. So these Java programs—*applets*, as they're commonly known—will run within the Navigator window. Web documents are no longer static—Java brings them alive with motion, sound, and interaction. ∎

What is Java?

Java is a sophisticated programming language with an important feature; a Java program can run on any operating system for which an interpreter is available.

Finding Java sites

You'll come across Java applications now and again, but to find the best available you'll have to go to a few important link sites.

Java made simple—JavaScript

JavaScript is like Java's little brother, a slightly simpler programming language in which the code is inserted directly into the Web page.

ActiveX

ActiveX is Microsoft's answer to Java. It's growing in importance, but at present it is not directly supported by Communicator—though you can install a plug-in that will run ActiveX programs.

What Can Java Programs Do for You?

What can Java programs do? They can bring sound and motion to Web documents. The following are a few ways that Java applets can be used:

- *Regular and frequent document updates*   The Web document may contain information that is updated regularly and frequently. As you view the document, the information changes before your eyes: stock quotes, weather reports, news reports, and so on.

- *Expert graphics rendering*   A Java applet may be used to display high-resolution graphics or video.

- *User interaction*   A Java applet may contain a game: a crossword puzzle, chess, a MUD (Multiuser Dimension, a role-playing game), tic-tac-toe, word-match games, Hangman, and so on. Or it could allow a user to search a database or enter information for a survey. In Chapter 15, "Gopher, Finger, Telnet, and More," you'll see an example of how Java is used to run a chat program at TalkCity.

- *Animation*   Web authors can animate their documents, with blinking text, embedded videos and cartoons, and scrolling text and images.

- *Sounds*   Web authors can now use Java to add sounds to their documents: background music, a voice speaking in the background, a welcome-to-the-page spoken statement.

- *Database connections*   Java applets may be used to connect databases to a Web site. In fact, Web sites can use Java behind the scenes to provide information to users and process data provided by them.

But Is It Safe?

Java applets are designed to be secure. If the applet provides interaction between you and the server—you might be able to enter information and receive information back from the server—the information is transferred securely. Java also has protection against viruses and tampering and, until recently, didn't allow applets to store information on your hard disk (except in the Cookie.txt file, which we'll look at later). As we go to print, Netscape Communications is adding new security procedures that will allow Java applets to be digitally signed; users will then be able to give permission to applets to use certain computer resources—such as the hard disk—if the digital signature identifies the program as being from a safe source.

Still, security bugs in Java come to light now and then—they're fixed, of course, but then some other bug appears. So if you want to be really paranoid and disable Java, you can. Here's how: Choose Edit, Preferences, click Advanced in the Category list, and clear the Enable Java check box. (You can disable JavaScript, too; clear the Enable JavaScript check box.) You'll still be able to view Web pages with embedded Java applets, but a blank space will be left where the applet should go.

Where Can I Find Java?

Right now, for all the Java hype, relatively few Web sites have Java applets. You'll probably run across them now and again, though just by chance. But if you want to go searching for them, try these places:

- *The Netscape site*   Currently, there are links to various demos from the Netscape site. You can find your way to them from the Netscape home page or go directly (**http://home.netscape.com/comprod/products/navigator/version_2.0/java_applets/index.html**).
- *The Gamelan Registry*   You'll find links to a lot of Java sites (**http://www.gamelan.com/**).
- *Sun's List of Cool Applets*   From the people who brought us Java in the first place, here is a list of neat ones (**http://www.javasoft.com/applets/applets.html**).
- *Jars.com*   "The #1 Java Review Service" (**http://www.jars.com/**).

Playing an Applet

What do you have to do to play one of these applets? Nothing. At least, nothing beyond what you normally do when entering a Web page: Click the link or type the URL and press Enter, or whatever. When the Web page opens, Navigator will load the Java applet at the same time (assuming, of course, that you haven't turned off Java in the Properties).

Of course, once the applet is loaded, you may have work to do, but that's up to the Java programmer. If the applet is a game, for instance, you'll have to know how to play the game; a good applet will provide instructions, of course. Each applet is different, so there are no general rules.

TIP

The progress bar doesn't work well with Java applets. It works for a short while, during the time that the Java applet is being transferred to your computer. But then the progress bar stops working even though nothing may be happening. You may see a blank gray box, for instance, and nothing else. However, listen for your hard drive or look for the hard drive light; your drive is probably churning away, preparing the applet. Also, note that at the time of writing the Macintosh version of Communicator did not handle Java very well; some Java applets will crash the system when loaded.

The majority of sites are simply demo sites with little real utility. Other Java applets are so simple they're not terribly exciting. If you dig around a little, though, you should be able to turn up something interesting. Currently, one of the most common uses of Java is for displaying animated or scrolling signs. For instance, some sites contain little boxes that display a variety of messages or news stories, one after another. Here are a few samples that I found.

The Abacus

An electronic abacus (see Figure 12.1); now there's an interesting concept
(**http://www.ee.ryerson.ca:8080/~elf/abacus/**).

FIG. 12.1

Learn how to use an
abacus through the
interactivity of Java.

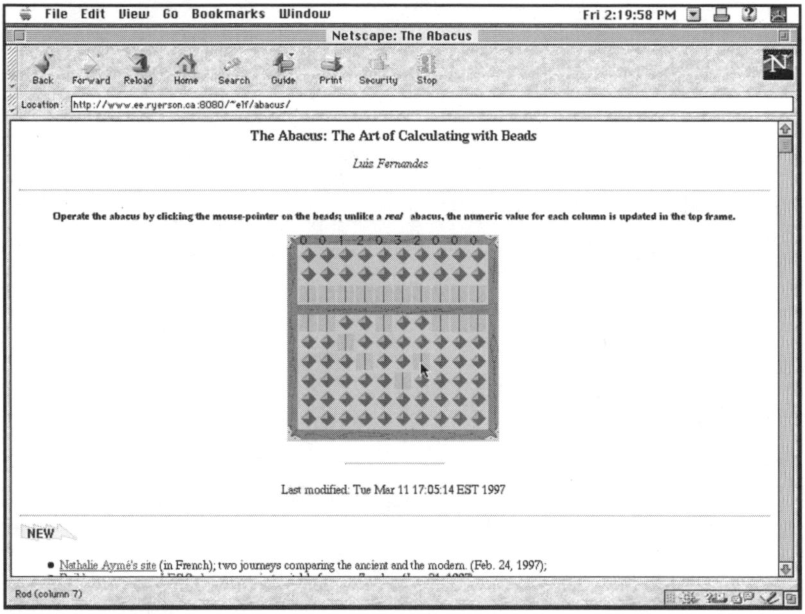

Control the Nuclear Power Plant

Control your own nuclear power plant (see Figure 12.2). Click valves to adjust the various flows
and, if you are lucky, you'll avoid a meltdown (**http://www.ida.liu.se/~her/npp/
demo.html**).

TIP If a Java applet is a play-once applet—a welcoming message in the Web author's voice, for instance—
you don't have to leave the page to replay it. Simply click the Reload button.

A Shopping Program

The Internet Shopping with Java applet can be used by Web sites to take orders from customers; the user drags a picture of an item into the shopping bag to order it (see Figure 12.3),
drags the shopping bag back onto the picture to remove the item from the bag, double-clicks
an item to see more information, and so on (**http://www.eastland.com/shopping.html**).

FIG. 12.2
One mistake and the power station blows!

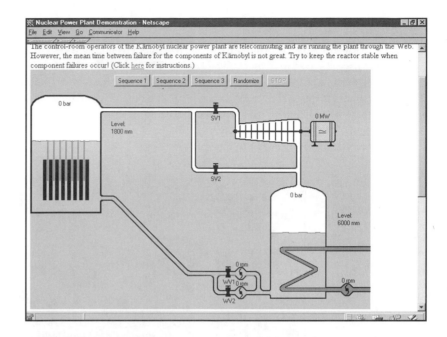

FIG. 12.3
The Internet Shopping with Java applet; drag an item into the shopping bag to make a purchase.

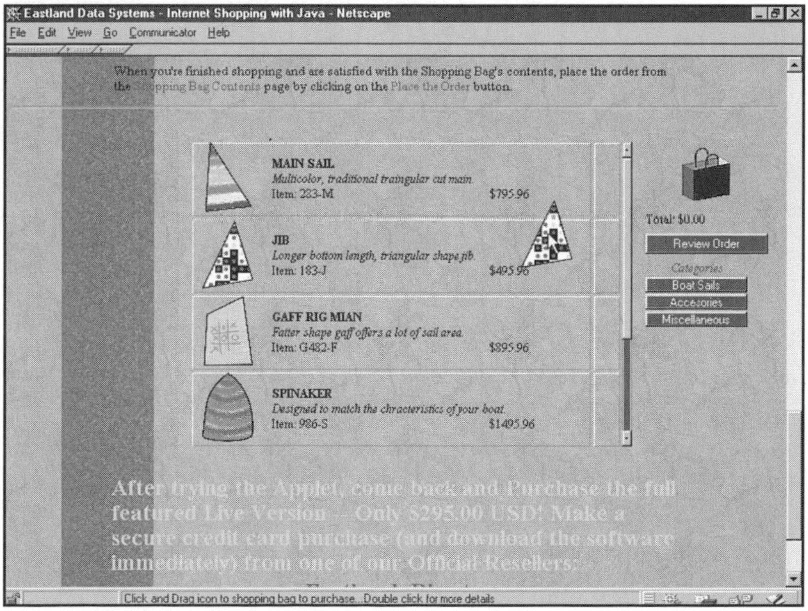

The Human Slice Viewer

Here's a strange little program, the NPAC Visible Human Viewer (**http://www.npac.syr.edu/projects/vishuman/VisibleHuman.html**). This allows you to pick a cross-section of a human cadaver and view it in a pop-up window. This program is from the Northeast Parallel Architectures Center (NPAC), which obtained the images from the National Library of Medicine's Visible Human Project. This project is creating a complete set of digital images of male and female cadavers, using photographs, magnetic resonance imaging (MRI), and computer tomography (CT) data (see Figure 12.4).

FIG. 12.4

Slide the lines around inside the image boxes to pick the cross-section you want, and then click Load to see the section in a pop-up window.

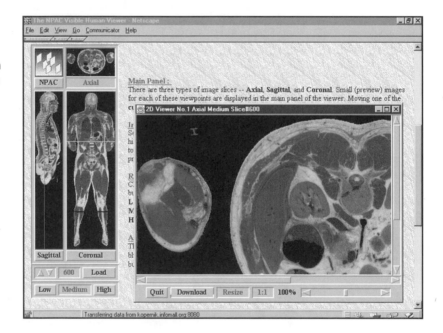

A lot has changed since the first edition of this book. At the time I wrote that book, most Java sites were hardly worth bothering with; most didn't work in Navigator (they were the wrong type of Java applet or simply too buggy), and many were slightly interesting but not worth coming back to. Now there are far more sites, and, as more programmers learn to use Java, the quality of the applets is definitely improving. Programs such as the NPAC Visible Human Viewer are really worthwhile, much more so than the simple bouncing head animations and the like that were the norm a year ago. It's a start, but there's still a long way to go.

Java is still not widely used; only a tiny proportion of Web sites have Java applets. That may change—perhaps very quickly—as the technology progresses, in particular as Java's ability to use computer resources is improved (and this depends on the new digital-signature security system that Netscape is introducing). Check the Java listings I've mentioned to see the current status of the Java world.

The Problem with Java

Java applets share a problem with most of the really neat stuff on the Web: They can be very slow if you are working through a modem. The introductory voice welcoming you to a Web page, for instance, may not play until you've read most of the page! The animation may be too slow to be fun. After the Java data has transferred, things work pretty quickly, but having to wait for the stuff to get over the Internet and to your computer spoils the effect to some degree. But hey, what can you do? If you are working on a network, it works well and the rest of us will just have to dream.

Another problem is that Java often simply doesn't work, however long you wait. There are different versions of Java, and the browsers each work a little differently. And even if it does work, the Java applet you're looking at may seem, well, rather dull. "Was it worth the wait?" you may think. Java is still young and has yet to live up to the hopes and claims of its proponents.

Troubleshooting Java

Navigator provides a troubleshooting tool for Java applets: A console that displays the Java program code being run. Click a link to a Web page containing a Java applet; then quickly choose Communicator, Java Console. A window opens and displays line after line of gobbledygook, which means little to the average user. This is really a tool for programmers who know what to look for. On the other hand, you may want to take a quick peek to see what a Java applet actually looks like.

A Simpler Form of Java—JavaScript

Part
II
Ch
12

There's another way that a Web developer can create *active* Web documents (documents that do things and allow you to do things to them). Developers can use *JavaScript*, Netscape's new scripting tool. (You may see the term *LiveScript*, too; this was the original name given to JavaScript.)

JavaScript is a simplified form of Java. To use Java requires programming skills; it's a true programming language, and developing applets is not to be undertaken lightly. JavaScript provides a slightly simpler way to jazz up Web pages. It's still a programming language, and to create anything sophisticated takes a programmer's skills. But it's possible for a Web author to do fairly simple things with JavaScript with minimal knowledge. For instance, a Web author could make message boxes pop up when someone entered or left a page, create lists of destination Web pages from which a user could pick (clicking a button could load the selected page), create simple databases that users could search, make slide shows that load Web pages automatically after a set time period, and so on.

TIP It's actually possible to create simple Web pages with very little HTML knowledge. An author who has created a simple Web page won't necessarily have the skills needed for JavaScript. But anyone who's willing to devote a few score hours to learning it should be able to figure it out.

So what can JavaScript actually do? It allows a Web author to script events, objects, and actions. The author can tell the document to "watch" for certain actions: When the document is opened by a browser, when the browser moves from the document to another one, when the reader clicks the mouse button on a button, and so on. It also allows the author to link the Web document to inline plug-ins and true Java applets—an author can take off-the-shelf Java applets and link them to a Web document by using JavaScript. It brings the power of Java to developers without the programming skills required to create Java applets.

The developer can use JavaScript to add sounds to a document—a sound may play when the document is opened by the browser or when the reader clicks the mouse button on an icon, for instance, or an inline picture may change according to the time of day. Web forms can now quickly check that the correct information has been entered, before that information is transmitted back to the server. A Java applet may open or may modify its actions, when the reader selects something from a form. For instance, the reader may choose a particular model, type, or color from an order form. The Java applet—on receiving JavaScript instructions generated when the reader makes his selection—then displays the appropriate object.

N O T E You may hear the term *JScript*, which is the name given by Microsoft to the version of JavaScript that is in Internet Explorer. It incorporates a slightly earlier version of JavaScript than that in Navigator 4, but also includes a variety of commands that are not present in JavaScript; it's intended to be a sort of hybrid system that links JavaScript and ActiveX together. (We'll look at ActiveX in a moment.) However, note that Navigator 4 does not work with the non-JavaScript commands that are present in JScript. ▓

When Do They Run?

When can JavaScripts run? Web authors can set up their documents to run JavaScripts when events such as the following occur:

- When your browser opens the document
- When you move from the document to another document by using the history list or bookmarks, for instance
- When "input focus" changes; for instance, when you press Tab to move the cursor from one field in a form to another
- When you select text in a field
- When you modify text in a field
- When you click a button
- When your browser sends the contents of the form back to the server
- When you click a link
- When you simply point at a link
- When you move the mouse pointer away from an object
- When an image hasn't loaded properly

Finding Samples

If you'd like to find some examples of JavaScripts and how they work, try these sites:

- Cut-n-Paste Javascript site located at **http://www.infohiway.com/javascript/indexalt.htm**
- Gamelan JavaScript List at **http://www-b.gamelan.com/pages/Gamelan.related.javascript.html**
- The JavaScript Index at **http://www.c2.org/~andreww/javascript/**
- LiveSoftware's JavaScript Resource Center at **http://jrc.livesoftware.com/**
- JavaScript 411 at **http://www.freqgrafx.com/411/**

If you are interested in seeing how to learn JavaScript and how to add a few simple JavaScripts to your own Web pages, take a look at my JavaScript site, at **http://www.netscapepress.com/support/javascript1.2/**.

At that site, there is an example of a JavaScript applet, the Area Code program that my brother and I created, at **http://www.netscapepress.com/support/javascript/firstarea.htm**; you can see this in Figure 12.5. This lets you search a "database" for an area code; you can search by code, city, or region.

FIG. 12.5
My Area Code program; search by code, area, or region.

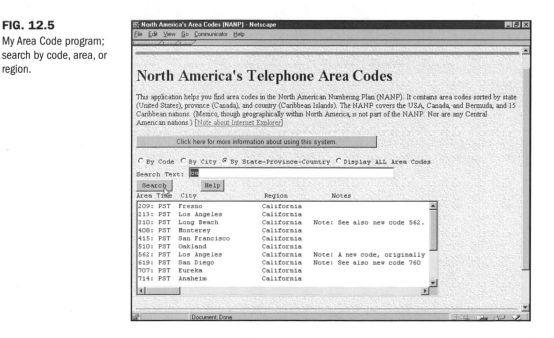

You can see another example, a Postfix notation calculator, in Figure 12.6. Go to **http://home.netscape.com/comprod/products/navigator/version_2.0/script/calc.html**. For an interest calculator, go to the same URL, except use the document name **interest.html**.

They don't look much different from a Java applet, which is the point of JavaScript. Authors can create objects and events in their documents that might be created by using Java, but with much less effort.

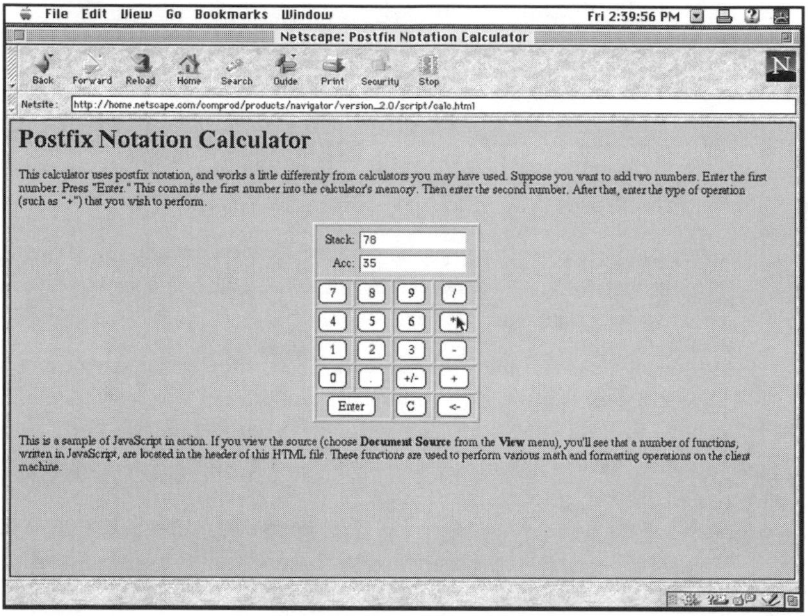

FIG. 12.6

You run this Postfix Notation calculator by using JavaScript.

In effect, these calculators are forms, but with much more interactivity than most forms you'll find on the Web. Most allow you to enter information and click a button to send the information. But these JavaScript examples do more; they respond by returning the results of your actions directly to the form. They work just like a calculator. (Of course, you have to understand reverse Postfix notation to use the first one; read the instructions above the calculator).

A Word About Cookies

Java and JavaScript can send something to your computer that's known as a *cookie*. A cookie is a bit of information that's stored in a file on your hard drive somewhere, often in a file called Cookie.txt (it depends on the browser and operating system being used). In theory, this is perfectly safe, because there are various limitations on Cookie.txt; there's a size limit, and a limit to how much information a Web site can store in the file.

The Cookie.txt file can be used to store information about the Web site and your visit. It might store the date you visited the site, for instance; the next time you visit it the Web site will be able to look in the Cookie.txt file and figure out how long it has been since you've been there. It may also be able to see what you did the last time you visited the site, and present information accordingly.

You have the choice whether to accept a cookie or not. When the server tries to send a cookie to you, a dialog box may appear telling you that the server is sending a cookie, telling you what the cookie will contain (though it may be unintelligible to you), and asking if you want to accept the cookie. The warning box is turned off by default; choose Edit, Preferences, then click Advanced in the Category list (see Figure 12.7). In the Cookies section of the Advanced pane, you'll see a Warn Me Before Accepting a Cookie check box; check this to see the warning message each time. The problem is, though, so many sites send cookies these days that you'll continually be seeing the warning box. You can refuse cookies altogether if you want. Look at the option buttons. You can Accept All Cookies, or Disable Cookies. You can also choose Accept Only Cookies That Get Sent Back to the Originating Server. This means that cookie information can be sent back only to the server that originally sent the information, not to another server. (Note, however, that there are already limitations built into the cookie system, and Web servers cannot generally retrieve information set by another server.) See Chapter 11 for information about security issues related to cookies.

FIG. 12.7
You can refuse cookies if you want, or choose to see a warning.

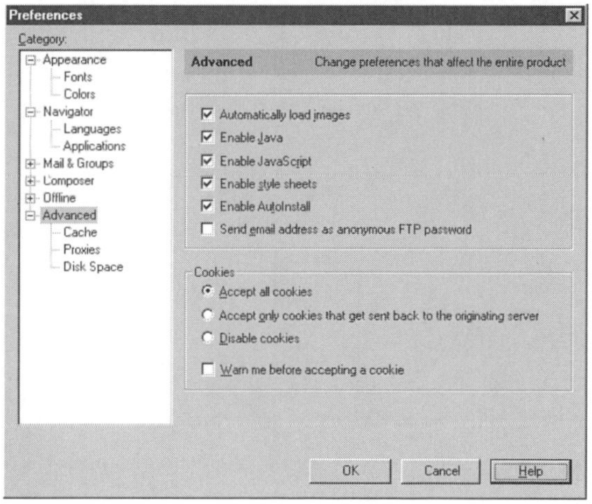

Putting It All Together—LiveConnect

I just want to say a little about LiveConnect, not because it's terribly important that you know about this feature, but because it's a word you'll see when reading through Netscape's marketing blurbs (and because I want the word LiveConnect to appear in this book's index!).

LiveConnect is the term that Netscape Communications has given to the ability of Java and JavaScript to communicate with each other. A JavaScript applet can communicate with a Java applet and vice versa. And both can use and communicate with plug-ins and inline objects.

That's all there is to it. It's really not a user feature; it's a developer feature, but it's a nice bit of marketing jargon that sounds good and helps to fill press releases. There's no way for you to "activate" LiveConnect. You'll only use LiveConnect if you run across a Java or JavaScript application that uses LiveConnect—and even then, you may not realize that LiveConnect is in action.

ActiveX: Microsoft's Answer to Java

ActiveX is Microsoft's answer to Java. It's another system for adding programs to Web sites, though it's nowhere near as popular as Java yet. It seems likely—perhaps I should say certain—that ActiveX will become very popular over the next year or two, as Microsoft pumps into the Internet enough money to buy a small country and as the Internet Explorer browser (the only browser that currently works with ActiveX) grows in popularity.

One reason for ActiveX's current lack of use, relatively speaking, is the fact that Netscape Navigator, the browser that most Web users work with, cannot run ActiveX programs. You can, if you want, install the NCompass scriptActive plug-in. This will run ActiveX, though perhaps not as well as a true ActiveX browser. For information about scriptActive, see Chapter 10. And, once you've installed it, go to **http://www-a.gamelan.com/pages/Gamelan.related. activex.html** to find examples and information about ActiveX. ●

The Internet: More than Just the Web

CHAPTER 13

Desktop Web Access: Using Netcaster

Communicator introduces a brand-new program to the Netscape family of Web tools: Netcaster. This program brings the Web to you. Rather than having to "travel" out onto the Web, back to sites you've visited before in order to find the information you need, you can tell Netcaster to do it for you. This is known as "push" technology; in theory, information from the Web is "pushed" to your desktop rather than you going to get it for yourself (actually the program grabs it for you automatically; but still, "push" is the popular word). There are a number of other push products that you may have heard of, such as PointCast, Castanet, and WebSprite. In fact, Communicator incorporates some of the Castanet technology. ■

Channels and updates

Netcaster manages "channels" that have been created from Web pages. Netcaster automatically updates the channels, getting the latest pages from the Web sites.

Adding channels

Channels can be added by choosing from a list provided by Netscape, or by configuring *any* Web site you want.

Displaying channels

Channels may be displayed at any time, by putting them in a browser window or in a Webtop, a special screen that replaces your operating system's desktop.

An Introduction to Netcaster

Netcaster is a Java applet that manages Web "channels." Each channel is a different Web page or Web site; in fact, you can set up a channel to retrieve one or more pages, several "layers" into a Web site. A channel can be displayed in a browser window, or as a Webtop display, a sort of desktop wallpaper. The channel is displayed when you select it from the Netcaster control panel, known as the *drawer*. And the channel is updated automatically, according to your specifications—every 30 minutes, every 12 hours, every week, and so on.

This is an interesting new program that can be very useful if you need frequent updates from specific Web sites; news, weather, and stock prices are the usual examples given for these technologies, but the Web sites you set up as channels can be *anything* you please—the Dilbert Web site, your best friend's Web site, your corporate Web site, and so on.

At the time of writing, the only version of Communicator that has Netcaster is the Windows 95/NT version, though that will change soon, with Windows 3.1 and Macintosh versions coming soon.

> **CAUTION**
> Netcaster was not included in the first public release of Communicator, upon which this book is based. Therefore, the information in the Netcaster section is based on preliminary beta-test information. The final release version of Netcaster may differ from this beta version in subtle or even significant ways.

Starting Netcaster

There are several ways to start Netcaster.

- Use the Netcaster icon in the Communicator folder.
- In any Communicator window, select Communicator, Netcaster.
- Set up Netcaster to open automatically each time you start your operating system. In Windows, you can do that by adding the Netcaster icon to your Startup program group (Windows 3.1) or menu (Windows 95 and NT). A startup option may be added to the Communicator Preferences soon, too.

You can see the Netcaster drawer in Figure 13.1. This is where you select the channels you want to add to your system, and where you pick the ones you want to view from your collection. This box is an "always on top" box, so it obscures whatever is below (at the time of writing, there is no option for changing this box so it is not always on top, but it might be available later).

However, note the little tab on the left side of the drawer; click this tab to hide the drawer. The tab will remain visible, at the edge of your computer screen; click it again to bring the drawer back.

FIG. 13.1
The Netcaster drawer is where you select channels.

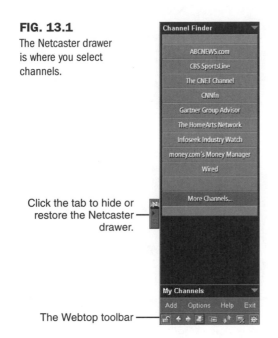

Click the tab to hide or restore the Netcaster drawer.

The Webtop toolbar

Adding Channels

The Netcaster drawer window has two sets of channels: Channel Finder and My Channels. My Channels is a list of channels that you've set up, channels that will automatically be updated for you and which are available for viewing at any time. The Channel Finder presents a list of popular channels from which you can select—so you can quickly add, say, the ABCNEWS.com channel, or the Home Arts Network, or one of a number of other channels already waiting for you.

You'll see in Figure 13.1 that the Netcaster drawer has two headings, each with a little triangle next to it; click this triangle to open that section of the drawer. For instance, click the triangle next to Channel Finder to see all the preselected channels.

There are actually two ways to add channels; you can pick one from the Channel Finder, but you can also set up any Web page you want as a channel. Let's look at both methods, starting with the Channel Finder.

Using the Channel Finder

Click the triangle next to Channel Finder to see all the preselected channels. If you'd like more information about a channel that is listed, click that entry and it will open up and display a logo or more details (see Figure 13.2).

FIG. 13.2
Click a channel button, then click +ADD CHANNEL to add the channel to your collection.

 If you decide you want to add the channel, click the + ADD CHANNEL button. You'll see another window, perhaps one that actually explains what the channel is all about. If you decide that you definitely want this channel, click the Add Channel button that you'll see near the top of the window; otherwise, click Cancel (see Figure 13.3).

FIG. 13.3
When you use the +ADD CHANNEL button in the drawer, another window opens and shows more information; click Add Channel to use this channel.

When you click the Add Channel button, you'll see the dialog box in Figure 13.4. This shows the name of the channel you're adding—you can change it if you want; this is simply the text that will appear in the My Channels drawer. It also shows the URL of the page you're adding. Note that you can tell Netcaster how often to update this channel—in other words, how often to automatically reload the Web page you're defining as this channel. Select an interval in the drop-down list box, from every 30 minutes to every week.

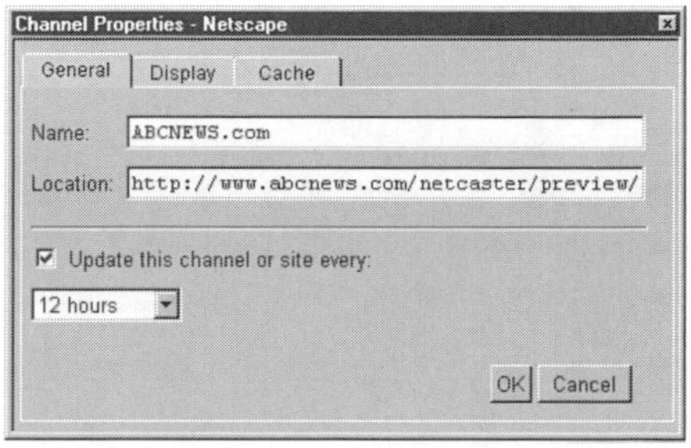

FIG. 13.4

Tell Netcaster how often to update the channel.

Click the Display tab to see the pane in Figure 13.5. This allows you to define how the Web page will appear—in a Default Window or in a Webtop Window. If it's displayed in a Default Window, it will appear in a normal browser window. But if it's in a Webtop Window, it appears on the desktop, as a sort of desktop wallpaper.

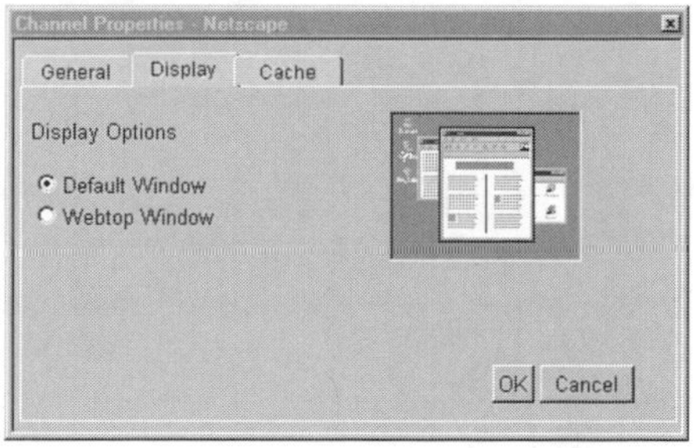

FIG. 13.5

Pick the window type.

Click the Cache tab to see the information in Figure 13.6. This allows you to set the size of Netcaster's special cache—it's separate from the cache used by Navigator (see Chapter 3 for information about the Navigator cache). But it also allows you to define how many "levels" deep the channel should go. For instance, if the channel goes one level deep, it will contain the main page only. If it goes two levels deep, it will contain the main page, plus all the pages linked to by that page. If it goes three levels deep, it will contain the main page, all pages linked to by the main page, and all pages linked to by *those* pages. Downloading several layers can make a channel *very* big, but it makes it quicker to read the pages. For instance, if you're downloading a news channel, you'll be able to see the headlines on the main page, *and* read the associated story. You'll be able to do that online or offline, and even if you are offline, the news stories won't have to be transferred across the Web; they'll come from the cache.

FIG. 13.6

Configure the cache and the number of levels that should be transferred from the site.

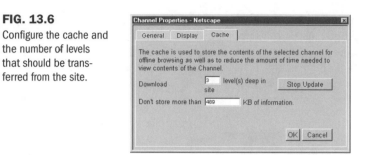

TIP Be careful with the levels setting. The channels you see in the Channel Finder have been created especially for Netcaster, so going down three levels is probably not a problem. But if you set up your own channels, going down three levels may be a real problem with some Web pages if they contain a lot of links.

Notice also that there's a Stop Update button that can be used later to stop a channel transfer (to open a channel's Properties dialog box later, open the My Channels area of the drawer, right-click the channel name, and select Properties).

By the way, if you *don't* see a channel that interests you in the Channel Finder, you can click the More Channels button in the drawer, and a Navigator window will open. This will show you more available channels, and also show a list of channels that will be available soon (see Figure 13.7).

FIG. 13.7

The drawer's More Channels button opens a page showing you (surprise) more channels.

TIP You may have problems with the display of colors in these Netcaster windows. As I mentioned, these are Java applets, so they don't work in quite the same way as the normal Communicator windows. The applets' color-display functions are not working well, at least in Windows. You may have to switch out of Netcaster, then switch back, to get the color to display correctly.

Adding Any Web Page

You can specify any Web page you want as a channel. In other words, you can have Netcaster automatically retrieve information from whichever of the tens of millions of Web pages are most important to you. To specify a Web page as a channel, simply click the Add button in the drawer, and you'll see the dialog box we saw before in Figure 13.3. Type a name for the Web page (whatever you want to appear in the My Channels area of the drawer), then type the URL of the page you want in the Location text box, set up whatever configuration options you want, and click OK. That's all there is to it.

Using Your Channels

To work with your channels, click the triangle in the My Channels bar in the drawer; you'll see a list of your channels (see Figure 13.8).

FIG. 13.8
Here's the list of channels you've added. Notice the little squares on some of the entries; these indicate a Webtop channel.

Channel Finder	▼
My Channels	▼
Netscape Channel	
ABCNEWS.com	
Macmillan	▣
Money Manager	▣

Add   Options   Help   Exit

Click the channel you want to view, and it will open. If you defined it as a Default Window channel, then a browser window opens; this is a good setting if you have a channel from which you often need to begin a Web session. If you defined a channel as a Webtop channel, though, all your windows and icons are replaced with a Webtop window, as you can see in Figure 13.9.

FIG. 13.9

Webtop windows take over your computer desktop.

You can use the Webtop just like a Web page in the browser; it's just that this Web page has taken over your screen, with the exception of the icons you can see in the lower-right part of the screen; the Netcaster tab, the Webtop toolbar, and a Netscape icon.

The Webtop toolbar contains these buttons that are used to manage a Webtop session:

 Displays Security information for a page displayed on the Webtop.

 The Webtop browser's Back button, to display the previous page.

 The Webtop's Forward button.

 Prints the current Webtop page.

 Displays or hides the Webtop; when you hide the Webtop your normal desktop reappears.

Moves the Webtop to the front or back (in front of or behind the normal operating system desktop). This feature is not currently working.

 Closes the Webtop.

 Opens a Navigator window.

Click links as normal to move around using the Webtop. You can also use the normal Navigator pop-up window to select commands.

Updating and Configuring Channels

You can modify a channel by selecting a command from a pop-up menu; right-click the channel name under My Channels and then select Delete (to remove the channel) or Properties (to modify the channel name, and the window and cache settings).

TIP Although the Mac version of Netcaster is not currently working, it appears that in the Macintosh version the pop-up menu will probably be available by pressing Option and then clicking the channel name.

You can also make Netcaster update the channel immediately, rather than having to wait for the next scheduled upates. From the pop-up menu select Start Update. You can cancel the update using Stop Update. You can also modify channels from Netcaster's Options dialog box, which we'll look at now.

Setting Netcaster's Options

Click the Options button at the bottom of the Netcaster drawer to see the dialog box in Figure 13.10. The Channels pane contains a list of your channels; click one and then use the buttons to set the properties, update the channel, or delete the channel. You can also add a new channel from here.

FIG. 13.10
You can also work with channels in Netcaster's Options dialog box.

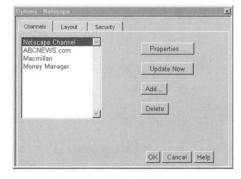

Part **III**
Ch **13**

Click the Layout tab to see the information in Figure 13.11. This area allows you to set up your overall Netcaster layout. You can select one of the options from the Attach Netcaster Drawer To drop-down list box; it can be on the left or right side of your screen (it's on the right by default). You can do the same for the Webtop, attaching it to the left or right of the screen.

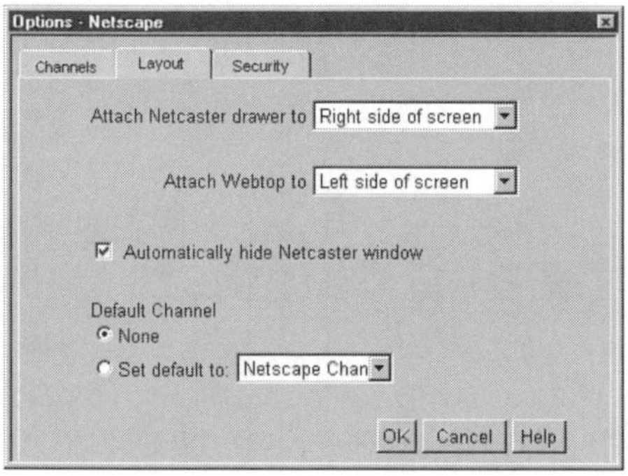

FIG. 13.11

You can also set up your layout in Netcaster's Options dialog box.

By default, the Netcaster window is hidden whenever you open a Webtop channel. You can keep the drawer visible by clearing the Automatically Hide Netcaster Window check box.

Finally, you can set up a default channel, one that will open each time you start Netcaster; simply select the Set Default To option button, then choose the channel from the drop-down list box.

Click the Security tab to see the settings in Figure 13.12. Netcaster uses technology from another "push" product called Castanet. This dialog box allows you to make certain Castanet settings.

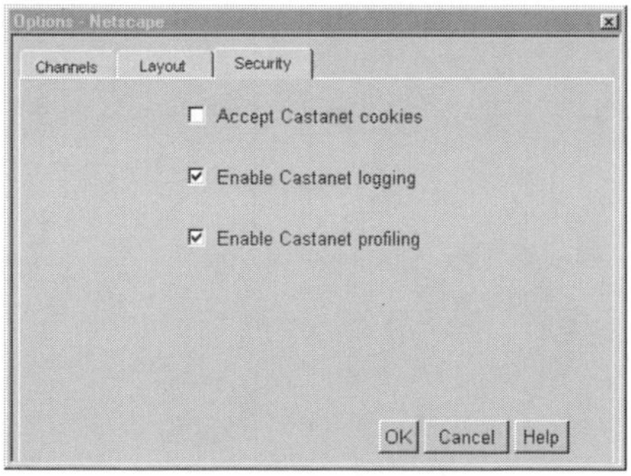

FIG. 13.12

Castanet settings can be made here.

CHAPTER 14

Accessing Files with FTP

The World Wide Web is relatively new to the Internet; there were plenty of other services running across the Internet long before the Web came along. Yet Web browsers have become the program of choice for users. The Web has taken the place of some of these services to a degree…but not completely. So Web browsers have become more than just Web browsers. They can now be used to work with a variety of non-Web services. The obvious services are e-mail and newsgroups, and we'll be looking at those in Chapters 16 to 18. But there are other services that are not quite so obvious; things like FTP, Archie, Gopher, Telnet, and more. That's what we'll be looking at in the next few chapters. And we'll start with one of the Internet's oldest services, File Transfer Protocol, more commonly known as FTP. ■

Using other Internet resources through Navigator

The http:// URL is not the only one; there are other URLs you'll see, such as ftp://, gopher://, telnet://, and mailto:. These URLs can be typed into the Location box, in the same way you do when going to a Web page.

Working with FTP

FTP provides access to huge file libraries all over the world. FTP used to be complicated; working through a Web browser it's just point and click.

Using Archie to search for computer files

There are thousands of FTP sites, millions of computer files spread throughout the world. How can you find the file you need? Using a service called Archie.

Using Other URL Types

So far in this book you've seen the standard http:// URLs. When your Web browser sees an URL that begins with http://, it knows that the destination is a Web document. But some URLs begin with other protocols, such as the following:

- *gopher://*   Takes you to a Gopher menu system (see Chapter 15).
- *ftp://*   Takes you to an FTP (File Transfer Protocol) site—a site set up so that you can transfer files back to your computer.
- *mailto:*   Used to send e-mail (see Chapter 16).
- *news:*   A special newsgroup protocol that enables you to read newsgroups from Web browsers (see Chapter 18).
- *telnet://*   Starts a Telnet session, in which you can log in to another computer on the Internet (see Chapter 15).
- *tn3270://*   Starts a tn3270-mode session, which is very similar to Telnet. (You're connecting to a different type of computer: an IBM 3270.) See Chapter 15.
- *wais://*   A relatively little-used URL. WAIS stands for Wide Area Information Servers—systems that are used to search databases. Navigator can use the wais:// protocol if you have a special proxy set up; if not, you can still use WAIS through special gateways.

N O T E   A *gateway* is a system linking one computer network with another or one networking system with another. Even though Navigator can't directly access WAIS sites, a gateway provides a way for it to receive information from a WAIS site. ▨

T I P   Note that the news: and mailto: URLs don't have // at the end. Earlier versions of Navigator allowed you to enter them into the Location box with the // (news:// and mailto://); at the time of writing, this seems to work for mailto://, but not for news://, so try to remember that these URLs do not generally have the slashes at the end.

In other words, you can use Navigator to access systems that are not true Web systems. You can use Gopher, FTP, and Telnet; you can send e-mail from Web links; and you can read newsgroup messages. There are even special gateways through the Web to systems for which your Web browser isn't prepared. For instance, your Web browser cannot communicate directly with Archie, a system used to search FTP sites for computer files. (You type a file name, and Archie tells you where to find it.) But there are Web documents that do the work for you by using forms. You type the name of the file into a form, and a special program at the Web server communicates with Archie for you (see "How Can I Find Files? Working with Archie," later in this chapter, for information about Archie).

Finding Internet Resources

If you'd like to find the sort of non-Web resources that you can get to through the Web, take a look at some of the following documents.

Inter-Links   Select a category to see lists of related documents and tools (**http:// www.nova.edu/Inter-Links/**).

Directory of Service Types   If you want to see where you can use WAIS, newsgroups, Gopher, Telnet, FTP, Whois, and other Internet services through your Web browsers, take a look at this Web document (**http://www.w3.org/hypertext/DataSources/ByAccess.html**).

ArchiePlex   This is a directory of ArchiePlex servers throughout the world—servers that let you search Archie directly from the Web. You'll find sites for browsers both with and without forms support (**http://web.nexor.co.uk/archie.html**).

The Yahoo! Web Gateways Page   This lists dozens of different gateway sites, ways to use your Web browser to use non-Web resources, from IRC to Finger, Lotus Notes to Teletext (**http:// www.yahoo.com/Computers_and_Internet/Internet/World_Wide_Web/Gateways/**).

Internet Resources—Meta-Index   This is a list of directories containing references to various Internet resources: the Web, Gopher, Telnet, FTP, and more (**http://www.ncsa.uiuc.edu/ SDG/Software/Mosaic/MetaIndex.html**).

FTP: The Internet's File Library

We've already seen how to transfer files from the Web back to your computer (see Chapter 8). The Web contains many files that you might find useful—shareware and demo programs, clip art, press releases, music, video, and plenty more.

But before the Web was born, there was already a system for grabbing files from the Internet: *FTP* (File Transfer Protocol). Using this system, you can log on to a computer somewhere on the Internet and then transfer files back to your computer.

There are many publicly accessible software archives on the Internet, which are known as *anonymous FTP* sites. With an FTP program, you can log in to a public FTP site by using the account name anonymous and then typing your e-mail address as the password. Those unfortunate souls still using the Internet through a UNIX command line actually type these entries when they log on to an FTP site. But Navigator can automate FTP sessions; Navigator will automatically log on to an FTP site for you.

TIP   Generally, your e-mail address is used for a password during anonymous FTP sessions. However, by default Navigator doesn't use your e-mail address during FTP sessions—it uses another generic word (such as *guest*). If you want to use your e-mail address, choose Edit, Preferences, click Advanced in the Category list, then click the Send Email Address as Anonymous FTP Password check box. You'll also have to enter your e-mail address into Mail & Groups (open that Category and then click Identity)—if you don't, Navigator will continue as normal using the generic word.

For example, here are a couple of FTP sites that contain many Windows shareware utilities:

ftp.winsite.com/pub/pc/win95/

ftp.wustl.edu/systems/ibmpc/win3

These sites have Macintosh software:

ftp://oak.oakland.edu/pub/macintosh/

ftp://mac.archive.umich.edu

ftp://sumex-aim.stanford.edu/info-mac/

ftp://wuarchive.wustl.edu

However, if you're looking for shareware, you should really check the Web sites first, such as Jumbo, Sharware.com, Tucows, and so on (see Chapter 10).

You might want to go to the **http://hoohoo.ncsa.uiuc.edu/ftp/** Web page, the Monster FTP Sites list, to find thousands of FTP sites. Or try the **http://www.yahoo.com/ Computers_and_Internet/Internet/FTP_Sites/** page. In general, though, you probably won't go to FTP sites looking for files. It's more likely that you'll use an FTP site that has been connected to from a Web page, or be given an FTP site address by a friend or colleague, or perhaps find an FTP address listed in a magazine.

Using an FTP Site

What does all the information in an ftp:// URL mean? It's pretty much the same as a Web URL. First, there's the ftp:// bit; that simply means, "this is an FTP site." Then there's the FTP site name (or host name): ftp.winsite.com, for instance. This identifies the computer that contains the files you are after. Then there's the directory name: /pub/pc/win95/. This tells you which directory you must change to in order to find the files.

FTP Path Names Use Forward Slashes

If you're used to working in DOS and Windows, FTP site directory names may appear pretty strange for two reasons. First, I've used a forward slash (/) rather than a backslash (\) to separate each directory in the path. In the DOS world, you use a backslash (\), but in the UNIX world—and most of the Internet still runs on UNIX computers—the forward slash character (/) is used instead.

Also, the directory names are often long. In DOS and Windows 3.1 you can't have directories with more than 12 characters in the name (including a period and an extension). Of course, in UNIX, Windows 95 and Windows NT, and on the Mac, you can, because these operating systems allow long file and directory names.

There are two ways to use the Web browser for an FTP session. You'll either click a link to an FTP site that some kind Web author has provided, or type an FTP URL in the Location text box and press Enter.

Let's say, for example, that you want to go the wuarchive.wustl.edu FTP site to see what shareware is available. You would type **ftp://wuarchive.wustl.edu/** into the Location text box and press Enter. Watch the status bar, and you'll see a progress message (Connect: Contacting Host). When you connect, you'll see something like Figure 14.1. (This site has a text message at the top of the directory listing; I scrolled down so you could see more of the files and directories.)

TIP As with the http:// URL, you don't always need to include ftp://. If the FTP site name begins with ftp, you can omit the ftp:// bit. For instance, you can type **ftp.winsite.com/pub/pc/win95/** instead of **ftp://ftp.winsite.com/pub/pc/win95/**.

FIG. 14.1
You can use Navigator as an FTP program.

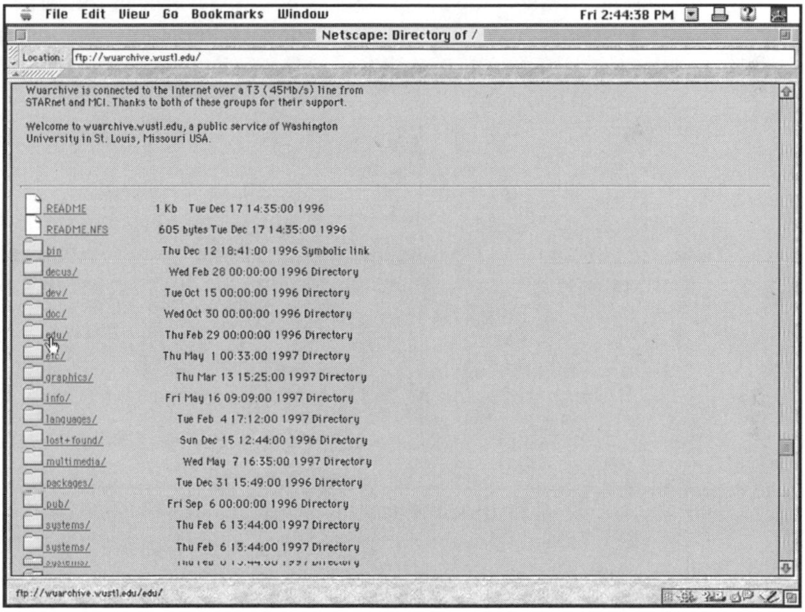

What You'll Find at an FTP Site

Each file and directory at an FTP site is shown as a link. On the left side of the window, you'll see a column of icons: Plain white sheets represent files of most kinds, white sheets with writing on them represent text files, white sheets with little colored symbols (a circle, triangle, and square) represent graphic files, white sheets with ones and zeroes represent program files, and yellow folders represent directories.

On the right side of the window, you'll also see a column with descriptions of each item (you may need to scroll to the right to see them), such as the following:

■ *Binary executable*   A program file.

■ *Compressed files*   A UNIX .z compressed file.

Part
III

Ch
14

- *Directory*   This represents a directory on the hard disk, which may contain files and subdirectories.
- *GIF Image*   A .gif file.
- *GNU zip compressed data*   A .gZ file, which is a compressed archive file used on UNIX systems.
- *Hypertext Markup Language*   An .htm or .Html file; click this and it'll be displayed in the browser.
- *JPEG Image*   A .jpg or .jpeg image file. The type of image used in Web pages; click to view an image in the browser.
- *BinHex*   An .hqx file, which is an ASCII text file that contains some form of binary file—a program file, graphics file,and so on—that has been converted to ASCII so it can be transferred across the Internet's e-mail system. BinHex is commonly used on Macintosh systems. In the UNIX and PC world, a similar system that is equivalent is UUENCODE (see Chapter 16).
- *Macintosh StuffIt*   A .sit file, which is a compressed archive file used on Macintosh systems.
- *Plain text*   A text file; click this file to read the file in the Navigator window.
- *Symbolic link*   These are special files, allowed by UNIX, that act as links to another directory and provide shortcuts through the directory system. Selecting a symbolic link is the same thing as selecting a directory.
- *TAR archives*   A .TAR file, which is another form of UNIX archive file.
- *ZIP compressed data*   A .zip file containing compressed data.

If there's no description shown for an item, then the item is a file of some other kind, one that Navigator doesn't recognize. But you may see various other descriptions, ones not shown here. Navigator looks at the list of plug-ins to see if you've set up one for the file type. For example, if you see a .spl file, it's probably a FutureSplash animation file. If you haven't configured the FutureSplash plug-in, the description will be blank; if you have, then the description will say FutureSplash.

You'll find more information about an entry, too. You can see that the file or directory's date and time of creation is shown (the date is very handy, providing an indication of how old the file is, and, therefore, whether it's worth downloading). And the size of each file, in bytes or kilobytes, is also shown.

Click a directory link to see the contents of that directory. Navigator will display another Web document showing the contents of that directory. There's also a link back to the previous directory—the Up to a higher level directory link, at the top of the listing. (This is not the same as the browser's Back command, of course. It takes you to the parent directory, the one of which the current directory is a subdirectory.)

TIP Don't forget Archie! Archie is a system that lets you search an index of FTP sites throughout the world for just the file you need. For more information, see "How Can I Find Files? Working with Archie," later in this chapter.

What happens when you click a link to a file? The same thing that would happen if you did so from a true Web document. If Navigator can display or play the file type, it will; if it can't, it will try to send it to the associated application. If there is no associated application, it will ask you what to do with it, allowing you to save it on your hard disk or define a new viewer. For instance, if you've set up WinZip as the viewer for .zip files, then when you click a link to a .zip file, Navigator transfers the file and opens WinZIP. If no viewer is set up for these files, then Navigator will ask what you want to do with them. If you click a link to an .exe file, Navigator asks you where you want to save it. See Chapter 9 for more information about how Navigator handles file transfers—whether the file is coming from a Web site or FTP site, the procedure's the same.

How Can I Find My Way Around?

Finding your way around at an FTP site is often a little difficult. There are no conventions for how such sites should be set up, so you often have to dig through directories that look as if they might contain what you want until you find what you're looking for.

Remember, though, that Navigator can display text files. When you first get to an FTP site, look for files that say Index, Readme, Directory, and so on. These often contain information that helps you find what you need. The more organized sites even contain full indexes of their contents, or at least a list of the directories and the types of files you'll find. And you'll sometimes find messages at the top of the directory explaining where to find the files you need. Click a text file in the Navigator window, and that file will be displayed. Then click the browser's Back button to return to the directory.

 TIP Many FTP sites are now accessible directly through Web documents. For example, instead of going to **ftp:// ftp.winsite.com/**, you could go to **http://www.winsite.com/**.

How Can I Use a Private FTP Site?

Many Internet users have private accounts at FTP sites. For instance, Que has given me a username and password so that I can access a private area of Que's FTP site. How can I use Navigator to get into that FTP site?

There are two ways. I can enter both my username and password in the URL, or just enter my username and let Navigator prompt me for the password. Here's how to do each one.

To create an URL in which you enter both your username and password, format it like this: **ftp:/ /username:password@ftp.site**. For instance, **ftp://pkent:23&*^12@ftp.mcp.com**. Press Enter; Navigator will connect to the site, passing the username and password information to the FTP host when prompted (you won't see it pass the information, it all happens in the background).

You can also enter the information like this: **ftp://username@ftp.site** (for instance, **ftp://pkent@ftp.mcp.com**). This time, when you press Enter, Navigator will display a small dialog box prompting you for your password; type it and press Enter again to continue. You might want to use this method if you work in a situation where people might be looking over your shoulder! When you type the password into the dialog box, each character you type is represented by an asterisk, so nobody can read what you are typing. (Type carefully.)

CAUTION

In some versions of Navigator, URLs typed into the Location box are saved and can be retrieved by clicking the little down arrow at the end; you'll find your ftp password there, too, if you use the first method!

Also, be careful after visiting a private FTP site; you may want to close Navigator so that the private site is cleared from the history list. If you walk away from your computer without closing Navigator, someone could use the history list to break into your site.

 Navigator's private-site FTP features are limited; though you can upload files, you can't delete files and create directories, for instance. So if you want a program designed specifically for FTP, go to one of the shareware sites mentioned in Chapter 10 and search, under your operating-system category, for the word ftp. You should find several options you can try. In the Windows world, WS_FTP is well known and very good. You might also try CuteFTP. In the Macintosh world, Fetch is very popular.

Uploading Files

You've seen how to download files from FTP sites to your computer, but how about going the other way, uploading files from your computer to the FTP site? For instance, I can upload files to the Que FTP site.

To upload a file to your private directory, simply choose File, Upload File. You'll see a dialog box from which you can select the file to upload (currently only one file at a time). When you select the file, Navigator transfers the file.

TIP To upload multiple files, position Windows Explorer and Navigator so you can view both. Connect to your FTP site in Navigator, and then drag multiple files from Explorer onto the Navigator window.

How Can I Find Files? Working with Archie

With millions of files to choose from and thousands of FTP sites spread around the Internet, it's difficult to know where to go to find the file you need. That's why Archie was developed.

Designed at McGill University in Canada, *Archie* is a system that indexes FTP sites, listing the files that are available at each site. Archie lists several million files at thousands of FTP sites and provides a surprisingly quick way to find out where to go to grab a file. Well, sometimes. As you'll find out, Archie is extremely busy and sometimes too busy to help you.

More Client/Server Stuff

As with many other Internet systems, Archie is set up using a *client/server* system. An Archie *server* is a computer that periodically takes a look at all the Internet FTP sites around the world and builds a list of all their available files. Each server builds a database of those files. An Archie *client* program can then come along and search the server's database, using it as an index. Your Web browser is *not* an Archie client. That is, there is no archie:// URL! Rather, you'll have to use an Archie interface on the Web. There are dozens of these. Go to **http:// pubweb.nexor.co.uk/public/archie/servers.html** to find a list. Just in case that's busy, the following are several Archie sites you can try:

> **http://www.lerc.nasa.gov/archieplex/**
>
> **http://hoohoo.ncsa.uiuc.edu/archie.html**
>
> **http://src.doc.ic.ac.uk/archieplexform.html**

When you arrive at an Archie site, what sort of search are you going to do? Most of these sites offer both forms and non-forms versions. Navigator is a forms-capable browser; that is, it can display the forms components we've seen earlier: text boxes, command buttons, option buttons, and so on. So select the forms search.

> **T I P** Many Internet users believe that it doesn't matter much which Archie server you work with because they all do much the same thing; some are simply a few days more recent than others. This isn't always true. Sometimes you may get very different results from two different servers. If, for example, one server finds two *hits*, another might find seven.

How Do I Search?

In Figure 14.2, you can see an example of an Archie form, this one at the NASA Lewis Research Center located at **http://www.lerc.nasa.gov/archieplex/doc/form.html**. The simplest way to search is to type a file name or part of a file name into the Search For text box and click the Submit button. For instance, if you are trying to find the WS_FTP program that I told you about earlier in this chapter, you can type WS_FTP and press Enter.

> **T I P** To cancel a search, click the Stop toolbar button or press Esc.

Archie searches are often very slow. In fact, they often simply don't work because the Archie server you are working with is busy (I'll show you how to choose another server in a moment). If you are lucky, though, you'll eventually see something like Figure 14.3. This shows what the Archie server found: links to the WS_FTP files. You can see that there are links to the host (the computer that contains the file you are looking for), the directory on the host that contains the file you want, and takes you directly to the file you want. For example, if you clicked one of the Ws_ftp.zip links, Navigator would begin transferring the file.

Part
III

Ch
14

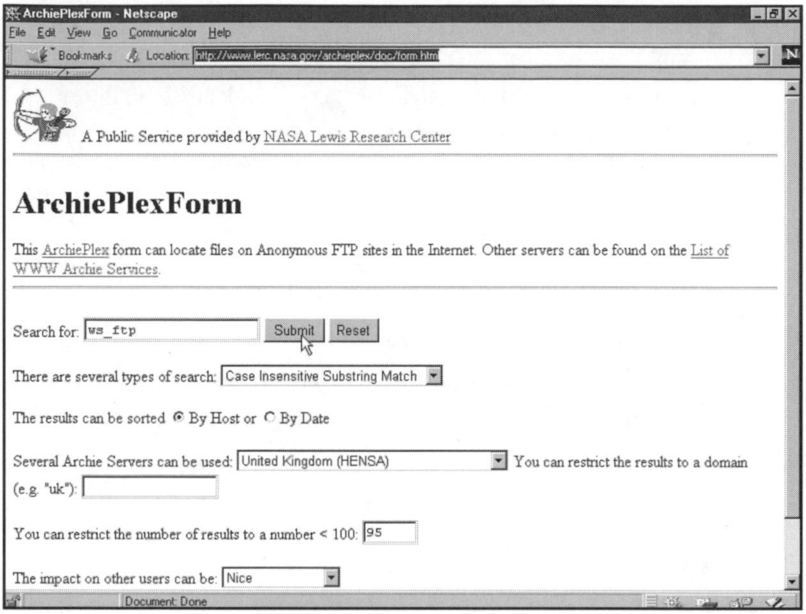

FIG. 14.2
The dozens of Archie Web sites provide a way for you to search Archie from your browser.

FIG. 14.3
If you're lucky, when Archie responds, you'll get a list of sites and files.

TIP Remember, you can choose Edit, Find In Page, to search the list of files. For instance, if you have Windows 95 and are searching for WS_FTP, you don't really want the Ws_ftp.zip files; those are probably the 16-bit versions for Windows 3.1. Rather, search the page for WS_FTP32 to find the 32-bit versions for Windows 95.

Archie's Options

The Archie form (refer to Figure 14.2) has other components that provide more options for your search. You'll find the following:

- *There Are Several Types of Search* There are four types of searches, which I'll explain in a moment.

- *The Results Can Be Sorted* The list of files that is returned to you may be sorted By Host (alphabetically by hostname) or By Date (chronologically by file date). The file-date search is a good idea, as it will help you pick the latest version of the file.

- *Several Archie Servers Can Be Used* There are Archie servers all over the world, and you can select the one you want to use from a list. If one Archie server is busy or it can't find what you want, try another. You might want to try servers in countries that are currently "asleep" and, therefore, less busy than during the day.

- *You Can Restrict the Results to a Domain* You can tell the Archie server that you only want to see files in a particular domain (a particular type of host computer): UK (FTP sites in the United Kingdom), COM (commercial FTP sites), EDU (educational FTP sites), and so on.

- *You Can Restrict the Number of Results to a Number <100* You can tell the Archie server how many results you want to see, though this setting is not always accurate.

- *The Impact on Other Users Can Be* You can tell Archie to be Nice (or Extremely Nice, Nicest, and so on) to other people, or to be Not Nice At All. Presumably this refers to how much of a hurry you are in, and whether you want to push your way as far forward in the queue as possible.

NOTE Each Archie form is a little different—the labels you see may differ from what I've shown here. Still, they're usually close to my example, so you'll be able to figure them out quite easily.

What Are the Search Types? Before you begin searching for a file name, you should figure out the type of search that you want to use. You have the following choices:

- *Exact or Exact Match* You must type the exact name of the file for which you are looking.

- *Regex or Regular Expression Match* You will type a UNIX regular expression. That means that Archie will regard some of the characters in the word you type as wild cards. (If you don't understand regular expressions, you're better off avoiding this type of search.)

Part
III

Ch
14

■ *Sub or Case Insensitive Substring Match*   This tells Archie to search within file names for whatever you type. That is, it will look for all names that match, as well as all names that include the characters you typed. If you are searching for ws_ftp, for example, Archie will find ws_ftp and ws_ftp32. Also, when you use this type of search, you don't need to worry about the case of the characters; Archie will find ws_ftp and WS_FTP. This is, in general, the easiest form of search to work with, so it's normally the default.

■ *Subcase or Case Sensitive Substring Match*   This is like the sub search, except you need to enter the case of the word correctly. For example, if you enter **ws_ftp**, Archie will find ws_ftp but not WS_FTP.

Remember the Find Limit!

The substring matches won't always find file names that contain what you typed. That is, if you type ws_ftp, it may not find ws_ftp32, or it may only find one or two when there are many files named ws_ftp32 at many FTP sites. Why? Because it will show you the ws_ftp matches before it shows you the ws_ftp32 matches; if there are a lot of ws_ftp matches, it may exceed the find limit (see "You Can Restrict The Number Of Results" in the list under "Archie's Options"). You can increase the number of results and search again, though, to see if there are any ws_ftp32 files. Or search for ws_ftp32.

You'll want to use the subsearch (case-insensitive substring match), which is frequently set up as the default. It may take slightly longer than the other types, but it's more likely to find what you are looking for.

You should know, however, that file names are not always set in stone. With thousands of different people posting millions of different files on thousands of different computers, sometimes file names get changed a little. If you have trouble finding something, try a variety of different possible combinations.

T I P   If you are looking for shareware, go to **http://www.shareware.com/**, **http://www.jumbo.com**, **http://www.filez.com** and the other sites listed in Chapter 10. These sites let you search for programs by description rather than by file name.

Why would you ever bother with Archie, when you can so often dig through shareware Web sites to find what you need? Well, Archie sometimes provides a quick way to find a file if you know the file name (or part of the file name), you know that the file is stored at a number of public FTP sites, and the file may not be one that is easy to find at a shareware site. ●

CHAPTER 15

Gopher, Finger, Telnet, and More

We haven't finished with the non-Web services yet—there are more Internet services available through Navigator. Most of these services are old, pre-Web services— Gopher, finger, and Telnet, for instance. But new services, not typically considered to be Web services, are appearing on the scene. In particular, Chat, a service that has been available off the Web for a long time, is now available on the Web. All these services can be accessed through Navigator (though, in some cases, Navigator must launch another application). ■

Gophering around in Gopherspace

Gopher predates the Web. In fact, in 1993 and even well into 1994, Gopher was supposed to be the next big thing on the Internet, the system that would finally make the Internet easy to use. Then came the Web…

Using Finger

Finger provides a very simple way for people to distribute information about themselves, their companies, and their interests.

Chatting through the Web

Chat has come to the Web in a big way. Chat "rooms" are now closely associated with Web sites.

Starting Telnet and tn3270 sessions

Log on to other computers that are connected to the Internet: Play games, search library catalogs, and dig through databases.

Traveling in Gopherspace

Before the World Wide Web become popular (Mosaic wasn't in wide use until the middle of 1994 and Navigator wasn't released until late in 1994), the really easy way to travel around the Internet was through Gopher. Compared to other Internet tools—which were about as easy to use as threading a needle in the dark—Gopher was a revolution.

The Gopher system provided a nice menu system from which users could select options. Instead of remembering a variety of rather obscure and arcane commands, users could use the arrow keys to select options from the menu. Those options could take the user to other menus or to documents of some kind. In fact, the Gopher system is, in some ways, similar to the World Wide Web. It's a worldwide network of menu systems. Options in the menus link to menus or documents all over the world. These Gopher menus made the Internet much easier to use (and accessible to people other than long-time "cybergeeks").

The Gopher system is still alive and well for a couple of good reasons. First, there were already many Gopher systems set up before the Web became popular. Second, there are still millions of Internet users who don't have access to graphical Web browsers, so Gopher tools are the easiest tools available to them. There's a lot of interesting information on Gopher servers around the world—fortunately, you can get to it with Navigator. Navigator may be primarily a Web browser, but you can use the Web to access Gopher.

Digging Around with Gopher

You can get to a Gopher server—a computer that maintains a Gopher menu system—in two ways: by clicking a link that some Web author has provided, or by typing the gopher:// URL into the Address text box and pressing Enter. For instance, typing gopher://wiretap.spies.com/ will take you to the Internet Wiretap Gopher server (see Figure 15.1).

In some cases, you can ignore the gopher:// bit. You've already learned that you can type an URL into the Address text box without including http://. Well, if the Gopher address starts with the word gopher, you can type the address and leave out gopher://. For example, you can type **gopher.usa.net** instead of **gopher://gopher.usa.net**. (Of course, the Wiretap address won't work this way.)

TIP For a list of links to Gopher servers, go to **gopher://gopher.micro.umn.edu/11/ Other%20Gopher%20and%20Information%20Servers**. If you don't want to type all that, go to **http://www.w3.org/hypertext/DataSources/ByAccess.html** and click the Gopher link.

How, then, do you use a Gopher server with Navigator? The Gopher menu options are represented by links. Click the link to select that option. If the option leads to another menu, then that menu is displayed in the window. If it leads to a file of some kind, the file is transferred in the normal way. And if Navigator can display or play it, it does so. If it can't…well, you'd better go back and see Chapters 8 and 9 for more information.

You'll find that most of the documents at Gopher sites are text documents; Navigator can display these text documents within its own window. Of course, you won't find any links to other documents within these text documents—they're not true Web documents, after all—so once you've finished, you'll have to use the Back toolbar button (or Alt+left arrow) to return to the Gopher menu. In Figure 15.2, you can see a text document that I ran across at the Wiretap site. I chose `Electronic Books at Wiretap` and then `Beowulf`.

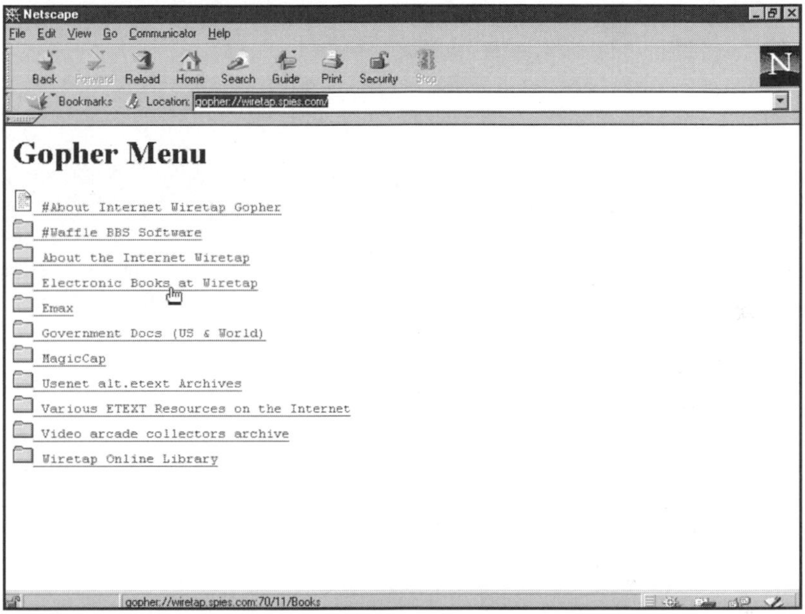

FIG. 15.1
The Wiretap Gopher contains a lot of interesting and strange documents.

FIG. 15.2
If you select a menu option that leads to a text document, you'll see it in the Navigator window.

Notice that the icons to the left of the menu options indicate what each option leads to, as follows:

 The folder represents a menu (or *directory* in Gopherspeak). Click this link to see another Gopher menu.

 The page represents a document or computer file of some kind. Click this link to read the document or view, or to transfer the file.

 The blank document represents an index that you can search. Click this link to see a form for conducting a word search.

Veronica and Jughead

Gopher servers have two types of search tools: Veronica (Very Easy Rodent-Oriented Netwide Index to Computerized Archives) and Jughead (Jonzy's Universal Gopher Hierarchy Excavation And Display). Do these acronyms mean much? No, but you try to create an acronym from a cartoon character's name!

Why *Veronica* and *Jughead*?

They are characters in the famous *Archie* cartoon strip. *Archie* arrived on the Internet first. Archie is a system that enables you to search the Internet for computer files (you learned about Archie in Chapter 14). Why Archie? The legend is that Archie is derived from the word "archive" with the "v" removed. Some say this is not how the name was derived, so who knows? Anyway, the people who created the Gopher search systems figured Archie needed company and named their systems Veronica and Jughead.

Veronica lets you search Gopher servers all over the world. Jughead lets you search the Gopher server you are currently working with (though many Gopher servers don't have Jugheads).

If you want to search Gopherspace—the giant system of Gopher menus that spreads across the Internet—find an appropriate menu option somewhere. For instance, at the **gopher:// gopher.cc.utah.edu/** Gopher site, you'll find menu options that say Search titles in Gopherspace using Veronica and Search menu titles using Jughead. (The Wiretap site is a bad example because it doesn't seem to have links to either Veronica or Jughead.) At other sites, you may have to dig around a little to find the menu options you need. Most sites have at least a link to Veronica.

Both systems are quite easy to use. However, you must understand that Veronica provides two ways to search and also allows you to choose a particular Veronica server. Veronica searches all of Gopherspace—Gopher servers all over the world. Something called a Veronica server stores an index of menu options at all of these Gopher servers, so you are actually searching one of these indexes—and you get to pick which one.

But at the same time, you have to decide whether you want to limit your search. You can search all menu options or only those menu options that lead to other menus. Let's assume, for example, that you went to **gopher://gopher.cc.utah.edu/** and then chose the Search titles in Gopherspace using Veronica option. You'll see something similar to Figure 15.3.

Part
III
Ch
15

FIG. 15.3

Veronica allows you to choose a server and pick the search type.

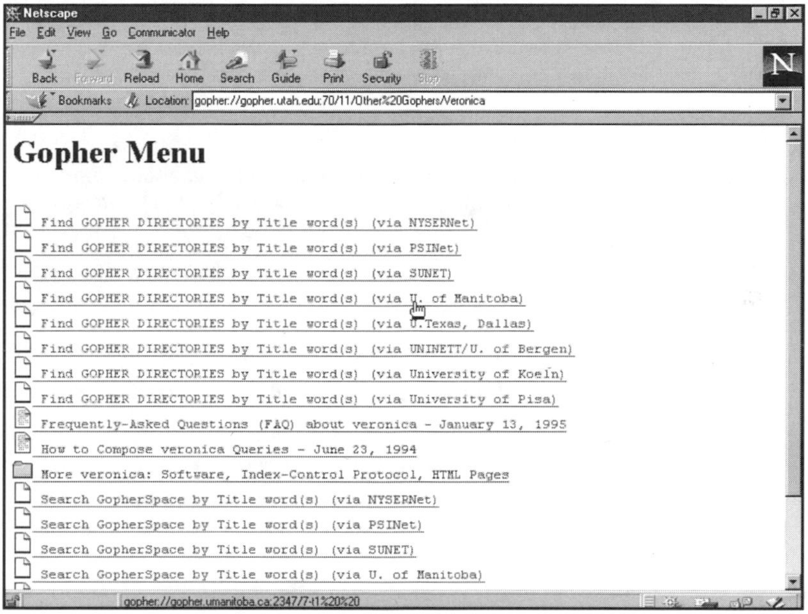

If you now select Find GOPHER DIRECTORIES by Title Word(s) (via U of Manitoba), you will be looking for menu options that lead to other menus (often called *directories* in Gopherspeak) using the University of Manitoba Veronica server. If you select Search GopherSpace by Title Word(s) (via PSINet), you will search all menu options—both directories and options leading to files and documents—at the PSINet Veronica server.

When you make your selection, a box into which you type the keywords appears. You might type electronic books, publishers, sports, or whatever your interest is. Then press Enter and the search begins.

What happens next? Well, there's a good chance you'll get a message saying *** Too many connections—Try again soon. *** or something similar. In this case, try another server. Or perhaps Navigator just seems to wait and wait, and nothing seems to happen. These servers are very busy, so it often takes a long time to get a result. Eventually, with luck, you'll get a list of links you can click to continue moving through Gopherspace to sites and documents related to your interests.

Using Jughead is similar to using Veronica, but easier. You don't get to pick a server or search type; you simply enter the keywords for your search.

N O T E   You can use Boolean operators in your search. Boolean operators allow you to mix keywords and define how they relate to one another. You can search for book or publisher or book and publisher or book not publisher and so on. For more information on how to search, read the information that most Gopher sites place close to the Veronica and Jughead menu options, such as How to Compose Veronica Queries or About Jughead. When using Jughead, you can search for ?help to see a link to the documentation. ■

Finger

The UNIX finger command lets you find information about someone's Internet account. Type **finger username@hostname** at a UNIX prompt and press Enter; you will see information about the user's real name, whether the user is logged on, and so on. More important, you'll see the contents of the user's `.plan` file. This is often used to distribute information about anything that strikes the user's fancy: sports scores, weather, earthquakes, and so on.

You can't use finger directly from Navigator; there's no finger:// URL. But there are finger gateways, such as **http://www-cs.indiana.edu:800/finger/gateway**.

Finger gateways provide a text box into which you can type the address you want to finger. For instance, fingering **smith@hostname** will produce a list of all the Smiths with accounts at that particular host computer. Or you can finger an account that is being used to distribute information. Try **quake@andreas.wr.usgs.gov**, for example. You'll see something like Figure 15.4.

FIG. 15.4

This earthquake report was obtained by fingering.

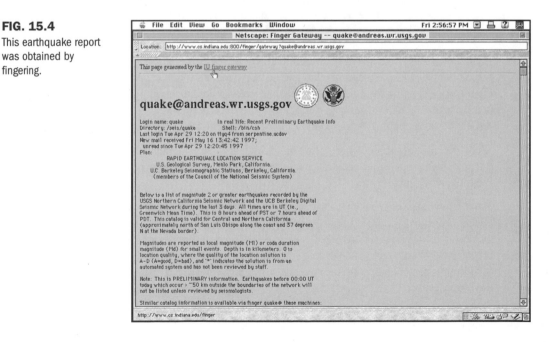

The sort of information you can get back depends on how the machine you are fingering has been set up. Some sites provide a lot of information, some just a little, and some won't give out any finger information at all.

T I P For more finger gateways, search Yahoo! or another search engine (see Chapter 6, "Searching for Information on the Web") for the word finger, or go to **http://www.yahoo.com/ Computers_and_Internet/Internet/World_Wide_Web/Gateways/Finger_Gateways/**.

Some Web pages have links that automatically use a finger gateway to grab finger information from a variety of sources on various subjects: auroral activity, NASA's daily news, a hurricane forecast, earthquake information, and all sorts of other, wonderful information. Unfortunately, it's now difficult to find such lists; as the Web grows, finger becomes much less important as a way of distributing information.

Some finger documents even contain small pictures; although .plan files are text files, they can contain links to images just like HTML Web documents can. If the document is retrieved through the right sort of finger gateway, those images appear in the document when it's displayed in your Web browser.

Chatting Online

A *chat system* is one that allows people to hold "conversations" in real time. You type a message, and others can read it almost immediately and respond to you. It's chatting without, well, the chat. It's chatting through the keyboard.

Chat is a service that still isn't well developed on the Web, but it's growing very quickly. At **http://www.rock.net/webchat/rwchat.html**, for example, you'll find the RockWeb chat system. Or try TalkCity (**http://www.talkcity.com/**), a Web site dedicated to hosting chat sessions. Some chat sites use Web forms to manage the chat sessions; others, such as TalkCity, use Java applications. Either way, you'll type messages into a text box and click a button or press Enter. Your message is sent to the main chat window, where others can see it and respond to it (see Figure 15.5).

On some systems, such as RockWeb's chat system, if you know a bit of HTML, you can even include HTML tags in your message so you can use bold, italic, underline, and so on—even include a link to somewhere. In other words, someone reading your message could click the link in your message to go somewhere else. (If you are going to do this fancy stuff, prepare it beforehand in a word processor, copy it to the Clipboard, and paste it into the chat.)

If you want to be really geeky, you can tell the system to display a picture next to your name each time you "say" something in the conversation. You'll have to provide the picture, though, and enter an URL pointing to the picture on a system somewhere. (From what I've seen, very few people are using the fancy features that are available in this chat system—mostly, it's just plain old text.)

FIG. 15.5
TalkCity is a Web site dedicated to chat. It uses a Java applet to manage the communications.

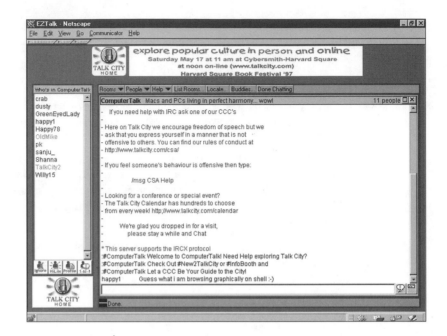

Netscape Chat and Ichat

Netscape Communications has a product called Netscape Chat, which can be integrated into Netscape Navigator. It provides a chat interface through which you can use Internet Relay Chat (an Internet-wide chatting system) or set up your own private chat links (similar to what is known as talk to UNIX users on the Internet). Those private chats can be between two people or an entire group, either with everyone in the group allowed to take part or with one person "presenting" to the group. You can find more information about Netscape Chat at the Netscape home page or at **http://home.netscape.com/comprod/chat.html**.

Netscape seems to be losing interest in Netscape Chat, though, and last time I looked I was unable to find where to download it. However, there is a chat plug-in, Ichat, which will work with both Internet Relay Chat and special Ichat sites. You can find this at the **http://www.ichat.com/** site.

Telnet Sessions

Telnet is a system that lets you log on to other computers that are connected to the Internet. You can play games, search library catalogs, dig through databases, and so on. Navigator can't do this for you directly; it doesn't support Telnet sessions. Instead, it can run a Telnet program that will manage the Telnet session. In the Windows versions of Communicator, this program is specified using the Windows file associations; a Telnet program can associate itself with the telnet:// URL, so it's automatically opened when a Telnet session is required. (At the time of writing, the Macintosh and UNIX versions had no way to specify a Telnet program, though this will probably be added to the Preferences.)

If you have Windows 95 or Windows NT, you'll have Microsoft Telnet available. Or you can find a Telnet program from elsewhere. Many commercial suites of Internet software contain Telnet programs, and there are a number of shareware programs you can use. Try looking at one of the shareware sites you saw in Chapter 10, such as Jumbo (**http://www.jumbo.com/**) or Shareware.com (**http://www.shareware.com/**).

As for tn3270, these programs are harder to find, because tn3270 sites are less common. You can find a commercial program called Host Explorer at **http://www.3270.mcgill.ca/**. There's also a freeware program called Windows Sockets 3270 Telnet Application, which should be available at **ftp.ccs.queensu.ca/pub/msdos/tcpip** or **ftp://ftp.sunet.se/pub/pc/windows/qws3270/** (search the FTP page for 3270). Or do an Archie search (see Chapter 6) for the qws3270 file.

If you have Netscape Communicator Professional, though, you already have a tn3270 program—Netscape IBM Host On-Demand.

Starting a Telnet or tn3270 Session

There are several ways to start Telnet sessions from Navigator. You'll occasionally find links from Web documents to Telnet sites (using a telnet:// URL). Clicking one of these links will launch the Telnet program you have specified. You can also start a Telnet session by typing telnet:// followed by a Telnet host address into Navigator's Location text box and pressing Enter. For instance, if you type **telnet://pac.carl.org** and press Enter, your Telnet program launches and connects to the Denver Public Library's site. (Type PAC and press Enter to log in.)

tn3270 sessions are started in the same way except that you (or the Web author) must use a tn3270:// URL. Or you can select Communicator, IBM Host On-Demand (Windows, IBM Host On-Demand on the Mac, of course) to open IBM Host On-Demand, then enter the host address into the tn3270E Server text box and click Connect to Host (see Figure 15.6).

Using HYTELNET

To get a taste for what's available in the world of Telnet, take a look at HYTELNET, the Telnet directory. You can view the directory at a World Wide Web site. Try **http://library.usask.ca/hytelnet/**. (You can also find a HYTELNET site at **http://www.cc.ukans.edu/hytelnet_html/START.TXT.html**, but it's rather out-of-date, and at a Gopher site, **gopher://liberty.uc.wlu.edu/11/internet/hytelnet**).

Each Telnet site is different. You can find Telnet sites at which you can play chess or search databases of satellite photographs or try experimental chat systems, and so on. But after you are connected to a Telnet site, that site's rules take over. Each system varies a little and may have different commands or menu options. So if you want to use Telnet, get to know your Telnet program first and then carefully read the instructions that are often shown when you enter a Telnet site.

FIG. 15.6

Communicator's IBM Host On-Demand program provides access to tn3270 hosts.

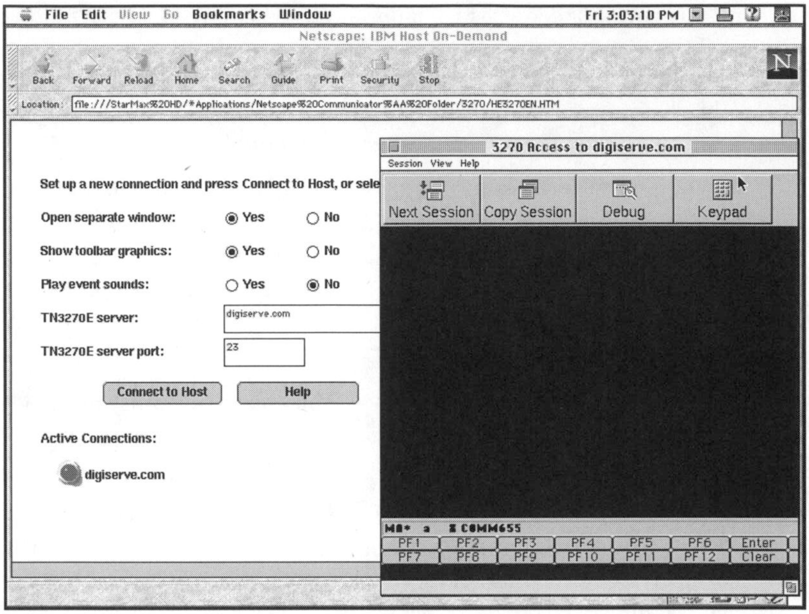

CHAPTER 16

Messenger:
World Wide E-Mail

Many browsers enable you to send e-mail. It's almost an essential browser function these days because so many documents use the mailto: URL. Click a link using this URL and the browser's e-mail program opens. The To field is already filled in for you with the address provided in the mailto: link. All you need to do is write the message and click Send.

Until recently, most browsers would let you send e-mail, but not receive it. Communicator, however, comes with a "full-featured" e-mail program, Messenger, which is linked to the Navigator browser. Not only can you send e-mail, but you can receive it, too. You can work with attached files, create folders, view your messages in a "threaded" view, use pictures and text formatting, create filters, and much more. ■

Preparing the e-mail program

You have some setup work to do before you can use your e-mail program.

Sending messages

It's a fairly simple point-and-click operation to send e-mail using Messenger.

Sending files and Web documents

You can send more than plain messages; you can also send computer files and Web pages.

Reading and managing messages

You'll use the Netscape Message Center and Netscape Folder/Messenger Mailbox windows to manage your messages.

Opening the Netscape Folder/Messenger Mailbox Window

We're going to begin by setting up the mail system and then sending an e-mail message. You'll write a message in the Message Composition window, which can be opened from a variety of places throughout Communicator. You actually manage your e-mail within the Netscape Folder/Messenger Mailbox window. There's another important window—the Message Center window—which we'll look at later in this chapter.

> **TIP** Note that although Netscape regards Messenger and Collabra as two distinct products, they are really combined into one system. In fact, they use the same windows to manage both e-mail and newsgroup messages. Many of the options and commands that you see while working with e-mail are also related to working with newsgroups, or even exclusively related to newsgroups, which we'll cover in Chapter 18.

Here are four different ways to open the Netscape Folder/Messenger Mailbox window:

- Double-click the Netscape Messenger icon.
- In Windows 95, select Start, Programs, Netscape Communicator, Netscape Messenger.
- Click the Mailbox button in the Component bar.
- In another Communicator window, select Communicator, Messenger Mailbox.

> **TIP** Just to confuse the issue a little, Netscape has used two names for the Netscape Folder window. To open the window, you'll use the Communicator, Messenger Mailbox command. But the window's title bar says Netscape Folder. I'm referring to the window as the Netscape Folder/Messenger Mailbox window.

Setting Up E-Mail

If you didn't enter all the necessary information when you created your user profile (see Chapter 2), the first time you start Messenger you'll see the Mail and Discussion Groups Setup dialog box. This allows you to enter the configuration information required by Messenger. We'll look at each pane of this setup dialog box; note that you can modify this information later. Select Edit, Preferences, click the Mail & Groups category.

You can see the first information pane in the Mail and Discussion Groups Setup dialog box in Figure 16.1. This is where you provide information about where and how to send and receive mail.

FIG. 16.1

Here's where you tell Messenger how to handle your e-mail.

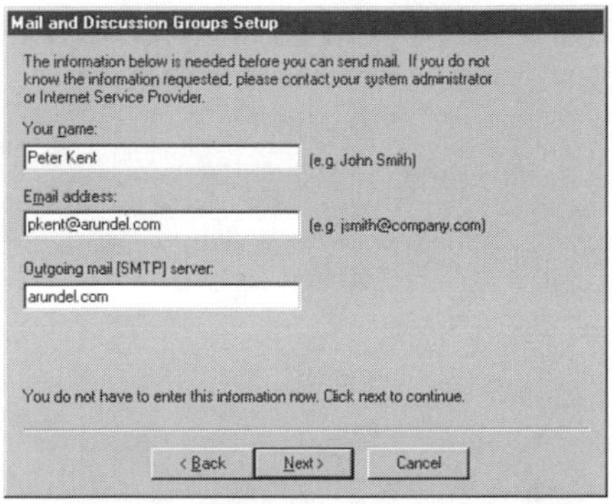

Part

III

Ch

16

Enter the following information:

- ■ *Your Name*   Type your name here. This will be included on the From line of your outgoing messages, along with your e-mail address.
- ■ *Email Address*   Type your e-mail address. Again, this goes on the From line.
- ■ *Outgoing Mail (SMTP) Server*   Enter the address of your SMTP (Simple Mail Transfer Protocol) server, the system to which Messenger will send e-mail messages. Ask your service provider or system administrator what to enter.

Click the Next button and you'll see the information in Figure 16.2.

FIG. 16.2

Enter more information about your mail servers.

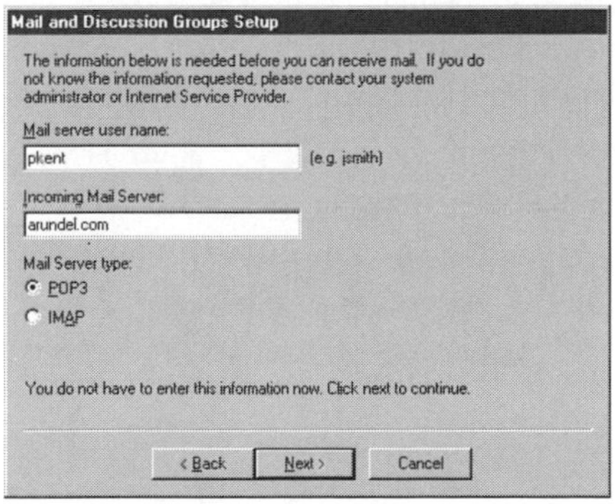

Enter the following information:

- ■ *Mail Server User Name*   This is your e-mail account or username, usually the same as the account name you use to log onto the Internet. Don't include the host name; for instance, I entered *pkent*, not *pkent@arundel.com*.
- ■ *Incoming Mail Server*   Enter the address of your POP3 (Post Office Protocol) or IMAP (Internet Message Access Protocol) server, the system that holds your incoming e-mail until you log on to retrieve it. Again, ask your service provider or system administrator what to enter here. Don't include your account name; for instance, I entered *arundel.com*, not *pkent@arundel.com*.

■ *Mail Server Type* There are two common types of incoming mail server on the Internet—POP3 and IMAP. Most Internet users are working with POP3; if you are not sure which type you have, ask your system administrator.

Click the Next button to see the information in Figure 16.3.

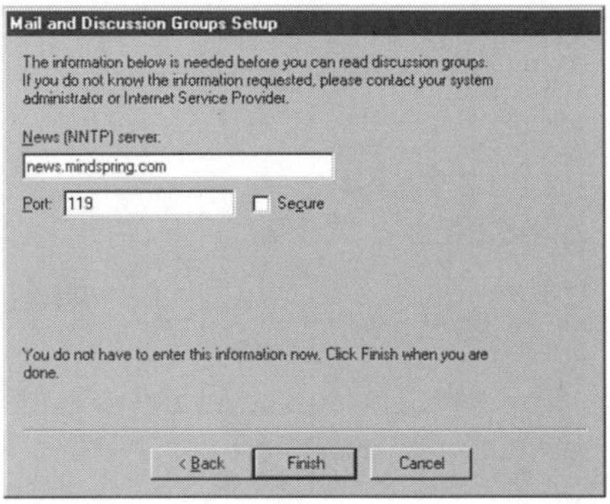

FIG. 16.3

You can enter the news
server information if you
want.

This pane is requesting information about the news server you use to read newsgroup messages. We'll be looking at this in Chapter 18. Enter this information:

■ *News (NNTP) Server* Enter the host name of your News (NNTP) Server, which is the computer that contains all the newsgroup messages (*NNTP* means *Network News Transfer Protocol*). You can get the host name from your service provider or system administrator. The news server may provide access to Internet newsgroups, or to private discussion groups set up by your company.

■ *Port* You probably won't have to change the port number; only do so if told to by your service provider or system administrator.

■ *Secure* If this is a secure news server, one that can encrypt incoming and outgoing messages, click this button. The type of news server used by most Internet services providers is *not* secure, but a company may set up a secure server for corporate communications.

Click the Finish button to complete your entries. You can now use Messenger, though I advise you to not do so until you've seen some of the other settings that are available. You've only entered very basic information, enough for the mail system to work, but not necessarily enough to avoid certain problems.

Setting Up More Preferences

Choose Edit, Preferences, and click the Mail & Groups category (see Figure 16.4).

FIG. 16.4

Tell Messenger how to display your messages.

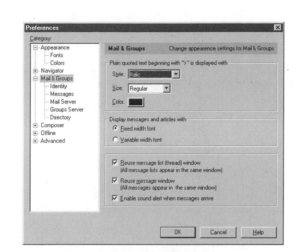

In this area, you can define what quoted message text looks like (that is, the text that is automatically inserted into your message from a message to which you are replying). You can select a font style, size, and color. You can also choose which font should be used when displaying normal (non-quoted) text in your messages: You can use a fixed-width font or a variable-size font. The variable-size font is easier to use, but the fixed-width font has an advantage; most Internet e-mail is sent using fixed-width fonts, and people often use spaces to line things up. If you use the variable font, the text is no longer lined up, while it *is* if you use the fixed font.

> **T I P** The fonts you have defined for the browser window are the same fonts that are used in the Composition and Message windows (see Chapter 2, "The Opening Moves").

You can also make the following choices:

- *Reuse Message List (Thread) Window*   If you leave this box checked, each time you open a message list by double-clicking a folder in the Message Center window, that folder's contents will be shown in the window already open. Clear this check box and a new window will open each time you double-click a folder (it can get very cluttered).

- *Reuse Message Window*   As you'll see later, there are two ways to view messages. In a pane at the bottom of the Netscape Folder/Messenger Mailbox window, or in a separate window. Single-clicking a message displays that message in the lower pane; double-clicking displays it in a separate window. If this check box is checked, when you double-click a message the message appears in the currently open message window, replacing the previous message. If this check box is cleared, each time you double-click a new window opens.

- *Enable Sound Alert When Messages Arrive*   If checked, each time a message arrives you'll hear an alert.

Entering More Identity Information

Click the Identity subcategory to see the pane in Figure 16.5.

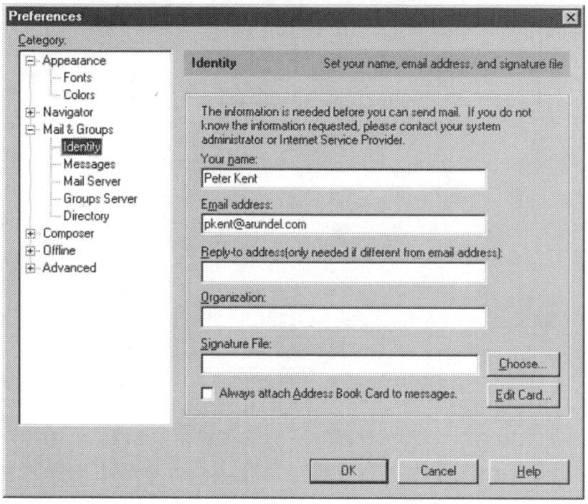

FIG. 16.5
More identifying
information for your
e-mail messages.

You can enter the following information:

- *Reply-To Address*   You can enter a different Reply-to address, if you want, so that replies to your e-mail are sent to a different address. Most users will ignore this option; it's useful if you have more than one e-mail address.

- *Organization*   This is used by many people when sending messages to newsgroups (see Chapter 18). You can, if you want, identify the organization you're associated with (your company, for instance). It's not necessary, though. (Note that the Organization line will be added to all messages, e-mail, and newsgroup messages.)

- *Signature File*   A signature file is a text file containing some kind of "blurb" that's inserted into the end of an e-mail message. You've seen other people use these—they often contain the person's name and address, phone numbers, other e-mail addresses, URLs, business ads, whimsical prose, and so on. If you want to use a signature file, type the text in a text editor. Limit it to about 65 characters across, and place a carriage return at the end of each line (you should probably limit yourself to about four or so lines, as many people find very long signatures offensive). Save the file as plain text, not in a word processing format. Then use the Choose button in this preferences pane to select the file.

- *Always Attach Address Book Card to Messages*   If you check this box, whenever you send an e-mail message a special "card" will be included with the message. This card is a block of information about you that the recipient can save in his Address Book. The card uses the vCard standard that many e-mail programs will soon use. (If the program receiving the message doesn't use vCard, the recipient will be able to read the contents of the card in plain text, including the Notes you've put in the card; it will act as a sort of signature.) You can use the Edit Card button to modify this card. See Chapter 17 for more information.

Entering Your Messages Information

Click the Messages subcategory in order to see the pane in Figure 16.6.

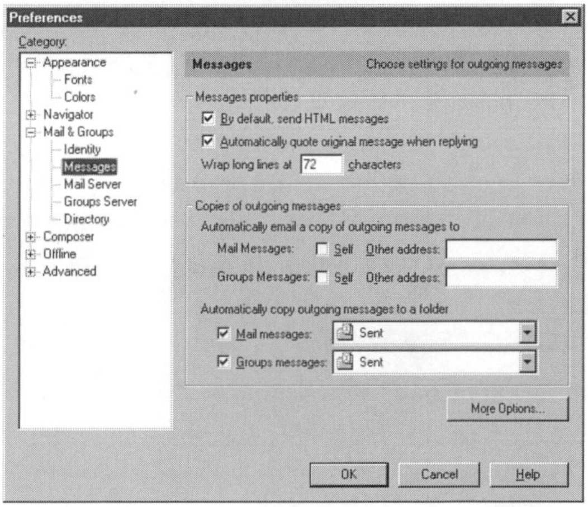

FIG. 16.6
Determine how
Messenger should
handle outgoing
messages

Make these choices:

- ■ *By Default, Send HTML Messages*   If this is checked, when you compose a message
  you'll be able to format the message text using HTML commands. You'll be able to color
  text, use the sorts of paragraph formats you see in Web pages—headings and lists, for
  instance—use bold, italic, and underlined text, and so on. If you clear this check box, the
  necessary toolbar will not appear in the Composition window.

- ■ *Automatically Quote Original Message When Replying*   "Quoting" in Netspeak is placing
  an original message inside a reply. Select this check box to automatically copy all of the
  original message's text into the reply. Each line of that text will be preceded by >, to
  indicate that it's quoted. If you're creating an HTML Mail message (a mail message that
  looks like a Web page), quoted text is entered using the Blockquote HTML format.

- ■ *Wrap long lines at___characters*   Some e-mail systems can't handle long lines very well.
  While the better, more advanced systems can "wrap" text, many can't. By wrapping, I
  mean that you can copy a paragraph of text from a word processor and paste it into a
  mail message, send that message, and the receiving mail system will contain the same
  paragraph; the recipient can copy the text into a word processor and the text will be a
  single paragraph, not a number of individual lines with line breaks at the end. However,
  some e-mail systems don't like long lines of text, or entire paragraphs. These systems
  may even break the text into individual lines, and insert strange characters (=20), for
  instance. You can stop these systems from inserting this weird stuff by telling Messenger to add line breaks to each line after the specified number of characters. In fact, this
  text box label is incorrect; Messenger doesn't *wrap* the lines, it breaks them.

■ *Automatically Email a Copy of Outgoing Message To*   You can have Messenger and Collabra send a copy of every e-mail and newsgroup message you send to another e-mail account. This is handy, for instance, if you use the Messenger e-mail system only for sending e-mail, and want to keep a record of all the messages you send in your main e-mail program. You can click the Self check box, in which case the message is sent to the address you entered into the Your Email text box under the Identity tab, or enter the e-mail address the message should be sent to.

■ *Automatically Copy Outgoing Messages to a Folder*   Messenger and Collabra will place a copy of every message you send via e-mail or to a newsgroup in the folder you select from the appropriate drop-down list box. There's generally no need to change this.

Click the More Options button to see the dialog box in Figure 16.7.

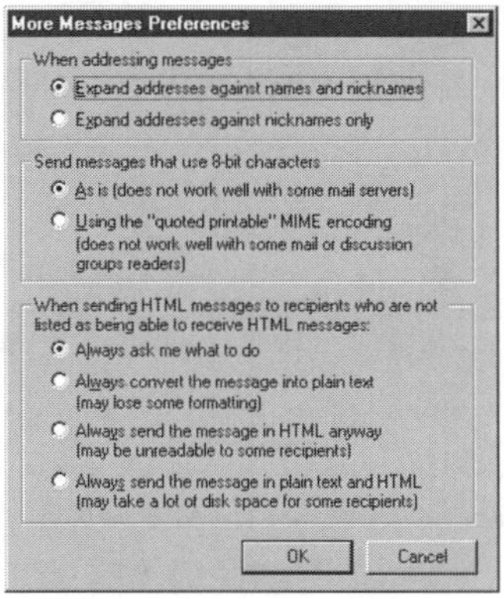

FIG. 16.7

More detailed message settings can be modified here.

Make these choices:

■ *Expand Addresses Against Names and Nicknames*   In Chapter 17, you'll see how to use the Address Book; this utility allows you to store mail recipients' information. If you select this option button, Messenger will automatically look at the Address Book's names and nicknames when you begin typing an entry into the Message Composition window's To: box; if it sees what it thinks may be a match, it enters it for you.

■ *Expand Addresses Against Nicknames Only*   Select this and Messenger won't look at names when you type a name into the To: box, only nicknames.

■ *Send Messages That Use 8-bit Characters*   The following options refer to the manner in which Messenger and Collabra transfer messages across the Internet. In some cases, special characters inserted into the message may not be transferred correctly. (For instance, special characters that you've copied into a message from a word processor. The ideal is to avoid sending special characters in your messages; stick to plain ASCII text messages.)

■ *As Is*   Keep this default setting unless you have problems transmitting messages; it may not work well in some cases.

- *Using the "Quoted Printable" MIME Encoding* Another method you can try, if you find that special characters sent from Messenger appear garbled on the recipient's system. Unfortunately this doesn't always work well, either.

- *When Sending Messages to Recipients Who Are Not Listed As Being Able to Receive HTML Messages* As you'll see, you can create messages that appear like Web pages, with colors, images, special character formatting, and so on. These options define what Messenger should do when you send a message to someone who is in your Address Book, but whose Prefers to Receive Rich Text (HTML) Mail check box has not been checked.

- *Always Ask Me What To Do* You'll see a dialog box prompting you to make a choice.

- *Always Convert the Message Into Plain Text* All the HTML formatting will be stripped out, and the message sent as plain text.

- *Always Send the Message in HTML Anyway* The message will be sent as HTML mail; note, however, that it may be illegible to the recipient.

- *Always Send the Message in Plain Text and HTML* The message is sent in both forms; the recipient will see plain text at the top of the message, then the HTML formatting at the bottom.

Entering More Mail Server Information

View the Mail Server pane in the Preferences dialog box to see the information in Figure 16.8.

FIG. 16.8

Some more important mail-server settings.

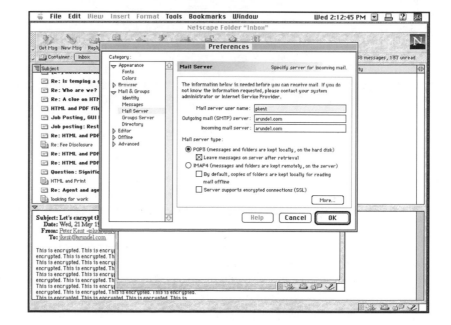

Part

III

Ch

16

There are some very important settings in this area:

■ *POP3 (Messages Are Kept Locally, On the Hard Disk). Leave Messages, on Server After Retrieval*   If you use a POP3 server, you can tell Messenger whether to remove the messages from the server once they've been copied to your hard disk. If this check box is cleared, once Messenger has retrieved your e-mail, it tells the POP server to delete the messages—if you try to retrieve them later using a different e-mail program, they won't be there. If you check the box, Messenger doesn't tell the POP server to delete the messages—you can retrieve them with another e-mail program later. This feature would be very handy if you need to access your e-mail from both home and work or if you travel a lot. (On the other hand, don't let too many messages build up on the server because they take up space that you may be charged for.)

■ *IMAP 4 (Messages and Folders Are Kept Remotely, On the Server)*   If you're using an IMAP server, your options are slightly different.

■ *By default, copies of folders are kept locally for reading mail offline*   Check this if you want to copy messages from the IMAP server to your hard disk so you can read them later. If you don't check this, you can only read the messages while connected.

■ *Server Supports Encrypted Connections (SSL)*   Check this if the server can encrypt messages when it sends them to Messenger.

Click the More Options button to see the dialog box in Figure 16.9.

FIG. 16.9

Some more important mail-server settings.

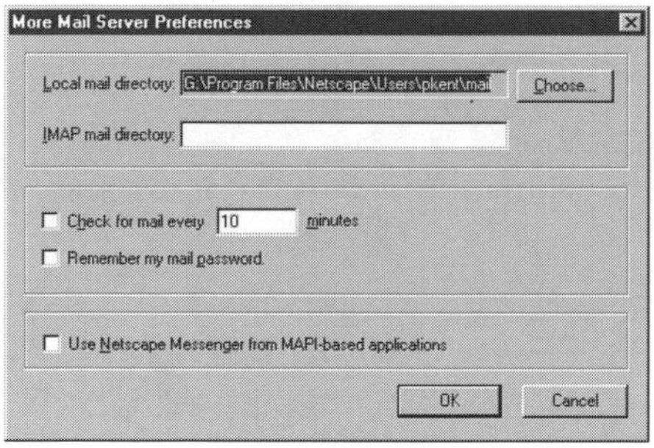

Make these choices:

■ *Local Mail Directory*   This is the directory on your hard disk where Messenger will store the mail-related files (the files containing the messages, for instance). There's generally no need to change this.

■ *Check for Mail Every*   You can tell Messenger to contact the incoming-mail server periodically to see if any messages have arrived; click the check box and then type an interval, in minutes, into the little text box.

■ *Remember My Mail Password*   The first time you retrieve your e-mail, you'll have to enter your password. If you check this box, Messenger remembers your password so you don't have to enter it again during the current session.

■ *Use Netscape Messenger from MAPI-Based Applications*   Check this if you have any programs that use Microsoft's Messaging Application Programming Interface. Those programs will be able to "call" and use Messenger.

Viewing the Phone Book Information

Finally, click the Directory tab to see the information in Figure 16.10. This area is used for setting up directories of e-mail users. As you'll see in Chapter 17, you have your own personal address book, but you can also search other directories. Communicator is already set up to work with several public directories of Internet users. The large list box shows you the order in which the directory is searched when you're looking for someone. Click an entry and use the arrow buttons to move the search order around if you want; by default, your personal phone book is searched first, which is fine in most cases.

FIG. 16.10

You can set up your phone-book directories here.

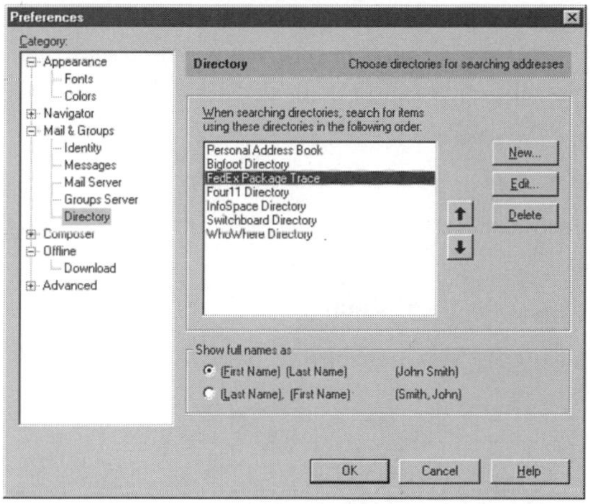

You can add new directories, too, by clicking the New button and entering the appropriate information. Where would you get this information? From your system administrator; for instance, your company may set up an e-mail directory for all its employees, and your system administrator will be able to tell you how to configure the directory. Directory information can be modified by clicking the directory and then clicking Edit.

The option buttons at the bottom of the pane simply allow you to define how names should appear in your address book, last name first or first name first.

TIP   Communicator works with LDAP directories. LDAP stands for *Lightweight Directory Access Protocol*, which is a simple method used for searching and updating directories over the Internet and intranets.

We'll be looking at the Groups Server tab in Chapter 18, as it's not related to working with e-mail. For now, let's move on and see how to send messages.

Sending E-Mail

We'll begin by looking at the basic browser e-mail function: sending e-mail messages. You can open the Composition window, the window in which you will write an e-mail message, several different ways. These methods work from the Navigator window:

■ Click a mailto: link in a Web document. You'll often see Internet e-mail addresses in documents that are colored and underlined just like any other link. Hold the mouse pointer over the link and you'll see the URL in the status bar, something like **mailto:pkent@arundel.com**.

■ Type the mailto: URL into the Location bar (type **mailto:robinhood@sherwoodforest.com**, for instance) and press Enter. (Try to remember to use mailto: and not mailto://; although mailto:// will open the Mail Composition box, it won't enter the address into the To" box.). You can even define a subject line, usingmailto:robinhood@sherwoodforest.com?subject=Maid Marion Kidnapped!. (A little geeky, perhaps, but a nice little party trick.) Make sure you put the ? between the end of the e-mail address and the word subject.

■ Select File, New, Message.

■ Select File, Send Page to send a copy of the current Web page.

Use these methods from the Netscape Folder/Messenger Mailbox or Message Center windows:

■ Click the New Message toolbar button.

■ Choose Message, New Message, or File, New, Message.

TIP If you have another e-mail program installed, it may interfere with the way in which Messenger works. For instance, the popular Eudora program has an option called Intercept Netscape Mailto URLs, in the Miscellaneous options. If this option is selected, then Eudora, not Netscape, will open when you click a mailto: link, or use mailto: in the Navigator Location box. Furthermore, it may interfere with other operations, such as (at the time of writing, at least), sending messages to mailing lists.

Whichever method you use, the Message Composition window opens; you can see an example in Figure 16.11 and 16.12 (as you can see, the Windows and Mac versions vary slightly at present). With the first two examples—using a link that has the mailto: URL, or entering the mailto: URL directly into the Location text box—you'll notice that the To: address is already filled in for you.

FIG. 16.11

Write your message and click the Send button.

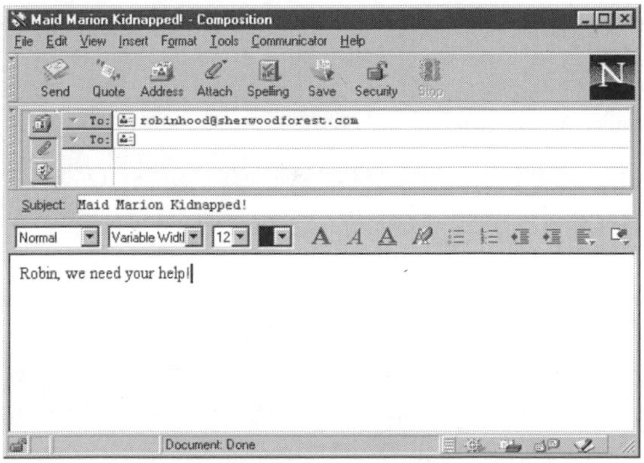

FIG. 16.12

Write your message and click the Send button.

 If the To: text box is not filled in, type an e-mail address into the text box, or click the Address button and select an address from the Address Book (see Chapter 17).

You can then click in the next box, below the first To: line, and another little button with a triangle appears. Click this little button and a pop-up menu opens, with some other choices:

- *To:* You can send the message to more than one person. Create another To line and enter an e-mail address, and each recipient will get what appears to be an original message—the recipient's address will appear in the message header on the To: line. The recipient will be able to see the other recipients' e-mail addresses on the To: line, as well.

- *Cc:* Enter the e-mail address of someone to whom you'd like to send a copy of this message. (Cc stands for carbon copy.) The recipient's address will appear in the message header on the Cc: line.

- *Bcc:* You can also enter the e-mail address of someone to whom you want to send a blind carbon copy (Blind Cc)—the recipient of the To: copy won't know that the Bcc recipient received a copy, though the Bcc recipient will know who the To: recipient is, as the To: line will still show that person's e-mail address.

- *Group*   You can use this to send a copy of the message to a newsgroup. This text box is really intended for use while working with newsgroups (see Chapter 18), but you can send a message to a newsgroup at the same time you send e-mail to someone. Simply enter the newsgroup name.

- *Reply To:*   The Reply To e-mail address is usually taken from the Mail and News Preferences dialog box, but you can use this option to enter a different Reply To address for this message if you want.

- *Followup-To*   This field is really a newsgroup feature. Some newsreader programs will look for a Followup To line on messages and respond to the specified newsgroup rather than the newsgroup in which the message was found. So this allows you to write a newsgroup message and get responses to your message in a different newsgroup.

Type something on the Subject line, a short description of the message. You don't *have* to have a subject, though if you try to send the message without a subject, Messenger will ask you if you want to add one.

There are several message options you can use, too. Click the Message Sending Options tab at the left, and you'll see an area in which you can select one of these:

Option	Description
Encrypted	Check this box if you want to encrypt the message (see Chapter 17).
Signed	Check this box if you want to digitally sign the message (see Chapter 17).
Uuencode Instead of MIME for Attachments	As you'll see later in this chapter, you can send computer files across the Internet by "attaching" them to e-mail messages. Generally a system called MIME is used, but if necessary you can select another system UUENCODE. This is a system used by some e-mail programs, particularly older ones.
Return Receipt	Check here if you want the recipient's mail program to send back a return receipt. This works only if the recipient is using Messenger or a compatible e-mail program.
Priority	This simply marks the message in both your Sent folder (you'll learn more about folders under "Working with Folders," later in this chapter) and the recipient's Inbox folder (assuming he's working with Messenger or a compatible mail system). As you'll see, there's a Priority column in these folders, and each message is marked with a priority ranged from Lowest to Highest (the text is colored accordingly, from light gray to red).

Option	Description
Format	These are the settings we saw earlier (the When Sending Messages to Recipients Who Are Not Listed As Being Able to Receive HTML Messages settings, in the More Options dialog box of the Messages Preferences category). Use these to decide what format to use when sending a message with HTML formatting in it.

After you've entered all the necessary information at the top of the window, place the cursor in the large text area and type your message. Then, when you've finished, click the Send button or choose File, Send Now. Messenger sends the message out across the Internet. You can select File, Send Later, and the message is placed in the Unsent Messages folder, but not sent yet. When you close Messenger, you'll be asked if you want to send the message, or you can send it at any time from the Message Center or Netscape Folder/Messenger Mailbox window by choosing File, Send Unsent Messages.

TIP There's a way to make a copy of a message that you might want to use again later. At any stage, choose File, Save Draft. A copy of the message is placed in the Drafts folder. Double-clicking a draft message in that folder will open the Compose window and load the message.

Using HTML Formatting

You can write messages using a variety of formatting tools. In Figure 16.11, you can see that there's a toolbar immediately above the message area. This is a toolbar from Netscape Composer, which you'll learn about in Chapters 20 and 21. You can use this toolbar to select a font, make text bold or colored, created bullet and numbered lists, and so on.

TIP The Composer tools are not present in the Composition window if the By Default, Send HTML Messages check box has been cleared in the Messages subcategory of the Preferences dialog box.

 There's an additional button at the end. When you click this one, a little drop-down toolbar appears, providing even more controls from Composer. These controls enable you to create links and tables, insert images, add horizontal lines, and insert link targets. And there are a number of commands on the Edit, Insert, and Format menus that are also from Composer, so you don't have to work with plain vanilla e-mail messages anymore! You can create messages that look like Web pages, with pictures, horizontal dividing lines, tables, and anything else that takes your fancy; you can even link to Java applets (if you know how, that is!). Whatever you can put in a Web page you can put in an e-mail message. However, note that all this is no good unless you are sending messages to recipients who are using Netscape Messenger, or another HTML-compatible mail program. If they're not, they'll see a jumble of HTML tags that will make reading the messages very difficult. As already noted, though, you can send messages in both plain text and HTML format, so a recipient is sure to be able to read it.

For more information about using these formatting tools, read Chapters 20 and 21.

TIP Recipients who don't have HTML-compatible e-mail programs can save the messages and then open them in a Web browser.

What are you really sending when you send a picture in a message this way (or place a Java applet in a message, for that matter)? For instance, if you choose Insert, Image and select an image file, what is being sent? If you used some of the early "preview" releases of Communicator, you may have noticed that the image file was not sent; rather, an HTML tag referencing the image was sent. So, for instance, if you inserted an image from your hard disk into a message, a link was made to the file, telling the e-mail program to go and grab the image, and insert it into the message when the message is displayed. The problem with this is that the user wouldn't be able to see that image, because it won't be in his cache, it's in yours. More recent releases of Communicator actually transfer the image with the message using MIME (see "Sending Computer Files," later in this chapter).

Incidentally, this feature (the ability to send e-mail that looks like a Web page) is known as HTML Mail. If you use any of the HTML Web-page features—the Netscape Composer features—Messenger won't treat it like a normal e-mail message. Rather, it will send it as a MIME attachment, as if you'd sent a separate computer file (which we'll look at in a moment). The recipient's e-mail program must be a program that can work with HTML Mail. It will recognize the attachment as a "Web page," and load it into the message window.

Sending the Web Document

Messenger provides several ways to send Web documents to other Internet users via e-mail:

■ In the Navigator window, choose File, Send Page, or File, Send Frame. The Message Composition window opens, with an URL indicating the file that you are sending. You can now type a message, above or below this URL, and send the message. If the recipient is using Messenger or another HTML-compatible e-mail program to read his e-mail, he'll see the Web document within the e-mail message (see Figure 16.13).

■ Open the Composition window, and click the Attach button and choose Web Page from the menu that opens. Type or paste the URL of the page and press Enter.

■ In the Composition box, select File, Attach, Web Page.

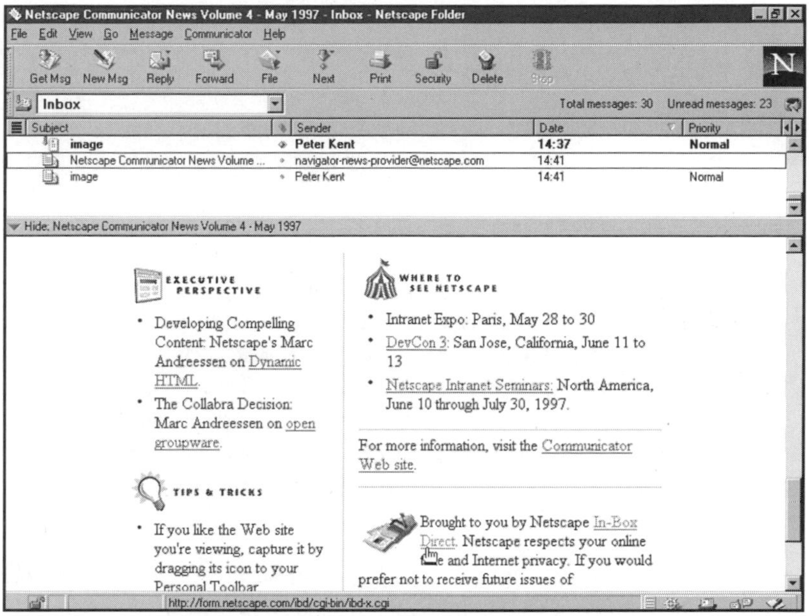

FIG. 16.13

This is a Web document sent to me from the Inbox Direct service. Notice that the links are active, too—you can see the little hand pointer at the bottom of the screen.

Sending Computer Files

Messenger is intended to be a full replacement for your current system. And no e-mail program would be complete without the capability to send binary files as attachments. When you send an e-mail message, you are sending plain text across your network connection; the program is not sending a complete computer file, just letters, one by one. But what if you want to send a computer file: a program, a picture, or a word processing file? In order to do this, you'll have to "attach" the file to the message.

There are three main ways to send attached files across the Internet: UUENCODE, MIME, and BinHex. (BinHex, a system often used on the Macintosh, is very similar to UUENCODE.) Messenger currently uses the MIME system by default, which means that the recipient of the message must be using MIME, too. Or you can choose to use UUENCODE if you know the recipient's program uses that method. (Yes, even if using the Macintosh, at least at the time of writing, the only alternative is UUENCODE, there's no BinHex option.)

N O T E MIME stands for Multipurpose Internet Mail Extensions, and is a system originally designed to allow Internet mail programs to attach files to e-mail messages. As you saw in Chapter 9, it's also used to identify files at Web sites. ■

To attach a file, click the Attach button in the Composition window, and select File from the menu that appears. (Or choose File, Attach, File.) Then use the Enter File to Attach dialog box to find the file you want to send.

You can also click the Attach Files & Documents tab on the left side of the Composition box and then click inside the list box that appears. The Enter File to Attach dialog box will open.

N O T E Some online services, such as CompuServe and America Online, use neither MIME nor UUENCODE. You can still send a MIME-encoded file to a someone at an online service, though. You can tell the recipient to get the Munpack program, which will take the MIME message—it will appear like a jumble of text—and convert it back to the original binary file. (You can find Munpack, along with Mpack, at **ftp.andrew.cmu.edu/pub/mpack/**, or by searching for munpack and mpack at various software archives; it's available for DOS, UNIX, and Mac machines.) If the recipient's program uses UUENCODE, you can use a special utility to convert the file into UUENCODE before sending it. You might use WinCode (a Windows program, which works with both UUENCODE and MIME) or Yet Another Base64 Decode (Macintosh, for both UUENCODE and MIME). You can find these by searching at software archives, also. ▪

If you know that the recipient is using UUENCODE rather than MIME, click the Message Sending Options tab, then check the Uuencode Instead of MIME for Attachments check box.

Receiving Computer Files

What happens when you receive a computer file that someone has sent to you? Simple. At the bottom of the message you'll see a box, similar to that shown in Figure 16.14. All you need to do is click the link on the left of the box, (Part *n.n*), and you'll see a Save As dialog box. Select the location in which you want to save the file, and click Save.

Netscape Messenger can work with files that were encoded using MIME, UUENCODE, and BinHex. Virtually all e-mail attachments are sent using one of these three systems, and Messenger can figure out which one has been used and automatically convert the file. So, if a correspondent asks you which method to use when sending a file, you can tell him to use whichever method is most convenient for him.

By the way, there are two ways to view attachments in messages:

- *View, Attachments, Inline*   With this menu option selected, Messenger will display attachments inside the message if it can. In other words, if it's a picture, in a format that Messenger can work with, you'll see the actual picture within the message. If it's a file type that Messenger cannot work with, then you'll see a link instead (see Figure 16.14).

- *View, Attachments, As Links*   With this menu option selected, Messenger always displays the link, even if it's capable of displaying the picture within the message.

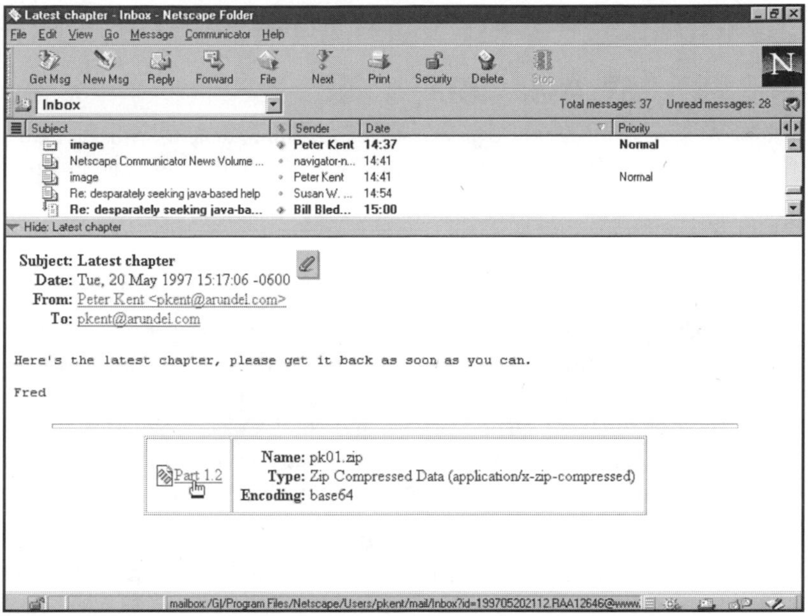

FIG. 16.14

To save a file you've been sent, simply click the link.

[A Netscape Folder window titled "Latest chapter - Inbox - Netscape Folder" with toolbar buttons: Get Msg, New Msg, Reply, Forward, File, Next, Print, Security, Delete, Stop. The Inbox shows messages including "image" from Peter Kent 14:37 Normal, "Netscape Communicator News Volume..." from navigator-n... 14:41, "image" from Peter Kent 14:41 Normal, "Re: desparately seeking java-based help" from Susan W... 14:54, "Re: desparately seeking java-ba..." from Bill Bled... 15:00. Below:

Subject: **Latest chapter**
Date: Tue, 20 May 1997 15:17:06 -0600
From: Peter Kent <pkent@arundel.com>
To: pkent@arundel.com

Here's the latest chapter, please get it back as soon as you can.

Fred

Name: pk01.zip
Type: Zip Compressed Data (application/x-zip-compressed)
Encoding: base64

Part 1.2]

Part III

Ch 16

More Composition Procedures

There are a few more things you can do in the Composition window when creating e-mail messages:

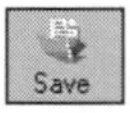

File, Save As—Use this to save a message in a text or HTML file.

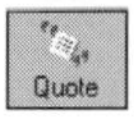

File, Quote Original Text—If you cleared the Automatically Quote Original Message When Replying in the Messages Preferences, you can use this command to quote a message you are replying to.

Edit, Paste As Quotation—Pastes text from the Clipboard and treats it as quoted text, adding the > symbol or setting it in the HTML Mail message as a Blockquote.

View, Show Paragraph Marks—Use this to show you where paragraphs end within your text.

Tools, Check Spelling—Spell check your messages before sending them.

The Message Center and Netscape Folder/ Messenger Mailbox Windows

Well, we've seen how to *send* e-mail. How about dealing with the tons of e-mail that you're going to *receive?* You'll do that in the Message Center and Netscape Folder/Messenger Mailbox windows.

But before we look at those, let's quickly talk about the relationship between Messenger, Collabra, and the Message Center window, a relationship that can at times be a little confusing.

Collabra is Netscape's newsgroup program. As you'll learn in Chapter 18, newsgroups are Internet discussion groups. Newsgroup messages are pretty much the same as e-mail messages, though. Both types of messages are primarily text messages, so Netscape Communicator uses the same system for managing both Collabra and Messenger messages. The windows you use to view your e-mail and newsgroup messages are almost exactly the same, with, in the main, the same buttons and menu commands.

This has both advantages and disadvantages: On one hand, if you learn how to use Messenger, you can quickly learn Collabra (and vice versa). But on the other hand, the mix of commands, some of which are appropriate and some not, may be a little confusing at times.

Communicator uses two common windows for Messenger and Collabra. First, there's the Netscape Message Center window. This shows a list of folders holding e-mail messages (handled by Messenger), and a list of newsgroups (handled by Collabra), as you can see in Figure 16.15 (don't worry for now about the newsgroups, we'll get to them in Chapter 18). You can display this window by choosing Communicator, Message Center in any of Communicator's windows—Navigator, Collabra, Messenger, and so on.

FIG. 16.15

The Netscape Message Center window shows you all your Messenger folders and subscribed newsgroups.

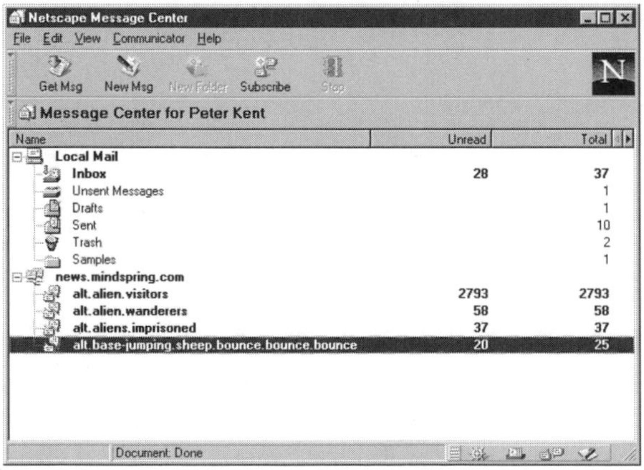

The Message Center window also appears when you open Collabra itself, by double-clicking the Netscape Collabra icon, or, in Windows 95, by choosing Start, Programs, Netscape Communicator, Netscape Collabra.

Think of the Message Center window as an overview of Messenger and Collabra, a way to get to a particular mail folder or newsgroup. You can see all the folders, and quickly see which ones have unread messages in them. I'm not going to discuss all the commands in this window, as they're duplicated in the Netscape Folder/Messenger Mailbox window…you'll learn about them there.

How do you open the Netscape Folder/Messenger Mailbox window, then? Use one of the methods we saw at the beginning of this chapter: Use Communicator, Messenger Mailbox, for instance, or click the Mailbox button on the Component bar.

When the Netscape Folder/Messenger Mailbox window opens the first time, it shows you two panes (as in Figure 16.16). The top pane displays a list of messages; the bottom pane displays the contents of the message selected in the top pane.

You can use the little triangle button on the bar that divides the panes (it's down in the lower left of the window if there's only one pane) to open and close the lower pane. Or use the View, Hide Message command.

This is the folder that's selected; select another mailbox from the drop-down list box

Click a message to view it in the lower pane

Click here to open the Message Center

FIG. 16.16
The Netscape Folder/ Messenger Mailbox window, showing the Inbox contents.

Open and close the lower pane by clicking here

Click here to view more columns

The lower pane displays the contents of the message selected in the upper pane

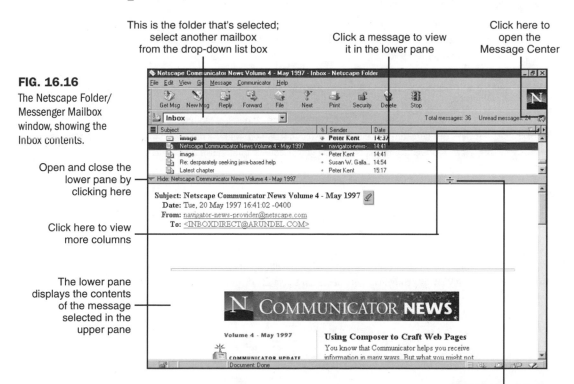

Use the mouse to drag the bar up and down

Getting Your Mail

The procedure for getting your e-mail is simple: Click the Get Msg toolbar button; or choose File, Get Messages, New. The first time you try to get your mail you'll see the password dialog box; type the password you use to retrieve your e-mail (if you're not sure, ask your system administrator), then click OK and Messenger retrieves your e-mail. In a few moments, you'll see new messages listed in the top pane.

TIP What, no e-mail waiting for you? Well, I can't teach you how to win friends and influence them to send you e-mail. But you can test the e-mail system by sending messages to yourself. Follow the instructions for sending e-mail earlier in this chapter, but enter your own e-mail address in the To text box. Or join Netscape's Inbox Direct program; see Chapter 17.

To read a message, you can simply click it. If the lower pane is open, the contents of the message will appear in that pane. If it isn't, you can click the triangle button in the lower-left corner of the window to open the lower pane.

Or you can open the message in a separate window; double-click the message, or right-click and select Open Message, or click once and choose File, Open Message. A new window opens, with all the same commands and buttons as the Netscape Folder/Messenger Mailbox window.

So what will you find in your message? You'll see the message header, which contains the Subject, Date, From, Reply To, and To information at the top of the message. Then you'll see the actual message text.

N O T E There's a lot more to a message header than is shown in the message in Figure 16.10. All sorts of data (Return-Path:, Received:, Message-Id: X-Sender:, and so on), which most people don't want to see and just clutters up the message pane, is hidden from view. If you *do* want to see this stuff (it's sometimes useful when trying to figure out where a message originally came from), choose View, Headers, All. Or you can select View, Headers, Brief to see a two-line header. ■

If someone sends you a message containing a MIME-encoded picture in JPEG or GIF format, that picture will be displayed in your message (see Chapter 18 for more details). If someone has sent you an HTML Mail message, you'll see it in the window in all its glory—Web-page formatting, links, pictures, and so on.

TIP If you've been sent HTML Mail—an e-mail message with Web-page features—you'll only see the Web document if View, Attachments, Inline has been selected (it's the default). If View, Attachments, As Links is selected, you'll see a link that you can click to view the document in Navigator. The same goes for pictures. If View, Attachments, As Links is selected, you'll see a link to the picture rather than the picture itself.

Moving Between Messages

When Messenger first transfers messages, it highlights the first unread message and displays the contents in the bottom pane. You can click any other message to see that message's text.

You can also use the following menu and toolbar commands (these commands also work in the message window that appears if you double-click a message, and are sometimes more useful in that window than the Folder window, in which you can simply click the message you want to use):

Choose Go, Previous Message to read the previous message.

 Click the Next button or choose Go, Next Unread Message to read the next message that you haven't yet read.

Choose Go, Next Message to read the next message in the list, whether you've read it or not.

Choose Go, Back to view the message you read just before the current one.

After using the Backtrack command, you can choose Go, Forward, to return to the message you've just come back from.

Replying to Messages

If you'd like to reply to or forward a message, you have a few options.

To reply to the person who sent the message, click the Reply button and choose Reply To Sender from the menu that opens; or choose Message, Reply, To Sender.

To reply to the sender and to all the people who received copies of the message, click the Reply: Mail button and choose Reply To Sender and All Recipients from the menu that opens; choose Message, Reply, To Sender and All Recipients.

 To send a copy of the message to someone else, click the Forward button or choose Message, Forward, or Message Forward Quoted to insert the forwarded text into the message in quoted form (with the > symbols or in HTML Blockquote format).

Working with Folders

When you begin working with Messenger, you'll find several mail folders:

Folder	Description
Inbox	This is the folder containing e-mail that you've received.
Unsent Messages	This is the folder which stores e-mail that you've written, but haven't yet sent.
Drafts	This is the folder in which you can save Draft messages (see under "Sending E-Mail," earlier in this chapter).

continues

Part
III

Ch

16

continued

Folder	Description
Sent	This is the folder holding copies of the messages that you've already sent (as long as the Automatically Copy Outgoing Messages to a Folder: Mail Messages check box is checked in the Messages Preferences Composition pane).
Trash	This is the folder where your messages are placed when you delete them.
Samples	A folder containing sample e-mail messages provided by Netscape Communications.

You can view any of these folders by double-clicking them in the Message Center window, or by selecting a folder from the drop-down list box near the top of the Folder window.

You can create your own folders, too. Choose File, New Folder, type a folder name, select from a drop-down list box where you want to place the folder, and press Enter. You might create a variety of folders for different purposes: Business, Family, Friends, one for each mailing list discussion group you join, and so on.

You can sort the messages in your folders. Choose View, Sort, and a cascading menu will open. You can then choose to sort the messages by Date, Subject, Sender, or Priority. You can also sort by Size, Status, Flag, Unread (we'll discuss Flag and Unread in a few moments), and Thread (which we'll look at in Chapter 17). You can also select Ascending or Descending sort on and off here. This controls the order in which the messages appear on your screen. For example, when sorting by date, select Ascending to put the newest messages at the bottom; select Descending to put the newest messages at the top.

TIP Messenger always puts incoming messages at the bottom of the Inbox list, regardless of the type of sorting you selected. Choose an option from the View, Sort menu again to place the messages in their correct positions.

Moving and Copying Messages Between Folders

You can quickly shift messages from one folder to another, using one of these methods:

- Select the message or messages that you want to move and then choose Message, File Message to open a small cascading menu showing all the folders. Select the folder into which you want to place the message.

- Use the same method to copy messages between folders, too: choose Message, Copy Message.

 Select the message or messages and then click the File button; a drop-down menu opens from which you can select the folder you want to use.

- Right-click a message and select File Message to see a menu with the folders listed.

■ Position the Message Center and Netscape Folder/Messenger Mailbox windows so both are visible, then drag messages from the Netscape Folder/Messenger Mailbox window onto a folder in the Message Center window. Hold the Ctrl key down while you drag to copy instead of move the messages.

> **TIP**
> You can carry out operations on several messages at once. To select multiple messages, hold the Ctrl key while you select each one; or, if the messages you want to select are in a contiguous block, select the first in the block, press Shift, and select the last in the block. Or you can choose Edit, Select Message, All Messages or Edit, Select Message, Flagged Messages (to select just those messages that have been marked—we'll look at that next).

Marking Messages—The Flag and Diamond Columns

In the top pane, the message-list pane, you'll see two small columns, one with a small flag at the top and one with what looks like a green diamond. The flag column shows if a message has been flagged. The diamond column shows if the message has been read. So when a message is first retrieved and placed in the Inbox, there's a green diamond in the diamond column— meaning the message hasn't yet been read—and a gray dot (no flag) in the flag column, meaning it hasn't been flagged.

> **TIP**
> The flag column may be all the way over to the right side of the window, perhaps even out of sight. You can adjust columns in three ways to make the ones you want more visible. You can drag the column headings left and right to move the column to another position; drag the line between the columns left or right to adjust the size of a column; or click the little triangle buttons on the right side of the column headings to scroll right or left through the columns.

You can flag a message by clicking the little dot in the flag column (or by selecting the message and choosing Message, Flag); Messenger replaces the gray dot with a small flag. Remove the mark by clicking again or by choosing Message, Unflag.

Why bother marking messages? Well, it's a way to group them for an operation. For instance, let's say you receive 20 e-mail messages (easy to do if you subscribe to one of the Internet's thousands of mailing-list discussion groups). As you read each one, you can mark the ones you want to shift to another folder. When you've finished reading and marking, choose Edit, Select Message, Flagged Messages. Messenger will highlight all the messages you have marked. Then choose Message, File Message, or Message, Copy Message, to move or copy those messages to another folder. You could also quickly scan the Subject lines of the messages you've received and flag the ones you are most interested in, then use the Go, First Flagged Message, Go, Previous Flagged Message, and Go, Next Flagged Message commands to read those messages.

Now for the diamond column, the one that shows if a message has been read or not. (The read status is also shown by the font used; bold-text means the message hasn't been read.) The View, Messages, All menu option displays all the messages in a folder, whether read or unread.

It is on by default. If you choose View, Messages, New, Messenger will show only your unread messages.

When Messenger retrieves your messages, each—except the first, which Messenger highlights—is marked with a green diamond in the diamond column. The green diamond indicates that you haven't read that message. After you open the message, the green diamond is replaced by a gray dot.

You can mark a read message as unread, however. You may want to do this if you open a message and don't have time to read it or if you want to reread it later. This is handy if you've selected View, Messages, New, or if you simply want to be reminded to return to it later. Click the gray dot in the diamond column, replacing the dot with a diamond again to mark the message as unread, or select several messages and choose Message, Mark, As Unread. You can also use Message, Mark, All Read (to quickly mark all unread messages as read), or Message, Mark, Read by Date (to specify a date—all messages up to that date will be marked as read). ●

CHAPTER 17

Messenger: Advanced Functions

In the last chapter, we covered most of the essential day-to-day operations you need to know to work with Messenger. But there's more. In this chapter, we'll look at a few other things, from working with threads and running Netscape Mail Notification (a program that checks for mail periodically), to working with e-mail filters, the Address Book, and even e-mail-message encryption. ■

Working with message threads

Messages can be sorted by "threads," list of associated messages.

Using the Address Book and searching directories

You can store e-mail addresses and other information in the Address Book, and retrieve such information from the Internet's directories.

Using Netscape Mail Notification

Have Messenger automatically inform you when e-mail is waiting.

Encrypting and digitally signing e-mail

Encrypt and digitally sign your e-mail to ensure the confidentiality of sensitive e-mail.

Using filters to organize e-mail

If you get a lot of e-mail, you need filters to help you sort through it all.

Working with Threads

A *thread* is a collection of associated messages. Someone sends a message, and then someone else responds to it; then someone responds to the first response, someone else responds to that response, and so on.

 The Folder window can display message threads. Simply click the button on the left side of the Folder window next to the Subject column to turn on thread mode. Or choose View, Sort, By Thread. To turn off thread view, click the button again.

You can see an example of threading in Figure 17.1. Notice the + and – icons. Clicking these opens and closes the thread. That is, you can see all the associated messages or just the first.

FIG. 17.1

You can view associated messages by using thread view.

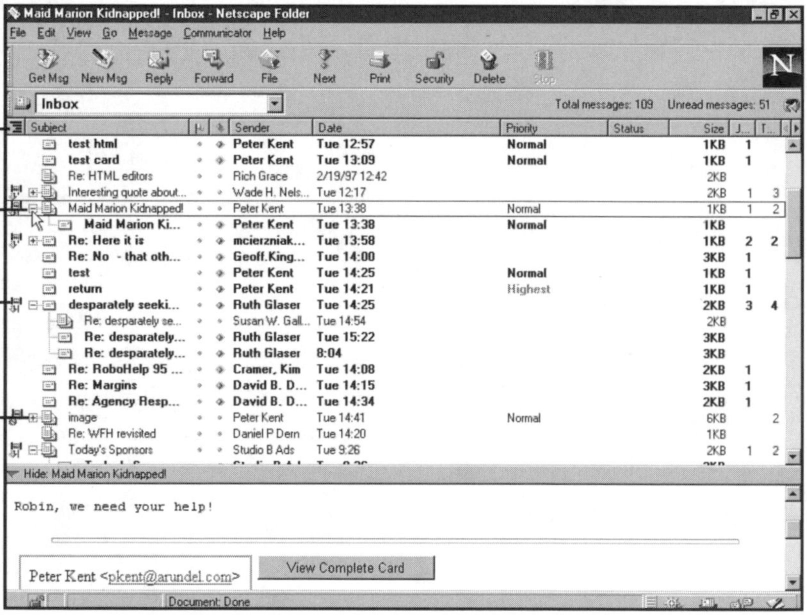

Click here to see thread view

Click a – to close the thread

Click the reel of thread to select all the messages in the thread

Click a + to open a thread and see all the messages

If you click the little "reel of thread" icon next to the first message in the thread, all messages within the thread are selected, a good way to prepare to move, copy, or delete all the messages. You can select multiple threads in this way; click several of the squares, and each thread remains selected. You can also select a thread by clicking any message in the thread and choosing Edit, Select Message, Thread.

T I P How does Messenger know which e-mail messages are associated? It looks at the messages' Message-ID and References lines, in the message headers. Each message has a unique ID number (in the Message-ID line), and when you reply to a message, the ID number from the message to which you are replying is placed into the References line. By tracking these numbers, Messenger can figure out message threads.

Note, however, that Messenger *also* looks at Subject lines. Thus if, by pure chance, two unrelated messages have the same title, they are both part of the same thread.

 You can tell Messenger to "watch" threads. Watched threads will be marked with an icon of a little pair of glasses. You can mark threads as watched using filters (see "E-Mail Filtering," later in this chapter), or you can right-click a thread and select Watch Thread (or click and select Message, Watch Thread).

More Messenger Functions

Before we move onto the Mail Notification program, here's a quick rundown of some procedures you'll want to carry out in Messenger now and again:

- *File, Empty Trash Folder*   You'll want to empty your trash folder now and then.
- *File, Compress Folders*   Compressing your folders now and again will save a little disk space; Messenger removes space left by deleted messages.
- *Edit, Folder Properties*   Select a folder in the Message Center, then select this command to see the Properties box, in which you can enter a new folder name.
- *Edit, Find in Message*   This command searches for text within the selected message.
- *Edit, Search Messages*   This command searches for a message, in your Inbox or any mail folder, based on text that you specify: text in various parts of the message, such as the From line, the body of the message, the subject, and so on.
- *Edit, Search Directory*   Use this command to search the Address Book and other directories (see "Using the Address Book" later in this chapter).
- *View, Document Source*   Just as with Navigator, you can view the message source within Messenger. You'll see all the text received in the message, including the full header, and all the HTML tags and attachments, if any.
- *View, Wrap Long Lines*   This command will take a long, single line in a message and wrap it down onto the next line so you can see it all.

There are more things you can do in this window, but they're mostly related to newsgroups and Collabra, which you'll learn about in Chapter 18.

T I P   You can also access many functions from a pop-up menu; right-click messages (Windows 95) to open this menu (there's currently no pop-up menu in the Mac version).

Part

III

Ch

17

Netscape Mail Notification

When Internet e-mail is sent to you, it's stored in a POP or IMAP server somewhere. That is the server that Messenger has to connect to retrieve your e-mail. But how does Messenger know you have any mail waiting? Unless you use Mail Notification, it doesn't. You can use the Get Msg button periodically to check, of course. Or you can run Netscape Mail Notification (the Windows 95 version is currently the only version with Mail Notification). This is a little program that runs quietly in the background, periodically checking to see if any e-mail has arrived for you. It's a good way to keep up with your mail, without having to expend computer memory to keep the Netscape Folder/Messenger Mailbox or Message Center window open and without having to tell Messenger to go and check now and again; Notification keeps checking for you.

To start the program, double-click the Netscape Mail Notification icon, or choose Start, Programs, Netscape Communicator, Utilities, Netscape Mail Notification. You can also place a shortcut to the icon in your Startup menu; that way, the program will start automatically each time you start Windows.

To configure the program, right-click the icon in the Windows 95 taskbar and choose Properties. You'll see the Netscape Mail Properties dialog box shown in Figure 17.2.

FIG. 17.2

Tell the Notification program when you want it to run and how to notify you.

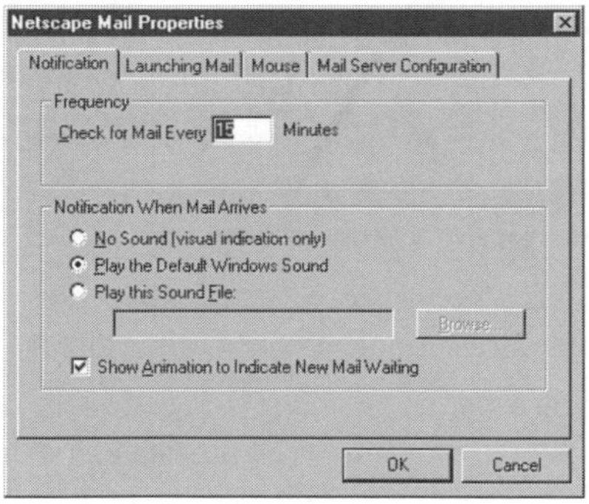

These are the options in the Notification pane:

- ■ *Check for Mail Every*   Enter an interval, in minutes, to define how often the program checks to see if you have waiting mail.

- ■ *No Sound*   Click this option button if you do not want a sound to play and let you know that there's mail waiting.

- ■ *Play the Default Windows Sound*   Click this option to play a sound picked for you.

- ■ *Play This Sound File*   Click this option button and then click Browse if you want to pick a particular sound.

Click the Launching Mail tab to see the sheet in Figure 17.3.

FIG. 17.3

Tell the program how to find Messenger.

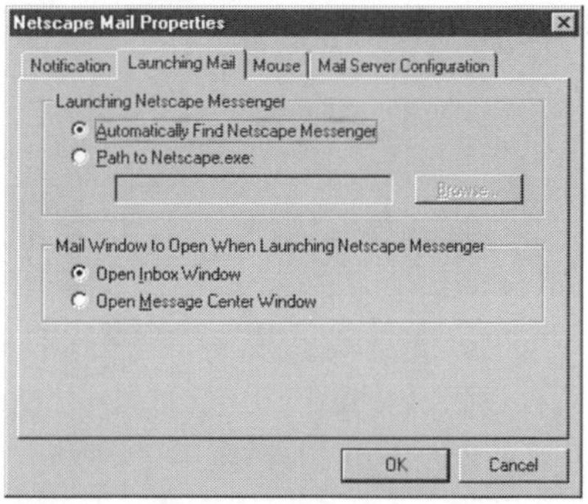

Here are the Launching Mail pane options. They define how Notification opens Messenger when you tell it to do so (which I'll explain in a moment):

- *Automatically Find Netscape Messenger*   By default, this is selected, and means that the program will find Messenger when it needs it. You can generally leave this selected.

- *Path to Netscape.exe*   If the program is unable to start Messenger for some reason, you can use the Browse button to find the Netscape.exe file, so Notification knows for sure where it is.

- *Open Inbox Window*   Select this option if you want Notification to open the Netscape Folder/Messenger Mailbox window.

- *Open Message Center Window*   Select this option if you want Notification to open the Message Center window.

You can also define what happens when you double-click the icon in the Windows 95 taskbar. Click the Mouse tab to see the pane in Figure 17.4.

FIG. 17.4

You can configure the taskbar-icon mouse action.

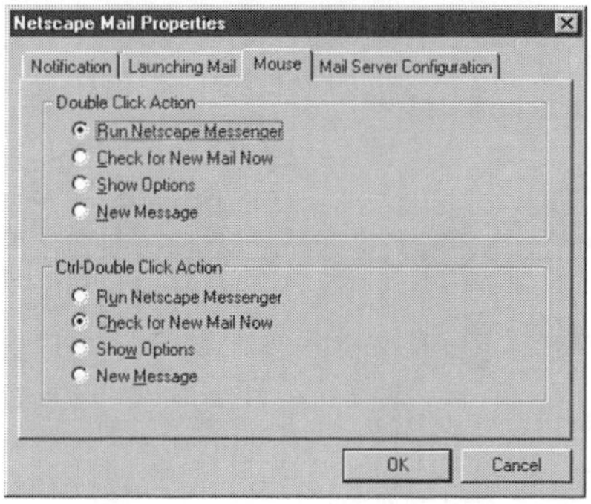

You can double-click the icon, or press Ctrl and double-click; these settings allow you to determine what happens when you carry out either action. You can open the Netscape Folder/ Messenger Mailbox window and retrieve your messages; check for new mail; open the Netscape Mail Properties dialog box; or open the Message Composition window.

Part
III

Ch
17

The final pane of this dialog box, the Mail Server Configuration tab, simply shows you the server information you entered in the Preferences dialog box, which we looked at in Chapter 16.

 Now, how do you use Notification? Well, you let it run. Now and then, it will check to see if there is mail waiting for you. You can also get it to do so by right-clicking the taskbar icon in Windows 95, or clicking the icon in other operating systems, and selecting Check Now. Or use one of the mouse actions defined in the Netscape Mail Properties dialog box—a double-click or Ctrl+double-click perhaps.

 If you do have mail waiting, it will play the sound you selected or look at the icon; you'll see a little flag to indicate that you have new mail.

To retrieve mail, you need to open Messenger and then use the normal method (click the Get Mail button). Open Messenger by double-clicking or Ctrl+double-clicking the icon (depending on what you set in the Netscape Mail Properties dialog box) or by right-clicking and choosing Run Mail.

Note that you can also quickly send a message using Mail Notification. You can right-click and select New Message. Or set up the mouse actions in the Properties box so you can double-click or Ctrl+double-click.

Using the Address Book

Messenger has a very simple Address Book. You can open it from the Navigator, Messenger, or Message Composition windows by choosing Communicator, Address Book. In the Composition window, you can click the Address button, too. You can see the Address Book in Figure 17.5.

FIG. 17.5
Here's the Address Book.

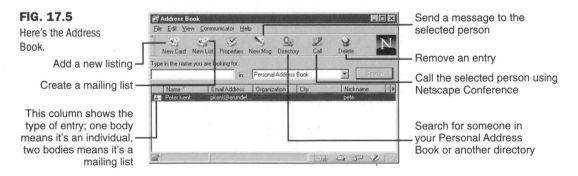

Add a new listing

Create a mailing list

This column shows the type of entry; one body means it's an individual, two bodies means it's a mailing list

Send a message to the selected person

Remove an entry

Call the selected person using Netscape Conference

Search for someone in your Personal Address Book or another directory

First, here's how you add a name to your Address Book:

1. Click the New Card button or choose File, New Card. You'll see the New Card dialog box in Figure 17.6.
2. Type the person's First Name, Last Name, and E-mail address.

FIG. 17.6
Use the New Card
dialog box to add
users.

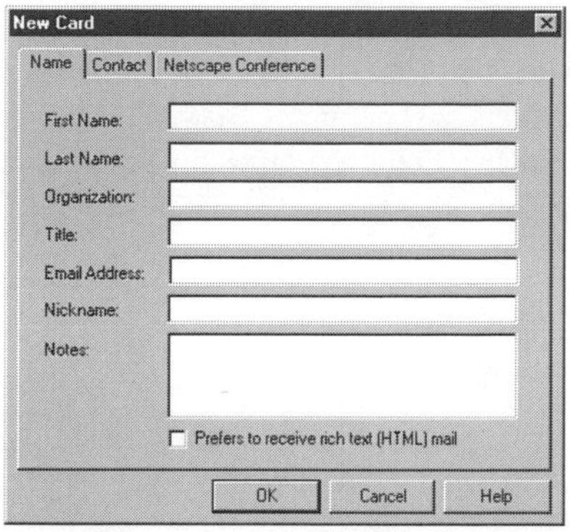

3. If you want, you may include an Organization entry and Title.

4. You may also include a Nickname. This is a name you can use when entering e-mail addresses into the text boxes at the top of the Message Composition window. For instance, if you want to add the robinhood@sherwoodforest.com e-mail address to your Address Book, you might type robinh as the Nickname. Then, when you want to send a message to Robin, all you need to do is type robinh into the Message Composition window's To text box, and Messenger will find the correct address for you.

5. Type some Notes, if you want. These can be any kind of information about the person.

6. If you know that this person uses Netscape Messenger or Netscape Navigator 3 (or another HTML Mail e-mail program) to manage his e-mail, you can check the Prefers to Receive Rich Text (HTML) Mail. That way, you'll be able to create messages with HTML formatting.

7. Fill in the information under the other tabs:

   - *Contact*   "Real world" contact information; the person's address and phone numbers.

   - *Netscape Conference*   This pane stores information about how to contact the person using Netscape Conference. See Chapter 19 for more information.

8. Click the OK button; the new person is added to the Address Book.

You can view (and modify) an entry's information later by right-clicking it and choosing Card Properties (in Windows; there's no pop-up menu on the Mac) or by double-clicking it (or click once and choose Edit, Card Properties).

Creating Mailing Lists

You can create mailing lists in the Address Book. These are groups of e-mail recipients. For instance, you might have one group called Family; everyone in your family will be in the list, so when you want to send a message to your entire family, you can select one Address Book entry—you won't have to type all the names in individually. You might have one group for customers, one for colleagues, one for the paint-ball team, one for…whatever group of people you need to send messages to.

Part
III

Ch
17

Click the New List button, or select File, New List. In the Mailing List Info dialog box (see Figure 17.7), type a name for the list: Family, Friends, Paint-Ball, or whatever else is suitable. You can also provide a nickname, again, a short name that you can type into the Address line of the Composition window. Include a Description if you want. On the Mac version, you can also drag entries from the Address Book itself onto the dialog box, a really quick way to create lists.

FIG. 17.7

Create a mailing list in moments using the Mailing List dialog box.

Mailing List	⊠
┌ Mailing List Info ────────────
List Name:
List Nickname:
Description:
To add entries to this mailing list, type names from the address book.
📇▾

| OK | Remove | Cancel | Help |

Then type the names of the people you want to add to the list. You can type a full e-mail address or the name or nickname of someone already in the Address Book; Messenger will fill in the address for you. When you've entered the information, press Enter to move to the next line and type the next one. When you've finished, click OK.

TIP If you type into the list an e-mail address that is not yet in your Address Book, Messenger will ask you if you want to add the address to the Address Book. You *must* add it, or you can't include it in the list.

You can now send messages to everyone on the list at once. Simply select the list as if it were a single e-mail user (I'll explain how to send mail to people listed in the Address Book next), and Messenger will automatically send a message to everyone on the list

Sending Mail to Someone in the Address Book

There are several ways to send a message to someone whose e-mail address is listed in the Address Book:

■ Open the Address Book, find the person (or mailing list), then right-click the entry, and select New Message (or click the entry once and then click the Compose button; or select File, New, Message). The Composition window opens, with the person's name and e-mail address in the To line.

■ In the Message Composition window, click the Address button to see the Select Addresses dialog box. Click a name, then click the To, Cc, or Bcc button to select that name. Enter as many names as required; then click OK to close the box.

- Begin typing the person's name or nickname into one of the lines in the Address area of the Composition window. As you type, Messenger searches the Address Book and shows you, in gray text, the name it thinks you are entering. If it's correct, simply press Tab (to move down to the message area) or Enter (to move to the next Address line) and the name and e-mail address is entered for you.

TIP Remember the Expand Addresses Against Names and Nicknames option button and Expand Addresses Against Nicknames Only option button in the More Messages Preferences dialog box (see Chapter 16). These options determine whether Messenger will recognize names that you type, or only nicknames.

Searching for E-Mail Addresses

You can search your Address Book, along with some other Internet-wide directories such as Four11 and Bigfoot. (See also Chapter 6 for information about searching for people on the Internet.) If your company has set up an LDAP (Lightweight Directory Access Protocol) directory on the corporate intranet, you could use that, too (see Chapter 16 for information about entering LDAP information).

To search for someone, start in this manner:

- Click the Directory button in the Address Book window.
- Choose Edit, Search Directory in the Address Book, Netscape Folder/Messenger Mailbox, Composition, or Message Center window.

Whichever method you choose, you'll see the Search dialog box, which has these options (you can see an example of this box, shown after completing a search, in Figure 17.8):

- *Search for Items* Select the directory you want to search, currently Four11, InfoSpace, Switchboard, WhoWhere, and Bigfoot. You may be able to search a corporate LDAP directory, too. (You can also search FedEx, but only for a package number, of course, not a person!)
- *Where The* Select the item you are going to enter: the person's name, e-mail address, organization, city, and so on.
- *The middle drop-down list* In the middle drop-down list box, select the type of search: contains (the item you are searching contains the text you're going to provide), is (the item exactly matches what you will provide), begins with, and so on.
- *The text box* In the text box, type what you are looking for: the person's name, phone number, and so on.
- *More* Click this button to add another line; you can provide several criteria to search for. However, note that in some cases the more information you provide, the less likely you are to find what you need because the more difficult it will be to match all the criteria. On the other hand, you can use this to narrow a search, by entering a city name, for instance.

Click Search and the search begins. With luck, you'll see something like Figure 17.8. I've found some of my numerous e-mail addresses. I was searching Four11, so, when I double-clicked the entry in the Search window, the Navigator window opened and showed me the information stored at Four11.

FIG. 17.8
I searched Four11 and found myself. Double-click an entry to see information about that person.

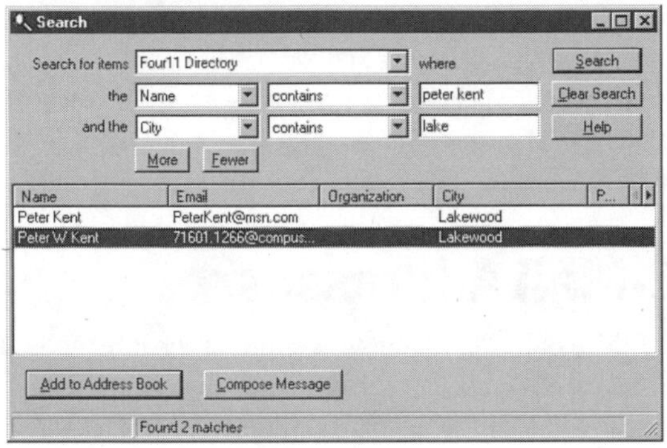

Search for your own information; you may find that you're not listed (you can add yourself to these directories by registering at their sites (for instance, **http://www.four11.com/** and **http://www.bigfoot.com/**). On the other hand, you may not be happy to discover just how much information these directories hold!

Note also that you can click the Add to Address Book and Compose Message buttons in the Search dialog box to…well, yes, add an entry you found to your Address Book or send a message to the person.

E-Mail Security—Encrypting Your Communications

Netscape Communications has been promising e-mail security for a long time now, since way back in the days of Netscape Navigator 2 in 1995. Finally, it's here. Well, almost here. It's actually not working particularly well at the time of writing but should be by the time you read this. (At the time of writing, it was working only on the Windows NT/95 version, not on the Macintosh.)

If you want to use e-mail security, begin by reading Chapter 11. Messenger uses the same public-key encryption system for e-mail that it does for the transmission of data from Web forms.

Here's a quick summary of how e-mail encryption works. First, in order to send an encrypted message to someone, you'll need that person's Personal Certificate. When you send a message to that person, Messenger will use the public key that's embedded in the certificate to encrypt the message—to scramble it so it's unreadable. You'll then send the message to the person, who will use his or her corresponding private key to unscramble it.

The system works the same the other way. In order to send you encrypted e-mail, a friend or colleague must have your Personal Certificate. And you'll use your private key to unscramble the message.

Where, then, do you get Personal Certificates? You can get them from the VeriSign key server, as explained in Chapter 11. Right now, only VeriSign is issuing Personal Certificates, so, if another Messenger user has one, you should be able to find it there (though other organizations may issue them later). Perhaps the best way, though, is to send the personal certificate to the people with whom you need to communicate in encrypted form. This is done by signing your e-mail.

Signing E-Mail and Transferring Certificates

Open the Message Composition window and enter the address of the person to whom you want to send your personal certificate. Then click the Security button to see the Security Info for this message (see Figure 17.9). Scroll down until you see Include My Security Certificate in This Message check box. Check this box to digitally sign your message. (Of course, if you don't have a certificate, you won't be able to do this.)

Part
III

Ch
17

FIG. 17.9
You can sign the message by checking this box.

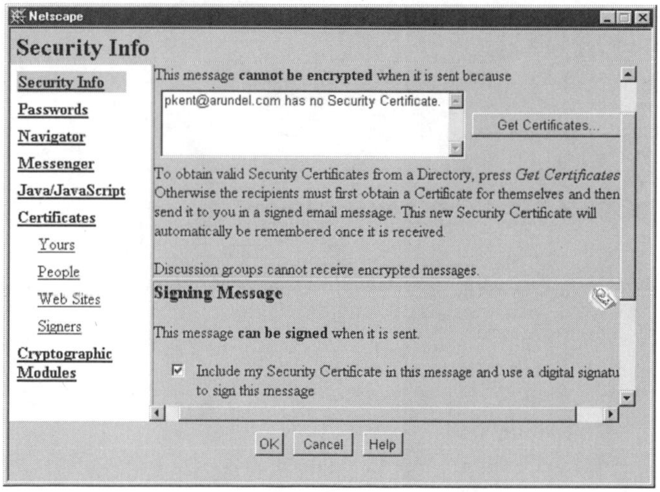

Note that you can also click the Message Sending Options tab on the left side of the Message Composition window, then click the Signed check box.

Note, by the way, that the Security button in the Composition window changes according to the security settings you choose:

The message has not been encrypted or signed.

The message has been signed, but not encrypted.

The message has been encrypted, but not signed.

 The message has been both encrypted and signed.

Now, send your message. You'll be prompted for your keyfile password if you have one (the dialog box won't say that, though; it will say something like "Enter the password or the pin"). See Chapter 11 for more information about certificates and passwords. Then your message will be sent with the certificate. You have actually *signed* this message digitally. What happens when the recipient gets your message? Well, if he's using Messenger or a compatible mail program, he'll see something like what's shown in Figure 17.10.

FIG. 17.10

This message has been signed by the sender.

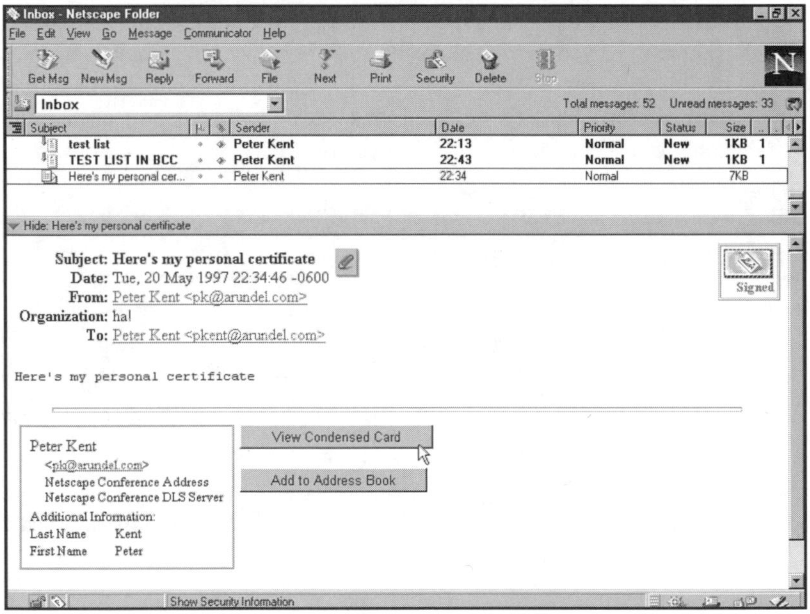

The recipient can click the Signed icon in the top right of the message to see the Security box shown in Figure 17.11. The recipient can click the View button to see the certificate. He could compare the fingerprint on the certificate with the one you have given to him; remember, there's no effective way to fake a fingerprint.

Certificates that arrive in this manner are automatically added to your list of People's cerficates in the Security dialog box. They can be used later to encrypt e-mail.

T I P A digital signature tells you two things. First, you know that the message was signed by the person who owns the personal certificate (or, more accurately, the person with access to that personal certificate). And secondly, you know that the message has not been altered. When the signature is added to the message, information about the message being signed is added to the signature. If the message is modified in some way after signing, the signature is no longer valid.

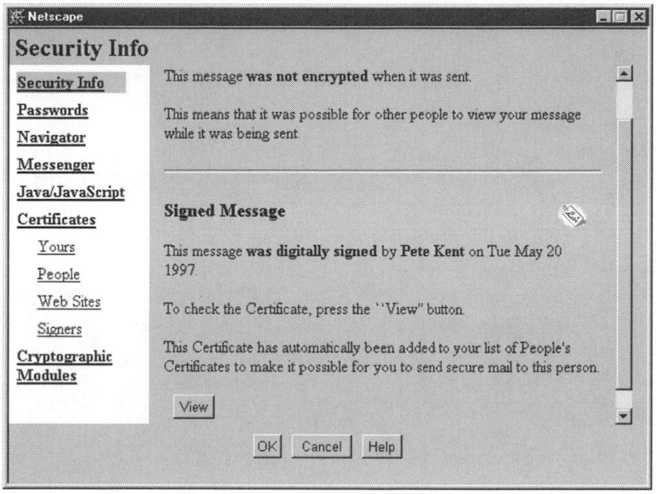

FIG. 17.11
The security box tells you the message has been signed, and allows you to view the certificate.

Netscape

Security Info

Security Info
Passwords
Navigator
Messenger
Java/JavaScript
Certificates
   Yours
   People
   Web Sites
   Signers
Cryptographic Modules

This message **was not encrypted** when it was sent.

This means that it was possible for other people to view your message while it was being sent.

Signed Message

This message **was digitally signed** by **Pete Kent** on Tue May 20 1997.

To check the Certificate, press the "View" button.

This Certificate has automatically been added to your list of People's Certificates to make it possible for you to send secure mail to this person.

View

OK Cancel Help

Part
III

Ch
17

About the vCard

Note, by the way, that in Figure 17.10 you can see two buttons in the message: View Condensed Card and Add to Address Book. These appear here because this message contains the vCard we discussed in Chapter 16 (the collection of information about the sender). The View Condensed Card originally said View Complete Card until I clicked it in order to see more information in the panel to the left of the card. Clicking the second button will, of course, automatically add the person's data to the address book.

TIP Directories can provide vCards, too. You can already download vCards from some directories, such as Four11. When you click a link that says something like Download this person's vCard, the card is automatically transferred to your computer and stored in Communicator's Address Book.

Encrypting E-Mail

You've seen how to send your certificate to other people; when you digitally sign a message, you are automatically sending your signature. Of course, you can reverse this process to get other people's certficates. Once the certificates are loaded into your system, you can encrypt e-mail to those people. You'll remember from Chapter 11 (which you have read, haven't you?) that in order to encrypt an e-mail message, you must have the recipient's personal certificate first. Messenger will use the public key embedded in that certificate to encrypt the message; the recipient will then use the corresponding private key to decrypt the message.

To send encrypted e-mail, simply check the Encrypted box in the Message Sending Options area of the Composition window. Which personal certificate will be used? After all, you may have several. Messenger uses the one originally defined during the certificate registration procedure (see Chapter 11) as the one to be used for e-mail signatures. However, you can pick another—see "Mail Security Settings," later in this chapter.

Another way to encrypt the message is to click the Security button, and you'll see something like Figure 17.12. As you can see in this case (unlike Figure 17.9), we *can* encrypt the message, because we have this recipient's personal certificate on hand. Click the check box at the top (Encrypt This Message), then click OK.

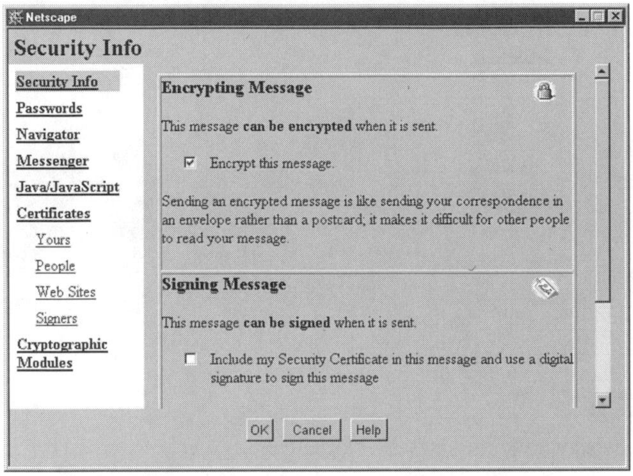

FIG. 17.12

This time, we can encrypt a message to this person, because we have his certificate.

Now, what happens when that person receives the encrypted message? Messenger will see that it's encrypted, and use the private key to decrypt the message. The recipient will see the message in its unencrypted form.

Mail Security Settings

There are a few e-mail security settings you should be aware of. Click the Security button and then click the Messenger heading in the list box on the left side of the dialog box. You'll see the pane in Figure 17.13 (scroll down the pane to see all this information).

The check boxes determine whether Messenger automatically encrypts and signs messages with you having to select those options in the Composition windows. That is, if the check boxes are checked, then the Encrypted and Signed check boxes in the Message Composition box are automatically selected when you start a new message.

The drop-down list box defines which certificate should be used to sign your mail. At the time of this writing, there was no way to quickly select a certificate while creating a new message; the certificate shown here is the one used for all messages, so if you want to use a different certificate for a particular message, you'll have to change this setting.

FIG. 17.13
Make sure you have
your security options
set correctly.

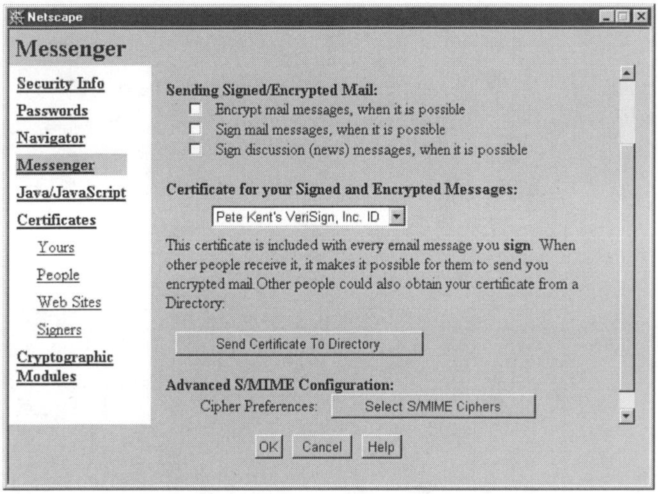

The Send Certificate To Directory button is used to transmit your personal certificate to a directory you select. That way, people will be able to download the certificate when they find your name in the directory, and send you encrypted messages.

Finally, the Select S/MIME Ciphers button allows you to enable and disable the encryption systems in use on your system. You'll probably never have to modify these settings.

E-Mail Filtering

I've received a few dozen e-mail messages today; some days I get many more. Many Internet users are being overwhelmed by the volume of mail they receive—they need a way to help them quickly organize their messages.

Messenger provides something called *filtering* to help you manage your messages. It works like this. You set up a filter, or series of filters, that tell Messenger what to do with messages that you receive. (Messenger filters only incoming messages, not outgoing.) Then, when Messenger retrieves messages, it examines each one and carries out your instructions accordingly. You can tell it to move messages from certain people to a particular folder—or delete them (a great way to ignore messages from your boss or ex-spouse). You can automatically modify the message priority for certain messages, too, marking particular subjects as high-priority messages, for instance.

Here, then, is how to create filters. Choose Edit, Mail Filters to see the Mail Filters dialog box, and then click New. You'll see the Filter Rules dialog box shown in Figure 17.14. (On the Mac, click the Filter Actions triangle—see Figure 17.15—to open up the lower part of this dialog box.)

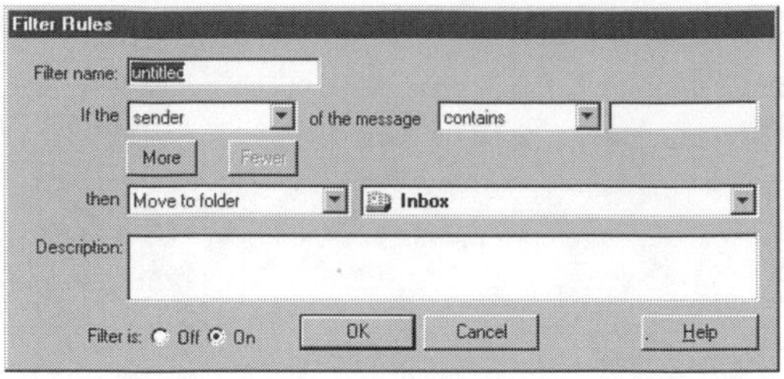

FIG. 17.14

Here's where you create a new filter.

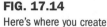

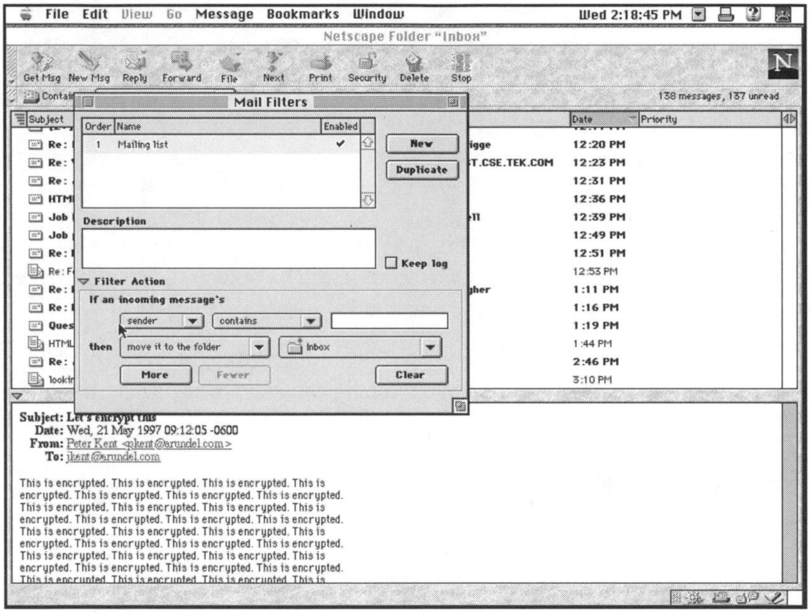

FIG. 17.15

On the Mac, all the filter information is built into one dialog box.

These are the settings you'll work with:

- *Filter name*   Provide a name for the filter; this name will appear in the big list in the Mail Filters dialog box.

- *If The*   Select what part of the message you want Messenger to look at before carrying out an action. Messenger will read the specified part of the message: From (the name and e-mail address of the person sending the message), Subject (the Subject line), Body (the message text itself), Date (the message date), Priority (the Priority setting, shown on the message X-Priority line), Status (the message Status line), To (the name and e-mail address of the person the message is addressed to), CC (the name and e-mail address in the CC line), To or CC (the information in either the To line or CC line).

- *Of the Message*   In this drop-down list box, you'll select the condition that must be met. And in the text box, you'll enter the text that Messenger is looking for. You can select

Contains (the action will be carried out if the text that Messenger examines contains whatever you type into the text box), Doesn't Contain (the action's carried out if the text does not contain what you enter into the text box), Is (the action's carried out if the text exactly matches what you've specified), Isn't (the action is carried out if the text does not exactly match what you've specified), Begins With (the text you've specified must be found at the beginning of the text Messenger is examining), Ends With (the text you've specified must be found at the end of the text Messenger is examining).

- *More* Click this button and you can create another set of conditions that must be met in addition to the first set.

- *Then* This specifies the action you want to be carried out if the conditions are met: Move to Folder (select the folder to move the message to from the drop-down list box that appears), Change Priority (select the priority to give the message from the drop-down list box), Delete, Mark Read, Ignore Thread, Watch Thread (specifies that these messages should be marked as watched threads, so you can quickly view them using View, Messages, Watched Threads With New).

- *Description* Type a description of the filter if you want, as a reminder of what it does.

- *Filter Is* You can turn the filter on or off by selecting an option button.

Click OK to save your filter. You can see your filters listed in the Mail Filters dialog box (see Figure 17.16). You may move the filters around using the arrow buttons if you want. This determines which filter is run first, so you may want one filter to run before another. For instance, you might filter messages with certain subjects into particular folders but then have a filter based on the To address. If Messenger doesn't move the message according to the subject line, it will finally move the message according to the To line.

FIG. 17.16
Here's where you can see your filters listed and modify the order in which they run.

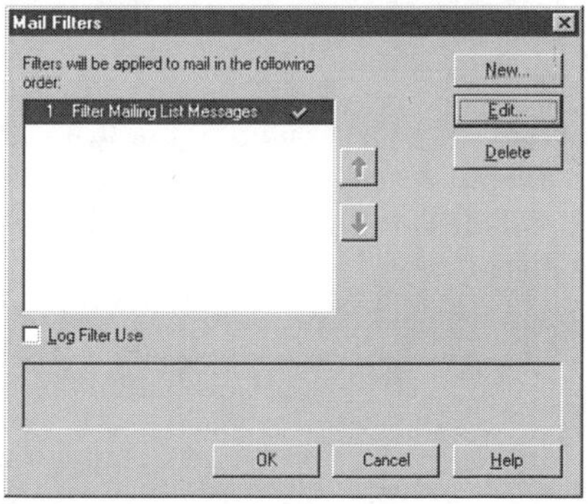

Note also that there's a Log Filter Use check box. This tells Messenger to keep a log file, a record of how the filters are used, which may be handy when trying to figure out why they're not working correctly.

Working Offline

If you have a connection to the Internet that you pay for by the minute, you may want to connect, grab your e-mail (and newsgroup) messages, then log off and read them. Communicator's Offline work Mode helps you do this. (I explained how to start Communicator in offline and online work modes in Chapter 2.)

You can tell Messenger to go online and grab messages, or to grab messages and go offline. Select File, Go Offline, or File, Go Online. You'll see the dialog box in Figure 17.17. Make any necessary changes to the check boxes; you can download (that is, retrieve) your mail messages, your discussion group (newsgroup) messages, and send any pending messages. Click the Go Offline or Go Online button and the action is performed. In the case of Go Offline, the actions are performed and the connection is closed. In the case of Go Online, Messenger connects, the actions are performed, and then Messenger remains in online mode.

FIG. 17.17
Tell Messenger to carry out mail and newsgroup procedures and then log off.

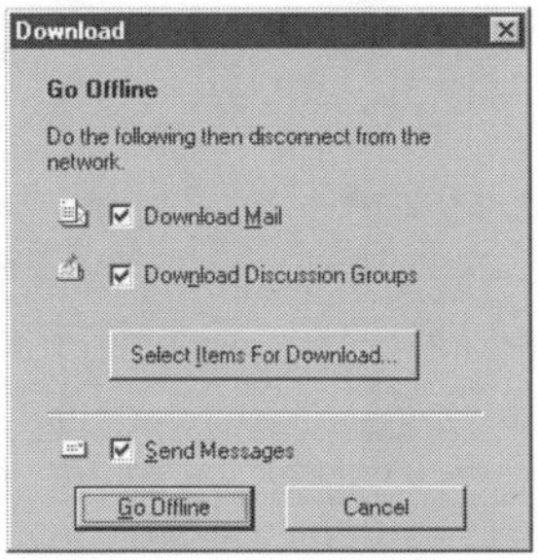

Free Stuff in Your Mailbox—Inbox Direct

Netscape Communications has set up a special program called Inbox Direct. This provides information delivered via e-mail, from a variety of sources. For instance, at the time of writing, there were over 50 services available, such as *TechInvestor*, *PC World Watch*, *Correo Expansión Directo* (a Spanish newspaper), the *London Daily Mirror Direct*, *Travel Discounts Direct*, *WeatherVane*, and *The New York Times Direct*.

The services work like this. Go to the Netscape Web site (**http://www.netscape.com/**) and find the link to Inbox Direct. Then click the Register Now button, fill out the information requested, and select the services you want by clicking a check box.

Within 48 hours, you should start receiving information, perhaps just a confirmation message, or perhaps the service itself will begin. The services vary from a couple of e-mail messages a day, to once a month. All services are free for at least 90 days, and some are free even after that.

The messages you will receive are HTML mail messages. In other words, they're created in order to take advantage of Messenger's ability to display Web pages. The messages will be text, but they'll contain links to images, sounds, and perhaps even Java applets, out on the Web. They'll also contain links to other pages on the Web. You can see an example in Figure 17.18.

FIG. 17.18

This is Netscape Communicator News, one of the Inbox Direct services.

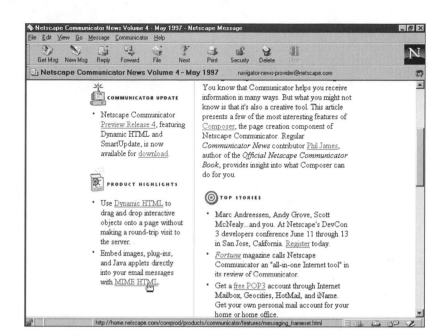

CHAPTER 18

Collabra: From Newsgroups to Corporate Communications

You may already be familiar with Internet newsgroups. These are discussion groups: Pick a subject, visit the group, read people's messages, respond, and start your own "conversations" or threads. There are tens of thousands of Internet newsgroups spread around the world, on every conceivable subject. Netscape Collabra is Communicator's newsreader program, a program that enables you to take part in these discussions. ■

Opening newsgroups from Netscape

Before you can use Collabra, you must tell the program where to find the newsgroup messages.

What is the newsgroup hierarchy system?

Newsgroups are part of a system in which groups are related to one another within subject hierarchies.

Reading newsgroup messages

There are several ways to open a newsgroup and read the messages.

Responding to messages and starting your own "conversations"

Newsgroups are an interactive medium; don't just sit there, get involved.

How to grab sounds and pictures from newsgroups

Newsgroups messages may contain sounds and pictures embedded in them. Collabra makes it easy to hear or view these inclusions.

Newsgroups and Discussion Groups

Netscape is "repositioning" its newsreader. Earlier versions of Netscape Navigator had built-in newsreaders, but with the release of Collabra, Netscape Communications is now calling the newsreader a "groupware" product, and their press releases talk of "public or private online discussion forums." In other words, it's not just a program for wasting time in Internet newsgroups, but it's a program that corporations can use on their intranets for employee communication. Netscape has gone so far as to remove the word "news" from references to Collabra. For instance, there's a Groups Server category in the Preferences dialog box, instead of the more traditional News Server. And they refer to groups as discussion groups rather than newsgroups. In the near future, though, most users will be working with it in the usual way, as a newsgroup program. And when you're actually using the program, the distinction is of no importance: Discussion group or newsgroup, the program works in exactly the same way.

There are tens of thousands of newsgroups. But you can't get to all these groups through your Internet service provider. Most Internet newsgroups are of local interest only and are not distributed throughout the world. But thousands of newsgroups—currently around 30,000— *are* distributed internationally, through a system known as UseNet. Each Internet service provider has to decide which of these UseNet newsgroups it wants to subscribe to. Service providers typically provide anywhere from 3,000 or 4,000 groups to around 10,000 or 12,000, and sometimes 20,000 or more. Enough to keep a chronic insomniac very busy.

> **N O T E** The term *news* is used rather ambiguously on the Internet. Often, when you see a reference to news somewhere, it refers to the messages left in newsgroups, *not* journalism. Newsgroups are, in most cases, discussion groups, although some newsgroups do contain real news stories and press releases. ■

Communicator's Newsgroup/Web Integration

Netscape Communicator provides a two-way integration of newsgroups: You can open newsgroups from Web pages and the Web browser, and open Web pages from newsgroup messages. It also combines e-mail and newsgroup messages into the same system. As you saw in Chapter 16, "Messenger: World Wide E-Mail," the Message Center window provides access to both e-mail and newsgroups, and the Netscape Folder/Messenger Mailbox window works in much the same way as the Netscape Discussion window. To use Collabra, you'll begin by opening the Message Center window, and using one of these methods:

- Double-click the Netscape Collabra icon on your desktop or program group.
- Choose Communicator, Collabra Discussions Groups from any of the Communicator windows.
- Click the Discussions button on the Component bar.
- In Windows 95, select Start, Programs, Netscape Communicator, Netscape Collabra.

When you open the Message Center window, you may see something like what's shown in Figure 18.1. You can see that this has a news server: news.mindspring.com. Below the server is a list of subscribed newsgroups: alt.alien.visitors, alt.alien.wanderers, and so on. You'll see how to subscribe to newsgroups a little later in this chapter, under "Displaying the Newsgroups and Subscribing."

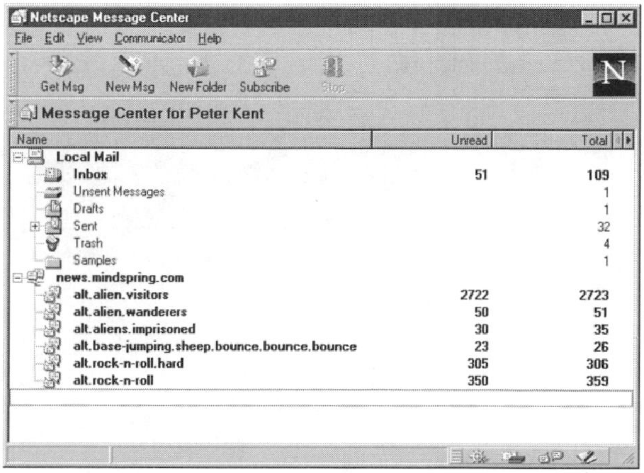

FIG. 18.1

If you've already entered the news server information, then you'll see the server listed in the Message Center window.

Of course, you may not have set up a news server yet, in which case you won't see one listed here. So let's see how to set up the newsgroup system. First, refer to Chapter 16, where I explained how to set up the e-mail system. Setting up the newsgroup system is almost exactly the same. In fact, once you've set up the e-mail system, you've entered most of the information that Collabra requires.

So return to Chapter 16 and follow the instructions for entering information into the Mail & Groups category in the Preferences dialog box. (You can open this from the Message Center window by choosing Edit, Preferences.) Make sure you've entered all the information discussed in that chapter. You'll also have to include the following items, under the Groups Server subcategory (see Figure 18.2), that I didn't cover in that chapter:

- *Discussion Groups (News) Server*   Enter the host name of your News (NNTP) Server, which is the computer that contains all the newsgroup messages (*NNTP* means *Network News Transfer Protocol*). You can get the host name from your service provider or system administrator. The news server may provide access to Internet newsgroups, or to private discussion groups set up by your company.

- *Port*   You probably won't have to change this setting; only modify it if told to do so by your service provider or system administrator.

- *Secure*   If this news server is a secure server, one that can send and accept encrypted messages, check this box; again, check with the service provider or administrator (few Internet news servers are secure, though many corporate servers will be).

- *Discussion Group (News) Folder* This is the name of the directory where Netscape will store information about the newsgroups you've subscribed to. There's generally no need to modify this.

- *Ask Me Before Downloading More Than xx Messages* You can tell Collabra not to download more than a specified number of newsgroup messages without asking you first.

FIG. 18.2

Enter the Groups Server information.

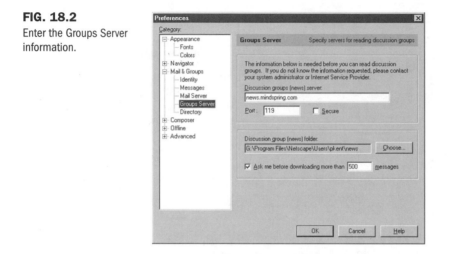

> **TIP** After you've set up the server, go to the Message Center, right-click the server, and select Discussion Group Server Properties (or click once and choose Edit, Discussion Group Server Properties). You'll see the box in Figure 18.3.

FIG. 18.3

The Group Server information.

This dialog box shows you the basic server information, but also provides a couple of options. You may need to provide a username and password in order to use the newsgroup. The options here allow you to ensure that Collabra does not access the server without asking for your information first (Always Ask Me For My User name and Password) or only the first time during an online session (Only Ask Me For My User name and Password When Necessary).

The Newsgroup Hierarchies

Before looking at ways to work in a newsgroup, you need to know about the newsgroup hierarchies. Internet newsgroups use a hierarchical naming system. The first name is the top level. For instance, in soc.couples.intercultural, the soc bit is the top level. Below that are sublevels. There's no soc. newsgroup; rather, below the soc. level are many sublevels, just one of which is couples. In fact, there's a soc.couples newsgroup, *and* sublevels below soc.couples. For instance, there's a soc.couples.intercultural group and a soc.couples.wedding group. The top-level UseNet groups are shown in the following table:

Top level	Subject
comp	Computer-related topics
news	Information about newsgroups themselves, including software used to read newsgroup messages and information about finding and using newsgroups
rec	Recreational topics: hobbies, sports, the arts, and so on
sci	Science topics; discussions about research in the "hard" sclMnces—physics, chemistry, and so on—as well as some social sciences
soc	A wide range of social issues, including types of societies and subcultures, as well as sociopolitical subjects
talk	Debates about politics, religion, and anything else that's controversial
misc	General topics: looking for jobs, selling things, a forum for paramedics

Not all newsgroups are true UseNet groups. Many are local groups, although they may be distributed internationally—through UseNet, just to confuse the issue. Such newsgroups are known as Alternative Newsgroups Hierarchies. The top-level groups are:

Top level	Subject
alt	Alternative subjects; often subjects that many people would consider "inappropriate," pornographic, or just weird; alt groups may also contain interesting and worthwhile information, but have been created in an "unauthorized" manner to save time and hassle
bionet	Biological subjects
bit	A variety of newsgroups from the BITNET network
biz	Business subjects, including advertisements
clari	Clarinet's newsgroups from "official" and commercial sources—mainly UPI news stories, press releases, and various syndicated columns

Part III

Ch 18

continued

continues

Top level	Subject
courts	Related to law and lawyers
de	Various German language newsgroups
fj	Various Japanese language newsgroups
gnu	The Free Software Foundation's newsgroups
hepnet	Discussions about high-energy and nuclear physics
ieee	The Institute of Electrical and Electronics Engineers' newsgroups
info	A collection of mailing lists formed into newsgroups at the University of Illinois
k12	Discussions about primary and secondary education
relcom	Russian language newsgroups, mainly distributed in the former Soviet Union
vmsnet	Subjects of interest to VAX/VMS computer users

You'll see many other categories, too, often local newsgroups from particular countries, towns, universities, and so on. And if your company has set up a news server, you'll be able to work with your company's own private newsgroups, too.

N O T E   It's sometimes said that "alt" stands for "anarchists, lunatics, and terrorists." The alt groups can be very strange; they're also some of the most popular groups on the Internet. ■

Getting the News

How can you view a newsgroup's list of messages? The following are several ways to start:

- Type a news: URL into the Navigator Location bar (news:alt.alien.visitors, for instance) and press Enter. Netscape will open the Collabra window and connect to your news server. (Note that the news: URL does not have the two forward slashes after the colon.)

- Click a link that contains a news: URL. The link may be in a Web page in Navigator, in an e-mail message in Messenger, or even in a newsgroup message in Collabra.

- Select a newsgroup from within the Collabra window (I'll explain that in a moment).

Now and again, you'll find Web documents that contain links to newsgroups. Go to Yahoo! (**http://www.yahoo.com**; see Chapter 6, "Searching for Information on the Web") and follow any hierarchy down a few levels; you'll eventually come to a list of newsgroups. For instance, follow the hierarchy to Entertainment:Music:Usenet. (You can go directly to this document with this URL: **http://www.yahoo.com/Entertainment/Music/Usenet/**.)

This document provides links to information about dozens of music-related newsgroups: a variety of alt.music newsgroups (alt.music.prince, alt.music.producer, and so on), rec.music.info, rec.music.marketplace, rec.music.misc, and rec.music.reviews. You'll find information about each newsgroup (a short description and the e-mail address of the person running the group) and a link to the group. When you click the link—a news: link—Netscape will open the Collabra window. If there are more messages in that newsgroup than the number you specified in the Groups Server category of the Preferences dialog box (the Ask Me Before Downloading More Than xx Messages setting), it will display the dialog box shown in Figure 18.4.

FIG. 18.4

Tell Collabra how many messages you want.

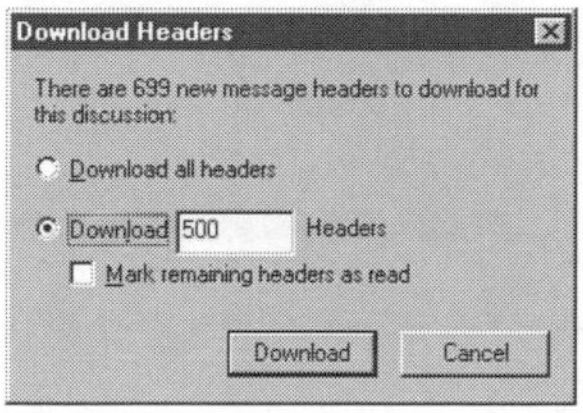

By default, the Download All Headers option button is selected, so you can simply click Download to get all the message headers (not the actual messages, just the header indicating what each message is about). Or you can click the Download xxx Headers option button, and enter a number into the text box, to download that many headers (perhaps you just want to see a few samples). You can also click the Mark Remaining Headers as Read check box. We'll discuss marking messages as read later in this chapter, under "Read versus Unread Messages."

When you click the Download button, Collabra transfers the messages from the news server; you'll see something like Figure 18.5.

T I P Another good search site that references newsgroups is Jump City (**http://www.jumpcity.com/**). You can select a subject, and you'll find a list of related Web sites and newsgroups. Also, try **http:// www.w3.org/hypertext/DataSources/News/Groups/Overview.html**, which is a large list of newsgroups with links that will open the groups.

N O T E Collabra may be unable to open the newsgroup. If the news server you've specified doesn't have the newsgroup, Collabra can't display it. Each news server subscribes to a different list of newsgroups, so now and again you'll run into a server that doesn't have the newsgroup referenced by the link you clicked. ▇

If you still want to read the newsgroup's messages, you may be able to choose another news server. See "Selecting Another News Server," later in this chapter.

Part
III

Ch
18

Reply to the selected
newsgroup message.

Post a message to the
newsgroup.

Get more e-mail messages
(not newsgroup messages).

Forward the selected
message to an e-mail user.

Save the message in
another folder.

View the next unread
message.

Select a subscribed
newsgroup here to see its
messages.

FIG. 18.5

The alt.alien.visitors
newsgroup is a window
on another world (well,
many worlds).

Return to the
previously read
message.

Click here to
close the
lower pane.

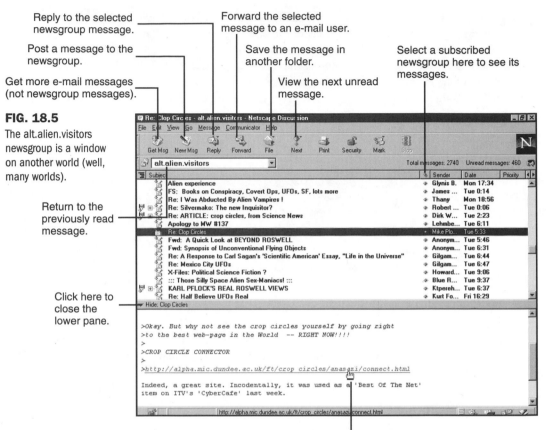

Newsgroup messages may contain
links to Web sites.

Working in the Newsgroups

What will you see when you open the newsgroup window? Perhaps something like Figure 18.5. To display the window like this, I typed news:alt.alien.visitors in Navigator's Location text box and pressed Enter. The window opened, and after a few seconds (it can take a moment), the list of messages appeared in the top pane. I then clicked a message, and the message text appeared in the bottom pane. Note that when you first see the list of headers, that's all you've got; the actual messages are still on the server. It's only when you click a message to see it in the lower pane (or double-click it to open a window) that the message is transferred.

TIP Some newsgroups are huge, and it can take a while to download the message listing. If it's taking too long and you don't want to wait, click the Stop toolbar button or press Esc.

If you've read Chapters 16 and 17, you're already familiar with the News window because it's very similar to the Mail window. The top pane shows a list of messages held by the newsgroup. The bottom pane shows the contents of the selected message (because the message is stored on the news server, it takes a few moments to view the message after clicking the entry in the top pane). You can also double-click a message to view it in a separate message window.

Displaying the Newsgroups and Subscribing

Collabra opens when you use a news: link, but you can also view newsgroups by going to Collabra and selecting the one you want. Here's what you need to do.

First, in the Netscape Discussion or Message Center window, choose File, Subscribe to Discussion Groups. Collabra will probably begin retrieving a list of newsgroups from the news server (if it doesn't, click the Get Newsgroups button). Retrieving this list may take a little while, depending on the speed of your connection and the number of newsgroups held by the news server. When Collabra has finished retrieving the list, you'll see something like Figure 18.6.

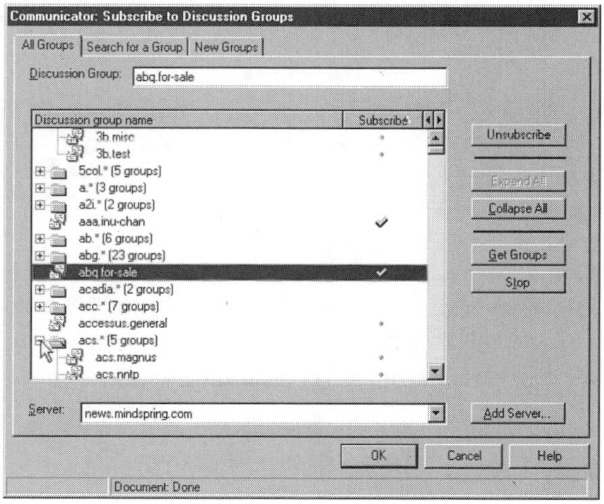

FIG. 18.6
Click in the Subscribe column to subscribe to a newsgroup.

Part
III
Ch
18

> **TIP** If all the names of the newsgroups are truncated, drag the column-heading border to the right to adjust the Discussion Group Name column size. Or use the little triangle buttons to shift the columns.

As you can see, some entries in this list have a folder icon, and others use the "speech bubble" icon. The folder icon represents a collection of newsgroups; click the plus sign (+) icon next to the folder to see the hierarchy expand, as you can see in Figure 18.6. (Use Expand All and Collapse All to open and close all the folders.) The "speech bubble" icons represent actual newsgroups that you can subscribe to.

Now notice the Subscribe column. Each newsgroup listed will have either a gray dot or a check mark in this column. A check mark indicates that you've subscribed to the newsgroup. That means the group will be listed in the Message Center window, below the news server.

TIP If you know the name of the newsgroup you are looking for, you can type it in the Newsgroup text box at the top of the dialog box—the list will scroll down to that newsgroup.

There are two more ways to find groups. Click the Search for a Group tab at the top of the dialog box to see the pane in Figure 18.7. Type a word into the Search For text box, then click the Search Now button. The list box will show all the groups that contain that word.

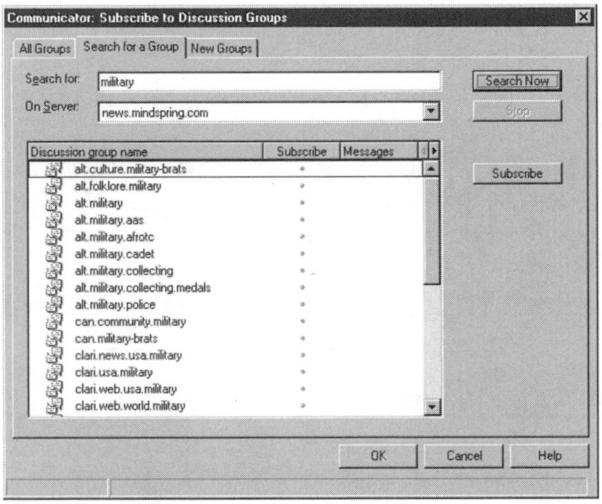

FIG. 18.7

Search for a keyword and Collabra shows you the matching groups.

If you click the New Groups tab, you'll see a list of groups that your service provider has recently added to its collection of newsgroups. There's a Clear New button in this pane; the list shows all the groups added since the last time you clicked this button. And if you click the Get New button, Collabra checks the news server for the new groups.

Click the gray dot in the Subscribe column—in any one of these three panes—next to a group that you want to read (or click a group and then click the Subscribe button). When you've subscribed to all the groups you want to work with, click OK. You'll find yourself back at the Message Center window. This time you'll notice a little plus sign (+) icon next to the name of the news server. Click this to expand the list of newsgroups. That is, you'll now see all the newsgroups that you've subscribed to, as we saw in Figure 18.1.

To read a newsgroup's messages, simply double-click the newsgroup name, and the Netscape Newsgroup window opens. This is pretty much the same as the Folder window which you saw in Chapters 16 and 17, so if you're not sure how to work in this window, look back at those chapters.

TIP Because newsgroup-message subject lines are often very long, you may need to drag the bars between the panes to the left or right to make more room for the text. You can also move columns around by dragging the column headers to different positions.

Automatically Subscribing to Groups

Unlike the newsreaders that came with earlier versions of Netscape Navigator, with Collabra you must subscribe to a group in order to view it. But there are three very quick ways to subscribe to a group and view it:

■ Type news:newsgroup.name into Navigator's Location bar and press Enter. Collabra's Netscape Newsgroup window opens and loads the newsgroup.

■ In the Message Center window, choose File, New Discussion Group. Type the newsgroup name and press Enter. The newsgroup is added to the list; double-click it to view it.

■ Click a news: link in a Web page, e-mail message, or newsgroup message. The newsgroup is loaded into the Netscape Newsgroup window.

In each case you are now subscribed to the group. If you only want to view it quickly, rather than subscribe to it, you'll have to unsubscribe; in the Message Center window, right-click the group and select Remove Discussion Group, or click once and press Delete (or select Edit, Delete Discussion Group).

The Newsgroup Message

What will you find in the message text? Well, the newsgroup message is very similar to what you saw in Chapter 16 when you looked at an e-mail message. You'll find the header: Subject, Date, From, and Organization. You'll often find Newsgroups and References entries, too, and you'll see that they're active links (colored and underlined).

The Newsgroups entry shows you to which newsgroups the message has been posted; many are posted to multiple newsgroups. Click a newsgroup name to open that newsgroup (and to automatically subscribe to that group). And the References entries show you related messages (other messages in the thread). Click a reference to see another message displayed in the main Navigator window (though you'll often find that the message isn't available).

Below the header you'll find the message text. (If you want to see the full header, all the strange routing stuff, choose View, Headers, All.)

You may see other things, too. If there's an URL in the message, Collabra converts it to an active link; click it and the referenced document will appear in the Navigator window.

TIP You may not have retrieved all the messages from the group. To get more, choose File, Get Messages, New, or File, Get Messages, Next 500.

Pictures from Words

Newsgroup messages are simple text messages. So if you want to send a computer file in a newsgroup message—maybe you want to send a picture, sound, or word processing document—you must convert it to text.

There are two ways to do this: You can UUENCODE a binary file, or you can use MIME. You saw in Chapter 16 how to attach files to messages, and the process is the same when posting to newsgroups—Netscape uses the MIME system by default, but as you saw in Chapter 16, you can use UUENCODE if you prefer.

But how about converting back from UUENCODE or MIME? Let's say you find a newsgroup message that contains a file you want—a picture, for instance. If you could see the newsgroup message before Collabra had a chance to convert it, it would appear to be full of garbage text, a huge jumble of mixed-up characters. But Collabra may be able to convert this text for you automatically. When it begins transferring a newsgroup message, it looks for evidence of a MIME or UUENCODE attachment. If it finds one, it tries to convert it and can do so if the binary file is a .jpg or .gif image file, as you can see in Figure 18.9.

FIG. 18.9

Collabra converted the UUENCODEd message to a picture automatically. I can now right-click and save the file.

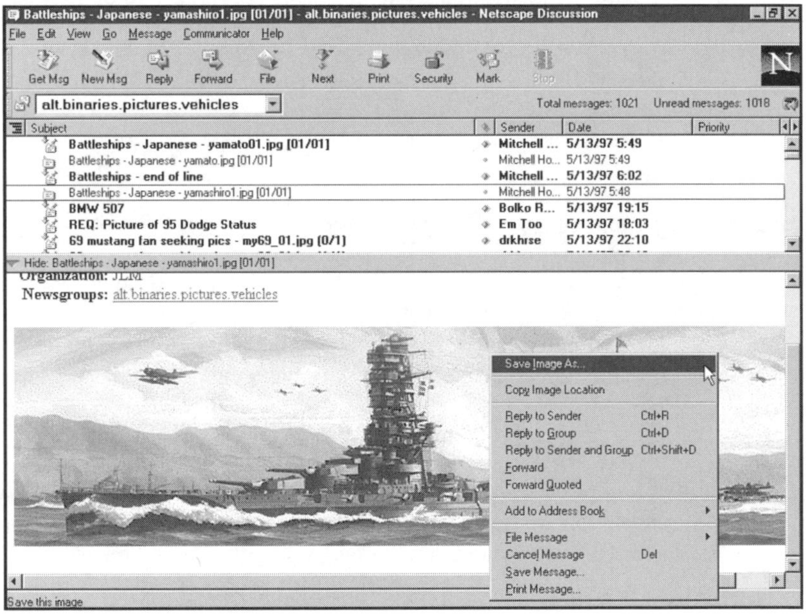

> **TIP** You can save a picture after it's converted by right-clicking the picture and choosing Save Image As. Or choose View, Attachments, As Links to see a link to the image in place of the image itself, then use the link's pop-up menu to save the image. However, many of the pictures you find in newsgroups have been posted illegally by people who don't own the copyright.

What if the file isn't a picture file, or is a picture type that Collabra can't display? As long as Collabra can convert it into a file of some kind, you'll see a link to the file. Click this link and one of two things will happen: Either Navigator will open and "run" the file (if Navigator can handle the file type or has a viewer or plug-in that can handle the file—see Chapters 9 and 10), or you'll see the Save As dialog box so you can save the file to your hard disk. For instance, if the message contains a .wav or .au sound file, Navigator will open and play the sound when you click the link.

There will be times when Collabra won't be able to convert the file—you'll see neither a picture nor a link to the file, or perhaps you'll see just part of the picture, or the link takes you to a picture fragment. Sometimes you'll see a link that's identified as a message/partial type. These things may happen for one of the following reasons:

- The file is split into multiple newsgroup messages. (Many binary files are coded with UUENCODE, then divided into several parts because the entire block of text is too big for a single message.) At the time of this writing, Collabra could not paste these pieces together, though a later version may—some other newsreaders can do so.

- It wasn't encoded properly in the first place. Somewhere between 10% and 20% of all the uploaded binary files are damaged in some way and can't be decoded (though the proportion of bad uploads is probably dropping quickly, as newsreader software improves).

> **T I P** Remember, there are two ways to view these attachments. If you've chosen View, Attachments, As Links, you won't see the pictures displayed correctly. Rather you'll see a link you can click to save the picture to your hard disk. In order to see the pictures, you must choose View, Attachments, Inline.

Working with Multiple Message Uploads

Collabra can't decode files that were uploaded in multiple messages, as many are; you'll often see message subject lines that say something like `Picture.jpg 1/3`, `Picture.jpg 2/3`, and so on. So if you find a file you really need, and Collabra can't get it for you, what do you do? Well, you might begin by finding a decoding utility such as Munpack (DOS and Windows, used to decode MIME), WinCode (Windows, used for UUENCODE and MIME), or Yet Another Base64 Decode (Macintosh, for UUENCODE and MIME). You may already have a converter, too, as they are increasingly built into other programs. For instance, if you have Norton Navigator, a Windows 95 add-on utility collection from Symantec, you already have a UUENCODE/DECODE utility built into Norton File Manager.

You'll have to save the newsgroup messages in text files (choose File, Save As). Some of these utilities, such as WinCode, can automatically string the component files together. Or you may have to open a word processor or text editor, copy the files into a single document, save the document, and then use the utility. You can find these conversion utilities at sites such as **http://www.jumbo.com/** and **http://www.shareware.com/** and at many other shareware sites.

The Gibberish Message—ROT13

Now and again, especially in the more contentious newsgroups, you'll run into messages that seem to be gibberish. Everything's messed up; each word seems to be a jumbled mix of characters almost as if the message has been encrypted. It has.

What you are seeing is ROT13, a very simple substitution cipher (one in which a character is substituted for another). It's actually very easy to read. ROT13 means rotated 13. In other words, each character in the alphabet has been replaced by the character 13 places further along. Instead of A you see N, instead of B you see O, instead of C you see P, and so on. Got it? So to read the message, all you need to do is substitute the correct characters. Easy. (Or *Rnfl*, I should say.)

For those of you in a hurry, there's an easier way. Choose <u>V</u>iew, Unscram<u>b</u>le (ROT13), and like magic, the message changes into real words.

TIP So what's the point? Why encode a message with a system that is so ridiculously easy to break? People don't use ROT13 as a security measure to make a message unreadable to all but those with the "secret key." After all, anyone with a newsgroup reader that has an ROT13 command has the key.

Encoding using ROT13 is a way of saying, "If you read this message, you may be offended, so if you are easily offended, don't read it!" ROT13 messages are often crude, lewd, or just plain rude! Converting a message into ROT13 forces readers to decide whether or not they want to risk being offended.

Threading and References

Many of the messages you will see in the newsgroups are replies to earlier messages. Someone sends a message with a question or comment, someone replies, someone else replies to the reply, and so on.

If all you saw were a chronological list of messages in the newsgroup, you'd find it very difficult to figure out what's going on. For this reason, make sure *threading* is turned on. If it isn't, click the button on the left side of the column heading bar, or choose <u>V</u>iew, S<u>o</u>rt, by <u>T</u>hread. Of course, the Netscape Newsgroup window is really the same as the Netscape Folder/Messenger Mailbox window, so threading works in much the same way as you learned in Chapter 17.

Also notice that many messages have a References line in their headers. This line shows a series of numbers, each of which is a link to a particular message—generally the message to which the one you're reading is a reply. Click one of these links to, perhaps, display that message in the main Netscape window.

NOTE You may not be able to find the original message in a message thread. Messages are not held in a newsgroup forever; the newsgroup files your service provider maintains have to be cleaned of old messages to make room for new ones. So if the thread is more than a few days old, you may not be able to find the message that began the thread in the first place. ▪

There are a number of special threading commands you can use:

Message, Ignore Thread	Select a message and then use this command to tell Collabra to ignore the thread.
Message, Watch Thread	Select a message and then use this command to tell Collabra to watch the thread. It will mark the thread with the little glasses icon.
View, Messages, Watched Threads with New	Select this to quickly see all the threads that you marked using the Watch Thread command.
View, Messages, Threads with New	Select this to see the new threads that have begun since the last time you viewed the newsgroup.
View, Messages, All	Select this to view all message threads.
View, Messages, Ignored	Select this to view the threads you marked using the Ignore Thread command.

Putting In Your Own Two Cents: Posting and Responding

You can just lurk in the newsgroups if you want (just read without taking any part in the discussions). Or you can put in your own two cents' worth by responding to messages or even starting your own discussion. The following are several ways to do this:

Part III

Ch 18

■ *Reply to a message*   Click the Reply button and a menu opens (or choose Message, Reply). Then select one of the following menu options:

  • *Reply to Sender*   Sends an e-mail message to the person who posted the message to the group.

  • *Reply to Sender and All Recipients*   Sends an e-mail message to the person who posted the message to the group, and to anyone who received an e-mail copy of the original message.

  • *Reply to Group*   Sends a reply to the newsgroup.

  • *Reply to Sender and Group*   Sends an e-mail message to the person who posted the message to the group, and also posts the reply to the group itself. (Nope, at the time of writing there was no "Reply to Sender and All Recipients and Group command!)

■ *Forward the message to someone*   To e-mail a copy of the selected message, choose Message, Forward, or click the Forward button.

■ *Send a new message*   To begin a new "conversation" in the newsgroup, choose Message, NewCompose Message, or click the New Msg button.

■ *Send an e-mail message*   You can send an e-mail message to someone while working in Collabra (anyone, not just a newsgroup correspondent), by choosing Message, New Message (or clicking the New Msg button); when the Composition window opens, delete the newsgroup name and change Group: to To:.

When you send a message, you'll be using the Composition window you saw in Chapter 16. That means, of course, that you can send newsgroup messages that are formatted using HTML—pages that look like Web pages, with pictures, links, colored text, and so on. Right now that's not a good idea for most newsgroups, as most newsreaders won't be able to display those pages properly. However, if you are using a corporate news server, and everyone in your corporation is working with Netscape Communicator, then you can safely format your newsgroup pages.

Read versus Unread Messages

When you click a newsgroup and Collabra retrieves the list of newsgroup messages, does it retrieve the entire list? No. It retrieves a list of messages that are marked as *Unread*.

How, then, does a message get marked as Read? Well, when Netscape displays the message contents, it marks the message as Read, removing the green diamond from the "Read" column in the top pane (the column with a green diamond at the top). But there are other ways to mark messages as Read, even if you've *not* read them. You can do this so that you don't see the message the next time you view the contents of this newsgroup. For instance, you might read a message's Subject line and know you're not interested in the message contents. Or maybe you've read the first message in a thread and know you don't care about the rest of the messages in the thread. So they don't appear in the list on your next visit to the newsgroup, mark them as Read by doing the following:

- Click the green diamond once in the Read column, removing the diamond.

- Select a message and choose <u>M</u>essage, <u>M</u>ark, or click the Mark button. Then select one of the following options from the menu that opens:

  As Read—The message is marked as read.

  Thread Read—All the messages in the same thread as the selected message are marked as Read.

  All Read—Every message in the newsgroup is marked as Read. The next time you view the newsgroup, you'll see only new messages listed.

  By Date—All messages up to the date you specify are marked as read.

Of course, you can go the other way, marking messages that you *have* read as Unread. Why bother? So that the next time you view the contents of the newsgroup, that message will still be there. (Maybe you're pondering something in the message, and want to reply to it later.) To mark a message as Unread, do the following:

- Click a message once and then choose Message, Mark, As Unread, or click the Mark button and select As Unread.

- Click the tiny dot in the Read column; Netscape will replace the dot with the green diamond, marking it as Unread.

Saving Messages

You can save newsgroup messages if you want. In fact, if you find a useful message, don't assume it will be there when you come back to view it later. If the message is removed from your service provider's computer—as it will be eventually—you won't be able to retrieve it.

 Choose File, Save As. You can also print the message; File, Print Page. Better still, why not create a folder into which you can save messages that you may want later? In the Message Center window, use the File, New Folder command to create the folder, then use the File button (or the various Move and Copy commands we saw in Chapter 16) to move messages to the folder. Whatever method you use, a copy of the newsgroup message will be placed into the folder. You can even drag a group of selected messages from the Netscape Discussion window onto the folder in the Message Center window; the message will be downloaded from the server and saved in the folder.

Searching for Messages

Collabra provides a nice way to quickly search a newsgroup's messages for a particular subject or participant. Choose Edit, Search Messages to see one of the search boxes you've seen already (in Chapter 17). Simply select either Sender or Subject in the first drop-down list box (currently most news servers will work only with Sender and Subject, not with Body, Date, or Any Text). Then type the word, e-mail address, or name you're looking for into the text box at the end of the line, and click Search. In a few moments, you may see a list of matching messages. Double-click a message to open it in a message window. (Unfortunately, this great little feature does not always work.)

Selecting Another News Server

Collabra lets you work with more than one news server. Why would you want to do that? For a variety of reasons:

- You may have a newsgroup server and a private corporate server as well.
- You may have several Internet Service Providers, each with a different selection of newsgroups.
- Some news servers provide access to a group of specialized newsgroups that are not widely available.
- Maybe you can't find a newsgroup you want on your service provider's news server, and your service provider can't or won't add the newsgroup; you can use a public news server to view that newsgroup.

In the Netscape Message Center, choose File, New Discussion Group Server. Type the Server address of the news server you want to use (if you're unsure of this, ask your system administrator or service provider). Make any other settings necessary (we've seen these before, earlier in this chapter), then click OK. Collabra will add the server to bottom of the list in the Message Center window. Select the server, then select File, Subscribe to Discussion Groups, and Collabra will connect to the news server and retrieve the list of newsgroups held by that server. You can now use this server in exactly the same way that you use your default host.

> **TIP**   If you need a public server, try the following sites for information:
>
> **http://www.yahoo.com/News/Usenet/Public_Access_Usenet_Sites/**
>
> **http://www.lipsia.de/~michael/lists/pubservers.html**
>
> **http://www.geocities.co.m/Hollywood/2513/news.html**

To remove a news server you no longer need, right-click the server in the Message Center window; then choose Remove Discussion Group Server. Or simply click it and press Delete.

Your Very Own News Server

Netscape sells a secure news server that some corporations are now using. This allows employees to send messages to a newsgroup and read messages from the group with complete security. The messages are encrypted between Collabra and the server. So a secure news server lets an organization set up private newsgroups. A company might have newsgroups in which employees all over the world could discuss private business securely, for instance. These newsgroups could be available over an intranet or even over the Internet itself. Employees in many different countries, using a variety of different private and commercial connections to the Internet, could carry out private discussions across this most public of networks.

Setting Newsgroup Properties

You can set a variety of properties for newsgroups, related to how Collabra saves and transfers messages. Open the Preferences dialog box (Edit, Preferences), then open the Advanced category and click the Disk Space subcategory (see Figure 18.10). This is where you define how Collabra transfers and saves messages—that is, how much disk space it will use for messages. (As you'll see in a moment, you are setting up system defaults, but you can in some cases modify individual newsgroups; for instance, you could allow Collabra to save more messages from a particular newsgroup.)

These are your options (note that the first two actually refer to both e-mail and newsgroups; the rest are specifically for newsgroups):

Do Not Download Any Messages Larger Than xx Kb—You can tell Collabra not to download very large messages.

Automatically Compact Folders When It Will Save Over xx Kb—Collabra can compact the databases holding the messages. You can use the File, Compress Folders command, or allow Collabra to do it automatically when a certain amount of disk space can be saved.

Keep Messages Which Have Arrived in the Past xx Days—Select this option button if you want to stop Collabra from removing messages that have arrived within a certain time period.

Keep All Messages—Select this to stop Collabra from deleting old messages entirely.

Keep the Newest xx Messages—Select this to stop Collabra from removing the most recent messages.

Keep Only Unread Messages—Allow Collabra to remove all but the unread messages.

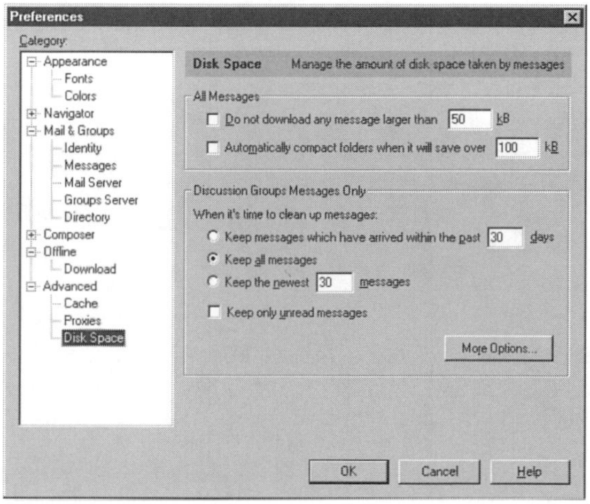

FIG. 18.10

You can define which messages are transferred, and how long they will be saved.

Click the More Options button and you'll see the dialog box in Figure 18.11. If you check this check box, Collabra will remove message bodies—the actual contents—but keep headers for messages over the specified age. Note, however, that just because there's a header doesn't mean you'll be able to retrieve the body; in fact, if it's 20 days old, you probably *won't* be able to retrieve the body later. (As mentioned before, if you want to keep a newsgroup message, save it in a text file or another folder.)

FIG. 18.11

You can save message headers and delete bodies if you want.

Well, you've set up the newsgroup defaults, but you can modify the settings for specific newsgroups. In the Message Center, right-click the newsgroup, then choose Discussion Group Properties. (Or choose Edit, Discussion Group Properties.) You'll see the box in Figure 18.12. This first pane shows you information about the group, and allows you to turn on HTML for that group; check Can Receive HTML, and you'll be able to use the formatting tools in the Message Composition window when sending messages to this group. (Very few groups are

Part

III

Ch

18

used by people who expect to see HTML messages; even discussion groups related to HTML generally don't have many HTML messages in them.)

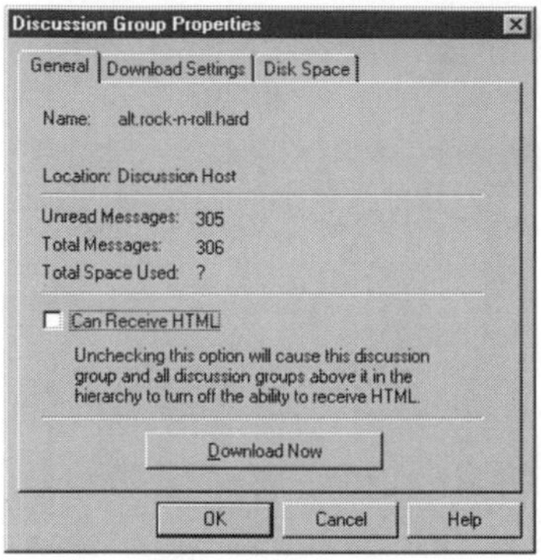

FIG. 18.12
Tell Collabra if the newsgroup can accept HTML messages.

The Download Settings tab is related to the offline-work mode, which we'll look at next. Click the Disk Space tab, though, and you'll see a dialog box that has the same message-expiration settings that we saw in Figure 18.10. So you can set this newsgroup to have its messages saved longer if you want.

Working Offline

As you've seen, a message is not transferred to your computer until you click a header. That means to read your newsgroups, you must be connected to the Internet…unless you use the offline-work mode. This allows you to transfer messages all at once, then log off your Internet connection and read those messages.

N O T E At the time of writing, the offline-work mode and message transfer system were not working correctly. ▨

First, set up the default Download settings. Select Edit, Preferences, then open the Offline category and click the Download subcategory (see Figure 18.13).

These are your options:

Download Only Unread Messages—Select this and Collabra won't download messages you've already got.

Download By Date—Check this and you can provide date criteria.

From—Select a time period from the drop-down list box.

Since—Specify a time period in the text box.

Select Messages—Click this button, then, in the dialog box that opens, select the newsgroups you want to download. (Click the Choose All button, or click next to a name in the Choose column.) These are the groups that will be downloaded when you use the File, Go Offline or File, Go Online command.

FIG. 18.13

This is where you define how Collabra should manage message downloads.

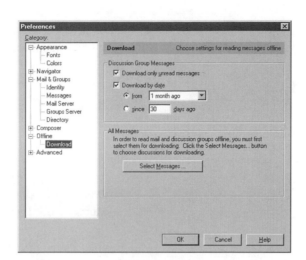

You can define settings for an individual newsgroup, too. In the Message Center, right-click the newsgroup, then choose Discussion Group Properties. (Or choose Edit, Discussion Group Properties.) Then click the Download Settings tab, and you'll see the pane in Figure 18.14.

FIG. 18.14

You can specify individual download settings for a particular newsgroup.

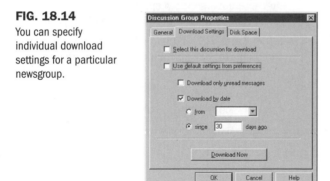

The Select This Discussion for Download check box is checked if you selected this newsgroup, as one of the ones to be downloaded, from the Preferences dialog box. You can use the box to quickly change a newsgroup's setting, of course.

If you clear the Use Default Settings From Preferences check box, you can now modify the message-selection settings you saw in Figure 18.13.

Now, how do you actually download your messages? Well, you can see the Download Now button in 18.14 (this button is in all three panes of the dialog box). Click this button and the download begins. When the process has finished, you can log off your Internet connection, open that newsgroup in a window, and read the messages.

The other way to download the messages is by using File, Go Offline or File, Go Online. When you select one of these commands, a dialog box opens. Click the Select Items for Download

Part

III

Ch

18

button if you want to specify the groups that should be downloaded (overriding the settings you made in the Preferences dialog box). Click the Go button and the transfers begin.

A Few More Procedures

Netscape Communications never sleeps. Its insomniac programmers are constantly plotting and adding handy little features, such as these:

File, Update Message Count	Select this Message Center command to get Collabra to see if any new messages have arrived in the newsgroup.
View, Show Images	Use this to turn the display of images in messages on and off.
Go, Next Group	Select this to open the next newsgroup in your subscribed list.
Go, Next Unread Group	Select this to open the next newsgroup containing unread messages.
File, Compress Folders	This compresses the databases that hold the messages, removing empty spaces created when messages were deleted and thus saving disk space.
Edit, Cancel Message	Select a message that you posted to the newsgroup and then use this command to remove the message from the newsgroup.
File, Edit Message	Puts the message into a Composition window so you can modify it and resubmit it to the newsgroup.

CHAPTER 19

Conference: Voice on the Net and More

Conference is Netscape's version of the VON (Voice on the Net) programs you've probably heard about. VON programs allow you to talk—literally, not figuratively—to other people on the Internet. You need a computer with a sound card, speakers, and a microphone, VON software (in this case, Conference) and you can talk with other Internet users with the same equipment, people all over the world. That's right, international calls at rates that will beat even the cheapest low-cost phone company.

Note that in order to successfully use Conference, you'll need a reasonably powerful computer, with at least a 14,400 bps modem (faster is better, of course) or a network connection. (If you have a 9,600 bps modem you'll still be able to use some features of Conference—the White Board and Chat—but you won't be able to use the sound features; you won't be able to talk to or listen to other Conference users.) ■

What is VON?

Voice on the Net is potentially a very important system, though for the moment it remains relatively little used.

Installing and setting up Conference

Before you can use Conference, you must tell it which directory and phonebook to use, and how to handle your sound hardware.

Making a connection

There are two ways to connect with Conference: by selecting someone from a phonebook, or by entering an e-mail address or IP number.

Sending text with Chat

Chat lets you send text to the other person.

Sending pictures with the White Board

You can draw, or load images from your hard disk, and the other person will see the images.

Sending files and browsing the Web together

File Exchange enables you to send files to the other participant, and even control that person's Web browser.

VON—Great Price, Reasonable Quality

Conference, and other VON programs, don't provide the sort of sound quality you are used to getting on your phone line. VON programs tend to be rather warbly, choppy even. But at this price, you may not care. You can make long-distance calls, even international calls, for next to nothing. Both parties to the call must connect to the Internet, so both parties are paying something, of course. But if you live in an area in which local calls are free, then your only cost is what you pay your online service or service provider for the time. And if you have a flat-fee service—$19.95 per month for as many hours as you want, for instance—then your calls are effectively free! Call friends in Europe, business contacts in Australia, people you just happen to meet on the Internet in Russia—all for free.

You might think this would worry the phone companies. And, to some degree, they are worried. An association of small telecommunications companies recently petitioned the FCC to ban the use of VON software. On the other hand, for a variety of reasons the phone companies have nothing much to fear, for a while at least. Only a relatively small minority of the U.S. population has Internet access, and a much smaller number has the hardware needed to use VON. And fewer still are prepared to put up with the inconveniences inherent in these systems. Still, what we're seeing is the beginning of something big, and perhaps the beginning of a big drop in phone-call prices.

Although Conference is primarily a voice program, if the person you want to talk to doesn't have sound set up on his or her computer, you can still communicate by using Conference. You can type messages to each other by using Conference's Chat tool. In fact, Conference contains five tools:

- Voice on the Net.
- White Board: A program that allows both participants to draw or send pictures.
- Collaborative surfing: Both participants can "travel" around the World Wide Web or intranet together, viewing the same sites and talking about them.
- File Exchange: Send computer files to each other.
- Chat: Type messages to each other.

Setting Up Conference

I'm going to assume that you already have a sound system configured for your computer; you have a card, speakers, and microphone (you can get a mike for about $10 from an electronics store).

Start Conference by double-clicking the Conference icon, or, in Windows 95, by choosing Start, Programs, Netscape Communicator, Netscape Conference. The first time you start Conference, the Conference Setup Wizard appears. This program walks you through the installation of Conference on your system.

The setup wizard is well designed and easy to use; just follow instructions, answering all the questions. You'll begin by entering your Business Card information, the information that identifies you to other Conference users (see Figure 19.1). The first entry is Name; this is the name you'll be identified with at the Conference Phonebook or Directory (a sort of giant address book of Conference users). You might want to use your real name or your Internet-access logon name, or a pseudonym.

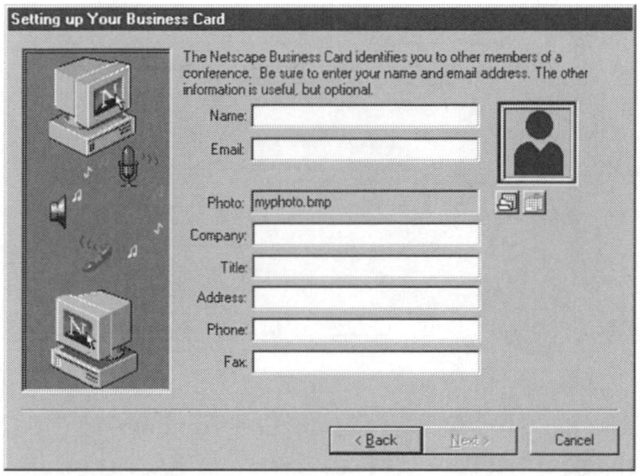

FIG. 19.1

Enter your personal information, and add a picture for the Business Card feature.

Fill in the rest of the information—your E-Mail address, Title, Address, and so on. You may not want to enter all of this information because it will be available to the Conference users you're talking to. You may want to leave some fields blank to protect your privacy. (At a minimum, you must include a name and e-mail address.)

Note Photo box; this shows the file name of the picture in the top-right corner of this dialog box. By default, Conference uses the myphoto.bmp image file, the blue picture of a torso and head, but you can use any image you want, such as a company logo or a picture of yourself. Click the little folder icon at the end of the text box and then find the graphics file you want to use; you can use a .tif, .gif, .bmp (Windows and OS/2 bitmap), or .jpg graphics file. Or use an image from the Clipboard; copy the image to the Clipboard from another application, then return to this dialog box and click the little Clipboard icon at the end of the Photo line. You'll see the image change.

After entering your Business Card information, you must select or enter the server and phonebook you'll be using to find other users and to list yourself so other users can find you; see Figure 19.2. (If you prefer not to be listed, simply clear the List My Name in Phonebook check box.) The server provides a way for people to place calls using e-mail addresses; when the user enters an e-mail address, Conference checks with the server for that address, to find the correct IP number for the person's computer. The phonebook provides a list of users from which you can choose the person you want to connect to.

At present, there are only two servers, though others may be set up soon and your company may even have its own private directory, or a directory on the corporate intranet. So enter

Part

III

Ch

19

whatever your system administrator tells you to use, or simply use the default selection. (By the way, DLS stands for Dynamic Lookup Server.) As for the phonebook, start off with the default selection; you can always change it later.

FIG. 19.2

Pick your Conference directory and phonebook.

The wizard will also ask you what type of connection you have to the Internet; you'll have several modem options (9,600, 14,400, or 28,800), ISDN, or LAN (Local Area Network) connection. You must also select the sound card you plan to use for the microphone and speakers; the wizard will probably be able to detect the sound card.

There's also a box in which you'll test your microphone (see Figure 19.3). Make sure you get these settings right, or the quality of your communications will suffer. Click the little microphone button, then speak into your microphone. You'll see little bars that move along the box to the right of the button. The blue Silence Level marker shows you at which point Conference will begin transmitting your voice. Sounds that are too quiet to move the bars across the blue marker will not be transmitted; it's not until the bars cross that marker that Conference begins sending sounds. So adjust this marker so that small and unimportant sounds are not transmitted—breathing, office background noise, and so on—yet when you begin speaking, your words *are* transmitted. (You are setting the sensitivity of the Recording/Playback Autoswitch, which we'll hear more about in a few moments.)

That's it, a fairly quick and easy setup procedure. If you ever need to run the setup wizard again—if you've changed your computer's sound hardware or are having problems working with the program—choose Help, Setup Wizard in the Conference window. You can also modify some of the settings you've made by choosing Call, Preferences.

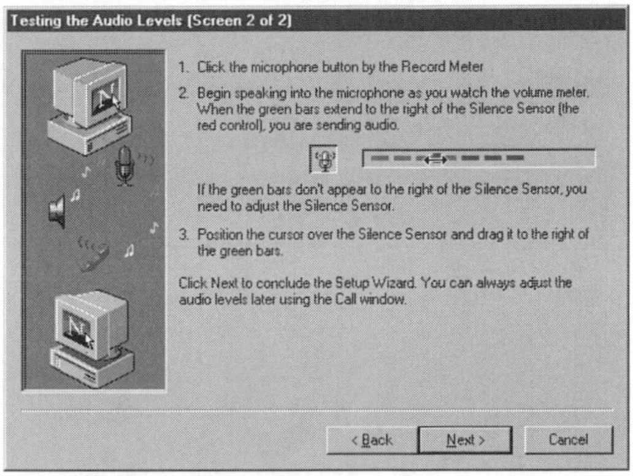

FIG. 19.3
Set up your microphone
correctly.

Setting Up the Options

There are a few more settings you can make, though you may not need to. In the Conference window (which opens as soon as you finish the setup wizard), choose Call, Preferences, and the Preferences dialog box opens. This has three tabs: Network, Business Card, and Audio. The Network and Business Card information was set in the wizard, but there are some settings we haven't seen yet in the Audio pane.

Audio Options

Click the Audio tab to see the dialog box in Figure 19.4. This is where you can set up the sound-card options, though most people won't need to modify these settings.

At the top, you'll see the Operation Mode. In this case, you can see that the mode is half duplex, which means that Conference can't transmit sounds and play at the same time. (Full duplex means that it can. If you have two sound cards or a full duplex sound card, you can use full duplex mode.) Next to that is the Recording/Playback Autoswitch check box. This is important; with a half duplex card, you have to take turns talking; you can't talk at the same time the other person is talking to you. This check box tells Conference to automatically switch between record and playback modes. If it hears you talking, it will assume you want to transmit your words, so it changes to record mode. When you stop speaking, it changes to playback mode.

How does it know if you're talking, or whether it's just hearing background sounds? Thanks to the sensitivity setting you made in the wizard (refer to Figure 19.3), Conference can distinguish between the two. You can modify the sensitivity in the Conference main window, as you'll see in a moment. If you have a lot of background noise, or want to be able to talk to someone next to you without that conversation being sent across the Internet, you may want to clear the Recording/Playback Autoswitch. You'll have to use the controls in the Conference window to determine when to transmit and when to play.

Part

III

Ch

19

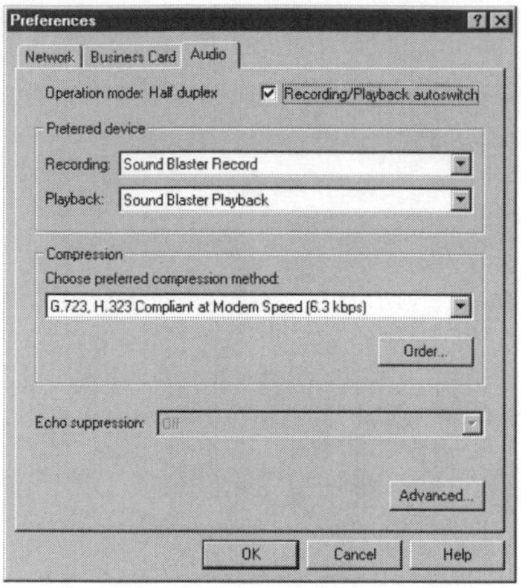

FIG. 19.4

The audio options allow you to adjust how Conference records and plays.

You probably won't need to modify the other settings in this pane:

Option	Description
Preferred Device	You made these choices in the wizard. If you have more than one sound card in your computer, you can select which one you want to use for recording, and which for playing the incoming sounds. If you have two cards, you can use both at once, in effect setting up a full duplex system even if the cards are actually half duplex cards.
Compression	There are a number of different methods for compressing the sounds that are being transmitted over the Internet. You can select the preferred method from the drop-down list box, or use the Order button to see information about each compression method. You can also modify the order in which Conference will try a compression method when it makes the connection. You probably won't have to modify these, though, unless told to do so by technical support or your system administrator.
Echo Suppression	The method used to stop echoes. Again, you probably won't need to modify this setting, though if you are using a speakerphone or headset, you can select another option. This option won't be available for all sound cards.
Advanced	If you're having problems with sound quality, you can click this button to find a number of arcane settings that might help.

Selecting the Answer Mode

There are three ways that Conference can handle incoming calls; select one of these options from the Call menu:

> Always Prompt—Conference will ask if you want to answer the call.
>
> Auto Answer—Conference will automatically answer the call.
>
> Do Not Disturb—Conference will never answer a call; it will send a message telling the caller that you're busy.

Note that each mode is indicated using a different icon in the large button to the right of the dial button.

Connecting Through the Directory

Let's begin by seeing how to connect to someone through the phonebook. You'll probably find lots of people experimenting with Conference; you can connect to another user and just chat for a while.

TIP If you are planning to go to the phonebook and find your own listing, wait a minute or two after starting Conference. It takes a little while for your information to be added to the directory (the directory shows users who are currently running Conference, not all people who use Conference). If you simply click Navigator's Reload button to get the latest version of the directory, you'll still see the directory from your cache. (You may be able to force the page to reload, though, by holding the Shift key while you click the Reload button.) So wait a few moments to give the directory a chance to load your information, then connect.

Click the Web Phonebook button in the Conference window, or select Communicator, Web Phonebook; Navigator opens and displays the Conference page. Use the directory to find someone. Depending on the directory, you might be able to search for a name or click a letter to see people whose names begin with that letter (see Figure 19.5). Click a link to someone you'd like to talk to, and Conference will try to connect to that person. Again, depending on the directory, you may have to click a Conference link. In some cases, there'll be other links that you can use to send the person an e-mail message or see directory information about the person. (You can bookmark a directory page, and go to that page *before* you start Conference. If you click a link to connect to someone before you've started Conference, Navigator will automatically open Conference for you.) Don't be afraid to try anyone—most people are experimenting with this technology and are quite happy to talk for a few minutes. You never know whom you'll meet.

FIG. 19.5

Find someone to talk to at the directory, and then click the link to make the connection.

Netscape Conference Directory - Netscape

File Edit View Go Communicator Help

Bookmarks Location: http://www.four11.com/cgi-bin/Four11Main?Conference

Directories
- E-Mail
- Telephone
- Yellow Pages
- ► Net Phone
- Government
- Celebrity

Cool Services
- Free iName
- Notifyme - *Free!*
- Address Book
- E-News - *Free!*
- dotCom yourself

My Listing
- Add Me
- Login

Information
- Free E-Mail
- *What's New*
- About Four11
- Help/FAQ

We Speak

English

Link To Us!

Netscape Conference Directory

Welcome to the Conference Net Phone Directory. You can look up Conference users who are online by name or browse any portion of the Net Phone Directory by using the letter controls. If you need assistance with Netscape Conference, contact Netscape technical support.

Viewing Users

List Directory entries with names beginning with:

[   ] Search

View All Entries

List Directory entries with names beginning with the following letter:

A B C D E F G H I J K L M
N O P Q R S T U V W X Y Z

Add Yourself To Four11

Why Register?

- People can search for you by name, by interests, by schools, etc.
- If someone finds your listing, they can see that you are on line with your net phone and call you right away.

http://www.four11.com/cgi-bin/con-phbook.cgi?index=k&XX=&FormId=.234.2.377FB00.3F70FA11

You'll hear a ringing sound as Conference tries to connect to the other person, and see a dialog box with a Cancel button. It may not be able to, of course. If the person is there, though, and agrees to "take the call," your session begins.

TIP In Windows 95, you can put a Conference icon in the taskbar's tray area. Select Call, Hide Window, and the window is removed. To reopen the window, simply double-click the taskbar icon.

Talking Through Conference

You can see the Conference window in Figure 19.6. Your window probably won't look like this yet; I clicked the Show Speed Dial button to open up the window and display the speed-dial buttons.

This window is where you control your conversation. Notice the sliders at the bottom of the box. The one labeled Microphone shows your voice as you speak into the mike. The one labeled Speakers shows the incoming voice. Also, you'll see a blue marker inside the Microphone bar. This is the sensitivity setting we saw in the wizard; you can drag this along the bar to control the sensitivity of the Recording/Playback Autoswitch that you read about earlier.

FIG. 19.6
Click the Show Speed
Dial and Show
Advanced Sound
Options lines to open
up the full Conference
window.

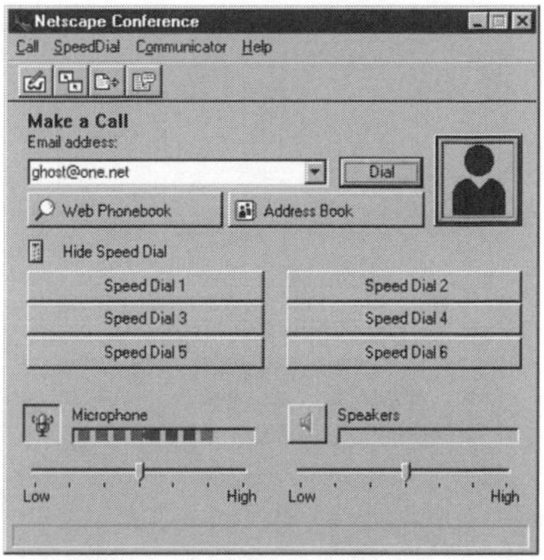

TIP Here's how to adjust this setting before you start a conversation. Click the Record Audio micro-phone button, then speak into your microphone. You'll see green squares appear in the Micro-phone bar. When the squares are to the left of the blue marker, it means the sound is too quiet to be transmitted. It's only after the squares pass the blue symbol that Conference would, if connected to another user, transmit the sounds. Adjust the silence setting—by dragging the marker along the bar—to where Conference transmits when you want it to, and isn't confused by background noise. The farther the blue symbol is to the left, the more likely that Conference will hear background noise and turn on record mode.

You can begin speaking. If you're using the Recording/Playback Autoswitch, Conference auto-matically switches between modes. (If not, you'll have to click the Record Audio button (the mike button) to turn recording on and off.) You'll see the squares in the Microphone bar—this is your voice. When the green bar crosses the blue symbol, Conference transmits your voice (if you have a half duplex system, when Conference transmits, you won't hear the other person speaking).

To modify the microphone sensitivity and speaker volume, drag the little arrow boxes along the sliders at the bottom of the box. Setting the microphone sensitivity adjusts how much the microphone amplifies sounds that it picks up; it's not the same as the Recording/Playback Autoswitch sensitivity, of course, though they're related, and you may need to adjust the Recording/Playback Autoswitch sensitivity after adjusting the microphone sensitivity.

TIP Remember to turn up your sound-system volume, not just your Conference volume controls. When you first start playing with Conference, you might want to use the highest volume you can, then reduce it to a more comfortable level.

When you've finished talking, click the Hangup button to end the session (the Dial button changes to a Hangup button when you are connected to another Conference user).

TIP Having trouble hearing? Try clearing the Recording/Playback Autoswitch in the Preferences dialog box. You'll then have to click the Record Audio button when you want to speak, and again when you want to stop and hear the other person. Also, try playing with the sensitivity adjustment on the Microphone bar.

More Ways to Connect

There are several other ways to start a call to someone:

- Type an e-mail address, IP number, or host address into the text box at the top of Conference, then click Dial.
- Choose Call, Direct Call, type an e-mail or host address into the text box that you see, then press Enter.
- Click the Address Book button and choose someone from your Address Book.
- Click the Show Speed Dial line to display the speed-dial buttons, then click one of the speed-dial buttons (see "Using a Speed-Dial Button," which follows).

TIP To automatically block incoming calls, so you don't need to decline to accept them, you can choose Call, Do Not Disturb. People trying to connect to you will be told that the "line" is busy.

Calling Someone Directly

There are two ways to call someone directly. You can type the e-mail address or host address into the text box near the top of the Conference window and click Dial; or select Call, Direct Call, type an e-mail address, an IP number, or a host address into the text box that you see, then press Enter. Conference then tries to connect.

How does conference know how to connect? Well, if you entered an e-mail address, Conference asks the directory how to connect to that e-mail address. If the person you want to contact is not currently listed at the directory, you're out of luck; you can't use that person's e-mail address. For instance, the person may be listed at a different directory, or may have chosen not to be listed at all.

If you entered an IP (Internet Protocol) number (something that looks like this: 206.133.160.32), Conference may be able to connect to the user's computer directly. You may, in some cases, be able to use a computer's host name, too. However, there's a problem with calling someone directly. When most users connect to the Internet via dial-up lines, the host computer assigns them a temporary IP number. Each time they connect, they get a different number. (When you start Conference, it checks your IP address and registers this with the Conference directory.) Furthermore, many host names are not real host names. For instance, I own a domain called arundel.com, and receive e-mail at pkent@arundel.com. But arundel.com is not my computer's host name; it's on a Web-hosting company's computer.

If you are working on an intranet, on which each computer has its own permanent IP address, this won't be a problem; you should be able to enter an IP address or host name and connect directly because the computer's identifying information doesn't change.

So there will be many people to whom you can't connect directly; rather, you'll have to arrange to "meet" at a server. At the predetermined time, you both connect to the Internet, start Conference, and use the same directory server. When the second person to connect sees the first person's entry in the directory, he can use that entry to make the connection.

> **TIP**
> To see what IP number you've been assigned, start Conference and then go to the directory and find your entry. Point at the link to your name and look in the status bar: At the end of the gobbledy-gook information you'll see your IP number. Most users working through a dial-up connection will find that this number is different each session.

Using the Address Book

In Chapter 17, you learned about the Communicator Address Book. The cards in the Address Book have a Netscape Conference pane that shows the server you want to use to connect to the person. You can enter the server you know this person uses.

 Open the Address Book from Conference by clicking the Address Book button, or by selecting Communicator, Address Book. When you find the person in the Address Book, click the entry and then click the Call button.

Using a Speed-Dial Button

You can add buttons to the Conference window to let you quickly connect to people you call frequently. To enter someone's information into a button, choose SpeedDial, Speed Dial x, Edit. Then enter the person's name, e-mail address, DLS server, and, if possible, an IP number or host address that can be used as a Direct Address (as mentioned earlier, this information is not available for most Internet users).

To use one of the buttons, click the Show Speed Dial line in the Conference window, and Conference will expand to show all the buttons. Simply click the button you want to use. Note, however, that at the time of writing the Speed Dial buttons did not work; clicking one of these buttons actually dialed whatever happened to be in the Make a Call text box near the top of the window.

Viewing the Business Card

You've already seen how to create your business card; but how do you see the other person's business card? When you connect to another person, that person's Business Card photo appears in the window in place of the large phone logo. (In many cases, of course, you'll see the default picture, as many people don't use a picture.)

Click this picture to open a dialog box showing you the other person's business card, along with some other information about the person's host computer and Conference information.

TIP Use the call log to keep track of calls you make. Choose <u>C</u>all, Call <u>L</u>og to see a list of all the calls, with each person's name and e-mail address, and the time and duration of the call.

The Answering Machine

If you must leave your desk with your computer connected to the Internet, and Conference running, you can still receive calls. When other Conference users call, and find that you are not available, they'll see a message asking if they want to leave a message on your answering machine. If they do, Conference will store the message on your hard disk, so you can listen to it later. (This feature is not yet functioning, though should be soon.)

If you reach someone who is not answering, but whose Conference is still online, you'll see a message asking if you want to leave a message. If you select Yes, you'll see the dialog box in Figure 19.7. Click the dot button to begin recording the message.

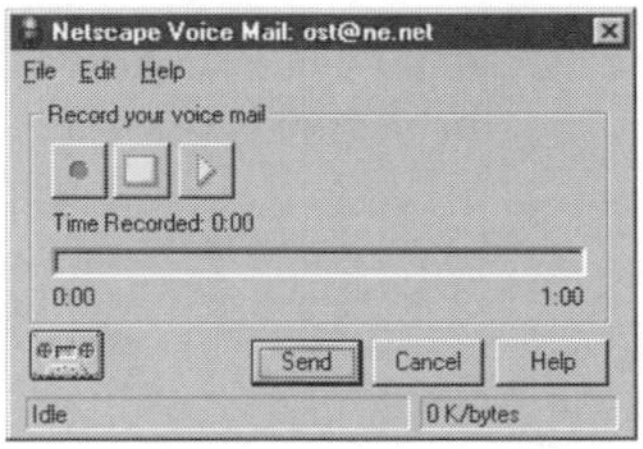

FIG. 19.7
Conference's Answering Machine.

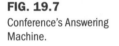

Typed Messages—Using Chat

Conference has a useful little Chat window. Chat, in Internet-speak, means a system in which you type a message to another person, and that person can immediately see the message and respond to it. Why use Chat if you've got voice? Well, maybe you haven't got voice. Perhaps your friends are using Conference, but you haven't yet bought a sound card. Or maybe you do have sound, but have connected to another Conference user who doesn't. You can still use Conference to communicate, by using the Chat window.

Or perhaps you want to talk *and* use Chat. For instance, two programmers collaborating on a project could use Chat to send bits of program code. They can talk about the piece of code that they're working on, and send the actual code via the Chat window. Or you can send poems, love notes, e-mail you've received, bits of a novel you are working on, whatever you want.

To open the Chat window, click the Chat button. You'll see the window in Figure 19.8.

FIG. 19.8
Conference's Chat tool lets you type at the same time you talk. A great collaboration tool.

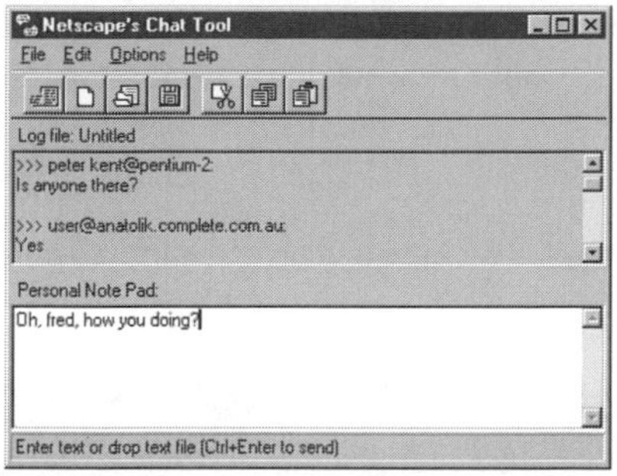

Type your messages in the bottom pane, then press Ctrl+Enter to send what you wrote (or click the Send button in the toolbar, or choose File, Post Note Pad). The other person's Chat window should open automatically (by default, the Options, Pop Up On Receive menu command is selected). You'll see the conversation—the messages you type, along with the other person's responses—in the upper pane, so that pane is a complete log of the "conversation." (This is why the name is titled Log File:.)

Use the File, Include command (or the Include button) to send the contents of a text file that you have saved on your hard disk; the text in the file will be placed into the lower pane, just as if you'd typed it. Or you can simply drag a text file from another program—from Windows Explorer or File Manager, for instance—and drop it into the lower pane. Again, that text is entered just as if you'd typed it. In neither case is it sent automatically, though; you can modify it, then press Ctrl+Enter to send it. And the Cut, Copy, and Paste buttons on the toolbar can be used in the normal way, to paste and copy text to and from the panes and other programs.

You can save everything that's "said" in the chat session, which is very handy in many cases; you can grab those pieces of program code or poems I mentioned earlier, for instance. Click the New button, or choose File, New to begin saving the log.

Before you close Chat, you'll be asked if you want to save the log. Or you can save the log at any time using the Save button, or by choosing File, Save, or File, Save As. You can also print the log, using File, Print.

TIP The Chat window is especially useful for getting a connection going; if the other person can't hear you, or vice versa, you can start a chat session and send a message—the other person's Chat window should open automatically.

Using the White Board

The White Board is to images what the Chat window is to text. You can send pictures while you're talking. Click the White Board button to open the window (see Figure 19.9). This is a fairly typical paint program, similar to many others, such as Windows Paint. You can use different colors, line sizes, shapes, and so on. And as you draw, the other person sees what you are

Part
III

Ch
19

drawing. (The White Board also has an Options, Pop Up On Receive command, so the other person's White Board will probably open as soon as you send something.) Unlike Chat, White Board sends images automatically as soon as you draw or open them. You don't need to click a button to do so.

Luckily for the graphically impaired, you don't have to be able to draw to use White Board. You can send other images, too:

FIG. 19.9

Conference's White Board lets you send pictures during your conversation.

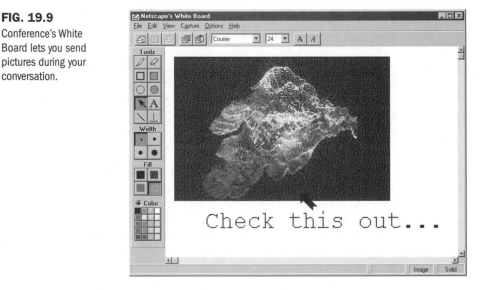

■ Choose File, Open, or click the Open button, to select an image file from your hard disk. Then click in the White Board to paste it where you want it.

■ Choose one of the Capture commands to remove the White Board window and take a picture of something on your screen. Then click in the White Board (which reappears) to position the image. Choose Capture, Window, and then click a window to take a picture of that window; Capture, Desktop, to take a picture of everything on your screen (except the White Board); or Capture, Region, to use a mouse tool to take a snap of a certain portion of the screen.

 ■ Copy an image from another application, then paste it into the White Board; press Ctrl+V or click the Paste button.

 ■ You can type notes onto images; click the big A button in the toolbar on the left side, click inside the workspace, then start typing. A great way to make notes about a particular portion of the image.

■ Point to parts of the image by clicking the Arrow button and then clicking next to the thing you want to indicate; a big black arrow is stamped into the image. It's moved when you click somewhere else. Or simply hold the mouse button and drag it around; the other person will see the pointer moving as you move the mouse.

Spend some time playing with the graphics tools to see what you can do; if you're familiar with other paint programs you'll quickly understand this one. You'll find that there are actually two layers. There's the image layer. That's made up of image files that you open from your hard disk and the "snapshots" captured using the Capture menu. Then there's the markup layer, made up of things you draw or write using the tools in the tool box, and things pasted from the Clipboard.

This is important to realize, because some commands operate on just one layer, others on both layers. For instance, Edit, Clear Markups clears only the markup layer, removing anything you've pasted from the Clipboard, drawn with the drawing tools, or typed onto the picture with the text tool. On the other hand, Edit, Clear Whiteboard operates on both layers, clearing both and giving you an empty workspace in which to start again.

Also, the eraser tool operates on one or both layers. Select Options, Erase Markups, and when you use the eraser, only markups are cleared; you won't be able to remove images loaded from disk or created through snapshots. Select Options, Erase Image, and the eraser operates on both layers, clearing both markups and the underlying images.

 There are a few more commands you might like to know about:

- *File, Save As*   When the person you are communicating with sends an image, you can use this command to save it to your hard disk.

- *Edit, Synchronize Page*   If, due to transmission problems, one image has not updated properly, select this option and your entire image will be repainted on the other person's White Board.

- *Edit, Paste Text*   If you want to paste text that you copied from another program, use this menu command; you won't be able to paste using Ctrl+V or the Paste button.

- *Edit, Paste Picture*   This pastes text, but in a slightly different form (as a "metafile" image). The previous menu option tends to provide better-looking pasted text.

- *The View Menu*   You can zoom in and out on the image using this menu.

- *Options, Compress*   This is intended to speed up transmissions, by compressing the data before it's sent. In some cases, with fast connections, it may actually slow down transmission.

Part III
Ch 19

Sending Files

 You may now and again want to transfer a computer file while in a Conference session. To do so, click the File Exchange button to see the window in Figure 19.10.

Click the Open button, or choose File, Add to Send List. A typical File Open dialog box appears. Select the file you want to send and click the Open button; the file is listed in the top pane. You can do this several times, to select multiple files.

When you've got all the files you want to send, click the Send button, or choose File, Send. The file will be transmitted to the other user, and will then be shown in the bottom pane.

FIG. 19.10
Use this window to send files to others.

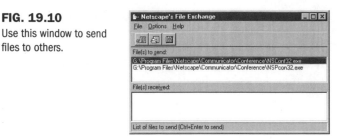

When you receive a file, you can click it in the bottom pane, then click the Save button, or choose File, Save. If you decide you don't want to keep the file, use File, Delete instead.

There are a few options you need to be aware of:

■ *Options, Compress*   With this selected, the file will be compressed before transmission, speeding up transmission in most cases.

■ *Options, Pop Up on Receive*   With this selected, if someone sends you a file, the File Exchange window will open automatically.

■ *Options, ASCII*   You only need to use this option if sending a text file to a computer using an operating system different from the one you use. For instance, if sending a text file from a Windows 95 computer to a UNIX computer, you should select this option, as it will ensure that the ASCII line endings are converted so they'll appear correctly in UNIX.

■ *Options, Binary*   In all other cases, the Binary transfer should be used.

Browsing the Web Together

The Collaborative Browsing tool is a great little utility for viewing Web sites together. For instance, two employees of the same company, in offices in completely different areas of the world, could browse through the Web together to view Web sites of competitors or Web sites that might be useful to the company's marketing efforts. One employee can lead the other through a series of Web sites, pointing out areas of interest.

To start browsing together, click the Collaborative Surfing button. Navigator will open, and the other person will see an invitation to join the session; if he accepts, his Navigator opens, too. One participant then clicks the Control the Browsers check box in the dialog box that appears, and then the Sync Browsers, to make sure both are starting off at the same point.

The leader then clicks Start Browsing, and begins his "journey" through the Web. As he moves around on the Web using all the normal Navigator tools, the other participant in the session can just sit back and watch. Both browsers will work in synchronization; when the lead browser displays a page, the following browser loads it, too. ●

IV

Creating Web Pages with Netscape Composer

Creating Your Own Home Page

Publishing on the Web is surprisingly easy, and creating your own home page is probably the best first step. It's a great way to get a feel for how HTML works, and you'll produce something you can use, too. How do you go about producing a home page? Well, you can use any of many freeware, shareware, and commercial HTML creation, or "authoring," tools. But in this chapter, you're going to learn about one tool in particular: Netscape Composer. ■

Opening Composer

Composer can be opened in numerous ways; it's all part of the integration of Communicator's different parts, making it easy to take or select a Web page and edit it.

Creating links to other Web documents

Working with Composer is similar to working with a word processor…until you begin creating hyperlinks.

How can I place pictures and horizontal lines into the document?

Inserting images and horizontal lines is a snap.

Setting your home page

Once you've created a page, you can quickly set it as Navigator's home page.

Netscape Composer is Communicator's built-in HTML authoring tool. Composer is an independent authoring tool—you'll learn in this chapter about the Composer window—but it's also integrated into other parts of Communicator. For instance, in Chapter 16 you saw that the Message Composition window contains some of Composer's HTML tools built into it, so you can create e-mail and newsgroup messages that look like Web pages.

Netscape HTML tags

Composer creates pages using the Netscape HTML tags. Some of these are not standard tags, so not all Web browsers will be able to view the formatting that you put into your document. That doesn't matter if you are creating a home page for your own use, but this issue should be considered if you plan to create pages and place them on the Web.

For instance, some of the special horizontal lines and text formats—the colors and the superscript and subscript characters—are not standard. Many of the other browsers will display them, though, and in most cases the formats don't create problems for browsers that can't use them—they're simply not visible.

Your First Home (Page)

What is a home page? The following list is a quick refresher:

- It's the page that appears when you open Navigator. (Assuming you have the Preferences set up to display a home page: Choose Edit, Preferences, then click the Navigator category.)
- It's the page that appears when you click the Home toolbar button or choose Go, Home.
- It's a "main page" at a Web site.

There's some ambiguity about the term *home page,* which has come to mean two things. The original meaning is the page that appears when you open your browser or use the Home command. The new meaning is a page that you have published on the Web, a page that others on the Web can view (the Rolling Stones' home page, for example). Whenever I use the term *home page,* I mean the page that opens when you open Navigator.

Why would you want to create your own home page? The following are a few reasons:

- On the Internet, one size doesn't fit all. Everyone uses the Internet in a different way. The page provided by Navigator may be okay to start with, but it won't have all the links you want and may contain plenty that you don't want.
- The History and Bookmarks lists are very handy, but if you are going to use certain items from these lists frequently, you'll find it more convenient to have them on your home page.

- You can customize your home page with links to your favorite sites across the Internet. Or you can have a home page plus a series of documents on your hard drive linked to that home page: one document for work, one for music, one for newsgroups, one for whatever else. Then you can have links from the home page to those separate documents. (I'll show you how in the section called, "Creating Multiple Documents.")

How Do You Open Composer?

The Composer window is shown in Figure 20.1. There are several ways to open this window, as follows:

- Double-click the Netscape Composer icon.
- In Windows 95, select Start, Programs, Netscape Communicator, Netscape Composer.
- In any of the other Communicator windows, select Communicator, Page Composer.

- Click the Composer button in the Component bar.
- In Navigator, choose File, New, Blank Page; a blank Composer window opens (the browser window remains open).
- To edit a copy of the document you are currently viewing, choose File, Edit Page. To edit a document within a frame, click the frame containing the document you want to use and select File, Edit Frame.
- To use the Wizard to help you create a page, choose File, New, Page From Wizard, and the Netscape Page Wizard page opens in the Navigator window (**http://home.netscape.com/home/gold4.0_wizard.html**). Follow the instructions, and a special program will build the page for you. When the page has been completed, choose File, Edit Page to save the document on your hard disk.
- To open one of the Netscape templates, choose File, New, Page From Template. In the dialog box that appears, click the Netscape Templates button and the Netscape Web Page Templates page opens in the Navigator window (**http://home.netscape.com/home/gold4.0_templates.html**). You can choose from a list of sample Web pages. When you find one that looks like what you want, choose File, Edit Page to save the document on your hard disk.
- To edit an HTML document that you saved on your hard disk, choose File, New, Page From Template. In the dialog box that appears, click the Choose File button, and find the page you want to use; it will be loaded directly into the Composer window.
- To edit a Web page you have not yet loaded into the Navigator, choose File, New, Page From Template. In the dialog box that appears, type a full URL (including the http:// bit). The page will be loaded directly into the Composer window.

Why would you want to edit an existing document? Eventually, you'll want to modify documents you created earlier, of course. But editing an existing document, one you've found on the Web, is a great way to create your first Web document. Find a document that you think looks good—one that you'd like to copy—and edit that document, replacing the original headings with your headings, keeping the images and links you need, and so on. Then save the modified document on your hard disk. In fact, that's the principle used by the Netscape templates and the Netscape Page Wizard. In the first case, you choose from a selection of pages already created for you by Netscape Communications. When you find one you like, you use the Composer edit mode to save it on your hard disk and make any modifications you want. And in the second case, the Wizard, you use a form in a Web page at Netscape's Web site to create a page, step by step. The form actually creates this page at the Netscape Web site, so when you've got what you want you can use Composer to make changes and then save it to your hard disk. (Or you can simply use File, Save As to save it directly to your hard disk from the Navigator window.)

> **CAUTION**
>
> Be aware that you don't own something you "borrow" from the Web. If you borrow something from the Web and simply keep it for your own use, there's generally no problem. But if you publish it by creating a Web site using pictures and text you grabbed from another Web site, for instance, you may be guilty of copyright infringement. If you use the borrowed stuff as a template, though, replacing everything in the page with your own stuff, there's no problem in most cases (though it's possible for a particular design to be copyrighted, too). However, the templates provided by Netscape are intended for this very purpose.

We're going to start with a clean slate—the blank document. We'll learn how to use the HTML-authoring tools and then later in this chapter, we'll see how to take an existing document and modify it.

FIG. 20.1

The Composer window provides the tools you need to create or modify a Web page. This is one of Netscape's templates.

Here's a quick summary of what each button in this window does:

- *New*   Display the Create New Page dialog box, which lets you choose a Blank Page, a Template, the Page Wizard, or open a file from your hard disk.

- *Open*   Click here to open a file on your hard disk.

- *Save*   This button saves the document on your hard disk.

- *Publish*   Click here to open the Publish dialog box. You use this function to specify which files you want to send by FTP to your service provider's Web server.

- *Preview in Navigator*   Click here to see how your document will appear in the browser. The document is opened in the Navigator window.

- *Cut*   Highlight text in the document and click this button to remove the text, placing it in the Clipboard.

- *Copy*   This button copies highlighted text to the Clipboard.

- *Paste*   Click here to paste text from the Clipboard to the document.

- *Print This Page*   Click here to print the page.

- *Find*   Opens the Find dialog box, so you can search the document.

- *Insert Link*   Insert a hypertext link to another document, or to a target within this document.

- *Insert Target*   Click here to place a target in the document. Targets are special tags, invisible to the reader, that allow you to link to a point in the document from hypertext links elsewhere in the document.

- *Insert Table*   Click here to insert a table.

- *Insert Image*   Click here to insert a picture into the document.

- *Insert Horizontal Line*   This inserts a horizontal line across the screen.

- *Check Spelling*   Click here to begin a spelling check.

- *Paragraph Style*   Composer uses a system of styles, much like most word processors. You can click text and modify it by selecting a style.

- *Font*   Select text and then select the type of font you want to use from this drop-down list box.

- *Font Size*   Highlight text and then choose a font size setting to make the text larger or smaller than the default for that paragraph style.

- *Font Color*   Highlight text and then click here to change its color.

Part

IV

Ch

20

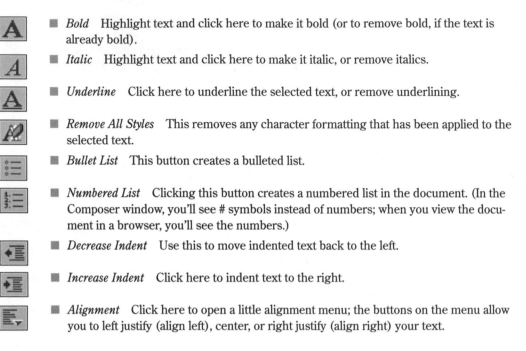

■ *Bold*   Highlight text and click here to make it bold (or to remove bold, if the text is already bold).

■ *Italic*   Highlight text and click here to make it italic, or remove italics.

■ *Underline*   Click here to underline the selected text, or remove underlining.

■ *Remove All Styles*   This removes any character formatting that has been applied to the selected text.

■ *Bullet List*   This button creates a bulleted list.

■ *Numbered List*   Clicking this button creates a numbered list in the document. (In the Composer window, you'll see # symbols instead of numbers; when you view the document in a browser, you'll see the numbers.)

■ *Decrease Indent*   Use this to move indented text back to the left.

■ *Increase Indent*   Click here to indent text to the right.

■ *Alignment*   Click here to open a little alignment menu; the buttons on the menu allow you to left justify (align left), center, or right justify (align right) your text.

Entering Your Text

If you'd like to experiment with the editing tools, why not start with a blank document and begin creating a home page. Type the following text into the Composer window (you can see an example in Figure 20.2):

My Home Page
This is my very own home page

Really Important Stuff
These are WWW pages I use a lot.

Not So Important Stuff
These are WWW pages I use now and again.

Not Important At All Stuff
These are WWW pages I use to waste time.

FIG. 20.2

Start typing the headings into Composer; you'll find it's just like working with a word processor.

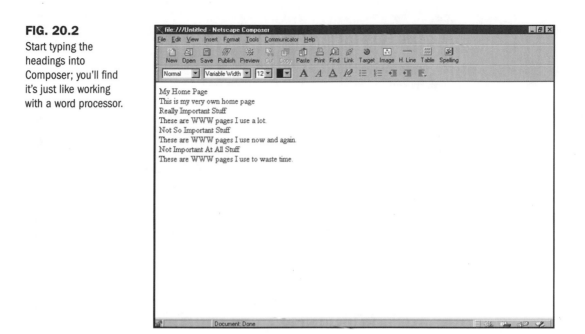

Right now, all you have is basic text; look in the Paragraph Style drop-down list box (the list box on the left side of the Format toolbar) and you'll see it shows *Normal*.

You can quickly change the paragraph styles. For instance, try the following:

1. Click in the My Home Page text, and then select Heading 1 from the Paragraph Style drop-down list box.

2. Click the Alignment toolbar button, then click the Center button (the second button on the menu that appears).

3. Click in the This is my very own home page text, then click the Alignment toolbar button and on the Center button.

4. Click in the Really Important Stuff text, then select Heading 2 from the Paragraph Style drop-down list box.

5. Click in the Not So Important Stuff text, then select Heading 2 from the Paragraph Style drop-down list box.

6. Click in the Not Important At All Stuff text, then select Heading 2 from the Paragraph Style drop-down list box.

Now what have you got? Your page should look something like that in Figure 20.3.

Part

IV

Ch

20

FIG. 20.3

A few mouse clicks and you've formatted the document.

Before you go on, save what you've done: Click the Save toolbar button, select a directory, type a name (homepage, if you want), then click the Save button. Composer will save the file with an .htm extension.

T I P   Want to see what you've just done? Choose View, Page Source, and you'll see the HTML source document that Composer has created for you. Advanced HTML users can also edit this source; choose Edit, HTML Source to open the source document in a text editor. (You'll have to save the document first, and provide it with a title. If you haven't yet defined an editor in the Preferences—which we'll look at in Chapter 21—Composer will open a File Open box from which you can select the text editor you want to use.)

T I P   If you make changes to your document, then change your mind, you can quickly return the document to the way it was the last time you saved it. Choose View, Reload. When you see a message box asking if you want to save your work, click No.

How About Links?

Now you're going to get fancy by adding an *anchor*, a link to another document. For example, you may want to add a link to the Netscape home page. (On the other hand, you may not; you can always click the N icon in the top right corner of the browser to get there, even if you are using your own home page.) Or perhaps you'd like a link to one of your favorite sites.

Click the blank line below `These are WWW pages I use a lot`, then click the Link button or choose Insert, Link. (You can also right-click in the document and choose Insert New Link.) You'll see the dialog box in Figure 20.4.

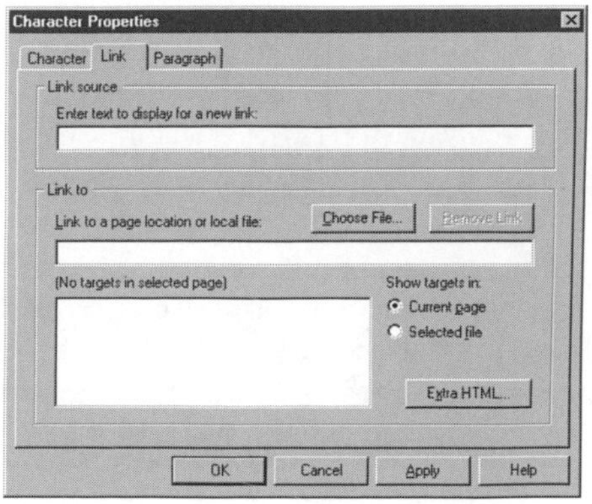

FIG. 20.4

Enter the text you want to see and the URL you want to link to.

FIG. 20.4

Enter the text you want to see and the URL you want to link to.

In the first text box, type the text that you want to appear in the document: the words you will be clicking to use that link. In the second box, type the URL of the page you want to link to, or use the Choose File button to find the file you want to link to on your hard disk.

Notice also the large list box at the bottom; if you'd created targets in the document you are working on, you'd see a list of those targets; you could then select the target you want to link to and create an internal link; we'll look at that process in Chapter 21.

You can even link to an internal target within another document, as long as it's a document on your hard disk. Click the Show Targets In Selected File option button, then choose the file using the Choose File button; you'll see a list of targets in *that* document and can link to any of them you want.

N O T E You can find URLs to link to in a number of places. You might use the Navigator window to go to the page you want and copy the URL from the Location bar. Remember also that you can right-click a link in a Web document and choose Copy Link Location. In Windows 95, you can also copy URLs from Windows 95 desktop shortcuts (see Chapter 5): right-click the shortcut, choose Properties, click the Internet Shortcut tab, then press Ctrl+C to copy the URL.

You can also get links from another document or elsewhere in the same document: Right-click a link in the Composer window and choose Copy Link to Clipboard to copy the URL to the Clipboard. ■

Notice the Remove Link button, too. This is active only if you click inside a link in your document and *then* open this dialog box. Clicking the button removes the URL so you can enter a new one, or so that you can retain the document text but remove the link from it. (You can also right-click a link in the Composer window and choose Remove Link. Or you can select a block of text, right-click the text, and choose Remove All Links in Selection. The links are removed, but the text remains.)

TIP Here's another way to create a link: Highlight text that you typed into the document earlier, then click the Link button (or right-click the highlighted text and choose Create Link Using Selected). The highlighted text will appear in the dialog box. All you need to do is enter the URL and click OK.

Notice the Extra HTML button in this dialog box. You'll see this button in other dialog boxes throughout Composer. If you click it, you'll see a large workspace into which you can type HTML attributes—so you can use advanced HTML tag features that are not provided by Composer. Of course, this is only of use if you understand how to use HTML, which we won't be covering in this book.

TIP You can add mailto: links, too. These, you'll remember, are links that open the user's mail program when clicked. Instead of typing an http:// URL into the Link to a Page Location or Local File text box, type mailto: followed by an e-mail address (for instance, mailto:robinhood@sherwoodforest.com). In the same way, you can create any other kind of link: gopher:// and ftp:// links, for example.

More Nifty Link Tricks

You can also create links by copying them from the browser window. Position the windows so that both are visible. Then click a link in the browser window, but hold the mouse button down. You'll notice that the link is highlighted. Now, with the mouse button still held down, drag the link from the browser window over to the Composer window (see Figure 20.5), move the pointer to the position you want to place it, and release the mouse button. (This won't work on the Mac, though.)

 You can also drag the Location icon (next to the text box in Navigator's Location bar) to use the current page's URL for a link.

Finally, why not grab links from your bookmarks? You've probably already created bookmarks to your favorite sites (see Chapter 5), and you can quickly create links from them. Choose Communicator, Bookmarks, Edit Bookmarks to open the Bookmarks window.

Now you can drag bookmarks from the Bookmarks window onto your document in Composer. As long as you don't click anywhere in the document—simply drag and release where you want the new link—the Bookmarks window remains above the Composer window.

 TIP To view your changes in the browser window so you can test the document you've created, choose File, Browse Page or click the Preview in Navigator button. You'll have to save your work on your hard disk before continuing.

FIG. 20.5
You can drag links from the "What's Cool?" page (or any other Web document) into Composer.

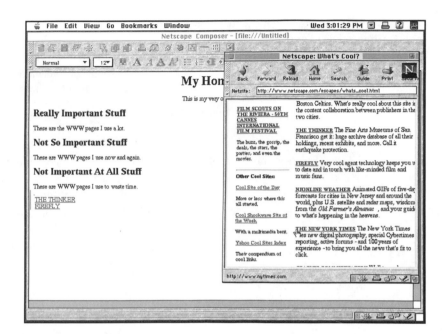

Inserting Pictures

No self-respecting Web page would be complete without a picture or two, would it? Luckily Composer provides a way for you to insert pictures. Place the cursor where you want the picture, then choose Insert, Image, or click the Insert Image button. You'll see the dialog box in Figure 20.6. First, note that there are three tabs at the top: Image, Link, and Paragraph. This is the Properties dialog box, and it's used for more than just image information; right now, of course, were are concerned only with the Image tab.

FIG. 20.6
There are lots of options to figure out when inserting images.

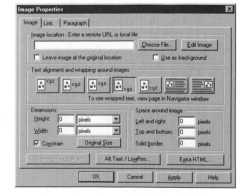

Begin by entering the file name of the image you want to use into the top text box—or use Choose File to find the image. You can, if you want, enter an URL here to insert an image stored somewhere out on the corporate intranet or World Wide Web. (How do you find the URL you'll need? In Navigator, right-click the image you want to use, then choose Copy Image Location. You can now paste the URL into the Image Location text box; press Ctrl+V.)

Here are the other settings in this dialog box:

Option	Description
Leave Image at the Original Location	If this is cleared (and it is by default), Composer will copy the image to the directory in which the document is saved.
Use As Background	Click here and Composer won't insert the image directly into the document; rather, it will use the image as the document's background image.
Edit Image	Click this button if you want to edit the image; if you haven't specified a graphics program to use in the Editor Preferences, Composer will ask you to do so.
Text Alignment and Wrapping Around Images	You have seven different alignment options, and you can see each one on the face of its button. Text can be aligned so that it sits next to the image (in various different positions) or wraps around it (on the left or right).
Dimensions	You can modify the size of the image if you want, in pixels or %. When you first insert an image, there's no need to change these settings; Composer will automatically figure out the image size and enter the correct numbers. Later you can shrink or enlarge the image by changing those numbers.
Constrain	You don't need to worry about this when you first insert a picture into the document. This setting is used when you decide to modify an image size later; if you clear the constrain box you can modify just one size setting, adjusting the image in one plane but not the other. If constrain is set on, adjusting one size will adjust the other one proportionally.
Original Size	Clicking this makes Composer check the image and reset the size to the correct numbers.
Space Around Image	You can also set the Space Around Image, to determine how much space should be left between the image and the text.

Solid Border	You can place a border around the image by entering a value into this box.
Remove Image Map	If you've copied a Web page, an image may be an image map; that is, it may have hotspots on it that contain links. Click this button to remove all hotspots.
Alt. Text/LowRes.	Click here to enter Alternate Text (the text that appears if a user views the document with inline pictures turned off, or when the user holds the mouse pointer over the image for a few moments) and a LowRes image (a low-resolution image that can load quickly first, while the primary, higher-resolution image, is still being transmitted).
Extra HTML	Allows you to add additional HTML attributes.

TIP There's a special command that makes sure that text placed after an image appears *below* the image, not "wrapped" around it. Let's say you've aligned the picture so that the text following it appears on the right side of the picture. You can now place the cursor inside that text at, say, the end of a paragraph, and choose Insert, Break below Image(s). The text that appears after the cursor is now moved down, below the image.

When you've got everything set up, click OK and the image is dropped into the document.

TIP Do you want to find some icons you can use in your documents? Go to an icon server: a Web site from which you can download icons or even link your documents across the Web to a particular icon. Try the following sites:

http://www.bsdi.com/icons
http://www-ns.rutgers.edu/doc-images
http://www.di.unipi.it/iconbrowser/icons.html
http://www.cit.gu.edu.au/~anthony/icons/

Part
IV

Ch
20

Where are you going to get pictures for your documents? You can create them yourself using a graphics program that can save in a .jpg or .gif format (many can these days). You can also grab them from the Web, remember! Find a picture you want, right-click it, and choose Save Image As. (Note, however, that if you're grabbing images from the World Wide Web, you don't *own* the image, as it's probably not in the public domain. You can use it on your own system, but don't put it on a Web or intranet site that is visible to other people unless you have permission to use it or know for sure that it's in the public domain.)

TIP To modify an image's properties later, double-click it, or right-click and choose Image Properties.

Adding Horizontal Lines

Horizontal lines are handy. You can use them to underline headers, as dividers between blocks of text, to underline important information, and so on. Composer allows you to create a number of different types of lines.

 To place a line across the page, place the cursor on a blank line or at a point within text where you want to break the line and insert a horizontal line, and click the Insert Horiz. Line button (or choose Insert, Horizontal Line). Composer will drop a horizontal line into the document. Now, double-click the line, or right-click and choose Horizontal Line Properties. You'll see the dialog box in Figure 20.7.

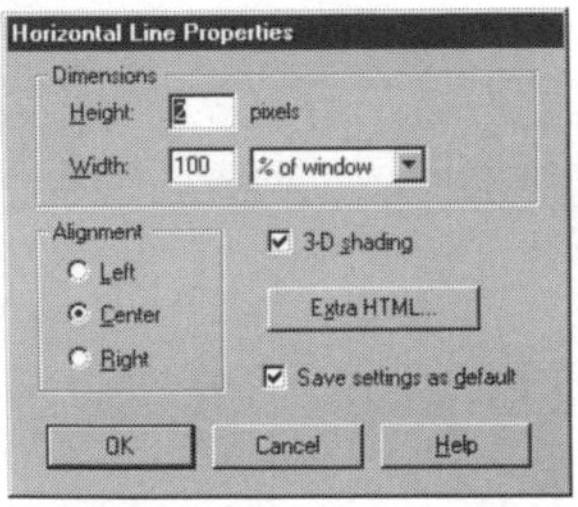

FIG. 20.7
This dialog box helps you create a line.

There are a variety of controls in this dialog box. First, you can adjust the height, which is measured in pixels. Then you can modify the line width—you can adjust the line's width by Percent or by Pixels (select one from the drop-down list box). The Percent setting refers to the width of the document (when the window is maximized). So a line that has a width of 50% will stretch across half the document.

The Pixel setting is harder to predict, though. A pixel is the smallest unit that your computer monitor can display. For instance, in VGA mode a monitor displays 640 columns and 480 rows of pixels. So if you create a line that's 60 pixels wide, it will be about 10% of the width of the document—in VGA mode. But what if the person viewing the document is using a different resolution—1024×768, for example? In such a case, the line that was 10% of the width in VGA is now about 5% of the width. Of course, this doesn't matter if you are creating a home page for your own use, but bear it in mind if you are creating documents that you plan to put out on the Web.

Next you can tell Composer where you want the line: aligned against the Left, in the Center, or aligned against the Right. Notice, however, that by default the line has a Width of 100 Percent (that is, it's 100% of the width of the document). The alignment settings have no effect until you modify the width setting. (If a line is 100%, how can you center it, after all?)

Then there's the 3-D Shading check box. The 3-D effect is created by using four different lines to create a "box,"—the left and top lines are dark gray, and the bottom and right lines are white. Clear the 3-D check box, and your horizontal line will be a single dark gray line. There's the usual Extra HTML button, allowing you to add any fancy new HTML attributes to the horizontal line (such as line color). If, that is, you happen to know the attributes.

Finally, there's the Save Settings as Default check box; click this if you want to use your new settings for all subsequent horizontal lines.

Creating Multiple Documents

You may want to create a hierarchy of documents. For instance, you could create a home page, a page that appears when you open Navigator, with a table of contents linked to several other documents. In each of those documents, you could then have links related to a particular subject: one for business, one for music, one for your kids, and so on.

This is very simple to do. Create and save several documents in Composer. (I suggest you put them all in the same directory, for simplicity's sake.) When you have completed all your documents, open your home page document again (click the Open File button or choose File, Open Page), and enter links to each page using the method previously described.

How Can I Use My Home Page?

You've created a home page; now how do you use it? Use the following procedure:

1. Click the Preview in Navigator button, or choose File, Browse Page. Navigator opens and displays your document.
2. Choose Edit, Preferences, and click the Navigator category.
3. Click the Home Page Location option button.
4. Click the Use Current Page button.
5. Click OK.

Now, the next time you start your browser, you'll see your very own home page. Simple, eh?

Here's a Good One—Let's Change It

Composer provides a wonderful way to quickly create Web pages by "borrowing" them from the Web and modifying them to your requirements. If you see a page you like—one that has many links that you'll need in your home page, for instance, or one that uses a particularly attractive format—you can open that page and make changes to it, and then save it on your hard disk.

As I noted earlier, this is the principle behind the Template (File, New, Page From Template) feature. Grab a template that Netscape Communications has created for you and modify it.

Part
IV

Ch
20

First, display the page you want to modify in the Navigator window. Then choose <u>F</u>ile, <u>E</u>dit Page. Make your changes to the document, and then save it on your hard disk (<u>F</u>ile, <u>S</u>ave).

N O T E Sometimes when you edit a document you find on the Web, you see yellow tags in the document that weren't there before. These indicate pieces of HTML code that Composer doesn't recognize. It keeps them, though; you can double-click them, or right-click and choose HTML Tag Properties, to see the HTML Tag dialog box in which you can see the tag contents. ▪

T I P If you understand enough about HTML, you may be able to edit these tags. Otherwise, you may want to delete them or simply leave them alone. (To delete one, simply click it and then press Delete.)

Now that you've got a document you want to modify, you can work in it as you would documents you created yourself. You can delete text and replace it with your own and change text using the formatting tools.

How do you highlight text? The Composer window works just like a word processor. Simply click in the text to place the cursor, then use the arrow keys to move around in the text. Also, you can use the mouse cursor to select text: Hold down the mouse button while you drag the pointer across text to highlight it.

T I P As with a word processor, you don't need to highlight text in order to modify *paragraph* formats. If you want to change the paragraph style, indentation, or alignment, simply click once in the paragraph and then make your change.

CHAPTER 21

Advanced Web Authoring

In Chapter 20, you learned how to use Netscape Composer to design and produce a home page and modify an existing Web page. But there's more. In this chapter, you'll find out about a few advanced features of Composer. You may want to make your home page really cool or even use your new skills to publish your own pages on the Web. ■

More paragraph and character formatting

Composer has a number of character and formatting tools that are similar to a word processors (though with a distinctly HTML flavor).

Creating lists

You can create bulleted and numbered lists, in a variety of formats, as well as several other list types.

Links within documents

Placing targets inside your document allows you to create internal links, that is, links from one part of the document to another.

Creating tables

Composer's Table tools make table creation a snap.

Publishing your Web pages

When you've finished your Web pages, here's how to transfer them to your Web site.

Lots More Formatting

There are a number of formatting tools I didn't get around to describing in Chapter 20. You can format a paragraph in many different ways by setting up indents and alignment as well as by choosing a paragraph style. And you can modify particular words or individual characters, too, by changing colors and type styles.

The Other Paragraph Styles

You've seen only a couple of paragraph styles so far, so let's take a look at the others. In Figure 21.1, you can see examples of all the different Heading levels as well as Normal text, the Address style, and the Formatted style. (I've also shown the HTML tags used to create each style.)

Normal	▼

You can apply any of these styles by placing the cursor inside the paragraph you want to modify and then selecting the style from the drop-down list box (or by picking the style from the Format, Paragraph or Format, Heading menus). Note that what you see depends on how you've set up Navigator; other browsers may display these styles in a different way.

> **T I P** At the time of writing the drop-down list box and the Format, Paragraph menu did not exactly match. The Paragraph menu contains an extra style, Blockquote. This, however, doesn't currently work, though it should be fixed sometime soon. The Blockquote is a style in which text is indented and centered. You can, however, create a Blockquote using the Paragraph Properties pane of the Character Properties dialog box, which we'll look at in a moment (see "Creating Customized Lists"). Also, note that the Description Title style is more properly known as the Definition Term, and the associated Description Text is more properly known as the Definition. (The Definition Term and Definition are typically used together, one after the other.)

> **T I P** Browsers normally remove blank lines and multiple spaces when viewing a document. The Formatted style tells the browser to keep the text format as it appears in the HTML document, spaces, blank lines, and all. Also, long lines of Formatted text will run off the side of the window—the text will not wrap down to the next line.

How About Creating Lists?

You can also use the Paragraph Styles drop-down list box, the Format, Paragraph menu, and a couple of the toolbar buttons to create lists. You can create bulleted lists, numbered lists, and definition lists.

You can create a bulleted list by clicking the Bullet List button or by choosing List Item from the Paragraph Style drop-down list box, or by choosing Format, List, Bulleted. (At the time of writing, it's best *not* to use the List Item from the drop-down menu, though, as it isn't correctly formatting the HTML code for the bullet list.) Type an entry, and then press Enter; each line will begin with a bullet until you select another paragraph style. You can see an example in Figure 21.2.

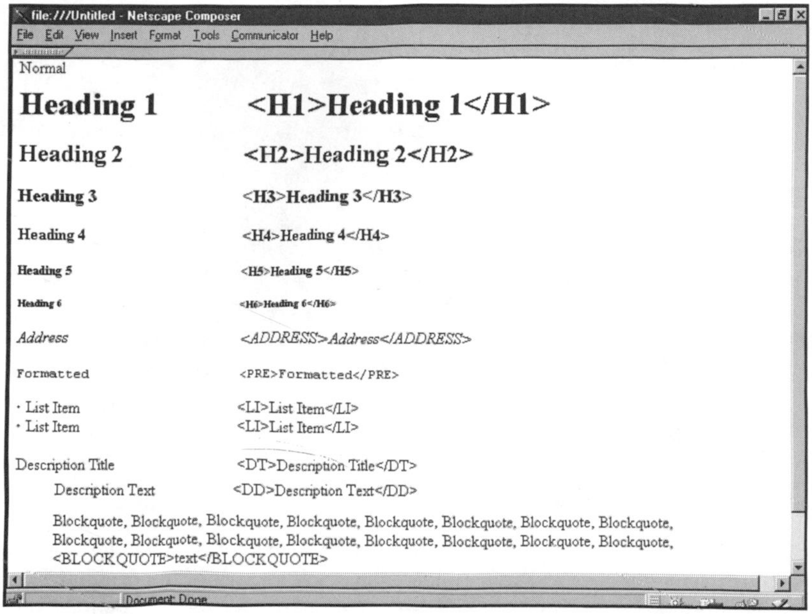

FIG. 21.1
The formatted paragraph styles. In the column on the right, you can see the HTML tags used to create each style.

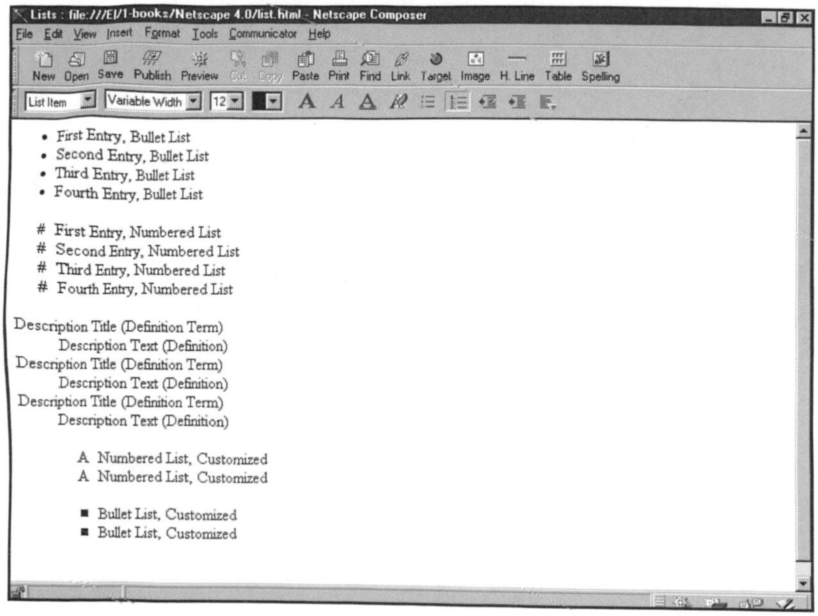

FIG. 21.2
You can create lists by using the paragraph styles.

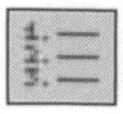

 To create a numbered list, click the Numbered List button, or choose Insert, List, Numbered. You won't see numbers in this list; you'll see the # symbol. When you view the document in a browser, though, the list will be properly numbered.

Another form of list is the definition list, which you can create by alternating lines between the Description Title and Description Text Paragraph styles (the HTML Definition Term and Definition styles).

There are more lists, though. There are two entries in the List submenu: Directory and Menu, though these currently don't work. They are presumably the <DIR></DIR> and <MENU></MENU> tag pairs. It's a little odd that these are here at all, as they are rarely used these days, and, in fact, Navigator displays them in the same way it displays bulleted lists—though some other browsers do display them differently. Note, however, that you *can use* these formats if you select them from the Paragraph pane of the Character Properties dialog box, as you'll see next.

Creating Customized Lists

You can also create customized lists. Right-click in the document where you want to place the list, and choose Paragraph/List Properties. (Or choose Format, Character Properties, then click the Paragraph tab in the box that opens.) Select List Item from the Paragraph Style drop-down list box and then a list style from the Style drop-down list box (see Figure 21.3). Some of these styles then allow you to make a further selection in the drop-down list box to the right. For bullet lists, you can select the bullet type. You can select Automatic (which means the browser picks the bullet type; it will usually be a solid black circle); Solid Circle; Open Circle; or Solid Square. If you pick one of the last three, a special attribute is added that tells the browser which type to use.

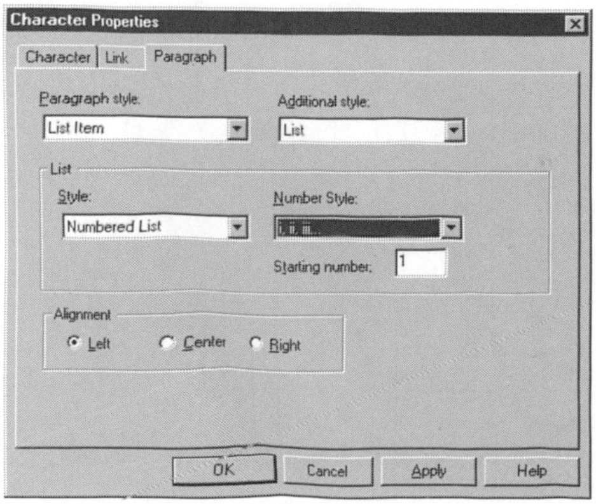

FIG. 21.3

Customize lists here; pick your numbering style and starting number, for instance.

For numbered lists, you can pick a numbering style: Automatic (it's up to the browser—usually 1, 2, 3); 1, 2, 3; I, II, II; i, ii, iii; A, B, C; or a, b, c. You can define the starting number, too. Finally, you can modify the style's alignment by selecting Left, Center, or Right.

Note also that the Directory List and Menu List formats *do* work if selected from this dialog box. And you can even use the Blockquote style if you select it from the Additional Style drop-down list box. (You can either select Normal in the Paragraph style drop-down list box and then select Blockquote, to create a Blockquote by itself, or you can select another style first to combine the styles together.)

TIP Composer's paragraph-formatting tools have a nasty habit of not cleaning up after themselves; they often leave little stray HTML tags in the document. You can't see these tags, of course (unless you choose View, Page Source), but the effect is that when you select the Normal style, the text doesn't always return to the left column. You can click the Decrease Indent button, or choose Format, Decrease Indent to move the text into the correct position.

Positioning Paragraphs

Now let's see how to move paragraphs around the page. You can use the three toolbar buttons on the right side of the Format toolbar to indent paragraphs, align them to the left, center them, and align them to the right. You can combine alignment settings and indentations, too (see Figure 21.4 for a few examples).

FIG. 21.4
You can position paragraphs in a variety of ways.

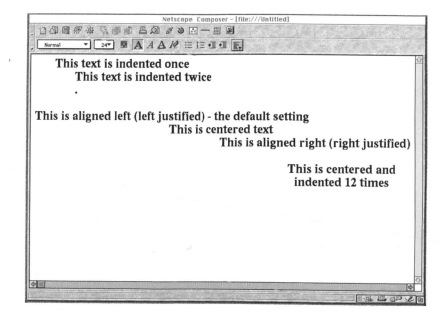

How Can I Modify Character Formats?

You have quite a bit of control over individual characters. In effect, you are telling your document to override the way in which the browser that opens your document displays the characters. A browser, for example, may have a default text color set, but you can override that color and define your own. (You looked at this and at how Navigator can be told to override this sort of overriding in Chapter 2.) Figure 21.5 shows a variety of character formats.

FIG. 21.5

Highlight text and click the appropriate button to modify it.

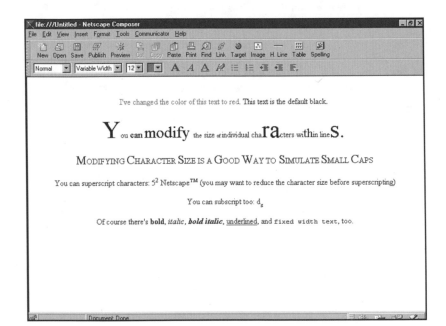

Simply highlight the characters you want to modify, and then click the appropriate button in the Character Format toolbar. Also, use the Format, Style drop-down list, where, in addition to the bold, italic, and underline that are available from the toolbar, you'll find Strikethrough (a horizontal line is put through the text), Superscript (the text is raised), Subscript (the text is lowered), Blinking (the text uses the Netscape "blink" feature, which causes it to disappear and reappear), and Nonbreaking (used to ensure that the selected text will always remain on a line together; the text will not be wrapped to the next line).

TIP There's also an Insert, Nonbreaking Space command. This inserts a space that is treated as part of the word's each side; that is, the text will not be wrapped at that point.

You can also select a font from the Font drop-down list box. The two safest selections are Fixed Width and Variable Width; these simply tell the browser to use whatever fixed-width or variable-width fonts happen to be set. The other options are all the fonts installed in your system…which may not be installed in the computers on which your documents will be displayed, of course.

You can also right-click text and choose Character Properties to see the Properties dialog box; or choose Format, Character Properties. In here, you'll find all the character formats that you can use. Until recently, this dialog box also provided the ability to add JavaScript; there were two special options—JavaScript (Server) and JavaScript (Client). These allowed you to set text as part of a JavaScript script; the text would appear in the document in Composer (in blue or red text) but wouldn't appear in the document when viewed in the browser. This is a feature that allowed JavaScript authors to incorporate their scripts into Web pages. However, the JavaScript support has been removed from Composer, and it's unclear when or whether it will return. In any case, JavaScript is complicated and way beyond the scope of this book! (For more information about JavaScript, see Chapter 12.)

TIP   To remove all formatting from text, highlight the text and choose Format, Remove All Styles, or click the Remove All Styles button.

Creating Links Within Documents

In Chapter 20, you saw how to create links to other documents. But it's often useful to be able to create a link to a position lower down in the same document. For instance, you may have a table of contents at the top of the document and want the reader to be able to click a link to jump down to the related section later in the document.

This is a two-step process. First, you must create a target within the document. Then you can link to the target. So begin by placing the cursor at the position you want to jump to (not from). Then click the Insert Target button, or choose Insert, Target. In the dialog box that appears, type a name for the target and then click OK. Composer will place a little target icon in the document. You can double-click the icon later to change its name if you want or click once and press Delete to remove it. (However, note that if you change its name, Composer will not update the name in any links you may have created to the target, at least at the time of writing.)

Now, to use this target, place the cursor where you want to create a link to the target (or highlight the text you want to turn into a link). Click the Insert/Make Link button, or choose Insert, Link. In the dialog box that opens, make sure that the Show Targets in Current Page option button is selected, click the target name in the list, and click OK.

Creating Tables

Composer also lets you create tables. Place the cursor where you want your table; then click the Table button, or choose Insert, Table, Table. You'll see the New Table Properties dialog box shown in Figure 21.6.

Enter all the information; this dialog box may look complicated, but it's really quite straightforward. Tell Composer how many rows and columns you want in the table. You can specify the table alignment (Left, Center, or Right). You can also choose to create a caption; check the Include Caption check box, then choose Above Table or Below Table. When you click OK,

Part
IV

Ch
21

Composer will create the table and place the cursor in the caption position, where you can type the caption.

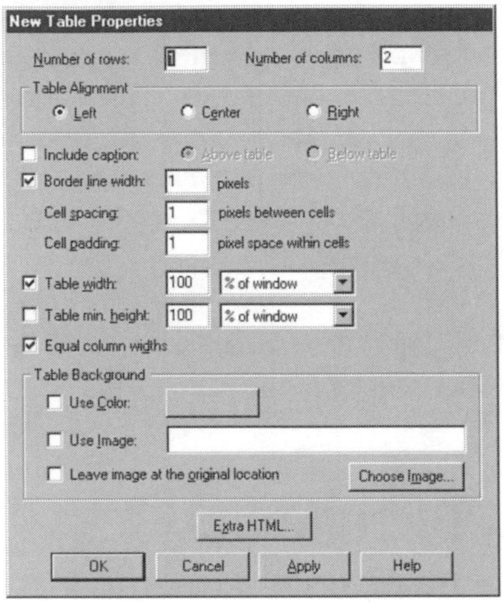

FIG. 21.6

Enter your table specifications.

You can set the width of the border lines around the table itself (the Border Line Width), as well as the space between the cells (Cell Spacing) and the space between the text within the cells and cell borders (Cell Padding). In effect, each cell in a table is a separate box, as you can see in Figure 21.7. All the boxes are within a large rectangular box; cell spacing specifies the distance between those boxes. Cell padding is the space within the cell between the border line and the text; a very small padding number means that the text is close to the border; a large padding number means there's lots of space around the text.

T I P

If you set the Border Line Width to zero, Composer creates a table that doesn't have visible cells, a good way to position text and images in fancy page layouts without making it obvious that you're using a table. You'll see dotted lines around each cell in Composer, but in a browser window the cells will not be apparent.

The Table Width setting is turned on by default; Composer will create a box that stretches all the way across the window. The Table Min. Height setting is turned off by default, though; if you want, you can force the table to be a particular height. You can choose to specify the sizes in Pixels or percentage of Window. As explained for the horizontal line in Chapter 20, percentage of Window is easier to work with. You may also want to force Equal Column Widths, to ensure that the table remains "balanced."

You can modify the table's background color, if you want. Click the Use Color check box and then the Choose Color button. Alternatively, you may want to use a background image; click Use Image, then either enter the URL of the image file, or click Choose Image to find it on your hard disk. As you saw in Chapter 20, the Leave Image at the Original Location check box defines whether you want to move the image to the same place as the document; leave the check box cleared if you do.

FIG. 21.7
Fooling with tables is fun. Experiment with modifying sizes, putting tables within tables, and so on.

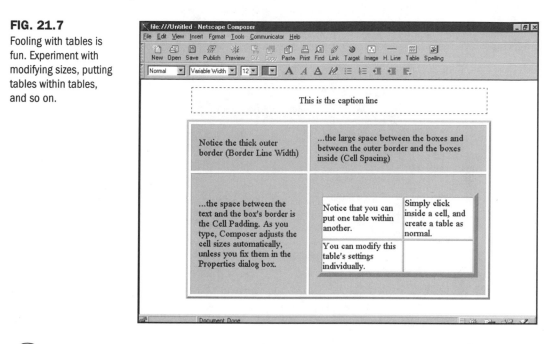

T I P To delete a table, click anywhere in the table and choose Edit, Delete Table, Table. You'll notice that the cascading menu has options that allow you to delete portions of the table: Row, Column, Cell. Note that you can also modify the settings of particular rows and cells—colors, sizes, text alignments, and so on. Right-click in a cell and choose Table Properties (or click in the cell and choose Format, Table Properties); then click the Row or Cell tab. Unless you fix cell sizes, Composer will adjust them for you as you add text.

Setting Up Page Properties

Each Web page contains information, hidden away from readers, that Web browsers can view to learn more about the way in which you want the page displayed. These are known as the page properties, and they control a variety of items, from the title shown in the browser's title bar when displaying the page, to the colors of the links and the background image. Let's look at how to set these properties.

To open the Page Properties dialog box, select Format, Page Colors and Properties, or right-click in the document and select Page Properties. We'll begin with the General pane of the Page Properties dialog box, which you can see in Figure 21.8.

Part
IV

Ch
21

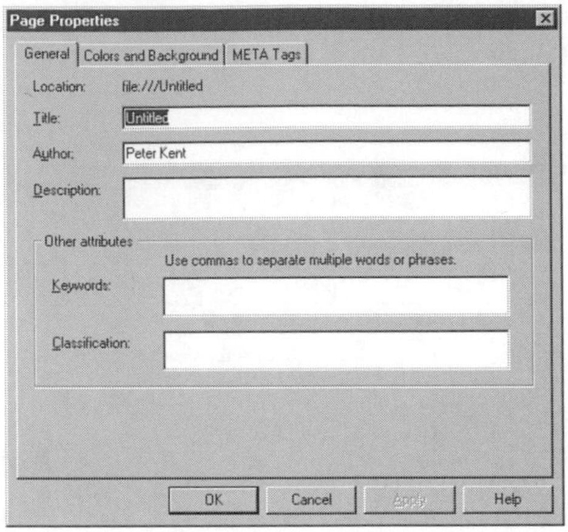

FIG. 21.8

This is the General sheet in the Page Properties dialog box, where you define the page title and other attributes.

Here are the settings you can make in this dialog box:

- ■ *Title*   This is the page's title, which is used to identify the page. It's displayed in the browser's title bar, in Bookmark lists, history lists, and so on. If you save a page without defining a title first, Composer opens a dialog box in which you can define one.

- ■ *Author*   This places text into a `<meta name="Author">` tag in the source document. It's used to identify the person who created the document. This tag, and the following three, may be used by indexing programs that are used by the Web search engines to classify Web pages (see Chapter 6).

- ■ *Description*   This one is the `<meta name="Description">` tag, and it's used to provide a quick description of the page contents.

- ■ *Keywords*   The `<meta name="Keywords">` tag. These are a few keywords, words that people searching for the sort of information held by your Web page are likely to enter into a search form.

- ■ *Classification*   The `<meta name="Classification">` tag, yet another way to classify the page's contents.

You'll use the Colors and Background tab (see Figure 21.9) to define the background and link colors and background image used in the document.

The first thing to decide is whether you want to set document colors or not. You have two option buttons:

- ■ *Use Viewer's Browser Colors (No Colors Saved in Page)*   This means that the Web page will contain no instructions, so the user's browser will decide for itself how to set colors.

- ■ *Use Custom Colors (Save Colors in Page)*   This means that you will be placing instructions in the Web page defining what colors should be used. The user's browser will read these instructions and, perhaps, use them (it may override them, though).

FIG. 21.9

Set up the background and colors here.

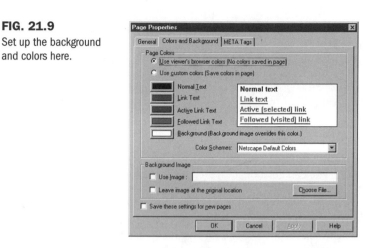

If you want, you can pick a color scheme from the Color Schemes drop-down list box. These are, presumably, mixtures of colors that work well. Select one and you'll see the effect in the sample box. Or you can define the colors for yourself by clicking each button and selecting a color.

Finally, there's the Background Image area of the dialog box. If you want to use a background image, click Use Image and then the Choose File button to find the image file. Or type the URL of a background image file that you want to borrow from somewhere out on the Web. And, again, there's the usual Leave Image at the Original Location check box; leave the check box cleared if you want to save the image with the document.

Note that there's another tab in this dialog box, the Advanced tab, but we're not going to look at it. It allows you to create more <meta> tags for providing more instructions to browsers. Of course, in order to do this, you have to understand <meta> tags, and that's out of the scope of this book (if you do understand them, you'll be able to use this feature without help).

Publishing Your Work

You may discover what hundreds of thousands of other people have done—that creating Web pages is quite easy. So why not do what many others have done, and publish your own work on the Web?

Composer provides a few tools to help you post your work online. Where can you post your work? Talk to your service provider about whether and where you can place your pages at their site. Most service providers these days allow each subscriber their own directory and some disk space for a personal Web site.

Relative versus Absolute Links

Before I talk about how to "publish" your Web pages, I'd like to talk a little about relative and absolute links. If you plan to move your Web pages onto a Web server somewhere, it's a good idea to use relative links. This means that a link doesn't describe the full location of the item being referenced: The image you've inserted or another document the reader can reach by clicking a link. Instead it describes where the item is relative to the document itself. An absolute link provides the full Web address of the item. For instance, the following is an URL used in an absolute link:

http://home.netscape.com/comprod/index.html

This URL provides the full Web address of the Index.html document. Within the Index.html document is a picture, taken from the company_and_products.jpg file (Index.html is a real document at the Netscape site; you can go and take a look if you want). But the picture is referenced using a relative link:

`/comprod/images/company_and_products.jpg`

Notice that this URL doesn't contain the http:// bit or a host name. It simply tells your browser where the .jpg file is relative to the position of the document you are viewing by giving the path through the computer's directory structure to the file.

If the file called company_and_products.jpg had been in the same directory as the Web page, then the author wouldn't have even had to provide the path; all that would be necessary is the name of the file in the link. No host name, no directory path, just the file name.

So the simplest way to create a Web site is to create relative links to all of your pages and graphics and place them all in the same directory: the same directory on your hard disk, and the same directory at your service provider's site. That way, you don't need to worry about adjusting links when you move your work from your hard disk to your service provider's.

N O T E   If you want to learn more about creating HTML files, your local bookstore has about eight
million books on the subject.

Que has a number of books that cover HTML. One of the best is *Using HTML*, Second Edition. This book contains very detailed and thorough information on how to use HTML to its fullest. Macmillan Publishing's Web page (**http:\\www.quecorp.com**) contains a list of all of Que's HTML books. ■

Moving Your Files to Your Service Provider

When you are ready to move the files from your system to your service provider's system, click the Publish button or choose File, Publish. You'll see the Publish dialog box shown in Figure 21.10. Make sure the Page Title and HTML Filename boxes are filled in; of course, they will be if you've saved the file before, but if you haven't, Composer will save the file before you transfer it. Also, note that you can change the file name, so that it has one name on your hard disk but another at the Web site. (A file with the same name will be overwritten by the one you are transferring.)

Next, enter the hostname you have to send your files to in the HTTP or FTP Location To Publish To box; you'll have to check with your service provider if you are not sure. You can enter an FTP URL (ftp://) or a Web URL (http://). No abbreviations here; you must include the ftp:// or http:// piece of the URL. You may also need to include the full path to the directory in which you'll place the files. If you're not sure what to enter here, ask your service provider.

FIG. 21.10

Composer even helps you transfer your Web pages to your service provider's site.

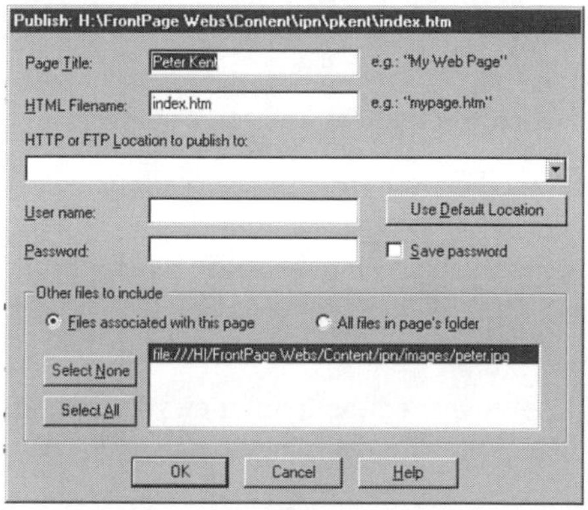

Enter your Uscr Namc and your Password. Notice also the Use Default Location button. This tells Composer to take the upload details from the Preferences dialog box, where you may have entered them earlier (see the following "The Composer Properties" section). Click the Save Password check box if you want Composer to keep your password for next time.

Now you must pick which files you want to send. If you choose Files Associated With this Page, only the open document and the files embedded in the document will be sent (the image files). But if you choose All Files in Page's Folder, all the files held in the directory in which the document is stored will be sent. It's a good idea to create a directory for your Web site and keep all the associated files in that directory, and nothing but files destined for the Web site. That way, you can use this command to quickly transmit the entire collection of files at once. Note also the Select None and Select All buttons which you can use to select files; or click individual entries to select and deselect them.

Now, click OK, and, with luck, Composer will log onto your service provider's system and upload the files. You may see a message box telling you if your document links to pages on your hard disk that you are not transferring. If so, you'll probably want to cancel the operation, then select those documents and transfer them, too. Remember, the simplest thing to do is place all your files in a single directory, make sure all the links are working correctly, then transfer all those files.

TIP There's another way to transfer files to your Web site, if you've been given an FTP directory. Use Navigator to connect to the FTP site, as described in Chapter 14. Then drag the files from Windows File Manager or Windows Explorer. Note, however, that Navigator does file transfers in binary mode, which is fine with image files but may cause problems with HTML files (which, ideally, should be transferred in ASCII mode).

The Composer Properties

Before we leave Composer, let's take a quick look at the Composer properties. Select Edit, Preferences, and click the Composer category (see Figure 21.11). These are your options:

- *Author Name*   The author name used in the `<meta name="Author">` tag (see the "Setting Up Page Properties" section earlier in this chapter).

- *Automatically Save Page Every*   You can make Composer automatically save your work every few minutes … just in case, you know.

- *HTML Source*   If you understand how to edit HTML tags, and want to do so, you can define which editor should be used. When you choose Edit, Source in Composer, the document will be loaded into the specified HTML editor.

- *Images*   You can define an image editor, too. When you click the Edit Image button in the Image Properties dialog box, the specified image editor opens.

- *Font Size Mode*   When you select a font size in the Composer window, you can do so from the Font Size drop-down list box. When Composer sets a font size, it does so by setting the <FONT SIZE=n> tag, where n is a size relative to the normal font size for the text (-1, +2, and so on). These option buttons define what will appear in the drop-down, and how Composer figures out the font size you want.

- *Show Relative Size As Points Based on Your Navigator Font Sizes*   In other words, Composer shows a point size in the drop-down list box. Then, when you select a point size, it looks at the font sizes defined in the Appearance/Fonts area of the Preferences dialog box, and figures out how to set the `<FONT SIZE=n>` tag. For instance, if the browser font size is set to 12 points, when you select 18 points in the Font Size drop-down list box, Composer figures out that it needs to use `<FONT SIZE=+2>` in order to get the appropriate font size.

- *Show Relative HTML Font Scale*   Select this and Composer shows you the actual number it's going to put into the `<FONT SIZE=n>` tag.

- *Show Relative HTML Scale and Absolute "Point Size" Attributes*   Select this and Composer includes both types of number in the drop-down list box: point sizes and the HTML attribute number.

Click the Publishing subcategory (see Figure 21.12) to define how Composer works when you save pages that you've found on the Web. These are your options:

- *Maintain Links*   This tells Composer that you want it to make sure that the links within the document you are transferring will still work. Any links to documents that are within the same directory as the one you are saving will be modified, if necessary, to be relative links, so when the files are transferred to your Web site, the links will still work. Links to documents that are not in the same directory will be made absolute, so they will still work—the files or images will be drawn from the original location (assuming that the document will be available on the Internet or intranet). You should normally leave this check box marked; if you clear it, you may find that some of the links within the document do not work.

FIG. 21.11

Make your general
Composer settings
here.

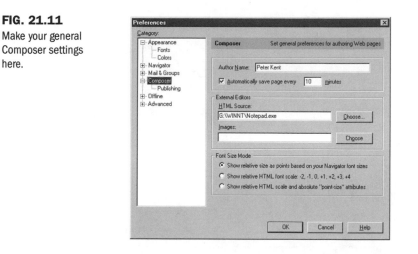

■ *Keep Images with Page*   With this selected, when you transfer a page, Composer will automatically transfer the images that were in the page. It will also modify the URLs that reference the images, making them relative URLs, so the images will always appear in the page, even if you move the page and images to another location.

■ *Enter a FTP or HTTP Site Address to Publish To*   This is the location used when you click the Use Default Location button in the Publish Files dialog box—the location to which you will transfer your Web pages when publishing them. You must enter a full URL, including either ftp:// or http://, and any directory path that is required. If you are not sure what to enter, ask your system administrator or service provider.

■ *If Publishing to a FTP Site, Enter the HTTP Address to Browse To*   This is a little ambiguous, and in fact, at the time of writing doesn't seem to actually do anything. There used to be a Browse To command in Navigator, which would take you to the Web site defined in this text box, but that command has been removed. Maybe it will reappear, or maybe this will remain as a vestigial component, unused.

FIG. 21.12

Tell Composer how to manage Web-site transfers.

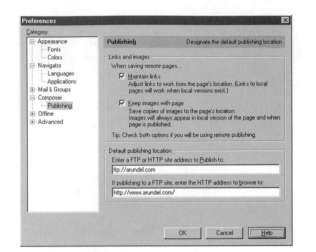

Index

D

MACMILLAN COMPUTER PUBLISHING USA

A V I A C O M C O M P A N Y

If you need assistance with the information in this book or with a CD/Disk accompanying the book, please access the Knowledge Base on our Web site at **http://www.superlibrary.com/general/support**. Our most Frequently Asked Questions are answered there. If you do not find the answer to your questions on our Web site, you may contact Macmillan Technical Support **(317) 581-3833** or e-mail us at **support@mcp.com**.

Complete and Return this Card
for a *FREE* Computer Book Catalog

Thank you for purchasing this book! You have purchased a superior computer book written expressly for your needs. To continue to provide the kind of up-to-date, pertinent coverage you've come to expect from us, we need to hear from you. Please take a minute to complete and return this self-addressed, postage-paid form. In return, we'll send you a free catalog of all our computer books on topics ranging from word processing to programming and the Internet.

Mr. ☐   Mrs. ☐   Ms. ☐   Dr. ☐

Name (first) ☐☐☐☐☐☐☐☐☐☐☐☐☐☐   (M.I.) ☐   (last) ☐☐☐☐☐☐☐☐☐☐☐☐☐☐☐☐

Address ☐☐☐☐☐☐☐☐☐☐☐☐☐☐☐☐☐☐☐☐☐☐☐☐☐☐☐☐☐☐☐☐

City ☐☐☐☐☐☐☐☐☐☐☐☐☐☐☐☐☐☐   State ☐☐   Zip ☐☐☐☐☐ ☐☐☐☐

Phone ☐☐☐ ☐☐☐☐☐☐☐   Fax ☐☐☐ ☐☐☐☐☐☐☐

Company Name ☐☐☐☐☐☐☐☐☐☐☐☐☐☐☐☐☐☐☐☐☐☐☐☐☐☐☐☐☐☐

E-mail address ☐☐☐☐☐☐☐☐☐☐☐☐☐☐☐☐☐☐☐☐☐☐☐☐☐☐☐☐☐☐

1. Please check at least three (3) influencing factors for purchasing this book.

Front or back cover information on book .... ☐
Special approach to the content .... ☐
Completeness of content.. ☐
Author's reputation .... ☐
Publisher's reputation .... ☐
Book cover design or layout .... ☐
Index or table of contents of book .... ☐
Price of book.. ☐
Special effects, graphics, illustrations .... ☐
Other (Please specify): _____ ☐

2. How did you first learn about this book?

Saw in Macmillan Computer Publishing catalog .... ☐
Recommended by store personnel .... ☐
Saw the book on bookshelf at store .... ☐
Recommended by a friend .... ☐
Received advertisement in the mail .... ☐
Saw an advertisement in: _____ ☐
Read book review in: _____ ☐
Other (Please specify): _____ ☐

3. How many computer books have you purchased in the last six months?

This book only .... ☐   3 to 5 books .... ☐
2 books................... ☐   More than 5 .... ☐

4. Where did you purchase this book?

Bookstore .... ☐
Computer Store .... ☐
Consumer Electronics Store .... ☐
Department Store .... ☐
Office Club .... ☐
Warehouse Club .... ☐
Mail Order .... ☐
Direct from Publisher .... ☐
Internet site .... ☐
Other (Please specify): _____ ☐

5. How long have you been using a computer?

☐ Less than 6 months   ☐ 6 months to a year
☐ 1 to 3 years   ☐ More than 3 years

6. What is your level of experience with personal computers and with the subject of this book?

	With PCs	With subject of book
New	☐	☐
Casual	☐	☐
Accomplished	☐	☐
Expert	☐	☐

Source Code ISBN: 0-7897-0982-1

7. Which of the following best describes your job title?

Administrative Assistant .... ☐
Coordinator .... ☐
Manager/Supervisor .... ☐
Director .... ☐
Vice President .... ☐
President/CEO/COO .... ☐
Lawyer/Doctor/Medical Professional .... ☐
Teacher/Educator/Trainer .... ☐
Engineer/Technician .... ☐
Consultant .... ☐
Not employed/Student/Retired .... ☐
Other (Please specify): _____ ☐

8. Which of the following best describes the area of the company your job title falls under?

Accounting .... ☐
Engineering .... ☐
Manufacturing .... ☐
Operations .... ☐
Marketing .... ☐
Sales .... ☐
Other (Please specify): _____ ☐

9. What is your age?

Under 20 .... ☐
21-29 .... ☐
30-39 .... ☐
40-49 .... ☐
50-59 .... ☐
60-over .... ☐

10. Are you:

Male .... ☐
Female .... ☐

11. Which computer publications do you read regularly? (Please list)

_____
_____
_____
_____
_____
_____
_____
_____
_____
_____

Comments: _____
_____
_____

Fold here and tape to mail.

Check out Que® Books on the World Wide Web
http://www.quecorp.com

As the biggest software release in computer history, Windows 95 continues to redefine the computer industry. Click here for the latest info on our Windows 95 books

Make computing quick and easy with these products designed exclusively for new and casual users

Examine the latest releases in word processing, spreadsheets, operating systems, and suites

Que

Desktop Applications & Operating Systems

new users

what's new?

Que's Publishing Areas

Windows 95

Internet And New Technologies

The Internet, The World Wide Web, CompuServe®, America Online®, Prodigy®—it's a world of ever-changing information. Don't get left behind!

Find out about new additions to our site, new bestsellers, and hot topics

Calendar of Events

DEVELOPER AND EXPERT USERS

ZD ZIFF-DAVIS PRESS

Que's Top 10 Titles

Macintosh & Desktop Publishing

In-depth information on high-end topics: find the best reference books for databases, programming, networking, and client/server technologies

A recent addition to Que, Ziff-Davis Press publishes the highly successful *How It Works* and *How to Use* series of books, as well as *PC Learning Labs Teaches* and *PC Magazine* series of book/disc packages

Stay on the cutting edge of Macintosh® technologies and visual communications

Find out which titles are making headlines

With six separate publishing groups, Que develops products for many specific market segments and areas of computer technology. Explore our Web Site and you'll find information on best-selling titles, newly published titles, upcoming products, authors, and much more.

- Stay informed on the latest industry trends and products available
- Visit our online bookstore for the latest information and editions
- Download software from Que's library of the best shareware and freeware

QUE®